STUDIES IN
AMERICAN SOCIOLOGY
UNDER
THE GENERAL EDITORSHIP OF
STANFORD M. LYMAN

VOLUME I

D1521520

SOCIAL
ORDER
AND
THE PUBLIC
PHILOSOPHY

An Analysis and Interpretation of
the Work of Herbert Blumer

Stanford M. Lyman
Arthur J. Vidich

The University of Arkansas Press
Fayetteville 1988 London

Copyright © 1988 by Stanford M. Lyman and Arthur J. Vidich
The University of Arkansas Press, Fayetteville, Arkansas 72701
All rights reserved
Manufactured in the United States of America
92 91 90 89 88   5 4 3 2 1

Designer: Chang-Hee H. Russell
Typeface: Linotron 202 Bembo
Typesetter: G & S Typesetters, Inc.
Printer: Thomson-Shore, Inc.
Binder: John H. Dekker & Sons, Inc.

The paper used in this publication meets the minimum requirements
of the American National Standard for Permanence of Paper for
Printed Library Materials Ze9.48-1984. ⊚

Library of Congress Cataloging-in-Publication Data

Lyman, Stanford M.
    Social order and the public philosophy.
    Bibliography: p.
    Includes index.
    1. Blumer, Herbert, 1900–1987.   2. Sociology—United States—
History.   3. Political science—United States—History. I. Vidich,
Arthur J.   II. Title.
HM22.U6B565   1988   301'.0973   87-30257
ISBN 0-938626-87-6 (alk. paper)

Dedicated to

Herbert Blumer (1900–1987)

Distinguished Scholar
and
Innovator of the Public Philosophy

CONTENTS

Preface   xi

Acknowledgments   xix

**The Problem of a Public Philosophy:
A Sociological Perspective**   3

Introduction   5

Blumer's Antecedents   10

   Sumner, Croly, and the Southern Comteans   10

   Walter Lippmann: Public Opinion versus a Public
   Philosophy   20

      Modernity and Democracy   20

      Obstacles to Enlightenment: Stereotypes and the
      Mass Media   23

      The Public Philosophy and the American Community:
      Inclusion and Exclusion   28

      The Public Philosophy and the 'Mandate of Heaven'   33

   A Public Philosophy for Mass Society: The Civic
   Sociology of Herbert Blumer   35

      Interaction and the Social Meaning of the Film   36

      Public Opinion, Propaganda, and War   42

      Morale, Truth, and Freedom of Speech   44

Race Relations and Inequality in the Democratic State   55

   The Relevance of Symbolic Interactionism for
   Race and Ethnic Relations   55

Race, Political Power, and Public Philosophy   61
Race Relations in the Labor Market: Affirmative Action   66
A Public Philosophy for Affirmative Action   76
Race and Labor-Management Relations:
Political Realism and Moral Order   92

Labor Conflicts in a Post-Protestant Era   95

Toward a Politically Realistic Public Philosophy   106
Mass Society: Beyond the Secularization Process   108
Industrial Conflict Resolution: A Model
for a Public Philosophy   114
Notes   121

Selected Works of Herbert Blumer   145

Public Opinion and Public Opinion Polling   147

Morale   161
The State of the Problem   161
The Nature of Morale   163
Inadequate Views of Morale   167
Forms of Morale   170
Morale in America   174

The Nature of Race Prejudice   183

Race Prejudice as a Sense of Group Position   196

The Future of the Color Line   208

Social Science and the Desegregation Process   223
Nature of Segregation   223
Segregation as a Social Problem   225
The Segregating Group   226
Desegregation   228
Role of Functionaries   230

Role of Organizations   231

Conclusions   233

The Rationale of Labor-Management Relations   234

The Nature and Function of the Labor Strike   246

Control of the Labor Strike   257

Industrialization and Problems of Social Disorder   270

The Alleged Role of Industrialization in
Producing Social Disorder   271

Assessment of Industrialization as a Source
of Social Disorder   282

Sociological Theory in Industrial Relations   297

Group Tension and Interest Organizations   309

Economic Power Blocs Natural to Society   309

Dynamic Organizations in a Mobile World   313

Nature of Group Tension   315

Continuous Workable Adjustments   316

Problems of Adjustment   317

Conflicts and the Public Interest   319

Proposals to Reduce Tension   320

Conclusion   324

Social Structure and Power Conflict   326

Introduction   326

Analysis of Power   329

Labor-Management Relations as Power Relations   333

The Concept of Mass Society   337

Selected Bibliography of Herbert George Blumer   355

Index   361

PREFACE

The question of the public philosophy was thrust upon us by our discovery—reported in an earlier book, *American Sociology: Worldy Rejections of Religion and Their Directions,*[1]—that the religious foundations of the original American social compact had become deeply eroded. In their place, some sociologists had suggested the necessity for and formulated the basis of a civil religion. We believe that the idea of a civil religion masks a latent commitment to the very religiosity that has already lost much of its social force and civic function. Our own searches and researches noticed that the writings of Herbert Blumer evince, if only implicitly, a persistent concern for the secular bases of a democratic public philosophy. Although we believe Blumer has come closer than any other contemporary social thinker to framing sociological problems that point to the basic themes of a public philosophy, he did not address this issue directly. In the present study we interpret selected portions of Blumer's corpus to develop our own statement of a public philosophy for the United States. Because any public philosophy for this country must concern itself with three fundamental issues—the influence of public opinion on political leadership, the conflicts among America's several indigenous racial and ethnic groups, and the adversarial relations between workers and employers,—we have drawn our own interpretation and commentary from Blumer's essays on these subjects.

As part of our project we hope to acquaint the reader with the work of one of America's well known but insufficiently appreciated social thinkers. Blumer is widely recognized for his essays on the principles of and methodologies appropriate to symbolic interaction. His applications of that perspective to empirical

[1] New Haven: Yale Univeristy Press, 1985.

studies of race prejudice and the color bar,[2] the rationale of labor-management relations and their attendant power conflicts, the realities of public opinion and mass sentiment in time of war, and the conditions and character of social change in modern societies are less well known. Many of them are found in his fugitive essays—published originally in regional journals, out-of-the-way places, in a foreign language, or in anthologies where editorial privilege submerged Blumer's originality. We have collected, reprinted, and in one case provided an English translation of these essays at the end of this volume.

Although Blumer always attuned his critical eye to the errors, misunderstandings, and faithlessness-to-empirical reality in conventional sociological formulations, he also—if only by indirection—suggested the basis for a new public philosophy. Transcending both the transvalued Protestantism that characterized his discipline's dominant outlook and the over-rationalized conception of the republic that flowed from Comteanism and America's Enlightenment heritage, his perspective aimed at outlining the conditions for equity and freedom. Our study delineates that public philosophy, sifting it from Blumer's theoretical statements and methodological critiques, and elaborating on it in ways that Blumer did not see fit to develop. In the course of our commentary, we present a new theory of free speech and an innovative justification for affirmative action programs. Although Blumer's work inspired our own thoughts on these matters, he is not responsible for the formulation presented here. Our version of a public philosophy extends Blumer's ideas in new directions that we believe are faithful to their spirit.

For the past 130 years much of American sociology has been guided by a latent and unacknowledged Comteanism overlaid with a steadily secularizing Protestantism. This attitude has been applied to resolving the problems of an industrializing, urbanizing, world-expanding, racially divisive and multi-ethnic society.

[2]See, however, Lewis M. Killian, "Herbert Blumer's Contributions to Race Relations," in Tamotsu Shibutani, ed., *Human Nature and Collective Behavior: Papers in Honor of Herbert Blumer,* (Englewood Cliffs, N.J.: Prentice-Hall, 1970), pp. 183–190; and Stanford M. Lyman, "Interactionism and the Study of Race Relations at the Macro-Sociological Level: The Contribution of Herbert Blumer," *Symbolic Interaction,* VII (Spring, 1984), pp. 107–120.

In a perspective that fuses positivism with functionalism, more recent American sociology has lent its support to an assurance of social progress that it sustains despite the disconfirmations of calamitous events. Comte had been convinced not only that "social development will ultimately regenerate social science," but also that he and his fellow Positivists would rediscover their true purpose as scientists by concentrating their efforts on ". . . the vanguard of the human race, . . . the greater part of the white race; or the European nations,—even restricting ourselves, at least in regard to modern times, to the nations of Western Europe."[3] Although Comte hoped that his "science of positive polity" would take hold in and guide the formation of a confederated union uniting England, France, Germany, Italy, and Spain,[4] his fundamental ideas—the cumulative build-up of a social system in developmental stages; the leading position of the white race and European industrial culture; the obligation that fell to men of knowledge to shape a socially instaurative public policy; and the preponderant importance of science and rationality in the social control of human conduct—resonated so favorably with early American sociologists that, while rejecting his nescient Religion of Humanity, they adapted them to their own proclamation of a scientifically invigorated and nationally reconstructive Social Gospel.[5]

Combining a socially conscious but exact science of society with Christian endeavor,[6] the Social Gospel became the single most important intellectual resource of *fin de siecle* American sociology.[7] It hoped to hasten America's destiny—becoming

[3] *The Positive Philosophy of Auguste Comte,* freely translated and condensed by Harriet Martineau, 2nd edition. (London: Trubner and Co., Ludgate Hill, 1875), II, p. 151.

[4] Richmond Laurin Hawkins, *Auguste Comte and the United States (1816–1853),* (Cambridge: Harvard University Press, 1936; reprinted, New York: Kraus Reprint Corp., 1966), pp. 3–13.

[5] *Ibid.,* pp. 14–24.

[6] In addition to the works cited in 7 *infra,* see Vidich and Lyman, *op.cit.,* pp. 53–194.

[7] See Washington Gladden, *Applied Christianity: Moral Aspects of Social Questions,* (Boston and New York: Houghton, Mifflin and Co., 1886); Walter Rauschenbusch, *Christianity and the Social Crisis,* ed. by Robert D. Cross, (New York: Harper Torchbooks, 1964. Originally published in 1907); Charles Howard Hopkins, *The Rise of the Social Gospel in American Protestantism, 1865–1915,* (New Haven: Yale University Press, 1940); Ronald C. White, Jr., and C. How-

the redeemer nation,[8]—and to establish for all the world to acknowledge its status as "the city upon a hill."[9] Against this proto-
Comtean and Protestant Christian illusion of the age there arose
few opponents and the most able of these—the doom prophet,
William Graham Sumner, and his rival, the atheistic champion of
synergistic progress, Lester Frank Ward,—could not defuse the
optimism of the sociological redemptionists. Later, when the re-
demptive dream seemed to recede in the face of a dimmer and
darker present, it would be reformulated to emphasize the importance of perfecting the methodological means that would
eventually achieve the promised end. Mid-twentieth century
neo–Comtean and post-Puritan sociologists speak less about the
older, grander vision and more about matters of technique that
need immediate attention.[10] In emphasizing the latter, however,
they ceased addressing the general question that had called their
discipline into existence—how could a democratic American society persevere in the face of racial conflicts, ethnic diversity,
labor-management antagonisms, and a public discourse that
could not be assured of following the rules of reason?

Blumer, though unique among his sociological contempo-
raries in his manner of addressing this question, is in the tradition of America's earlier public philosophers: William Graham
Sumner, Herbert Croly, and Walter Lippmann. Moreover, by
couching his discussions of race prejudice, industrial conflicts,
public opinion, social morale, and mass society in terms of a sustained critique of the received wisdom and reigning paradigms
of America's melioristic sociology—and especially of the discipline's claim that social equilibrium would always renew itself
despite outbursts by disaffected blacks, oppressed aliens, angry

ard Hopkins, *The Social Gospel; Religion and Reform in Changing America*, (Phila-
delphia: Temple University Press, 1976); Cecil Greek, "The Social Gospel
Movement and Early American Sociology, 1870–1915," *The Graduate Faculty
Journal of Sociology*, III:1 (Fall, 1978), pp. 30–42.

[8] See Ernest Lee Tuveson, *Redeemer Nation: The Idea of America's Millenial
Role*, (Chicago: University of Chicago Press, 1968, 1974); and Mona Harring-
ton, *The Dream of Deliverance in American Politics*, (New York: Alfred A. Knopf,
1986).

[9] Despite its polemical tone, there is much of value in Loren Baritz, *Backfire:
A History of How American Culture Led Us into Vietnam and Made Us Fight the
Way We Did*, (New York: William Morrow and Co., Inc., 1985), pp. 17–54.

[10] Vidich and Lyman, *op.cit.*, pp. 281–310.

workers, and anguished patriots—Blumer placed his work on the sound empirical ground of, and in relation to the achievement of justice in, a permanently pluralized and segmented mass society.

Sumner, Croly, and Lippmann had chronicled the decline of a moral basis for civic action, but had—each in his own way—treated the problem of secularization in terms of the transference of religious themes to a secular order. Blumer's approach is secular in a quite different way. Where Sumner recounts the passing of the Puritan order and prophesies a permanently disordered future unless its moral equivalent is reestablished in America; where Croly hopes to impose a Comtean techno-industrial religion of humanity on America's deracinated people; where Lippmann seeks to revive the Greco-Roman philosophy of reason and infuse it with a reinvigorated Protestant ethic, Blumer speaks to the fundamental problem of modernity: how freedom and equity can be assured when institutional arrangements and interpersonal relations are threatened by disparate groups and desperate peoples, disinterested publics and deep-interested factions. He visualizes the quest for justice and equity in an America where religions have become ethical interest groups competing with one another for an unlikely monopoly on individual souls and civic virtue; where race conscious groups struggle to maintain, manipulate, or deconstruct the bulwarks that defend the reigning color and culture bar; and where labor and management face each other armed with the power, strategy, and tactics to achieve ends that fall within, against, or in no recognizable relation to the public interest.

We have chosen to contrast Blumer with Sumner, Croly and Lippmann because each of these social-political philosophers is an exemplar of a different approach to the public philosophy. We have not compared Blumer's work with that of other sociologists because with rare exception—the outstanding example being Talcott Parsons whose work we do address briefly—few have directed their attention to the central concerns of our study.

Herbert Blumer was born in 1900 and grew up in St. Louis, Missouri. He received his A.B. and A.M. from the University of Missouri and served as an instructor there from 1922 to 1925. Appointed instructor in sociology at the University of Chicago, he played professional football for the Chicago Cardinals while working on his Ph.D. He received that degree from the University of Chicago in 1927, writing on "Method in Social Psychology," and incorporating the perspective of social philosopher George Herbert Mead. Except for his public service during World War II and his visiting appointments at the University of Michigan (1936), and the University of Hawaii (1939, 1950–51), he served as instructor (1925–1930), assistant professor (1930–31), associate professor (1931–1947), and professor (1947–1952) at the University of Chicago for twenty-seven years. In 1952 he became professor and chairman of the newly-formed Department of Sociology and Social Institutions at the University of California at Berkeley. Although regarded as something of a maverick within the discipline, and certainly one of its most formidable critics, Blumer carried out the duties of secretary-treasurer of the American Sociological Society from 1930 to 1935 and was elected that association's president in 1956. After the outbreak of World War II he became Principal Liaison Officer in the Office of War Information (1943), and Public Panel Chairman of the War Labor Board (1943–45). His wartime service helped sharpen his focus on morale, public opinion, and collective behavior, subjects on which he was regarded as an independent-minded expert. From 1945 to 1947 he chaired the Board of Arbitration of the United States Steel Corporation and he saw firsthand the processes—and machinations—that characterized labor-management relations in the United States. From 1952 until 1975 he led in the development of a comprehensive sociology curriculum at Berkeley that brought the perspectives of symbolic interactionism together with those of comparative, historical, and institutional sociology. During the same period he elaborated on the theory of racial prejudice, conducted comparative studies of the effects of industrialization on traditional social orders in Brazil and Puerto Rico, and supervised a study of drug usage among adolescents. All of his work is characterized by close attention to the empirical world, a refusal to accept *a priori* reasoning, and concern for the social conditions of and institutional obstacles to social justice and democratic conduct in mass society. In 1983 the American Sociological Association honored Blumer with its Award for a Career of Distinguished Scholarship. Herbert Blumer died on April 13, 1987.

Over the course of more than a half century, Herbert Blumer investigated virtually all of the critical issues and significant crises affecting American society, with the one possible exception of religion and its effects. In the concluding section of our book we have reprinted twelve of his essays. These include two works on the problem of public opinion and social morale, four studies of race prejudice, America's color line, and the desegregation process, and five articles on labor-management problems, industrial conflicts, and power relations. Finally, we present for the first time in English translation, Blumer's essay on mass society— "Über das Konzept der Massengesellschaft." This essay has been translated by Brian Willson from Dorly Frey's and Heinz Otto Luthe's German version of a lost English original and edited by Michael Hughey and the authors. For those readers who wish to peruse Blumer's other works, a bibliography has been appended at the end of our book.

In the course of researching and writing this book we have incurred debts which we here acknowledge in lieu of payment that their value insures cannot be made. First and foremost we wish to thank Herbert Blumer for critically appraising our earlier study of his contributions, providing us with many bibliographic leads, encouraging our continued research in this area of study, and expressing a lively curiosity about how we would derive a public philosophy from his work. Among the small but significant coterie of symbolic interactionists, we would also like to express our gratitude to Tamotsu Shibutani and S. Frank Miyamoto for their contributions to social research on race relations and the social process, Thomas J. Morrione for his helpful suggestions, and Peter Adler for convoking a special session on "A California School of Interactionism?" at the 1986 annual meetings of the Society for the Study of Symbolic Interaction at which we presented some of the ideas adumbrating this study. Our analysis of affirmative action has been informed and aided by the researches as well as the critical advice of Herbert Hill. We have benefited from the critical appraisals of the manuscript by Michael Banton and Marvin B. Scott. Miller Williams and his editorial staff at the University of Arkansas Press have proven the value of excellence in publishing. Ann Barron has done yeoman service in preparing the typescript, keeping the records, and assisting in all phases of our research and writing. Ron Childress prepared the index. Although each has contributed, we alone are responsible for the theses presented here.

S. M. L.
A. J. V.

ACKNOWLEDGMENTS

Permissions to reprint essays by Herbert Blumer are gratefully acknowledged and have been obtained from:

"Public Opinion and Public Opinion Polling," pp. 542–549, *American Sociological Review,* Vol. 13:5, October, 1948, The American Sociological Association.

"Morale," pp. 207–231, in *American Society in Wartime,* ed. William Ogburn, The University of Chicago Press, 1943. Copyright © 1943 by The University of Chicago. All rights reserved.

"The Nature of Race Prejudice," pp. 11–20, in *Social Process in Hawaii,* V (June, 1939), University of Hawaii.

"Race Prejudice as a Sense of Group Position," pp. 3–7, in *Pacific Sociological Review,* I (Spring, 1958), published by Sage Publications, Inc.

"The Future of the Color Line," pp. 322–336, in *The South in Continuity and Change,* eds. John McKinney and E.T. Thompson, 1965, Duke University Press.

"Social Science and the Desegregation Process," pp. 137–143, in *The Annals of the American Academy of Political and Social Science,* CCCIV (March, 1956), American Academy of Political and Social Science.

The Rationale of Labor-Management Relations, 1958, Rio Piedras: Labor Relations Institute, Rio Piedras, Puerto Rico.

"Industrialization and Problems of Social Order," pp. 47–58, published by permission of Transaction, Inc., from *Studies in Comparative International Development,* Vol. V (1969–1970). Copyright © 1970 by Transaction, Inc. All rights reserved.

"Sociological Theory in Industrial Relations, pp. 271–278, in

American Sociological Review, Vol. 12, June, 1947, The American Sociological Association.

"Group Tension and Interest Organization," pp. 1–15, in *Proceedings of the Second Annual Meeting, Industrial Research Association,* 1950, Industrial Research Association.

"Social Structure and Power Conflict," pp. 232–239, in *Industrial Conflict,* eds. Arthur Kornhauser, Robert Dubin, A.M. Ross, McGraw-Hill, 1954. Copyright © 1954, by the McGraw-Hill Book Company, Inc. All rights reserved.

"Über das Konzept der Massengesellschaft," pp. 19–37, in *Militanter Humanismus,* ed. by Alphons Silbermann, S. Fischer Verlag, 1966, Frankfurt, Germany.

SOCIAL ORDER
AND
THE PUBLIC PHILOSOPHY

The Problem of
A Public Philosophy:

A Sociological Perspective

Introduction

The problem of a public philosophy for the United States of America took on its modern form after the Civil War. That war—fought to end chattel slavery, preserve the Union, and elaborate the human promise contained in the Declaration of Independence—succeeded only in its first two aims. The ideals that had served to buttress stable group life before 1861 became a casualty of that war; new ideals to replace them did not seem to be arising. As intensive industrialization, rapid urbanization, massive immigration, and new forms of racial subordination challenged whatever moral conscience or civic consciousness remained in the reconstituted Republic, the void in common values evoked a pessimistic sociological formulation: William Graham Sumner (1840–1910) expounded the thesis that a government of laws depended on a prior covenant of *folkways* and *mores*. He claimed that in the United States the originating Puritan covenant had flourished briefly, but been broken irrevocably by the calamitous war and its chaotic aftermath. "The mores which once were are a memory. Those which anyone thinks ought to be are a dream."[1] Hence, until a new social compact emerged—and Sumner was unsure when that would happen and not able to predict what values that covenant might espouse—no social legislation could be effective. Within this moral and political void, Sumner noticed an unpromising "philosophical drift . . . towards state regulation, militarism, imperialism, towards petting and flattering the poor and laboring classes, and in favor of whatever is altruistic and humanitarian."[2] Furthermore, this drift was accompanied by federal indifference to the lynching of Negroes in the South,[3] a breakdown of civility in the relations among blacks and whites in the North,[4] and a moral fervor in behalf of Christianizing but otherwise ignoring the brown-skinned Filipino subjects acquired as a spoil of the Spanish American War.[5] Convinced that a rampant materialism, pitting democracy against plutocracy,[6] had all but supplanted what was left of the venture into civic virtue and social progress undertaken by the original settlers, Sumner declared that "We have no grounds for confidence in these ruling tendencies of our time."[7] Holding that America's republican government had been corrupted by money and eroded by bureaucratization,[8] Sumner relegated the public good to what an individual might accomplish in the isolated pursuit of self-interest: "The man who makes the most of himself and does his best in his sphere is doing far more for the public good than the philanthropist who runs about with a scheme which would set the world straight if only everybody would adopt it."[9] For a reconstituted America to become morally solvent, Sumner seemed to say, the Protestant ethic (or its functional equivalent) would have to become the guiding spirit of democracy.

Herbert Blumer began his writing two decades after Sumner's death, at the onset of the Great Depression and with the emergence of the welfare state. He recognized that the spirit of Protestantism could no longer be the basis for America's public philosophy. For him, the spirit of democracy expressed in the epoch of *laissez-faire* capitalism had been challenged to find a new justification by the rise of giant corporations and national labor unions; moreover, its *elan* had been chastened by the consolidation of a centralized administrative state, the professionalization of political party leadership, and the expansion of mass communications. President Franklin D. Roosevelt's program for American national recovery had called into being a policy of economic and social Keynesianism—federal intervention into what had hitherto been free market economic operations as well as the seemingly inexorable dynamics of the social process. In the midst of these great changes in America's politics, culture, economy, and ways of life, Blumer analyzed an emerging social order that was transforming older and outworn conceptions of the public philosophy.

Blumer's sociology encapsulates a public philosophy that is neither shrouded in the metaphysical mysteries of historical processes nor placed beyond the capacity of individuals—or their elected representatives and appointed officials—to determine and direct. Anchoring his perspective in a consistent epistemology, he implicitly formulated a political sociology in the face of the bankruptcy of virtually all received paradigms of social science. Most of what passed for theoretical sociology, he argued, had failed to grasp the nature of human nature. Blumer rejected all religious eschatologies and secular utopias; he remained outside of and in opposition to prevalent ideologies; and he believed that a social scientific approach to a democratic public philosophy must be faithful to the essential character of that ethos. His approach emphasizes the collective construction of meaning that imparts definition to the various schemes of social reality, repudiates the allegedly irrevocable effects of structural arrangements, and allows for—indeed, expects and encourages—opposition, individuality, and idiosyncracy within the social order. Moreover, he developed this new sociology on the basis of systematic investigations of the major problems that trouble American public life: the race question; the problems of work and management under incipient and advanced industrialization; and the moral issues that plague a civil democratic society.

A sociological approach to a public philosophy transcends the usual descriptions of the statics and dynamics of a stratified order; the latter are the conventions of American sociological thought. It requires, in Howard Brotz's fine phrase, "the understanding that society must have some over-all principle that establishes what is respected and [acknowledges] that even the presence of conflicting standards in itself exhibits a principle."[10] What that principle (or set of principles) is, how it is translated into belief and policy, and whether it is accepted, modified or repudiated by the citizenry constitute central problems for a civic sociology.

Whereas Blumer holds that any general societal principle is formulated in the course of the collective acts and responses that define a novel situation, and is subject to reconsideration, repudiation, or reaffirmation as part of the ongoing process that accompanies important public events, many sociologists have virtually accepted the thesis—put forward at various times by Gunnar Myrdal, Talcott Parsons and Seymour Martin Lipset,— that America's public philosophy is patterned within a contradictory value complex of liberty and equality and effected through a dynamic process that insures stability in the midst of change. However, the latter perspective has led each of its proponents to quite different conclusions about one of America's most pressing social issues—the race question. In 1944, Myrdal, holding that fundamental contradictions of liberty and equality could not endure, predicted a beneficent conclusion to that question: the "higher" values of democracy would drive racism out of both the individual American conscience and the collective consciousness of America's public institutions.[11] More than two decades after Myrdal's prediction had failed to materialize, Parsons assured Americans that an "inclusion" process—derived from the Founding Fathers' commitment to both freedom and equality— would absorb the several racial and ethnic aspirants one at a time; however, he warned that an economic base-line from which each group might rise must be established first, and that a public policy aimed at realizing this goal must be adopted. Hence, Parsons reasoned, with the consolidation of the New Deal's economic aid to blacks and other classes of the deserving poor, full citizenship for the Negro was close at hand—as long as nothing occurred to interfere with America's social conscience or legislative imperatives.[12] Least optimistic was Lipset. Holding that American society achieved its balance as a result of pushes toward conformity and equality evoking pulls toward liberty and individuality, he bitterly acknowledged that full democracy would be denied to America's blacks until a surge of voluntary affirmative action, producing *more* than equality, would alleviate their plight.[13] Blumer's position on this issue is quite different; it belongs to an approach recently characterized by Glenn Tinder as *civility,* i.e., it "sustains bonds of a kind with all human beings . . . [but, while] many feel historical despair [and] others remain fiercely determined to transform society . . . , [it] is an effort to stand clear of both extremes, neither falling into political despondency nor counting on historical transformation."[14]

The racial question is but one illustration of a multiplicity of situations toward which a public philosophy must be directed. Others include industrial problems, morale in wartime, and mass opinion. Functionalist and positivist sociologists adapted older ideas of a moving-but-stable social system to the newly established welfare state and prophesied progressive if gradual transformations of American life and society. Postulating that society would necessarily be moved and yet always remain in a state of equilibrium, they nominated themselves as scientifically disinterested but democratically inclined navigators for the ship of state.[15] Blumer worked out of another tradition entirely, one foreshadowed by, but different in its particulars from that inspiring Sumner, Herbert Croly, and Walter Lippmann. That tradition takes as its starting point the necessity of formulating a public philosophy for an American society that no longer relies on sanguinary eschatologies and is not assured of permanent social or dynamic equilibrium.

10

Blumer's Antecedents

SUMNER, CROLY, AND
THE SOUTHERN COMTEANS

Sumner came to the conclusion that the problems of modernity that challenged democracy could best be met by limiting the federal power. "In the present case," he wrote, "I maintain that the way to minimize the dangers to democracy, and from it, is to reduce to the utmost its functions, the number of its officials, the range of its taxing power, the variety of its modes of impinging on the individual, the amount and range of its expenditures, and, in short, its total weight. . ."[16] However, there remained the problem of a philosophy that could guide even a limited democratic republic. Sumner could not see what that philosophy would be—he left its formulation and praxiology as a bequest from the nineteenth century to the twentieth: "For the present and the immediate future the purification of political institutions is the most urgent task which demands our effort. . ."[17] A Puritan moralist, Sumner believed that America had been sunk in corruption and that it could only be redeemed by the moral probity of its leaders and the personal integrity of its citizens.

Although Sumner had treated the problem of the public philosophy as central for a reconstituted sociology in a reconstructed republic, most sociologists demurred from that challenge, opting instead to reinvigorate the disintegrating moral fabric of the American populace by establishing a new covenant. This social compact would combine civil faith with scientific endeavor. Steeped in the recently proclaimed Social Gospel, most nineteenth and early twentieth century sociologists sought solutions to the problems of poverty, alienation, and disorganization in settlement houses or set forth scientific proposals to control or eliminate altogether those dependent, defective, and delinquent persons whose presence in America made the Social Question manifest.[18] It was left to such figures as Herbert Croly, a self-proclaimed disciple of Auguste Comte, Walter Lippmann, a scion of a new Enlightenment, and Herbert Blumer, a leader in what should be seen as a sociological instauration, to address Sumner's problem. Although none achieved closure on the issue, each posed questions in ways that attested to the need for a new political sociology, one that would be faithful to the distinctive nature of its subject matter: multivalent man in pluralistic society.

Taking his point of departure from the philosophy of Auguste Comte, Herbert Croly attempted to define a public philosophy that would suit a unified corporate society—a society in the throes of industrial advance and their concomitant social and moral problems. Although Comte's *Cours de philosophie positive* (1830–1842) had been a basic intellectual resource for America's antebellum sociologists—Henry Hughes, George Fitzhugh, George Frederick Holmes, and Joseph Le Conte[19]—it did not exert a similar influence on those of the post Civil War era. Insofar as it continued to influence American sociologists, it provided a scientific imprimatur supporting the fulfillment of the Social Gospel. Even after Luther Lee Bernard rediscovered Henry Hughes' Comtean *Treatise on Sociology* in 1927 and attempted through it to revive the theoretical perspective and public policy orientation of the man who had given sociology its name,[20] little interest was aroused among academic and professional practitioners in America. However, outside of the academic discipline, Comteanism found a foremost publicist, first in David Croly (1829–1889) and later, and more comprehensively, in his son, Herbert (1869–1930). Just as Comte's social philosophy was a response to the French Revolution and its European aftermath, Herbert Croly's "new nationalism" hoped to redress the social and economic inequities that troubled America's Industrial Revolution and provide a new vision of an industrializing, progressive American republic.

Croly's Comtean analysis not only reconceptualized what Sumner had called the threat posed by plutocracy, but also reappraised the issue that had divided the Federalists and Democratic Republicans in the Revolutionary era: whether unregulated commercial capitalism would support or subvert a democracy rooted in civic virtue. The Federalists had relied on the hidden hand that guided the operations of a liberal economic policy, while the Jeffersonians hoped to insure the common good through limited government and each American's freehold of a productive farm. Each party's ideal was thwarted from the start by events and policies that eroded its spirit: the practice of chattel slavery, the military conquest and forced sequestration of the Indians, transcontinental advance, and the rise of cities, commerce, and manufacturing. Croly's Comteanism virtually repudiated the limitations on governmental action established in the Constitution of 1787 and called, in Comte's words, for government to "intervene in the performance of all the various functions of the social economy, to keep up the idea of the whole, and the feeling of the common inter-connection: and the more energetically, the more individual activity tends to dissolve them . . ." Together with Comte, Croly believed that "The very nature of its action indicates that it cannot be merely material, but also, and much more, intellectual and moral; so as to show the double necessity of what has been called the temporal and spiritual government . . ."[21] Comte's interventionism, although far more pervasive than that put forward a century later by John Maynard Keynes, envisioned a concentration of economic power in ever-enlarging corporate structures.[22]

Croly's proposals for reconstructing the American economy echoed Comte, calling not for the dissolution of monopolies and trusts, but for governmental "discrimination in their favor."[23] He proposed establishment of a regulated industrial organization that would invigorate national development by stimulating "the peculiarly efficient individual . . . , offering him opportunities for work commensurate with his abilities and training."[24] Excessive profits would be reduced by new corporate taxes and the governmental encouragement of "enlightened shrewdness" on the part of capitalists and entrepreneurs.[25] Moreover, in Croly's vision of a reconstructed America, labor unions would be recognized officially, but such recognition would not license their unrestricted demands on the political economy. Rather, as in the proposal affecting corporations, governmental recognition would subject them to "an effective fight . . . against their unjustifiable demands . . . The state will recognize the kind of union which in contributing to the interest of its members contributes also to the general economic interest."[26] Croly believed that a public philosophy could only be developed within a framework that recognized the value of, but regulated the relations among, modern society's large scale units of production.

In Croly's Comtean vision, the individual could best realize his or her own potential in a society guided by a collectivized techno-industrial public philosophy. Like Sumner, Croly looked to the individual to perfect his talents—"that is, by doing his own special work with ability, energy, disinterestedness, and excellence,"[27]—but he insisted that "no one shall be admitted to the ranks of the thoroughly competent performers until he is morally and intellectually, as well as scientifically and manually, equipped for excellent work." Moreover, Croly continued, "These appropriate moral and intellectual standards should be applied as incorruptibly as those born of specific technical practices."[28] Implicit in the latter is the establishment not only of an untrammeled standard of excellence, but also, and more importantly, of a techno-moral magistracy empowered to judge and reward those who prove their worth through their work. Such a magistracy would be composed of those who had already achieved the Comtean ideal of human self-reconstruction, i.e., those who had succeeded conscientiously and independently to the highest stage of Positivist philosophical consciousness: "[Such a] disinterested and competent individual is formed for constructive leadership just as the less competent and independent but well-intentioned individual is formed more or less faithfully to follow on behind."[29] Moreover, these leaders possess the "intellectual and moral ability required, not merely to conceive, but to realize a policy of social reorganization . . . ," and their capacity to exercise these abilities "is far higher than the ability to carry on an ordinary democratic government."[30] Indeed, Croly concluded, "Such leadership, in a country whose traditions and ideals are sincerely democratic, can scarcely go astray."[31] For Croly personal probity and technomorally virtuous leadership—incorruptibility—were essential to the survival and enhancement of modern American democracy.

Croly's program for an America reconstructed in terms of collective individualism constitutes an unacknowledged elaboration of the public philosophy put forward a half-century earlier by the Southern Comtean, Henry Hughes (1829–1862).[32] Like Hughes, he allowed for social controls over those workers who could or would not become part of any collective. And, again like Hughes, he imagined that the element of labor least amenable to self-directed personal ambition and effortful achievement was likely to be found among unskilled farm workers. Inspired as much by Calvin as by Comte, Hughes had proposed that governmentally sanctioned coercion be implemented to insure that everyone complied with the universal obligation to work—a system he called "Warranteeism" and urged in justification of black slavery. Croly, mindful of the fact that since 1863, institutionalized slavery was no longer possible, and knowing that, once urban industrial workers were organized by labor unions, "the only important kind of non-union laborer left in the country would be agricultural," believed that a permanent supply of farm workers could be assured only if exacting competency tests would be administered to all who sought escape from the rural sector, and if federal legislators and the general citizenry came to recognize that the large-scale farm, like its predecessor, the plantation, provided a technical as well as a moral training ground for workers "of the most inferior class." " . . [F]arm labor," he wrote, "is, on the whole, much more wholesome for economically dependent and mechanically untrained men than labor in towns and cities. They are more likely under such conditions to maintain a high moral standard."[33]

Like his Southern Comtean predecessors, Croly linked the race question to that of labor and saw in both a need to keep blacks and other supposedly inferior classes out of the urban industrial mainstream. Writing about slavery, he praised the plantation owners for being "right . . . in believing that negroes [sic] were a race possessed of moral and intellectual qualities inferior to those of the white men," and for seeing "clearly . . . that the Abolitionists were applying a narrow and perverted political theory to a complicated and delicate set of economic and social conditions."[34] When Croly addressed the situation whereby "Agriculture suffers in this country from the scarcity, the instability, and the high cost of labor," and warned that "unless it [i.e., agricultural labor] becomes more abundant, less fluid, and more efficient compared to its cost, intensive farming, as practiced in Europe, will scarcely be possible . . . ," he echoed the claims and complaints put forward by California's incipient agribusinessmen. In California, a variant of Hughes's "warranteeism" had been put into practice in order to rationalize the labor needs of the owners of erstwhile Mexican *latifundia,* plantation-size farms that had remained intact in accordance with a provision of the Treaty of Guadalupe Hidalgo. Guided in part by the sociological observations on race and agriculture put forward by the University of California's first professor, the former slaveholder and Southern Comtean, Joseph Le Conte,[35] the State's large-scale farmers embarked on a program experimenting with various foreign-born, non-white and non-Anglo workers—Chinese, Japanese, East Indian, Filipino, and Mexican—in an effort to discover the most efficient, least rebellious, and best exploited agricultural labor force. Croly's assertion "that the least intelligent and trained grade of labor would be more prosperous on the farms than in the cities, because of the lower cost of living in an agricultural region [and because their] scale of wages would be determined in general by that of the lowest grade of industrial labor . . ."[36] serves not only to link the applications of antebellum to postwar Comteanism, but also to indicate the accommodation of his public philosophy to the surviving vestiges of slavery.

Croly's federal-interventionist proposals adumbrated the Keynesian public policy that Franklin D. Roosevelt would later effect. However, they also recalled Henry Hughes's demand that the state enforce every American's obligation to work in an appropriate calling. Croly's philosophy entailed a democracy ensconced within a techno-moral meritocracy while Hughes's "warranteeism" envisioned an agricultural republic guided by a landed seigneurial aristocracy. Common to both was a distrust of the masses, a commitment to an orderly stratification of classes (and, in Hughes's case, of races and sexes), and an exhortation that the right kind of people must both reign and rule.

Croly proposed a form of collective individualism that would at once be moral, practical, and liberating. His "new nationalism" hoped to evoke a new set of civic virtues: ". . . success in the achievement of the national purpose will contribute positively to the liberation of the individual, both by diminishing his temptations, improving his opportunities, and . . . enveloping him in an invigorating rather than an enervating moral and intellectual atmosphere."[37] As Croly conceived of the matter, a person's "actual occupation may tend to make his individuality real and fruitful; but the quality of the work is determined by a merely acquisitive motive, and the man himself thereby usually debarred from obtaining any edifying personal independence or any peculiar personal distinction . . ." His programmatic philosophy would inspire a collective effort that would not only emancipate Americans from the hazards of "unlimited competition," but also and more significantly deter them from compromising their individual integrity in behalf of worldly success.

Croly also meant his new philosophy to apply to the new class of businessmen, who, he believed, " . . . are forced into a common mold, because the ultimate measure of the value of their work is the same, and is nothing but its results in cash."[38] Ultimately, he concluded, "The man whose motive is that of money-making will not make the work any more excellent than is demanded by the largest possible returns; and frequently the largest possible returns are to be obtained by indifferent work or by work which has absolutely no social value."[39] In modern society work as such did not necessarily contain any social values. However, work might be infused with social value if a "national structure . . . encourages individuality as opposed to mere particularity . . . [and] creates innumerable special niches, adapted to all degrees and kinds of individual development." Under a national industrial and educational policy inspired by such goals, the "individual becomes a nation in miniature, but devoted to the loyal realization of a purpose peculiar to himself, [while the] nation becomes an enlarged individual whose special purpose is that of human amelioration, and in whose life every individual should find some new but essential function."[40]

Croly's vision of a corporatist state promised a final outcome: "The ultimate end is the complete emancipation of the individual . . ." But, "that result depends on his complete disinterestedness. He must become interested exclusively in the excellence of his work." Moreover, such disinterestedness could not be achieved so "long as heavy responsibilities and high achievements are supposed to be rewarded by increased pay . . . The only way in which work can be made entirely disinterested is to adjust its compensation to the needs of a normal and wholesome human life."[41] A public policy appropriate to a democratic corporatist state would take as its goal the cultivation of the citizen as a total person.

America might achieve its national purpose, not by seeking

to differentiate itself from feudal Europe, but rather by tearing away the providential shibboleth of its Christian heritage: "The bondage from which Americans needed, and still need, emancipation is not from Europe, but from the evasions, the incoherence, the impatience, and the easy-going conformity of their own intellectual and moral traditions."[42] These traditions included that part of the Puritan heritage holding that "somehow a special Providential design was effective on the American people, which permitted them as individuals and as a society to achieve their purposes by virtue of good intentions, exuberant enthusiasm, and enlightened selfishness."[43] In place of all this—and Croly admitted that clearing away the debris of such a debilitating heritage would be an arduous and time-consuming task—there was needed a new Positivist disinterestedness, inspired by the ethic of producing socially valuable and high-quality work. There was required a moral re-education of the American people, a building up of a new set of what Sumner had called mores and folkways. And this could be accomplished only by means of a thorough-going, dedicated, nationalistic and authoritative pedagogics. Moreover, "the process of educating men of moral and intellectual stature sufficient for the performance of important constructive work cannot be disentangled from the process of national fulfillment by means of intelligent collective action." Ultimately, it would require the establishment of a new stratum of Positivist leadership; for "American nationality will never be fulfilled except under the leadership of such men; and the American nation will never obtain the necessary leadership unless it seeks seriously the redemption of its national responsibility."[44]

Although Croly was aware of the difficulties that lay ahead, he thought he saw signs of the coming Positivist age in the fact that recently, "Those who were able to gain leadership in business and politics [had] sought to justify their success by building up elaborate and political organizations which gave themselves and their successors peculiar individual opportunities"; while "The men of more specifically intellectual interests [had] tacitly abandoned the Newer-Worldliness of their predecessors and . . . discovered that the first step in the acquisition of the better standards of achievement was to go abroad."[45] Croly was enthusiastic over the fact that a "similar transformation has been taking place in the technical aspects of American industry," that of "late years even farming has become an occupation in which special knowledge is supposed to have certain advantages," and that in "every kind of practical work specialization, founded on a more or less arduous course of preparation, is coming to prevail."[46]

Like Henry Hughes before him, Croly found in Comteanism a secular theodicy of work that he converted to a national public philosophy of productive effort. But, whereas Hughes had been confident that intellectuals, professionals, plantation owners, and skilled workers naturally possessed the instinct of workmanship and the call to public service (while only unskilled workers and slaves needed the coercive threat of state-enforced punishment to instill effort),[47] Croly, writing a half-century later, was less sanguine: "The comparatively zealous and competent individual performer . . . has still much to contend against in his social, economic, and intellectual environment. His independence is precarious . . . What the better American individual particularly needs, then, is a completer faith in his own individual purpose and power."[48] And this, Croly hoped, might be achieved by a collective process of ethically structured symbolic interaction: "The principle of democracy *is* virtue," Croly insisted, and the "common citizen can become something of a saint and something of a hero, not by growing to heroic proportions in his own person, but by the sincere and enthusiastic imitation of heroes and saints, . . . [But,] whether or not he will ever come to such imitation will depend upon the ability of his exceptional fellow-countrymen to offer him acceptable examples of heroism and saintliness."[49] In this, Croly anticipated the development of the heroes and heroines of the mass media, but he would have hoped that they would represent an image of public morality, rather than pubescent patriotism or cavalier commerce.

Croly's hope for an America born again under the inspiration of work-for-its-own-sake and his faith in a leadership stratum comprised of disinterested social technocrats has not come to pass. Writing in 1986, more than seven decades after Croly proposed his new nationalism, Lawrence M. Mead, an admirer of Croly and an advocate of a kind of neo-Crolyism to solve America's race and work problems, asserts that the welfare state is a failure because it never set efficient production standards nor did it enforce obligations to work among the recipients of governmental largesse.[50] Although he does not invoke Henry

Hughes's public philosophy of warranteeism—the social obligation of every "warrantee" to produce in return for the "warran-
tor's" beneficence, both to be regulated and administered by the
magistracy of the state—Mead argues a virtually identical thesis.
Just as Hughes had insisted that blacks needed a regime of warranteeism in order to be both productive and secure in a perfectly
coordinated hierarchy of labor, so Mead insists that in an age of
equality, "The most vulnerable Americans need obligations, as
much as rights, if they are to move as equals on the stage of
American life."[51] Invoking the shade of Croly, Mead laments the
fact that, despite the brilliance of his thesis, its message has not
been received. Belief in either *laissez-faire* freedom or the social
obligations of beneficent democracy has led both liberals and
conservatives to misconstrue the duty of leadership: "Neither
will use authority in social policy in a benevolent *and* directive
way."[52] Like Croly before him, Mead perceives the contemporary Social Question in terms of the need to re-educate, indeed,
to re-socialize the poor, the blacks, the unwed mothers and the
unemployed youth: "What is missing is the idea of obligation.
Work is normative for the poor, but it is not something they feel
they must do, whatever the personal cost."[53]

Whereas Croly had little to say about the condition of black
freedmen, Mead is reminiscent of Hughes in the latter's concern
for coercively obligating the Negro to work and to see his purpose in life as the discharge of his labor obligation. Mead insists
that the "need to enforce work is clearest in the case of young
black men, the group most central to the work problem."[54] After
summarizing a number of explanations of black youth joblessness, Mead argues that "however we explain their joblessness,
the overriding fact is that their behavior is not controlled by the
normal expectations supporting work." Indeed, Mead goes on to
describe young blacks as persons living outside of the social system: "They are, in Hobbes' phrase, 'masterless men' living in
many ways outside their social norms."[55] Fearing the moral
effects on the social order that a large number of masterless
Negroes would produce, Henry Hughes had once mulled over a
proposal that manumitted slaves to be exported to Africa in exchange for new batches of black "warrantees," the latter to be
educated as docile obligees of the South's peculiar institution;[56]
Mead, writing long after the black population might be consid-

ered for foreign export, proposes that work be made an obligation for black youths and a basic support of community survival:
"Community has indeed dissolved in the low-wage market. For
it to be restored, work must apparently become a duty for the
least skilled, not just a matter of self-interest."[57] And, like Comte,
Hughes, and Croly, Mead believes that in the absence of compelling moral suasion from within, "Only public authority in
some form can restore order." For blacks and other "masterless
men" Mead's version of Comtean-Crolyeanism relegates the
public philosophy to an American variant of *Arbeit macht frei,* and
fails to see that work as such no longer provides the moral foundation for either a meaningful life or a public philosophy.

WALTER LIPPMANN:
PUBLIC OPINION VERSUS
A PUBLIC PHILOSOPHY

Modernity and Democracy

In a letter to Quincy A. Wright, dated January 25, 1955,
Walter Lippmann, (1889–1974) perhaps twentieth century America's foremost philosopher of democracy, observed, "I do, of
course, distinguish the public philosophy from the ideology or
religion of any particular group . . . [The] public philosophy is
necessary for a plural society and . . . it assumes the existence of
diversities of belief."[58] Lippmann—an assimilated Jew who ma-
triculated at Harvard, collaborated with Herbert Croly in founding *The New Republic,* and in the first six decades of the century
established himself as a national public conscience—had observed in 1910 that "Those who are young today are born into a
world in which the foundations of the older order survive only as
habits or by default."[59] Pessimistic in a way that recalls Sumner,
Lippmann came to espouse a different view from his. Where
Sumner had despaired of "stateways" making the foundation for
"folkways," Lippmann couched his vision of a saving public philosophy in the rule of law, the superiority of reason over passion,

and the triumph of the Enlightenment in America. Lippmann's emphasis on law and rational procedures derived in part from his conclusions about the severe limitations of religious precepts and about the moral gaps in a life governed by the spirit alone: "The deposit of wisdom in The Bible and in the classic books does not contain a systematic and comprehensive statement of moral principles from which it is possible to deduce with clarity and certainty specific answers to concrete questions."[60] A twentieth century Positivist, Lippmann placed his faith in the Comtean ideals of careful experiment,[61] adjudicative reason,[62] and a deliberative approach to the solution of public problems.[63] However, for him each of these was constrained and sometimes threatened: passions all too often overwhelmed public opinion; while political competitiveness sapped the spiritual strength of democratic governance.

Lippmann credited Croly's *The Promise of American Life* with being "the political classic which announced the end of the Age of Innocence with its romantic faith in American destiny and inaugurated the process of self-examination."[64] However, for Lippmann the consciousness under self-analysis was by no means mature: A young man of the modern era "faces an enormously complicated world, full of stirring and confusion and ferment. He hears of movements and agitations, criticisms and reforms, knows people who are devoted to 'causes', feels angry or hopeful at different times, goes to meetings, reads radical books, and accumulates a sense of uneasiness and pending change."[65] Lippmann hoped that his book, *Drift and Mastery* would provide a new perception on and a new praxis for this general unease.[66] Americans, he noted in 1914, would have to choose between "drift"—a mindless acquiescence to the forces that seemed to be shaping their destiny—and a conscious effort at mastering their history in the very making of it. If they chose the latter, they could forge their own futures. Mastery, however, would require dedication and effort. Early in his career, Lippmann looked to the social sciences as a source for both wisdom and guidance in this task.

As part of his Enlightenment heritage, Lippmann accepted and elaborated upon Bacon's distrust of ordinary man's capacity for reason. And, like Bacon, he put his faith in scientific knowledge. In his critical analysis of the vagaries of public opinion, published in 1922, he proposed that a synthesis of theoretical and applied social science become a regular, indeed, indispensable resource for government and a guide in the making of public policy. America, for Lippmann "The Great Society," could not be governed " . . . by men who thought deductively about rights and wrongs, [but it] could be brought under human control only by the technic which had created it."[67] Paradoxically, Lippmann observed, although elected officials had solicited the advice of "statisticians, accountants, auditors, industrial counsellors, engineers of many species, scientific managers, personnel administrators, research men, 'scientists,' and sometimes just plain private secretaries . . . , [they were] slow to call in the social scientist."[68] The latter had much to offer the makers of public policy, Lippmann believed, but only if the positions that presently ordered relations between men of affairs and academics could be reversed: "Today the sequence is that the man of affairs finds his facts, and decides on the basis of them; then, sometime later, the social scientist deduces excellent reasons why he did not decide wisely . . . The real sequence should be one where the disinterested expert first finds and formulates the facts for the man of action, and later makes what wisdom he can out of comparison between the decision, which he understands, and the facts which he organized."[69]

Lippmann's views in 1922 are not dissimilar from Lester F. Ward's earlier proposal for an American technocentric sociocracy; moreover, they adumbrated William Fielding Ogburn's and Charles Merriam's 1933 proposal that the positivist-oriented Social Science Research Council become the principal planning agency of the Executive branch.[70] However, by the mid-1930s, Lippmann, unhappy with many of President Franklin D. Roosevelt's New Deal policies, began to express skepticism about the benefits that social scientific knowledge might provide: "The essential limitation . . . of all policy, of all government, is that the human mind must take a partial and simplified view of existence. The ocean of experience cannot be poured into the little bottles of our intelligence . . . It is, therefore, illusion to imagine that there is a credible meaning in the idea that human evolution can be brought under conscious control."[71] Repudiating Ward's idea of a collective social telesis, Lippmann, after having read L. J. Henderson's edition of *Pareto's General Sociology,* asserted that

"The logic by which it might become possible to analyze the 'mutually dependent variations of . . . variables' is such an abstruse logico-mathematical undertaking that it is as much beyond the lay mind of a minister of public affairs or his technical advisers as chemistry is beyond a cook."[72] Lippmann consigned the effective application of social science to public policy to some future time, "when the higher logic will have been sufficiently developed to enable thinkers to analyze the whole relevant social order, and from the analysis to predict successfully the real, not merely the apparent and immediate, effect of a political intervention."[73] Until that time, the public policy would have to depend for its formulation and support on the application of human reason and the rule of law.

Obstacles to Enlightenment: Stereotypes and the Mass Media

When decisions on public issues and the election of officials are to be carried out, a representative democracy requires that each citizen exercise the deliberative faculty, and more significantly, ensure its sovereignty over the passions. However, it was precisely the capacity and willingness to employ reason that Lippmann worried about. Subjecting the Enlightenment's faith in reason—best represented in James Mill's statement in *The Liberty of the Press:*

> Every man possessed of reason is accustomed to weigh evidence and to be guided and determined by its preponderance. When various conclusions are, with their evidence, presented with equal care and with equal skill, there is a moral certainty, though some few may be misguided, that the greatest number will judge right, and that the greatest force of evidence, whatever it is, will produce the greatest impression.[74]

—to a searching examination, Lippmann concluded that the Utilitarian's faith in the ultimate triumph of right reason had been premature. ". . . [T]aking it all at the most favorable estimate, the time each day is small when any of us is directly exposed to information from our unseen environment."[75] As a result perception is modified and reception restricted. Information comes to us not as events or persons intrinsic to their situation and status, but rather in stereotypes. "There is a connection between our vision and the facts," Lippmann showed, "but it is often a strange connection."[76] Ordinary people do not "first see, and then define," but rather "define first and then see." Further, their definitions are not original works of creative intelligence; instead, out from "the great blooming, buzzing confusion of the outer world we pick out what our culture has already defined for us."[77] A central characteristic of modernity, Lippmann observed, is the separation of the individual from direct and immediate information about persons and matters that are relevant for decision-making and judgment.

Among the stereotyped forms of information that Americans regularly receive and act upon are their conceptions of alien peoples, exotic races, and foreign nationalities. "What does the word 'Japan' evoke?" Lippmann asked, and then inquired: "Is it a vague horde of slant-eyed yellow men, surrounded by Yellow Perils, picture brides, fans, Samurai, banzais, art, and cherry blossoms?"[78] National stereotypes not only affected the perception of the mass in the street, but also and more significantly, the politicians and statesmen who met to decide the fate of the world. At the Paris Peace Conference that concluded the First World War—where Lippmann served as a member of the American Commission—"Clemenceau [when dealing with the German representatives] . . . saw the type, and . . . took to heart those reports . . . which fitted the type that was in his mind. If a junker blustered, that was an authentic German; if a labor leader confessed the guilt of the empire, he was not an authentic German."[79] Lippmann held that the source of perceptive distortions and partial or misinformation is not humankind's biological heritage; rather, they arise from society's fundamental institutions of socialization. "In so far as political habits are alike in a nation," Lippmann observed, "the first places to look for an explanation are the nursery, the school, the church . . . [I]t is a solecism of the worst order to ascribe political differences to the germ plasm."[80] However, Lippmann noted, it was precisely the parents, teachers, and churchmen who seemed least amenable to the dictates of reason.

Modernity itself—and especially the communicative media's alienating effects—had separated the individual from first-hand experience, denying him that clarity of information that is indisputably necessary for making an informed judgment. At the same time, the findings of modern psychology seem to challenge the Enlightenment's assurance that human reason could reign supreme over the individual. Lippmann, who had been impressed during his Harvard days by Hugo Munsterberg's demonstrations of everyday distortions in ordinary human perception, became especially distressed by the reason-disturbing effects of two of the popular mass media—movies and newspapers.[81] On March 22, 1915, Lippmann sought to enlist the aid of John Collier in restricting the showing of D. W. Griffith's *Birth of a Nation,* the film version of Thomas Dixon's fictional glorification of the Ku Klux Klan, *The Clansman.*[82] Seven years later Lippmann was still sufficiently disturbed by the negrophobic incitements of *Birth of a Nation* to utilize the movie as an example of how "Photographs have the kind of authority over imagination today, which the printed word had yesterday, and the spoken word before that . . . [O]n the screen the whole process of observing, describing, reporting, and then imagining, has been accomplished for you . . . The shadowy idea becomes vivid; your hazy notion, let us say, of the Ku Klux Klan . . . takes vivid shape when you see the *Birth of a Nation.* Historically it may be the wrong shape, morally it may be a pernicious shape, but it is a shape, and I doubt whether anyone who has seen the film and does not know more about the Ku Klux Klan than Mr. Griffiths, [sic] will ever hear the name again without seeing those white horsemen."[83] Moreover, Lippmann accused movies of evoking unwarranted passions from their audiences and berated them for introducing erotic motifs into their tales about issues of public importance. "Only in moving pictures, novels, and some magazine fiction are industrial relations, business competition, politics, and diplomacy tangled up with the girl and the other woman."[84] Yet, he was forced to admit that film was a new source for discovering the truth about disputed matters and for verifying discrepant observations: "It was the moving pictures which finally settled a real doubt in many reporters' minds, owing to the slowness of the human eye, as to just what blow of Dempsey's knocked out Carpentier."[85] Precisely because movies and other popular media seemed so accurate and evoked such powerful feelings, Lippmann despaired of any constructive role that they or any other institution of mass culture might play in public affairs.

Movies are screened fictions that convey pseudo-facts and express and invite passionate emotions; news media, on the other hand, are supposed to present the unvarnished truth about matters vital to the rational decisions and informed judgments that the modern citizen of a democracy must make. But Lippmann was skeptical of the truths in reports that appear in newspapers and magazines. In a letter to Oliver Wendell Holmes, Jr., he observed " . . . [The] difficulty is that in addition to men's natural limitation in apprehending truth about society, there have grown up institutions such as the press, propaganda, and censorship which block the road to truth. At best these institutions put truth second to what they think is morality or patriotism; at worst they are downright liars."[86] In 1922, bitter about the fact "that no American student of government, no American sociologist, has ever written a book on news-gathering," Lippmann complained that "practically everywhere it is assumed that the press should do spontaneously for us what primitive democracy imagined each of us could do spontaneously for himself, that every day and twice a day it will present us with a true picture of all the outer world in which we are interested."[87] That true picture could not be provided, he argued, because of the pressures of the profit motive on editors and reporters, of stereotypes on the observations of news-gatherers and news-writers, of preconceived prejudices on the readers, and, finally, because the "truth about distant or complex matters is not self-evident, and the machinery for assembling information is technical and expensive."[88] Impressed by the quantitative techniques used in Paul U. Kellogg's Pittsburgh Survey, Lippmann contrasted the truth values available from statistical reports with those obtained from news reporters' investigations. "In order to tell the truth about the steelworker in the Pittsburgh district, there was needed a staff of investigators, a great deal of time, and several fat volumes of print. It is impossible to suppose that any daily newspaper could normally regard the making of Pittsburgh Surveys . . . as one of its tasks."[89]

Because they could not be operated as organs of social scientific reporting, Lippmann considered newspapers incapable of sustaining a public philosophy or guiding public policy. "The press is no substitute for institutions . . . [M]en cannot do the work of the world by this light alone. They cannot govern society by episodes, incidents, and eruptions . . . For the troubles of the press, like the troubles of representative government, be it territorial or functional, like the troubles of industry, be it capitalist, cooperative, or communist, go back to a common source: to the failure of self-governing people to transcend their casual experience and their prejudice, by inventing, creating, and organizing a machinery of knowledge."[90] The individual in a large scale organized society could not obtain access to the information and knowledge necessary for making rational political choices.

According to Lippmann, one prerequisite for a democratic public philosophy is "a reliable picture of the world." Such a picture was unlikely in modern societies, he complained, because "apathy, preference for the curious trivial as against the dull important, and the hunger for sideshows and three-legged calves"[91] tended to prevail. In this matter Lippmann's pessimism corresponded to that of Sumner, who had despaired of the masses' capacity to rise above sensual responses and who observed how the press catered to their lack of taste and inability to make deliberative judgments. Because "thinking and understanding are too hard work," Sumner claimed that ordinary people "use routine, set formulae, current phrases, caught up from magazines and newspapers of the better class."[92] Moreover, he argued, once the news medium had become a capitalist industry in its own right, "its managers are hampered by considerations, and obligations, and if they try to do justice to them all, they dare utter only colorless platitudes." The result was that the newspaper became at one and the same time "an institution of indispensable social utility, and . . . a foul nuisance." In the latter capacity, its editors, if "they get a chance to 'pitch into' something or somebody who has no power of defense . . . seize the opportunity to manifest freedom and independence . . . [and the] result is blackguardism."[93] The social fact that the masses preferred trashy novels, popular advertisements, humor-laden news reports, and yellow journalism was to Sumner a symptom of the inherent mentality of people in mass society and indicated how their prejudices and trivia would be continuously strengthened as the capacities for reason and critical understanding declined.[94] Sumner had supposed that the irrationalities of the new masses were still another bequest from the nineteenth to the twentieth centuries. Sadly, Lippmann seemed to agree, and he concluded that "the primary defect of popular government, a defect inherent in its traditions, . . ."[95] is its persistent activation of stereotypes and slogans.

The Public Philosophy and the American Community: Inclusion and Exclusion

In the same letter in which he distinguished the public philosophy from political ideologies and religious doctrines, Lippmann observed that "the public philosophy must be applicable to the entire community." But, although he would "not attempt to define a priori who is in the community and who is not," he believed that "the community really consists of those who accept and abide by the public philosophy."[96] With this statement Lippmann introduced a covenant of commitment that hoped to define and decide upon the qualifications for new members of the American commonwealth. Adherents of the public philosophy act in behalf of the rational pursuit of the public interest; for that "interest may be presumed to be what men would choose if they saw clearly, thought rationally, acted disinterestedly and benevolently."[97] In his effort to hold to reason as a foundation for a public philosophy, Lippmann was prepared to exclude the unreasonable members from the community.

Rationality in matters of public affairs required that the citizen true to the public philosophy decide "where he will strike a balance between what he desires and what can be done."[98] Lippmann's suspicion of ideologies, ancient religions, and cultural superstitions led him to worry over the distribution of rationality in a multi-ethnic society and to express serious doubts about the community *bona fides* of Jews, Blacks, and Japanese-Americans. In the case of Jews, Lippmann espoused unreserved assimilation as a way of avoiding "that rather Jewish feeling of not belonging," and asserted about himself, "I can find nothing in myself which responds to the specific Jewish ethos in religion or culture as it appears in the Old Testament . . . I have understood the classical and Christian heritage and feel it to be mine, and always have."[99] America, Lippmann believed, provided a setting— "for the first time on a large scale in the history of the Jewish

People"—in which "Jewish racial mysticism rationalized by Jewish theological exclusiveness would (. . . where there is no legal discrimination) break down under the impact of modern criticism and science." For this very reason Lippmann favored the quota of fifteen percent that Harvard University placed on the admission of Jews. "When . . . a large number of Jews are concentrated in a university like Harvard . . . [y]ou get not a spiritual conflict in which there might be first argument, then understanding, and finally perhaps conversion, but a conflict of manners and appearances inspired more by irritation than by conviction." Lippmann's sympathies were with the non-Jew: "His personal manners and physical habits are, I believe, distinctly superior to the prevailing manners and habits of the Jews." Moreover, Lippmann looked forward to the day when "Jewish exclusiveness" would be broken down and Jews, becoming more settled, would "assimilate these habits and . . . lose their racial identity."[100] Lippmann subscribed to the belief that Jewish distinctiveness, Jewish economic habits, and Jewish manners, customs, and ethnic exclusiveness were the main contributors to antisemitism.[101] Hence, he rejected Zionism,[102] opposed Randolph Bourne's pluralistic and pro-Zionist proposal for a "trans-national America,"[103] and did not agree with Horace Kallen's thesis that democracy thrived in and through the preservation of minority cultures.[104] In general, he anticipated the suggestion put forward in 1933 by Chicago sociologist Ellsworth Faris, that Jews dissolve their religio-ethnic identity utterly in the benevolent solvent of WASP America.[105] Until they had completed a thoroughgoing assimilation, Lippmann seemed to be saying, they belonged outside the community that formulated and was protected by the public philosophy.*

Lippmann's subscription to the war aims of the United States from 1941–1945 did not place emphasis on rescuing Jews or rooting out antisemitism. Rather, he envisioned an apocalyptic victory of Greco-Roman ideals of reason and law that would

---

*Lippmann's attitude toward the Jews expressed itself in a remarkable diffidence with respect to Hitler's persecution of them. He offered a half-hearted proposal that Europe's beleaguered Jews be resettled in Africa, but was silent about victims of the impending holocaust. It was the *nouveaux riches* eastern European Jews that outraged Lippmann's sense of a community. In a noteworthy newspaper column (May 19, 1933) Lippmann described one of Hitler's speeches as "the authentic voice of a genuinely civilized people," and he urged his readers

come about when America assumed its rightful place "at the center . . . of Western civilization. . . ." He issued a proclamation: "The American idea is not an eccentricity in the history of mankind . . . It is no accident—it is indeed historical and providential—that the formation of the first universal order since classical times should begin with the binding together of the dismembered parts of Western Christendom."[106] That universal order seemed to have room only for assimilated Jews. In 1948 Lippmann extended his thesis about Jews to the international world; he opposed the formation of a separate Jewish state in Israel, favoring instead an Arab-Jewish confederation.[107]

The race question was a different matter for Lippmann.[108] Racial violence, he wrote in 1919 in response to the race riot that had thrown Chicago into turmoil, arose because America's "planless, disordered, bedraggled, drifting democracy" had not yet "learned to house everybody, employ everybody at decent wages in a self-respecting status, guarantee his [i.e., the Negro's] civil liberties, and bring education and play to him . . ." Until it did learn to do these things, American pious talk about solving the race problem would "remain a sinister mythology." However, Lippmann believed that the Negro problem was peculiarly complicated by its entanglement within the anti-miscegenationist code precluding intimate interracial contacts. Moreover, he believed that the castelike character of America's racial order encouraged demoralization among and terrorism by insecure whites, who were themselves degraded and terror-stricken. Lippmann held that the constant proclamation of white superiority arises from "the parvenue, the snob, [and] the coward" and that it "evokes imitation in his victim." However, "so long as the status of the white man is in every way superior to that of the colored, the advancement of the colored man can mean nothing but an attempt to share the white man's social privileges." It was

not to judge the Germans by Nazi intolerance, asserting that that would be like judging "the Jews by their parvenus." More than a decade earlier, in an essay published in The American Hebrew on April 14, 1922, he had written that the "rich and vulgar and pretentious Jews of our big American cities are perhaps the greatest misfortune that has ever befallen the Jewish people," and were in fact the "real fountain of antisemitism." By 1933 he was prepared to accept the thesis that it was Jewish behavior that had brought about their misfortunes at the hands of the Nazis.

in this latter arena—in what Blumer would later designate as the inner citadel of the color bar—that Lippmann believed integration would have to wait on socio-economic uplift. Because he regarded the "terrible confusion between the idea of social equality and the idea of social mixture" to be at the core of the race problem, but also was sure that "permanent degradation is unthinkable and amalgamation undesirable for both blacks and whites," Lippmann proposed a vague resolution of the race problem in what he called "race parallelism." "We shall have to work out with the Negro a relationship which gives him complete access to all the machinery of our common civilization, and yet allows him to live so that no Negro need dream of a white heaven and of bleached angels." Although Lippmann wished to restrict Jews insofar as they had become parvenus, he hoped his program of race parallelism would bring blacks up to a position wherein "a dark skin is no longer associated with poverty, ignorance, misery, terror and insult." Only when race pride among blacks equalled that among whites would the latter "be able . . . to enjoy the finest quality of civilized living—the fellowship of different men." However, Lippmann did acknowledge a special feature of his proposal for race parallelism: "Parallel lines may be equally long and equally straight; they do not join except in infinity, which is further away than anyone need worry about just now." Equality could be achieved without social mixture. Full-fledged community might be put off until that equality had become fact.

Lippmann's identification of the public philosophy with the reign of reason, the Occident's legacy from the classical Mediterranean civilizations, did not extend to empathy with or concern for the civil rights and fundamental liberties of Americans of Asian descent. Moreover, military decisions made in World War II led him to compromise his philosophy and to develop casuistries designed to rationalize these defaults. The case in point is that of Japanese in the United States. He advocated the mass imprisonment of both Japanese aliens and American citizens of Japanese ancestry soon after Japan's attack on Pearl Harbor. " . . . [W]hat happened at Pearl Harbor," he wrote on December 18, 1941, "is the very pattern and image of the deadly illusions and moral failings which have prevailed among us since the other war . . ."[109] Consulting with the notoriously anti-Japanese General John L. DeWitt, Commander of the Western Defense Command that embraced Washington, Oregon, and California, Lippmann, writing under the headline "The Fifth Column on the Coast," asserted that "It is a fact that communication takes place between the enemy at sea and enemy agents on land." He went on to dismiss the embarrassing "fact that since the outbreak of the Japanese war there has been no important sabotage on the Pacific Coast" by invoking a conspiracy theory that recalled the "Yellow Peril" stereotype that he had criticized two decades earlier: "It is a sign that the blow is well-organized and that it is held back until it can be struck with maximum effect." Lippmann lamented what at first seemed "The unwillingness of Washington to adopt a policy of mass evacuation and mass internment of all those who are technically enemy aliens" and saw no problem in abrogating the civil rights of the sixty-five percent of Japanese American Pacific Coast residents who were citizens of the United States: "Nobody's constitutional rights include the right to reside and do business on a battlefield."[110] When certain of President Roosevelt's advisers expressed skepticism about the wisdom of removing and incarcerating the entire Japanese American population living along the West Coast, Lippmann rebuked Attorney General Francis Biddle about "the great gap between what you know in Washington and what was known [about Japanese Americans] on the Pacific Coast."[111] Lippmann proposed that the entire coast be declared a "combat zone" in which "everyone should be compelled to prove that he has a good reason for being there."[112] When in later years other pro-internment leaders began to regret their participation and recant their belief in the rightfulness of this wholesale incarceration, Lippmann remained adamant. However, he modified his rationale for supporting what the American Civil Liberties Union called the "worst single violation of civil rights of American citizens in our history,"[113] holding that it was necessary for the protection of the Japanese Americans from mobs. "There is no doubt that the rights of the citizens were abridged by the measure," Lippmann wrote to Palmer Hoyt, editor and publisher of the *Denver Post* on February 26, 1968, "but I felt then, and I still do, that the temper of the times made the measure justified."[114] Whatever else Lippmann's conception of the public philosophy entailed, it did not include the protection of a minority's fundamental rights when international crises aroused the passions and prejudices of the white citizenry. Reason itself, as Lippmann conceived of it, would not be sufficient to ground a public philosophy.

The Public Philosophy and the 'Mandate of Heaven'

Lippmann's pursuit of a public philosophy for democracy led him to inspect and reject religious doctrines, to applaud but then become skeptical about truths to be discovered by social science, and finally to return to an exhortation that Americans revive the political culture of civility. As a basis for this renewed civility, Lippmann called for a revival of respect for the principles of natural law. However, he warned that "we must be careful" in this matter. "They are not scientific 'laws' like the laws of the motion of the heavenly bodies. They do not describe human behavior as it is. They prescribe what it should be." These natural laws describe a rational order that "consists of the terms which must be met in order to fulfill men's capacity for the good life in this world." However, principles of natural law "do not enable us to predict what men will actually do."[115] Hence the old faith in a Positive philosophy that would predict and control human conduct is repudiated in Lippmann's ultimate formulation. In its place Lippmann evokes the image of the American citizen: "[T]he inwardness of the ruling man—whatever his titles and his rank—[is] that for the sake of his realm, of his order, of his regiments, of his ship, of his cause, he is the noble master of his own weaker and meaner passions."[116] Further, he argued that "the radical error of the modern democratic gospel is that it promises, not the good life of this world, but the perfect life of heaven." In Lippmann's later formulation, the good life of this world is limited on the one hand by what Montesquieu had said about freedom, that it "can consist only in the power of doing what we ought to will, and in not being constrained to do what we ought not to will,"[117] and, on the other, by what William James had spoken of as the "flux of things," i.e., the thesis that "Whatever equilibrium our finite experiences attain to are but provisional . . . [I]t will inevitably meet with friction and opposition from its neighbors. Its rivals and neighbors will destroy it unless it can buy them off by compromising part of the original pretensions."[118] Hence, the activation of the will to do right in a world of changing meanings requires improvisation and the employment of less-than-extreme rules. More significantly, it would entail acceptance of a mean "at the tension of push and pull, of attraction and resistance among the extremes," an outcome that is "imprecise and inconclusive."

Lippmann doubted that "The wisdom of the world can ever rise above these imperfections."[119] Nevertheless, he insisted on reasserting the existence of a distinctive public realm and the necessity to preserve and protect it. Its security would depend on the citizenry's ability to overcome the "terms of discourse in public controversy [that] are highly unfavorable to anyone who adheres to the public philosophy . . . , [that are] against the credibility and against the rightness of the principles of the constitutional state . . . , [and that] are set in favor of the Jacobin conception of the emancipated and sovereign people."[120] Set against these enemies of the public philosophy is the requirement that democracy be recognized as a government rooted in laws, and that these laws arise out of a deliberative and public discourse that gives them legitimacy "when they have the title of being right, which binds men's consciences."[121] Such a binding was ultimately religious, Lippmann eventually conceded. Unwilling to see it as part of a Christian heritage, Lippmann looked to Confucian ideas—the sound political ideas that would rise in a state steeped in legitimated law would have the "mandate of heaven."[122]

After serving fifty years as a public conscience for American politics, Lippmann was unable to define a wholly secular public philosophy. He accepted but was unable to transcend the exclusiveness of the American Protestant covenant, and in this respect his philosophy could not cope with the pluralism of American society after World War II. However, his hope for a politics that would be guided by a mandate from heaven, while suggesting a sense of desperation, does not vitiate the importance of his understanding of the role of mass communication, public opinion, and propaganda in modern politics. That mass behavior and its manipulation in politics and racial matters were of central concern for him and led him to a less than democratic attitude provides us with a base line from which to approach Blumer's conception of the public philosophy.

A Public Philosophy for
Mass Society:
The Civic Sociology of Herbert Blumer

Herbert Blumer's approach to a public philosophy proceeds indirectly. Its beginnings are to be found in his conception of meaning as the basis of action and his emphasis on the inextricable intertwining of action and meaning. Blumer eschews the dichotomy that divides reason from emotion and the hierarchy that positions rational understanding over passionate feeling. Each had aroused the fears of Croly and Lippmann. Blumer understands meaning to be a perspective that arises out of interaction itself. Meanings occur in and through situations and form by means of an interpretive process. Moreover, the emotions form an inseparable part of that process: "It is the affective element which ensures the attitude of its vigor, sustains it in the face of attack, and preserves it from change"[123]—and therefore, Blumer seems to infer, the cathexes cannot be derogated as expressions of some lower, inferior, and surmountable aspect of the human condition.

Attitudes and opinions—including public opinion—embrace both the definition of situations and the feelings about them. If a public philosophy is to be founded on a politico-sociological perspective that is faithful to the character of its subject matter, it would have to include a fundamental respect for the variations in human expression; moreover, as a logical extension of that respect, it could not restrict freedom of speech to what Lippmann had designated as "the ark of the covenant of the public philosophy. . . : [an] unchangeable commitment to rational determination."[124] Lippmann had supposed that "in the absence of [deliberative] debate unrestricted utterance leads to the degradation of opinion" and that by "a kind of Gresham's law the more rational is overcome by the less rational, and the opinions that will prevail will be those which are held most ardently by those with the most passionate will."[125] Furthermore, Lippmann believed that "the modern media of mass communication do not lend themselves easily to a confrontation of opinions."[126] At one time Lippmann had proposed that films that inflamed social antipathy be censored, and he later warned that if "there is no effective debate, the unrestricted right to speak will unloose so many propagandists, procurers, and panderers upon the public that sooner or later in self-defense the people will turn to the censors to protect them."[127] Blumer's orientation toward the media of mass communication is quite different; it developed out of his researches into a concrete situation—a proposal that film content be regulated in accordance with a moral code, in relation to which he investigated the cinema's effects on the moral virtues and social conduct of its audience.

INTERACTION AND
THE SOCIAL MEANING OF THE FILM

Blumer's film inquiries took place at the time movies had begun to have a serious impact on American society. The American film industry had been under intermittent attack by ethnic, religious, and moralistic groups since 1897, when a policeman closed down the showing of the silent movie *Orange Blossoms* for being what a court later declared to be an "outrage [to] public morals." Eighteen years later, the attack against *Birth of a Nation* launched by the National Association for the Advancement of Colored People, Walter Lippmann, and many others led to that film being banned more frequently than any other American movie.[128] In 1916 social psychology's first major contribution to film study—*The Photoplay* by Harvard University's Hugo Munsterberg—was published. In films Munsterberg found the basis for a science he had previously supposed to be impossible of formulation, a *Geisteswissenschaftliche* psychology that could envision the actual operations of the human mind. Precisely because of its great power of emotional representation and political persuasion, Munsterberg called for public and pedagogic controls over the film industry and for the establishment of a state-sponsored cinematic lyceum that would produce photoplays in the public interest.[129] Although Munsterberg's book had considerable influence on media studies undertaken by his erstwhile student, Robert Park, and on other members of the latter's Chicago school of sociology,[130] it did not bring about major changes in public policy on movies.

In the late 1920's Hollywood was again under attack. Although in 1922 the major studios had hired former Postmaster General Will Hays to preside over the newly formed Motion Pictures Producers and Distributors Association,[131] their approach to limited self-censorship had not satisfied the various self-appointed guardians of public and private virtue. In 1928, the University of Wisconsin's preeminent sociologist, Edward Alsworth Ross, had warned that movies had already made "more of the young people who were town children sixteen years ago or less . . . sexwise, sex-excited, and sex-absorbed than . . . any generation of which we have knowledge." Ross went on to excoriate the immoral effects of the cinema on non-delinquent children: "Thanks to their premature exposure to stimulating films, their sex instincts were stirred into life sooner than used to be the case with boys and girls from good homes, and as a result in many the 'love chase' has come to be the master interest in life."[132] The Motion Picture Research Council, supported by the Payne Fund and directed by a pious opponent of popular films, Rev. William H. Short, formed a Committee on Educational Research that included, in addition to Herbert Blumer, the Chicago sociologists Robert E. Park, Philip M. Hauser, Frederick M. Thrasher, and Paul G. Cressey. That committee undertook a series of thirteen studies between 1929 and 1932 to determine "the degree of influence and effect of films upon children and adolescents."[133] The first two, by Herbert Blumer and Blumer and Philip M. Hauser, were published in 1933.[134] According to I. C. Jarvie, The Payne Fund Studies "marked the high point of the campaign begun in the twenties in America to agitate about the immorality of Hollywood and its films" and coincided with the codification of the highly restrictive Motion Picture Production Code.[135] Although Blumer's researches were widely interpreted to lend support to the Rev. Short's view that movies contributed to delinquency and immorality, their comprehensive orientation and basic outlook were not so directed and were lost on both his employers and his audience.[136]

Blumer approached the effect of movies on social conduct and human understanding through an elaboration of the problem of the mores that had originally been set forth by William Graham Sumner. Attendance at and responses to movies belonged to a kind of collective behavior found exclusively in modern societies: mass behavior arising in societies wherein the folkways have become attenuated. American moviegoers form such a mass, Blumer observed. They are drawn from all walks of life, composed of persons who occupy different class positions, belong to distinctive racial and ethnic groups, hold a variety of occupations, and have attained quite disparate degrees of cultural understanding. Formed out of lone individuals or small primary group clusters, a movie audience constitutes an aggregate that does not possess a social organization, a body of customs, a heritage of traditions, a set of rituals or rules, a structure of roles and statuses, or an established leadership. In contrast to the conduct of audiences, collective mass behavior arises out of the convergence of "a congeries of individual lines of action" which, sometimes has "far reaching effects on institutions . . ." For example, Blumer points out, "a political party may be disorganized or a commercial institution wrecked. . . ."[137] However, Blumer's film studies emphasized the fact that audiences rarely engaged in any concerted, joint, collective action or reconstituted themselves into a social movement. Rather, the filmgoer responds to the cinematic situation as an individual within the mass, and in terms of whatever needs he or she is seeking in the situation. Blumer and Hauser noted that "one manner in which the motion pictures may lead to delinquent and criminal behavior is through inciting desires for luxury, fine clothes, automobiles, and pleasure . . ." and showing how these might be illegally obtained. However, they added that while "Sometimes this combination [of incitement and pictorially depicted criminal techniques] may lead directly to criminal behavior; more frequently its influence is confined to imagination and yearning." Blumer and Hauser also added a qualifying caveat to those who thought that a film scenario describing criminal conduct could have only a determining imitative effect on the viewer. "In the end it may work unwittingly to make the individual more susceptible to undertaking crime. Or it may reenforce motives already responsible for the criminal careers of those who are already participating in crime."[138] Thus, in the complex and highly differentiated society whose folkways had disintegrated and whose mores lacked coherence, the filmgoer received influences from the screen, but these influences by no means had a definite mimetic effect on the movie watcher's conduct.

The mass, Blumer noted in 1935, "represents an alienation from and attack upon folk life . . ." The ultimate effect of the movies is "a reaffirmation of basic human values but an undermining of the mores." In the stories told on the screen, he explained, "one finds the constant portrayal and approval of such qualities as bravery, loyalty, love, affection, frankness, personal justness, cleverness, heroism and friendship." Nevertheless, although the screen plays "are tuned to the old and simple theme of conflict between what has our sympathy and what has our antipathy, between the good and the bad, between the desirable and the reprehensible . . . , the social patterns or schemes of conduct inside of which these primary human qualities are placed are likely to be somewhat new, strange, and unfamiliar."[139] Precisely because the characters, settings, events and forms of life shown on the screen are novel, and must be in order to attract popular attention, they permit these exotic persons and unusual situations to be penetrated by basic human values. Films in this sense invade precariously situated folkish, local, and pre-modern moral structures, but in doing so, they "fill gaps left by the school, by the home, and by the church, . . . [and] they may also cut athwart the standards and values which these latter institutions seek to inculcate."[140] The guardians of public virtue who sought to censor films were, in fact, fighting a rear-guard battle to preserve America's rural small town, and Protestant values against the celluloid intrusions of modern, urban and secularizing forces and formulations.

In presenting his findings this way Blumer laid new groundwork for a public philosophy in defense of freedom of expression. He sets aside the idea that truth invariably arises in a marketplace of ideas. In its place is an assertion that the changes and innovations that Americans are willing to accommodate entail risky acceptance of information that, while possibly subversive to established ways of thinking, opens the minds of the custom-bound citizenry to new ideas and different social arrangements. To this end it is worth noting that Blumer's studies emphasize that movies had as their greatest effect "the emotional agitation which they induce." Precisely because popular films "have at hand in such an effective fashion the implements of emotional stimulation yet do not employ them consistently towards any conscious goal," he observed, "their effects, ultimately, are likely to be of confusion."[141] Confusion might be said to play an incipient part in the onset of what W. I. Thomas had earlier called a *crisis* in habitual orientations toward conduct.[142] Or, to employ the more recent formulation of Alfred Schutz, to first stir the individual to recognition of a *crisis in the lebenswelt*.[143] Such confusions, the first stage in human response to intrusions into the settled life world, might, in turn, lead to what Frederick Teggart called a *release* from the constraints of custom and social convention.[144] Once liberated from habit and established understandings, individuals are free to introduce new forms, propose different social arrangements, adopt other moral outlooks. Without such interruptions of everyday life, true social changes might never come to the fore of thought or action.

Essentially populist and democratic in spirit, Blumer and his small coterie of fellow theorists approached the problem of a public philosophy in recognition of a world given over to contingency, idiosyncracy, and the permanent vulnerability of values and beliefs to manipulation and subversion. If freedom, justice and equality are to advance and persevere, they would have to survive and thrive in an ever-precarious moral environment.

"In our society," Blumer wrote, "the girl or boy of adolescent age is usually being ushered into a life which is new and strange."[145] There are no guarantees in such a society. No assurance can be given that the truth will triumph, or that the good will win out over the bad. Movies that celebrate love, loyalty, courage, and patriotism nevertheless incite some youths to commit delinquent acts or to engage in immoral conduct; others have their imaginations stimulated to prurient fantasies or to daydreams of ill-gotten gains. But still others are aroused differently and less heinously. In popular movies these young people find their interests in the larger world enhanced, their commitment to cherished beliefs reenforced and turned in new directions, or their concern for social issues sharpened. Blumer argued that in "the detachment of the mass from local culture and the turning of their attention towards an outside world, the influence of motion pictures seems to be felt most in the realm of reverie."[146] The consequences of these film-stimulated musings are not clearly evident. "We do not know how to interpret the meaning of this reverie nor are we able to trace its effects," acknowledged Blumer. However, although some regarded the fanciful daydreaming that moviegoers confessed to as providing a "harmless satisfaction of disturbing and dangerous impulses," he pointed to findings that indicated that it "whets appetites and stimulates impulses, leading to tension and not relaxation, to excitement and not quiescence, to disequilibrium and not organic harmony."[147] As Blumer put it, "The play of reverie, whether ordered as in the motion picture or free as in individual day dreaming . . sketches schemes of possible conduct, and launches the individual upon vicarious journeying in new social worlds."[148] Once unleashed from the chains of conventional thought and action, people may exercise their imaginations freely and innovatively. What the outcome of such exercises would be could not be foreseen. But, Blumer concluded, "[M]ass reverie not only reflects the spirit and feelings of people, but also invigorates and moulds this spirit and these feelings."[149]

Blumer enunciated a new rationale for a public philosophy that would secure the movies as well as other admittedly stimulating media from censorship. The Utilitarians had justified their support for freedom of expression by a presupposed assurance that truth would always prevail in a free and open marketplace of ideas. In our interpretation of Blumer's formulation, unfettered freedom of expression does not depend upon either an assurance of truth triumphant or the rule of untrammeled reason. Truth in a modern, complex society of competing interests and quarreling definitions of all situations rises and falls as a result of power struggles in the aftermath of which victors seek legitimations of their newly won constructions of social reality. Reason is so enmeshed in the web of meanings that entangle it with passion, feeling, and struggle that its independence and dominion cannot be counted upon. Rather, censorship should be opposed and freedom of expression encouraged because a democratic society should always be open to the widest possible play of the human spirit, to the greatest possible chance for emancipation of the human imagination. To secure these ends, governments should ensure the unrestricted possibility for—and be willing to accept the risks involved in—communications that are likely to undermine taken-for-granted dogmas, doctrines, truths and mores.

Blumer had no illusions about the actual interests pursued by the movie-makers: "The motion picture industry has no cultural aim, no cultural policies, no cultural program."[150] Movies "are the product of secular business groups with commercial interests . . . Were the motion picture industry to seek to become a cultural institution inside of a society of free masses it would probably quickly collapse."[151] Nevertheless, the imaginative and liberating effects of watching movies went far beyond the profit motives of the industry that produced them. "[T]he cinema," Blumer suggested, "despite its lack of culture, may be operating unwittingly to help prepare an *order* of life in a free and secular society." The reverie of the movie-going masses, Blumer went on, "does not represent inevitably an endless period of disintegration." Instead, it "may be merely transitional and preparatory to a new order of life measuring to a newly developed taste."[152] Because censorship would block activation and expression of a liberated imagination and to that extent restrict the possible construction of new orders of life and constrict the potential development of new canons of taste, a democratic public philosophy should eschew it.

PUBLIC OPINION, PROPAGANDA, AND WAR

Public opinion is another aspect of collective behavior that Blumer carefully examined. Lippmann had based much of his case for an enlightened American public philosophy on the development of a rational, intelligent, and dispassionate public opinion. However, his philosophical investigations and his experiences as a journalist led him to considerable skepticism about whether media producers—editors, journalists, radio and newsreel commentators—could accommodate the deliberative and unbiased approach necessary for the analysis of public issues with the financial responsibility they owed to the corporate controllers of the mass communications industry,[153] and an even deeper pessimism about whether "the prevailing public opinion [that] has been destructively wrong at . . . critical junctures"[154] in American history could ever coincide with "what men would choose if they saw clearly, thought rationally, acted disinterestedly and benevolently."[155] Having reconceptualized the general issue in a manner that transcended exclusive dependence on a ubiquitous rationality, Blumer approached the problem of public opinion in terms of the concrete realities of American political life. "Public opinion," he observed, " . . . can be thought of, perhaps, as a composite opinion formed out of the several opinions that are held in the public, . . . as being shaped by the relative strength and play of opposition among them . . . Public opinion is always moving toward a decision even though it never is unanimous."[156]

Citing Lippmann, Blumer defines the public as a complex unit of collective behavior; it is composed of various sometimes cooperating, more often contending interest groups on one hand, and a disinterested spectator-like, arbitrating and judging citizenry on the other.[157] When a genuine instance of public opinion arises, it does so because the disinterested citizenry are able to employ a common universe of discourse to evaluate and decide upon the claims and arguments put forth by the several interest groups. Precisely because "the public interacts on the basis of interpretation, enters into dispute, and consequently is characterized by conflict relations, . . . [the] individuals in the public are likely to have their self-consciousness intensified and their critical powers heightened."[158] At the same time, however, the "efforts made by interest groups to shape public opinion may be primarily attempts to arouse or set emotional attitudes and to provide misinformation."[159] Although Blumer believes that "Public discussion today . . . is likely to be hampered by the absence of a universe of discourse . . . [and by] groups or parties in the public adopt[ing] dogmatic and sectarian positions . . . , [thereby bringing] public discussion to a standstill,"[160] he does not rule out the role that rationality could play in judgments: "One must recognize," he observed, "that the very process of controversial discussion forces a certain amount of rational consideration and that, consequently, the resulting collective opinion has a certain rational character."[161]

Blumer believes that the quality of public opinion depends on the effectiveness of public discussion and that the latter in turn "depends on the availability and flexibility of the agencies of public communication, such as the press, the radio, and public meet-ings."[162] Although he is aware of the many constraints on the free formation of public opinion—propaganda campaigns that oper-ate "to mold opinions and judgments not on the basis of the mer-its of an issue, but chiefly by playing upon emotional attitudes and feelings;"[163] public opinion polls that actually gauge un-deliberated attitudes of disparate aggregates;[164] polls that employ "a conception of public opinion that is a gross distortion," in fact, "an untenable fiction of its empirical character;"[165] media study designs that treat the public as creatures "responding to stimuli;"[166] and the not uncommon judgment that, although it might be "accurate to say that public opinion is rational, . . . [it] need not be intelligent,"[167]—he nevertheless holds, "If certain . . . contending views are barred from gaining presentation to the disinterested public or suffer some discrimination as to the possi-bility of being argued before them, then, correspondingly, there is interference with effective public discussion."[168] Fundamental to the effective use of newspapers, radio, and public meetings, Blumer asserted, "is the possibility of free discussion."[169]

MORALE, TRUTH, AND
FREEDOM OF SPEECH

The case for a public philosophy supporting untrammeled freedom of speech is perhaps best tested in "worst-case" sce-narios, i.e., situations of war wherein the public is aroused by or vulnerable to propaganda and likely to be inflamed by passionate appeals to patriotic sentiment.

Modern warfare poses a severe challenge to freedom of speech, to the maintenance of morale, and the preservation of the nation's material interests and moral integrity. War demands that thousands and sometimes millions of people be activated for pa-triotic endeavor. To accomplish this, agencies of mass persuasion become participants in official propaganda campaigns, while vir-tually all mass media are pressed into serving the goal of national solidarity. In 1943, Blumer observed that the fact that military forces in modern societies are conscripted from the civilian citizenry, and are not supplied to any significant extent by professional or mercenary groups, "has compelled attention to the so-called spiritual factor."[170] However, a government's employment of such supposedly spirit-enhancing practices as lying and falsification, censorship, and nationalistic propaganda threatens the very democratic freedoms and moral convictions that the mobilized citizens are fighting to defend. Blumer's approach to this dilemma, developed in response to the problem of national morale during World War II, stands in clear contrast to that of two other scholars concerned with an appropriate public philosophy for a democratic society at war: Talcott Parsons and Walter Lippmann.

Even before America's entrance into the war against Germany and Japan, Talcott Parsons (1902–1979), soon to be recognized as the foremost exponent of structural-functionalist sociology, had become seriously concerned about the state of American morale and the extent of the American citizenry's commitment to democratic values.[171] Parsons was convinced that America's "mission and great responsibilities on the world stage" would not be carried forth unless "the national morale problem" was solved. Serving as vice-chairman of the committee on morale of Harvard University's Faculty Defense Group, he put forward a diagnosis of the nation's vulnerability to enemy propaganda and a prognosis for its remission. The American social order was still in a formative stage, Parsons argued, such that in the wake of the dynamic processes at work, "social disorganization and the attendant personal disorientation and conflict are particularly widespread . . . at the present time." The particular sources of these "strains," as Parsons called them, were four-fold: They arose out of dilemmas and contradictions in the system of stratification, ambivalent orientations of the nuclear family, Americans' commitments to various religions, and the differential rates of assimilation of immigrants.

Because only "a very small number can ever reach the top," Parsons believed that America's occupational structure and mobility pattern lend themselves to "widespread frustrated ambition . . . in the lower middle class." The "strain of adjustment" that accompanies rural to urban migration coupled with disruptions of opportunity that are brought about by rapid technological change, contribute to an accumulation of career frustrations and tend to engender "'irrational' reactions." These often include "defensive formation of solidary groupings," and in general they provide "one of the most important sources of explosive material in our society." The equilibrium so devoutly to be sought in Parsons's formulation of the problem required that careful controls be placed over socio-economic dynamics, insuring that an appropriate balance would be struck "between disorganizing processes and reintegrating processes."

One institution in which Parsons perceived the struggle between dis- and re-integrative processes taking place was the American family. According to Parsons's perspective, the family was "the most important repository of all those elements of tradition and cultural pattern which are not readily capable of reduction to universalistic terms and terms of efficiency." Precisely because of its embeddedness in particularism and ascriptive solidarity, the family fostered a permanent but painful strain on the coordination of universalistic values and competitive individualism that the world of work and the imperatives of worldly success demanded. Some individuals might employ family connections or inherited wealth to gain a competitive advantage over those whose family situations did not permit such opportunities. Because he believed that virtually nothing could be done to reduce the differential effect of family support on opportunities for advancement, the presence of a relatively fixed hierarchy of families constituted, in Parsons's words, "one of the central points of strain in our social system," a permanent source of that sense of injustice felt by all those who resented the discrepancy between their actual status and desired aspirations.

However, Parsons worried even more over his additional claim that religion, a major source of value and commitment, was itself subject to divisive and alienating "strains." Although Parsons believed that "in general the Anglo-Saxon Protestant traditions supply the solidest foundations for . . . loyalty," he regarded Calvinism as the strongest basis for a national sentiment invulnerable to fascist propaganda. A severe problem arose because of the presence of non-Calvinist traditions in America's open and multi-denominational religious structure. Parsons singled out Catholicism and Lutheranism for their proneness to an unacceptable authoritarianism. The "authoritarian element in the basic structure of the Catholic Church . . . ," he wrote, weakens "individual self-reliance and valuation of freedom"; while those

Americans of "Lutheran background . . . are apt to be partial to a political authoritarianism and old fashioned legitimist conservatism." Parsons attributed the attractiveness of Germany's Nazism and Italy's Fascism in part to the respective Lutheran and Catholic denominations prominent in those countries. He warned that America's Calvinist tradition would have to superimpose the liberal values of its secular counterpart, the democratic State—(according to Parsons's interpretation of Calvin, "the state is coordinate with the church in promoting God's kingdom on earth; the two have a common purpose but different spheres of influence")—over Lutheranism's and Catholicism's weaker commitments to democracy. Practically speaking, this would require sufficient readjustment of attitudes toward leadership to allow "emergency powers [to be placed] in the hands of the executive" so that the national leader would be able to "act quickly" in the face of any emergency and at the same time be assured of widespread public support.

However, Parsons was less than sanguine about the necessary unanimity of support for the struggle against Fascism. As he perceived the matter, a significant portion of the American populace was composed of unassimilated immigrants. A less-than-fully-Americanized element, these people lacked "the strong Anglo-Saxon tradition of responsibility in the affairs of the community . . . [and] are . . . apt to be particularly pliable material in the hands of any strong leadership which is able to exploit their characteristics and position." Indeed, Parsons hinted that the leaders of the war against German Nazism, Italian Fascism, and Japanese militarism could only be sure of the unalloyed support of those Americans who had assimilated "the Anglo-Saxon traditions," experienced a certain level of "prestige and success," and were "relatively free of exploitable resentments and senses of inferiority." In contrast to the British, who Parsons believed were fully in support of their government's entrance into the war against the Axis Powers, the people of the United States had "failed to develop a culturally homogeneous community . . ." and were likely to be divided about the war effort. In the face of the many frustrations that immigrants would encounter in the natural course of things, Parsons believed that "there is a strong tendency to resort to what appear to be strong anchorages" i.e., that there would be powerful resistance to surrendering the secure wrappings of their own foreign traditions to the uncertainties of new-found Americanism. Concluding his observations about the strains affecting the prosecution of a war against Fascist authoritarianism and Nazi tyranny, Parsons asserted that "the American nation constitutes . . . a relatively badly integrated social system with an unstable orientation on the part of large numbers of individuals, and many internal differences and conflicts." Because many "of the sentiments associated with these strains are capable of exploitation by the great movements of the present which are attacking our institutions," it might be necessary to take concerted action to enhance national morale and encourage patriotic endeavor.

Parsons's proposed solution to the dangers America faced took the "spiritual factor" as its point of departure. A security-conscious America would have to institutionalize practices that were a secular equivalent of the Calvinist state's instrumental actions. Although he allowed that this might require the forcible suppression of dissidents, Parsons placed greater emphasis on the powers of persuasion that might be employed. He held that Fascism and Nazism threatened something greater than democracy: they challenged rational–legal authority, the very basis of Occidental civilization. In light of the immensity of the danger, Parsons suggested that democracy and its attendant civil liberties would have to be reconceptualized: the fundamental Calvinist imperative, he asserted, obliged each individual performing a useful social function to act in the interest of society as a whole, rather than in pursuit of any personal goals. Hence, in a letter to Representative Edith Nourse Rogers, Parsons admonished the Congresswoman, "[O]n matters . . . which touch the most vital questions of the national welfare at this time, opposition for the sake of opposition seems to be both politically unwise and morally reprehensible."[172] Generally, he favored "a more positively functional conception of rights and liberties," one in which liberties would "be conditional on performance of a functionally important role—or at least pulling one's own weight in the boat." If those who dissented might be obliged to accept an abridgement of their civil liberties, so, in turn, it followed that America's privileged elite was obliged in the national interest not merely "to maintain its privilege solidly," but more significantly to make sure that "its claim . . . [is] broadly in harmony with the more general value system of the community." Prosecution of the war seemed to require reenforced legitimation of the stratified order and renegotiation of the rights of those who objected to it.

Parsons's enunciation of a Calvinized America offered a new public service role for social scientists. The wartime emergency called not only for a drastic reorganization of priorities, rights, and liberties, but also for a massive program of reeducation that would enlist the patriotic support of the citizenry for the duration. In such an effort, Parsons pointed out, "there is an opportunity to use sociological analysis in such a way as to redefine the situation in terms of a more realistic and less distorted version of the liberal democratic view."[173] Parsons's proposal in fact included employing his recently enunciated analogy of the Calvinist clergyman to the psychotherapist for the purpose of effecting a nationwide program of social control. Just as the clergyman, "in his role as personal adviser and spiritual guide . . . has been known to perform functions which have . . . an element of unconscious psychotherapy . . . [and which] bring—or keep—his parishioner in conformity with a normative tradition,"[174] so the competent, disinterested, and patriotic social scientist is, if given the opportunity and resources, in a position to manipulate "the mechanisms by which unconscious control operates on the social level [and thereby to] . . . contribute significantly to the formation of propaganda policies."[175] Should the government be willing to accept and act on his proposal for the solution of the problem, Parsons suggested that sociologists be enlisted to staff propaganda agencies that would "assume a role as closely analogous to that of physician as is possible in the circumstances . . . [and] so far as possible identify itself with those elements of the institutional patterning of government and other structures . . . which are symbolic of the integration of the society as a whole." Parsons's solution to the pressures that war imposes on truth was a social scientific propaganda agency that—in the face of an imperfectly integrated society, many unresolved social problems, and deep personal resentments—would produce patriotic constructions of social reality as its contribution to the preservation of Occidental civilization.

Walter Lippmann did not trust wartime governments or their soldier or civilian conscripts to present a disinterested truth.

Indeed, he believed that truth would be martyred to war, dying in behalf of the national emergency. During the first World War, Lippmann had noted how wars seemed to call for a sacrifice of honest reporting and deliberative discussion. "If . . . a general [is] planning an attack, he knows that his organized military units will scatter into mobs if the percentage of casualties rises too high." Similarly, on the home front, a politician feels he must underreport the number of battlefield casualties lest he undermine the positive "state of mind in the rank and file about its leaders." Confidence in their leaders enhances the morale of the citizenry, and that, in turn, is conducive to keeping the war effort at its appropriately feverish pitch. Morale, Lippmann concluded, "is said to be good when the individuals do the part allotted to them with all their energy . . ."[176] However, he believed that the energy could only be activated with fiery patriotic propaganda and chauvinistically nationalist rhetorics.

The conduct of leaders and media during the Second World War indicated to Lippmann that nothing had changed since 1914: "Once again it seemed impossible to wage the war energetically except by inciting the people to paroxysms of hatred and to utopian dreams."[177] Americans would sacrifice their lives and fortunes so that "The Four Freedoms would be established everywhere, once the incurably bad Germans and the incurably bad Japanese had been forced to surrender unconditionally."[178] Lippmann lamented that the "war could be popular only if the enemy was [made to appear] altogether evil and the Allies very nearly perfect."[179] Worse, Lippmann regarded this apparently unavoidable "mixture of envenomed hatred and furious righteousness" as not only a *sine qua non* of wartime morale, but also conducive to "a public opinion which would not tolerate the calculated compromises that durable settlements demand."[180] So long as an impassioned morale was needed to win the war, Lippmann concluded, the "inherent tendency in opinion to feed upon rumors excited by our own wishes and fears" would ensure that "the public opinion of masses cannot be counted upon to apprehend regularly and promptly the reality of things."[181] Lippmann based his assessment on an analysis of the content of propaganda alone; hence morale seemed to necessitate making truth and deliberation into the first casualties of combat.

Blumer approached the problem of morale in wartime quite

differently than either Parsons or Lippmann. He posed the question, what degree and kind of commitment is actually sufficient to carry on a war effectively? Hence, while he acknowledged "that the development of morale in a [social] movement is essentially a matter of developing a sectarian attitude and a religious faith,"[182] he pointed out that morale in a war might be grounded in less fervent feelings. Morale, Blumer observed, could be "organized around . . . aims that embody very different conceptions of life and widely diverse sets of ideals."[183] Not convinced that morale is a *sine qua non* for joint group action, Blumer considered that "it is distinctly conceivable, although unlikely, that a collective enterprise, with even the huge dimensions of winning a national war, may be carried on effectively with a minimum of morale."[184] Classifying the forms of morale in accordance with the character of the objective to be achieved, Blumer distinguished

> [that which is a] consecration of effort . . . caused by practical expediency;[185] [that which] develops around a romantic goal . . . [and] is colored with a variety of emotional and imaginative qualities which make it appealing, magnetic, and glorious;[186] [and that which] represents the primary as well as the ultimate value in life . . . , when the goal is sacred . . . [and where] its achievement becomes a matter of irrevocable duty and of divine injunction.[187]

Blumer pointed out that the morale arising in behalf of America prosecuting the fight against the Axis Powers was of the first type. Neither romantic illusions nor sacred obligations need play a significant role in invigorating the war effort.

Blumer believed that "on the whole . . . American people are united on the basis of winning the war . . . [and that their] morale remains high and their unity stable to the extent that they believe one another to be seeking this end."[188] In putting the matter this way Blumer separated his characterization of wartime morale from that of Parsons and Lippmann. "The American people do not hearken to the urgings that the war should be won to establish a new order of life or to extend and materialize an ideal philosophy. They are not animated by the sense of cause, of engaging in a crusade, of carrying out a sacred mission; or of affirming new conceptions of themselves in terms of glory, prestige, power, or esteemed position."[189] For Blumer the American people conceived of winning the war against Germany and Japan as "a necessary job that has to be done."[190] Whereas Lippmann had supposed that American morale was most effective when its emotional focus was an inflamed hatred of the very peoplehood of the enemy, and Parsons worried over the divisive effects that an inequitably stratified social order would have on the patriotism of its several minority groups, Blumer regarded the workmanlike attitude toward the war held by most Americans as likely to override such prejudices. "[O]ur alien and minority groups: Italians, Germans, Japanese, East Europeans, and Negroes . . . on the whole have not endangered our morale," he asserted. In effect, Blumer held that a public opinion appropriate to arousing and preserving American morale in wartime did not require the exacerbation of racist sentiments or ethnic prejudices against the enemy or against any segment of the American populace inappropriately identified with the enemy. On the part of any American, Blumer argued, "An inertia, a hesitation, or a failure to act in a required way must be identified as arising from a refusal to understand the importance of what is asked or a refusal to act on such an understanding, before being taken as a sign of poor morale."[191]

In treating American wartime morale during World War II as a product of practical necessity rather than glory-seeking chauvinism, religious crusading, or ethnocentric prejudice, Blumer meant "no impugning of the genuine character of patriotic sentiment."[192] Nevertheless, he had no illusions about the contexts out of which that morale grew. As Blumer saw it the "background for our morale was none too propitious." Indeed, recalling the interwar period, Blumer noted that the large number of divisive occurrences and disparate feelings—

> conflicts between races, between the native population and minority groups, between labor and industrialists, between various economy blocs, between political groupings, and between alignments on New Deal legislation . . . [as well as the] disillusionment following in the wake of the first World War, the presence of a substantial pacifist philosophy, especially in youths . . . the vigorous presentation of a traditional isolationist position . . . [and the] fact that participating in the war had become a bitter issue of the first magnitude . . . [193]

—not only boded ill for the development of national morale but also assured that if such morale did arise, there "was practically nothing in the situation that would favor the formation of a romantic or sacred goal."[194] In the face of all these unsettled and unsettling conditions, however, he asserted that the "attack on Pearl Harbor, following upon an increasing apprehension and suspicion of Axis intentions . . . [had evoked] the high value placed on the nation, on what it stands for, and on what it implies in individual life [so] that the winning of the war becomes a matter of practical necessity."[195]

Despite its dispassionate formulations, Blumer believed that American morale was not deficient, nor was the extent of its felt sense any cause for either alarm or major policy changes. The typical American's view was, he observed, "Let's get it over with." Such an outlook did enough to arouse "a sense of duty and . . . a willingness of co-operation."[196] Blumer cast doubt upon the widespread supposition that the actions associated with patriotic feeling—"purchase of bonds, acceptance of rationing restrictions, response to draft rules, increased industrial production, etc."—occurred solely because of a heightened emotional enthusiasm and wondered whether "mere acquiescence in a collective program" might not be a sufficient explanation.[197] Despite the fact that "the . . . continuing struggles between labor, farmer, [and] industrialist . . . [are] disquieting" and that the "[s]trikes, opposition to labor regulation, question of parity prices, pressure for special interest legislation, . . . effort to revoke previously enacted laws of welfare, [each with its] attendant charge, countercharge, and propaganda, suggest a picture such as Hitler had in mind when he wrote of being able to induce dissension and revolution in this country whenever he wished," Blumer pointed out that "each major interest and bloc . . . [is] committed to the winning of the war."[198]

There were real threats to morale, but Blumer discounted each of them after careful analysis. Short-wave propaganda broadcasts, although said "to be the source of rumors and malicious assertions subsequently to be planted in our population by enemy agents" were in fact "listened to by relatively few people, many of whom are animated chiefly by curiosity."[199] Among the contending interest groups in the United States, the "suspicion that one group or the other is seeking to use the war situation to its own advantage" was being allayed to the extent that "events occasion a vivid reaffirmation of the need of winning the war."[200] Finally, the concern over the "sizable heterogeneous group suspected to be lukewarm" about America's aims in the war, supposed also to be moved "by political bitterness and personal enmity and intrenched in the possession of a significant press" had been misconstrued. Although it was believed "that this group, keystoned by certain powerful newspapers, is ready to sabotage the war effort when opportunity arises. . . , [i]t seems clear . . . that such a group is controllable by the general attitude in this country [in favor] of winning the war."[201] Although Blumer conceded that the emergence of a romantic or sacred goal would have profound and disturbing consequences for the postwar world order, he felt that neither posed a serious threat to America's Second World War effort. As a result, the postwar era might very well be characterized by a sense of letdown. Morale might "be low or nonexistent . . . [and the nation] might not be able to form a collective goal of reconstruction which will command a high order of determined effort and co-operative spirit."[202] After the war had been won, Blumer seemed to say, a democratic public philosophy and its concomitant and supportive policies would have to deal justly with those problems of racial conflict, class warfare, intergroup hostility, and industrial development that seemed to be endemic to the United States and had not yet found a resolution.

Race Relations and Inequality in the Democratic State

THE RELEVANCE OF SYMBOLIC INTERACTIONISM FOR RACE AND ETHNIC RELATIONS

Race relations has occupied a central place of melioristic concern in American sociology. In one very prominent sociological formulation, that of Talcott Parsons and his followers, American society is preconceived as a social system into which minorities gain full participation by a queuing process that admits new racial, ethnic, and religious groups as each acquires the requisite economic and social characteristics. Although this system is regarded as imperfect and generates such inherent "strains" as racial, ethnic, and religious prejudices together with their "deviant" forms of institutionalized discrimination, it is expected that ultimately blacks, Jews, Asiatics, Hispanics, and Amerinds will be granted recognition as full-fledged citizens—unless some other element or strain should interfere.[203]

An older formulation of this general inclusion process was expounded by Robert Park and his disciples as the race relations cycle. According to this theory, each new racial and ethnic group would pass through three progressive and irreversible stages—contact, competition, and accommodation—and then finally be assimilated.[204] In still another formulation, that of the researchers working with T. W. Adorno, a leader of the Frankfurt School during its emigre period in the United States, venomous antisemitism and virulent negrophobia would remain as embedded attitudes of already assimilated Americans because each prejudice is a product of socialization and a feature of its widely prevalent mental impairment, the authoritarian personality.[205] Central to each of these perspectives is a background assumption of predetermined conduct and human unfreedom. Despite Parsons's assertion of "voluntarism" in his version of an individual's conduct in the universalistic-achievement, i.e., American social system, we believe this determinative assumption holds true for his approach as well. In Parsons's systems theory emphasis is placed on the performance of individuals within socially defined "roles" rather than on the conduct of persons attempting to learn how to act in specific situations. In these various orientations, several prior determining factors produce the mental life of what is in effect regarded as a dependent variable, the human personality. In contrast to all of these orientations, Blumer takes as his point of departure individuals acting as reflective and self-reflective persons; by means of an interpretive process, each defines as he or she shapes responses to the many different situations that human beings encounter in their many-sided lives.

Human action, as Blumer conceives it, arises out of the distinctively human capacity to engage in self-interaction, i.e., to note things, define objects and situations, and determine the significance of these interpretations for carrying forth a line of action. Many socio-psychological approaches tend either to treat conscious mental life as arising out of an internal interaction between a postulated id, ego, and superego, or to treat the self as an organization of needs and motives, or in Parsons's scheme, to hold that each act requires the individual to make a prior choice among opposed action orientations in five sets of basic "pattern-variables." Blumer's symbolic interactionist approach argues that "to perceive one's 'ego' puts one in the position of doing something with regard to it" and that "self-interaction puts the human being over against his world instead of merely in it, requires him to meet and handle his world through a defining process instead of merely responding to it, and forces him to construct his action instead of merely releasing it."[206] Society in this perspective is not a systemic entity that operates as a whole, that controls and governs the action of each of its parts, and that exercises its control and governance through the interplay among them.[207] Rather, it is "made up of different participants, engaging in divergent lines of action, some which fit together very neatly, others which are clearly incongruent with one another, others which have no discernable relation to each other—and with new alignments coming into being, with old alignments breaking down, with new dynamic thrusts emerging in different sectors of group life, and with previous dynamic areas becoming staid and fixed." Societies have no fixed, predetermined, or system-generated shape. They are and become what people define them to be or become.

They are given their shape by and through "this process of actors handling their situations . . ."[208]

At another level, societies are composed not only of numbers of individuals, but also of numbers of powerful, less powerful, and virtually impotent interest groups of all kinds. Blumer asserts, "[I]n our type of society it is natural for a multitude of interest groups of the most diverse nature to arise and flourish, each seeking in its own way to advance or defend its own interest."[209] This plurality of interest groups—including groups representing the interests of the various racial minorities—constitutes a principal component of "the wide array of different forms of . . . interaction" that occurs in any large-scale association of human beings: "venomous conflict, moderate conflict, pretended conflict, persecution, exploitation, protection, limited aid, intense cooperation, live and let-live arrangements, amused toleration and indifference."[210] The play of protest, power, accommodation, and defeat are aspects of the social process that a free society does and should countenance if it is to allow its members to pursue the goals of justice, of relegitimated power, and of redistributed prestige, status, and opportunity. Blumer's conceptions of the individual and of society constitute a testimony to human freedom, self-control, and to the quest for freedom and equity in a society that holds out the possibility for melioristic, ineffective, or destructive social changes to occur.

Blumer states that the setting in which race relations come to constitute a problem is one of hierarchy and subordination. "The setting . . . exists . . . in the form of a social arrangement in which a given racial group occupies a superordinate or superior position in the social order while another racial group occupies a subordinate or inferior social position."[211] Such a codified system of invidious stratification might go unchallenged, with its complex structure of barriers and its rigid lines of exclusion observed by all parties, producing racial relations that are essentially peaceful and orderly. However, in the United States "such relations have always been subject to critical evaluation from one quarter or another, in terms of a democratic ethic."[212] Race relations become a social problem, Blumer observes, "when the respective social positions are upset, . . . especially when the subordinate racial group challenges the superior social position of the superordinate race, [and] the racial groups enter into conflict."[213] Precisely because of their tendency to engender conflict, undemocratic race relations invite melioristic approaches redefining them as moral or political issues.

Most sociological and social psychological approaches to the race problem have been "guided by a framework which presupposes that non-democratic relations are improper;" researchers have focused on the scientifically postulated variables that are said "to hinder or block the establishment of democratic race relations."[214] As a result, the main thrust of social scientific research repudiates beliefs in the innate grounds that are said to justify racial hierarchies; finds causes for racial prejudice and proposes ways for the reduction of intergroup tensions; delineates the structural (i.e., economic, cultural, or sociopsychological) conditions that facilitate, preserve, and protect racial discrimination; discovers bases for and ways of achieving inter-racial harmony; uncovers unrecognized but operant democratic trends in social relations; and locates the stages and phases through which a racial group passes before it reaches a democratic relationship with other races.

These researches have been formulated on the basis of a philosophy that perceives little room for state action in securing a just and equitable solution to the race problem. As Blumer put the matter in 1958, after reviewing the bulk of the postwar studies on the subject, "In my judgment, race relations research in the last decade has not contributed a great deal to policy knowledge."[215] Nevertheless, he noticed that some researches had begun to focus on the nature and character of power relations and pointed out that "Attention is being focused on such devices as legislative enactment, administrative regulation, formulation of official policy, managerial arrangements, use of a power structure, and new living and working arrangements of groups." Although these studies had not yet produced "a body of theory . . ., they have given rise to a variety of ideas which are 'in the air' and which point to the possible emergence of a new theoretical framework."[216]

By 1980, however, a new theoretical framework for the study and improvement of race relations had not been developed in the social sciences, despite the enormous changes in those relations that had taken place since 1945. Reviewing the situation

once again, Blumer, together with Troy Duster, found it necessary to critically evaluate such major theories of race relations as
biological determinism, the prejudice-discrimination approach,
structural-functionalism, assimilative utopianism, and the more
recent elaboration of colonial-exploitative models.[217] The wave of
urban racial uprisings in America's cities and the rise of black nationalism among a people once said to be thoroughly accultur-
ated in the United States, led Blumer to point to the fact that
prevailing social scientific schemes of racial relations had failed
the test of empirical validation and to emphasize that a proper
understanding of the actual variation in collective definitions of
self, group, and situation would take account of the shifting
grounds of those definitions and could in turn help explain the
different notions of racial justice that were invoked at any period
of history.

Minorities in America face a seemingly permanent but paradoxical condition fostering contradictory goals and ambiguous
identities. On the one hand, there are reasons for defining their
situation in terms of separatism and nationalism; on the other, in
behalf of inclusion and assimilation.[218] The assimilationist orientation with its push toward integration arises out of the following: "Blacks are now and always have been predominantly in the
labouring class; . . . [D]uring prosperous times that seemed almost limitless and unending . . . [t]hey . . . would take the position, at least through the organizations that acted as the conduits
for their political expression, that the society as constituted could
incorporate them within existing structures, *simply by opening
up the gates* or lowering the barriers . . . In times of economic
boom and prosperity, cultural assimilation surfaces as the dominant side . . ."[219] A nationalist-separatist orientation is likely to
arise, Blumer believes, if there is an ideological change and an organizational shift in the associations representing the subordinate
group; such in fact occurred when the black leadership exercised
by the National Association for the Advancement of Colored
People began to decline after achievement of its most prominent
goal, passage of the Civil Rights Act in 1964, at the same time
that black-power groups that had taken over the once integra-
tionist and interracial Congress of Racial Equality moved into a
temporary period of ascendancy. But, although the "nascent nationalism of black organizations in the middle 1960s can be seen

as a reaction to . . . those organizations losing the financial support of whites, thus imposing a strategy of self-help and autonomy,"[220] Blumer and Duster regard the rise of separatist quests for redemption and justice as counsels of despair: " . . . members and representatives of the subordinative racial group may come to feel that nothing substantial can be expected to ever come from the dominant group . . . They come to believe that their efforts to escape from their social plight and to achieve the better life which they seek can be done only by developing their own order of life in place of trying to fit inside of that dominated by the superordinate racial group." However, in the United States at any rate, "these subordinate group members may find that they do not have the resources or facilities to move in . . . a separatist direction."[221] Unable "to break through the line of exclusion . . . nor . . . able to break away from their unfavoured position by developing their own separate institutional world," a disappointed minority group becomes ambivalent, "setting its two major divergent directions of effort (the assimilationist and the separatist orientations) and . . . flip-flopping from one to the other . . ."[222] While understandable, in light of the majority's resistance, Blumer and Duster concluded that the separatist-nationalist orientation has little chance of accomplishing its objectives.

Race and ethnic relations in the United States have for the most part taken the form of power relations, guided by more or less organized representative interest groups, each seeking to establish, confirm, reform, or reconstruct the stratification of rights, opportunities, privilege, status, authority, and deference that currently prevails. These relations are then a quest for justice, insofar as that term refers to the equitable distribution of the desiderata that are objectives of the contending groups' actions. Whatever stability exists in the relations between the several racial and ethnic groups arises out of and through temporarily established codes of law, custom, and etiquette. Indicative of a momentarily decisive victory by one or a coalition of racial groups over the others in what has been, and likely will continue to be, an unceasing conflict, these codified relationships—which might also be accompanied by what Blumer calls "sympathetic relations," i.e., personal sentiment, sympathetic concern, and a modicum of care extended to alien and remote groups—constitute a structure of inequity to which the losers might grudgingly acquiesce, or against which they may continue to fight.[223] As a temporarily vanquished segment of the American populace, the latter tend to perceive themselves as one or a congeries of "minorities," disprivileged bodies appealing and struggling for their yet-to-be-established status as full citizens. The quest for racial justice that proceeds toward full citizenship and equal rights via appeals, demands, power actions, legislative reforms, and judicial rulings within the existing institutional framework of the society has the same chance of succeeding, or failing, that all such movements have.

RACE, POLITICAL POWER, AND PUBLIC PHILOSOPHY

The transformation of the racial order, as Blumer conceives of it, takes place in and through the processes of the public arena.[224] Sociology itself has become an unacknowledged part of this public arena, but in Blumer's judgment, it is a rather poor citizen: the discipline mistakenly supposes that it can objectively and independently recognize a social problem such as racial inequality in accordance with its scientifically postulated designations of "dysfunctions," "pathologies," "disorganization," or "deviance" and then provide policymakers with a ready-to-hand system-centered solution; in fact, "sociologists discern social problems only after they are recognized as social problems by and in a society . . ." He observed that while, "Racial injustice and exploitation in our society were far greater in the 1920s and 1930s than they are today; . . . the sociological concern they evoked were little until the chain of happenings following the Supreme Court decision on school segregation and the riot in Watts."[225] The race problem proceeded apace, with most of sociology trailing behind it.

The race question, which, as noted earlier, only arises as a social problem in Blumer's formulation when one or a number of subordinated racial groups challenges the superior position of the superordinate racial group or groups, would have to struggle for its recognition as a legitimate problem in the public arena. Leaders and spokesmen of the superordinate race are in a position, Blumer and Duster observed, because of their "monopolistic access to the superior posts of the society and [their] control of the major institutions . . . , to resist efforts which seem to threaten such possession and use."[226] One strategic way a superordinate body might resist such a challenge to its established group position is to thwart the very recognition of the inequitable situation as a public issue. As Blumer notes, "a social problem must acquire social endorsement if it is to be taken seriously and move forward in its career."[227] He points out that the social endorsement of a subordinate group's claim for equity gives it "a necessary degree of respectability which entitles it to consideration in the recognized arenas of public discussion . . ." In the United States, he goes on, these arenas " . . . are the press, other media of communication, the church, the school, civic organizations, legislative chambers, and the assembly places of officialdom."[228] Without "the credential of respectability necessary for entrance into these arenas," a potential social problem such as the racial question "is doomed" as far as its recognition as a legitimate social issue deserving public deliberation and policy consideration is concerned. It is precisely here that a public philosophy affirming every group's right to enter into the public arena with an unrestricted right to freedom of speech becomes imperative.

Should the race question achieve recognition and endorsement as a legitimate social problem, it is by no means insured of a fair hearing or an honorable resolution. The superordinate group, as Blumer and Duster point out, might be divided into segments, some favoring protection or even enhancement of their established position, others, less threatened by the subordinate group's claims, encouraging the latter's efforts, while still others remain indifferent to consideration of the issue.[229] The clash of opposed interests virtually insures that discussions of the race problem will be characterized by "[e]xaggerated claims and distorted depictions, subserving vested interests, . . . advocacy, evaluation, falsification, diversionary tactics," and whatever other rhetorics and tactics are necessary to constitute "a mobilization of the society for action . . ."[230] The original conception of the social problem is likely to be reconsidered amidst this debate and redefined in response to strategic considerations and the shifting outlooks of public opinion. The race question, like other precariously legitimated social problems, could even "languish, perish, or just fade away"[231] at this point. The outcome of any essentially political process is uncertain. Any prior restraint on the nature, kind, quality, or content of speech permitted in the public argument over claims and counterclaims would probably work to the advantage of the censor. Toleration of every form of speech and each kind of rhetoric would seem to be a prerequisite to ensuring fair procedure in the public fray.

The racial situation that emerged after the Second World War succeeded in producing both a revolution of rising expectations among the colonialized peoples of the world and an improved economic and political position for minorities in the United States. In the two decades after 1945, the political, economic and social situation of the Afro-American population was subjected to such a profound redefinition that it eventually resulted in public acceptance of the subordinate group's designation of itself as "black" in place of its long-established denomination as "Negro." No longer willing to acquiesce to the white majority's assignment of "Negroes" to unskilled, menial, and non-unionized labor; the urban ghetto; the sharecropper's hovel; the segregated school; or to disenfranchised quasi-citizenship and the legal status of an endogamous caste, aroused blacks, led by both old and new representative groups, launched a movement designed to secure the broad panoply of civil rights that the Constitution seemed to promise to every American. The variety of means employed by the movement propelled it through and across the several institutional complexes of America as it instituted sit-ins, freedom rides, strikes, marches, and peaceful as well as violent actions. At the same time, the more traditional approaches of the older civil rights groups—seeking legislative reforms and judicial remedies—resulted in Court-ordered desegregation of all public facilities and Congressional passage of voting and civil rights acts. The hierarchical racial order that had flourished during the last two centuries began to crumble. However, the dismantling of this particular racial order did not usher in the disappearance of all racial or ethnic classifications nor did it herald an end to race relations.[232]

The Civil Rights Movement not only introduced a second Era of Reconstruction (the first one had occurred in the first dozen years after the Civil War) but also weakened the prejudicial views and discriminatory actions of the dominant racial group. As early as 1955, Blumer observed that social thought on race relations had been largely concerned "with the establishment and maintenance of a hierarchical racial order within a given society," and he urged consideration of "the question of what arrangement of race relations may be expected to follow in its wake."[233] Blumer suggested that in the era succeeding the old order race relations would be considerably affected by

> increased diversification of groups and organization; increased technological and occupational change; increased territorial movements of individuals; quickened vertical mobility; increased exposure to new definitions of objects and situations; rapid turnover in the objects of attention and interest; increased alignment and realignment of groups on the basis of interests; and intensification of the play of pressure groups and interest groups.[234]

Amidst this interplay of shifting forces and dynamic processes, however, there would still be

> occasion . . . for peoples to identify each other as racial groups . . . , [a] perpetuation of memories stemming from the racial order . . . , areas of exclusiveness from which they will be barred . . . , [and] clannish tendencies which will perpetuate some separateness of racial groups—particularly in intimate circles such as that of marriage, home life, social circles, and networks of personal relationships.[235]

Racial identification would continue, and the purposes to which their classification would be put would be a major issue for the next phase of the race issue in the United States.

Blumer placed the method for dismantling an unjust hierarchical racial order squarely within the arena of an active public philosophy. Unlike those social scientists who supposed that racial segregation could be eliminated by the putatively inexorable rationalization of social life that industrialization introduces,[236] or only after first ameliorating the conditions that evoke prejudicial attitudes and their discriminating expression, he sought social justice in a procedure that would "block the process [i.e., prejudice $\Rightarrow$ discrimination $\Rightarrow$ segregation] from achieving its end result."[237] This could be accomplished by means of an authoritative administration of just decision-making, more specifically "by controlling the decisions of the main functionaries who carry a given form of racial segregation into actual execution."[238] Changes could be introduced if Americans recognized that a "different setting is formed if the conscious efforts at desegregation are along lines which force functionaries to take cognizance of solicitations, demands, and pressures made on them to carry out a different line of decision."[239] Such solicitations, demands, and pressures arise most effectively from organizations mobilized to achieve desegregation and sufficiently influential to bring their message to bear on decision-makers and on those who supervise them. "The vehicle of procedure is strategical maneuvering," he observed, "designed to marshal and utilize the potentials of power and prestige available in the given situation."[240] However, functionaries who administer the vast array of institutions that come under public scrutiny can best be guided—or coerced—to make decisions that accord with a desegregationist philosophy when there exists a "kind of setting . . . brought into being by the enactment and application of laws against segregation or by the impositions of regulations and expectations against segregation by leaders . . ."[241] Once legislatures see that such laws are enacted, once judges make rulings that forbid particular acts of discrimination, once organizational and association leaders promulgate orders for desegregation, they clothe these laws, judgments, and proclamations with a mantle of authoritative legitimacy and moral rectitude. For this reason, Blumer pointed out,

> Agencies seeking to achieve racial desegregation have a particularly strong strategic weapon . . . in focusing on . . . *applying* the transcending legal or moral standard . . . [so that a functionary's decisions turn on] a question of obedience to the transcending legal or moral standard.[242]

Moreover, Blumer suggested that the imposition of authoritatively ordered desegregation on people of varying and perhaps mutually antipathetic attitudes might help to reduce race prejudice by changing the human heart and mind: "[I]n allowing the members of the racial groups to associate as equals in the new situations they lay the groundwork for acting toward one another on a human and personal basis . . ."[243]

Blumer points out that public deliberations over the resolution of the race question must take account of the fact that race relations are embedded in a wide variety of situations, occur in a vast array of different institutions, and include considerations of formal conduct, intimate behavior, and ideological perspectives, all occurring along what he calls "the color line."[244] Recognition of the diversity of situations and outlooks that are involved entails a further acquiescence to the fact that once agreement has been reached on a programmatic reconstruction of the racial order, the specific policies that arise therefrom are subject to bargaining, compromise, concessions, tradeoffs, and judgments of what might be workable. And even after a particular policy has been adopted, it is likely to be modified, twisted, bent, redirected and to take on unforeseen accretions. The forging of a public policy deriving from an egalitarian public philosophy is likely to engender new definitions of the racial situation, innovative remedies for long-festering inequities, and the enunciation of controversial proposals.[245]

RACE RELATIONS
IN THE LABOR MARKET:
AFFIRMATIVE ACTION

In twentieth-century America, what Blumer refers to as the second rampart of the color line is to be found in the arena where blacks suffer economic subordination and restriction of opportunities. In this arena there is a likelihood that new definitions will emerge and seemingly radical remedies be suggested to reconstruct and equalize the economic position of the subordinated group. The debate over affirmative action, a new doctrine embedded within current programs designed to eliminate the effects of America's racist heritage, is a significant example of the character and form of challenge that such approaches to racial reorganization pose. Blumer's consideration of the historical origins, geographical variation, and reason for decline of the color line suggests the lines of an argument that would justify affirmative action as a part of a Constitutional strategy for assaulting the barriers to equal opportunity in the labor market. Moreover, it is worthy of noting that what we regard as Blumer's implicit and emergent public philosophical orientation on current issues affecting the race question stands in sharp opposition to that developed by such opponents of affirmative action as Nathan Glazer[246] and Thomas Sowell.[247]

In the United States race relations are now and have long been governed by the organization and maintenance of a color line. Blumer points out that that demarcation is accurately represented not "by a single, sharply drawn line but . . . rather as a series of ramparts, like the 'Maginot Line,' extending from outer breastworks to inner bastions."[248] The intent as well as the effect of this color line is to separate whites and non-whites, "assigning to each a different position in the social order and attaching to each [racial group] position a differential set of rights, privileges, and arenas of action."[249] Although the concept of the color line is conventionally associated with black-white relations in the states that comprise the former Confederacy,[250] Blumer observes "that a color line exists not only in the South but in all sections of the nation."[251] In the North and the West, he goes on to note, the color line "expresses the fact that in these sections the two racial groups occupy different social positions along the axes of dominance-subordination and exclusion-inclusion."[252] Although "Northern and western whites have been much less aware of their color line and much less sensitive about it, . . . Negroes have felt its impact keenly."[253] In these parts of the United States, investigations had shown that blacks had been "barred, by tacit agreement if not by law, from equal access to many parts of the public arena; . . . restricted predominantly to the lower levels of industrial occupations; . . . scarcely ever allowed to enter the area of white management; . . . subjected to strong residential separation; and . . . excluded generally from private circles of white association."[254] The Civil Rights Movement that was active in the 1950s and 1960s succeeded in breaching "the outer band of the color line, . . . gain[ing] what is customarily referred to as 'civil rights,' that is to say, . . . remov[ing] the segregated position of Negroes *in the public arena*."[255]

However, the "achievement of civil rights merely peels off . . . the outer layer of the color line . . . not alter[ing] significantly the social positions of the two racial groups."[256] The next inner band of the line consists of "the crucial area of economic subordination and opportunity restriction—an area of debar-

ment . . . which is exceedingly tough because it is . . . complicated by private and quasi-private property rights, managerial
rights, and organizational rights."[257] The assault on this inner line
of defense of the color line involves attacking "barriers [that] are
extensive, varied, and formidable," indeed "a much more formidable part of the color line than is represented by the debarment . . . from the exercise of civil rights . . ."[258] As a result of
these difficulties there has developed "a large variety of scattered
efforts . . . tak[ing] such forms as pressure for fair employment
legislations, widening of civil service to Negroes, administrative
acts by branches of the federal government on behalf of equal opportunity in employment, greater admission of Negroes to labor
unions, scattered voluntary efforts by large business corporations
to increase the number of Negro employees and to open higher
positions to them . . . ,"[259] etc. However, in 1965 Blumer concluded that these several lines of attack on the line of white
economic privilege "have done comparatively little to improve
the economic and opportunity base of Negroes in American
society."[260]

Blumer argued that if the people of the United States wished
to avoid severe "discord and overt strife . . . [from becoming]
persistent marks of the color line," they would realize that "the
dictates of national interest" require public support of governmental programs that "effectively improve the economic and
community position of the urban Negro."[261] The large-scale
postwar migration of blacks from the rural South to the urban
ghettos in all parts of the country had concentrated "Negroes in
the deteriorated and deteriorating areas of our large cities" at the
same time that "technological changes . . . [had been] closing the
doors to conventional fields of Negro employment."[262] The net
effect has been the recent appearance in America's cities of "a vast
urban Negro proletariat with a high incidence of unemployment, . . . no secure foothold in the occupational structure, . . .
[and] restricted opportunities to escape or rise . . ."[263] The urban
black enclave is at one and the same time "an ecologically segregated and socially ingrown community . . . [and] a poor and
underprivileged group . . . marked by considerable community
and family disorganization . . . [It] suffers a considerable loss of its
better trained and economically successful members through migration; . . . its economic sights and hopes are low."[264] However,

Blumer observed, "There is no conceivable likelihood that a social code . . . could be developed that would hold the disparate social positions of the two racial groups in an orderly relation . . ."[265]

Because their social and economic disadvantages coincided with their urban situation and civic enfranchisement, blacks in American cities are likely to develop "a strong disposition to fight back, a fuller appreciation of their civil rights and a greater readiness to use them . . ." In addition, their situation would tend to catalyze "a conduciveness to agitation . . . , formation of protest movements, and . . . [efforts to retain] possession of strategic political power."[266] These considerations lead Blumer to favor "a massive attack" on the color line debarring blacks from employment opportunities, an assault that "raises significantly the economic position of the Negro, opens to him all doors in the occupational structure, makes available to him the level of training and preparation to enter such doors, and allows him free residential movement . . ."[267] Such a movement in behalf of racial justice would have to be mounted "chiefly in the large cities of the North and West, in the headquarters of national organizations," but, because "the nation cannot ignore the problems that converge on a depressed urban Negro proletariat," the principal arena of struggle would have to be "the seats of government, particularly the federal government."[268]

Blumer observed that "the future of the color line in this intermediate band remains a highly problematic matter." In part his cautionary statement bespoke the fact that the arena of employment practices lies on the border of the public and private sectors of American life and is difficult to regulate—especially if the matter under regulation is perceived as the expression of an unfortunate attitude that has originated in the confines of the family and as a consequence of child socialization. On the other hand, however, if the racist practices of business corporations and labor organizations are conceived not as idiosyncratic prejudices but rather as historic and cultural legacies of black bondage, surviving badges of involuntary servitude and vestiges of slavery, i.e., effects which the Thirteenth, Fourteenth, and Fifteenth Amendments to the United States Constitution and the Civil Rights Acts of 1866, 1870, and 1875 intend to eliminate, they might be subjected to judicial revocation and to legislative correction. Blumer's emphases on the historical rather than the psy-

chological origins of race prejudice and on the institutional embeddedness of racist practices serve as a significant catalyst to any
public policy enlisting the agencies of government in the construction of just such a definition of the sociology of race relations in America. It also could help protagonists of affirmative
action programs and advocates of the beneficent usage of racial
classifications to justify their proposals to effect race conscious employment policies and reorganize education admission programs.

Race prejudice, Blumer asserts, arises as a sense of group
position formulated in the futherance of a precariously codified
hierarchical order.[269] The prejudices speak at one and the same
time to a legitimation of the admittedly inequitable order and to
an apprehension that the justifications for institutionalizing unequal treatment do not enjoy universal acceptance. Specifically,
they are resented by most members, friends, and allies of the subordinate group, and will likely become targets of an impending
attack of some sort.[270] In respect to the United States, although
historians might continue to debate the precise causal nexus relating racial prejudice to Negro slavery,[271] there can be little doubt
that more than two hundred years of black enslavement fostered
a deep sense of racial hierarchy, locating the white race at its apex
and the blacks at its base. Moreover, once this racial hierarchy
was in place, other alien peoples deemed to be races or quasi-
races were located along the spaces in the vertical hierarchy in
accordance with anatomical, social, and moral attributes said to
justify their placement. Hence, although the specific prejudicial
allegations employed with respect to blacks, Asians, Hispanics,
and Amerinds are quite different from one another (and are not,
strictly speaking, always *race* prejudices), we contend that the institution of slavery is *a* if not *the* principal contributor to a heritage of racism still active in America.

If we accept the thesis just enunciated, viz., that current
prevalent racist attitudes and the various discriminatory practices
of professional associations, corporations, labor unions, and other
organizations that though private are charged with a public responsibility are surviving badges of a now prohibited servitude
or are vestiges of an unconstitutional slavery, then their manifestations are subject to legislative and judicial scrutiny and can
be recognized as lawfully appropriate objects for the courts and
Congress to eliminate. Blumer's several observations on the na-

ture, origins, persistence, and decline of race prejudice are helpful in reaching this conclusion. He has designated as at least scientifically questionable the idea that race prejudice arises out of some factor or cluster of factors affecting the individual personality, or that it is an expression of individual attitudes, or that it represents aggressiveness stemming from frustrated desires, or that it is a peculiar form of cultural expression. In place of these hypotheses, he offers seven theses that argue that race relations arise within the political process and occur in the public arena. First, he asserts that the various forms, contents, and modes of expression of racial prejudice are "formed by complicated and varying factors in complex processes of historical experience."[272] Second, he urges social scientists and policy makers to recognize that "the process by which racial groups form images of themselves and others . . . is fundamentally . . . *collective* . . . [and that it] operates chiefly through the public media in which individuals who are accepted as the spokesmen of a racial group characterize publicly another racial group."[273] Third, although Blumer had earlier pointed to the varying intensity, differing qualities of feeling, and regional variatons that comprise the variety of expressions of race prejudice, he recognizes that it is a real and obtrusive phenomenon in social life, "so impressive in its extensiveness, persistency, and apparent spontaneity that many students [mistakenly] regard it as inevitable."[274] Fourth, Blumer identifies the most general manifestation of race prejudice as the strongly entrenched and vigorously defended *color line* that powerful spokesmen for a superordinate group's interests have drawn across institutional complexes such that the subordinated races are restricted in their placement and advancement or excluded altogether.[275] Fifth, he shows that the alleged benefits of modernization, industrialization, and urbanization are not unambiguous insurers of a decline in racist practices.[276] Sixth, he rejects the notion that racial antipathies are ineradicable, showing that race prejudice declines when the subordinate group is no longer felt as a threat either because it has acquiesced to its place on the color line, retiring into a segregated arena wherein it builds up a parallel structure of institutions and contributions to the creation of a biracial society, or because the dominant group has become persuaded to regard it as inoffensive to its interests and acceptable to its members and instituted a gate-opening process that, in effect, begins to erase the color line.[227] Seventh, he emphasizes the pivotal role played by the interrelated political, executive, administrative, legislative, and judicial organs of the society in bringing about a new conceptualization of the racial order, giving it official legitimation, and promulgating and enforcing the regulations that will guide it.

The racial subordination of American blacks—and of Asians, Hispanics, and Indians—constitutes a remarkable example of the codified hierarchical organization that Blumer believes is typical of unjust race relations. Much of its historic legitimation grew out of the rhetorics employed to justify the institutionalization of Negro slavery and to draw a color line across the opportunities and social encounters of all non-whites and some non-Anglos after slavery had been abolished. The antipathies toward blacks were so heavily re-enforced by the more than two centuries of legalized slavery that they tended to spread out and engulf free blacks in the North and, after slavery had been abolished, to survive and become institutionalized in black codes, racially restrictive employment practices, urban ghettoization, and racially segregated education, transportation, and recreation. "If the Negro had been freed in the late eighteenth century rather than in 1863," writes historian Winthrop D. Jordan, " . . . he would have suffered far less degradation . . . He would have undergone a shorter period of association with a radically debased status."[278] As matters actually stood, however, abolition took place after a century of antislavery debate had hardened the slaveholders' opposition to the fundamental equality that Negroes deserved. The writers of the Thirteenth Amendment to the Constitution intended their codified addition to the fundamental rights of Americans to eliminate not only the institution of slavery but also all the burdens, badges, and indicia of slavery that were borne by blacks, bond or free.[279] It would be consistent with Blumer's conception of the historical origins of the color line and of its function as an expression of racial prejudice to regard them as continuing badges and vestiges of the system of slavery. It would be part of a public philosophy dedicated to realizing the intent and aims of the framers of the Civil War Amendments to support policies and proposals that seek to break down the remaining bulwarks of the color line, slavery's legacy.

One such proposal that has found various forms of codification and received an uneven and sometimes hostile response from the courts and the public, consists in such activities as reordering the admission requirements of medical schools, establishing new qualifications for apprenticeship training programs, and contracting new bases for hiring and laying off workers. Common to these different practices is the use of racial and ethnic classifications for beneficent purposes, specifically: assuring blacks and other disadvantaged minorities that the opportunity for a medical education is practically available to them; insuring that the changing bases for technological employment will not freeze out blacks hitherto denied opportunities to learn new techniques; securing the job-opening effects of employment made by the civil rights movement against racially insensitive seniority and retrenchment procedures. Common to the opposition to these and other programs of "affirmative action" is the charge that they institute "reverse discrimination" against whites and ought therefore to be as unconstitutional as the recently discredited laws and practices that supported the old color line. Opponents of affirmative action assert that blacks and other minorities are owed administrative and judicial protections only if it can be shown that they are victims of prejudice and discrimination in the particularity of their situation and in their own life-experience, and they insist that a public policy in behalf of constructing egalitarian racial relations has done all that it can when all official and administrative barriers to equal opportunity have been removed.[280] An approach consistent with that of Blumer would, we believe, lend some support to the affirmative action philosophy. This support is best expressed through a critique of the opposition's case against affirmative action.

Proposals that benign racial classifications be used to undo those occupational disadvantages created by employers' and labor unions' discrimination arose years before the Supreme Court had declared segregation in public facilities inconsistent with the Fourteenth Amendment's guarantee of equal protections of the law. Such proposals belong to that class of actions that Blumer has described as likely to arise when a "subordinate racial group seeks to break through the line of exclusion . . . [and employs organizational] pressures to secure better employment, the training necessary for such employment, access to institutions . . . and so forth."[281] A pertinent incident of this kind occurred in

1938 when The New Negro Alliance, "a corporation composed of colored persons," got into a picketing dispute with The Grocery Company, a Delaware corporation operating 255 retail grocery, meat, and vegetable stores in the District of Columbia. The NNA made a vain request that The Grocery Company, "in the regular course of personal changes in its retail stores, give employment to Negroes as clerks, particularly in stores patronized largely by colored people." The Grocery Company countercharged that the Alliance had made "arbitrary and summary demands" and then had unlawfully picketed the stores in order to secure them. Because in that proceeding the Supreme Court had only to decide upon the First Amendment rights of the picketers, it did not rule on the demand for counterracist preferential hiring, but notice should be taken of the grounds for opposing such in the dissent filed by Justice McReynolds: he rebukes the Court's majority for giving Constitutional legitimation to a situation wherein "no employer . . . who prefers helpers of one color or class can have adequate safeguard against intolerable violations of his freedom if members of some other class, religion, race or color demand that he give them precedence."[282]

Whether preferential hiring was a matter of strictly private concern or a matter in the public interest arose more directly in another picketing dispute brought to the Supreme Court from California in 1950. The issue before the Court was whether the State might enjoin Progressive Citizens of America, a reform group, from picketing Lucky Stores, a grocery chain, in order to induce the corporation to adopt an employment procedure whereby, at its store where approximately fifty percent of the customers were black, it would hire Negroes to replace only those white clerks who quit, retired, or were transferred until such time as the proportion of black to white clerks approximated the proportion of black to white customers.[283] The Supreme Court upheld the injunction against the Progressive Citizens of America, agreeing with California's highest court that the picketing which the latter had enjoined "would encourage discriminatory hiring . . . [and] give constitutional protection to petitioners' efforts to subject the opportunity of getting a job to a quota system."[284] In its own decision, quoted approvingly by Justice Frankfurter, the California Supreme Court not only rebuked the petitioners for "seeking to make the right to work for

Lucky dependent not on fitness for the work nor on an equal right for all, regardless of race, to compete in an open market, but, rather on membership in a particular race," but also predicted that, should the petitioners succeed in winning their demand, "then other races, white, yellow, brown, and red, would have equal rights to demand discriminatory hiring on a racial basis."[285] Frankfurter went even further, suggesting that if picketing in demand of racially selective hiring were to be permitted, "there could be no prohibition of the pressure . . . to secure proportional employment on ancestral grounds of Hungarians in Cleveland, of Poles in Buffalo, of Germans in Milwaukee, of Portuguese in New Bedford, of Mexicans in San Antonio, of the numerous minority groups in New York, and so on through the whole gamut of racial and religious concentrations in various cities."[286] He warned of the exacerbation of community tensions and conflicts that would occur if hiring practices would be made to proceed beyond the melting pot. "The differences in cultural traditions instead of adding flavor and variety to our common citizenry might well be hardened into hostilities by leave of law."[287]

In conceiving that blacks had no peculiar claim on the affirmation of their equality through classificatory preferences and in comparing their judicially unacceptable claim to that which might be put forward by other ethnic groups, the Court gave no recognition to the possibility that the virtual absence of black workers in retail clerkships might be a surviving heritage of slavery—an expression of the color line drawn specifically against Negroes. Recognition of the intimate relationship between Negro slavery and the color line that, after emancipation, restricted occupational and other opportunities for blacks in most institutional settings might have led the Court to a different definition of the situation: to affirm—or at least not to unalterably oppose—the use of a racial classification that sought to carry forward the Civil War Amendments' and postwar Civil Rights Acts' intentions of eliminating one of the badges and incidents of slavery. To this end, it is worth calling attention to the central argument of Justice John Marshall Harlan's dissent in the *Civil Rights Cases* (109 U.S. 3) decided in 1883. Observing that "there are burdens and disabilities which constitute badges of slavery and servitude," and that the removal of these badges was the "moving or principal cause of the adoption of . . . [the Thirteenth] Amendment," he asserted that as slavery as an institution "rested wholly upon the inferiority, as a race, or those held in bondage, their freedom necessarily involved immunity from, and protection against, all discriminations against them, because of their race, in respect of such civil rights as belong to freemen of other races." Moreover, Harlan had gone on to state that "Congress, . . . under its express power to enforce that amendment, . . . may enact laws to protect that people against the deprivation, because of their race, of any civil rights granted to other freemen in the same State; and such legislation may be of a direct and primary character, operating upon . . . such individuals and corporations as exercise public functions and wield power and authority under the State."[288] In light of Harlan's opinion—which the Court might have seen fit to elevate from its status as a dissent—might they have also seen that to grant the Progressive Citizens of America's petition to picket in demand of preferential hiring was not to invite a plethora of petitions for similar preferences from other peoples not similarly situated, i.e., not suffering from a legacy of inferiorization and a color line that derive from black enslavement, but to act in consideration of the intent of the framers of the Thirteenth Amendment?

A PUBLIC PHILOSOPHY
FOR AFFIRMATIVE ACTION

The issue for a public philosophy of racial equality that would support affirmative action programs turns on whether a beneficent use of racial classifications is seen to further or to retard the desired egalitarian objective. Much of the argument against affirmative action has proceeded as if the matter was one involving public opinion or mass sentiment alone. Hence, Nathan Glazer alleges that the adoption of benign racial quotas will arouse widespread resentment among the people excluded from their benefits, that it will encourage ethnics of all hues to clamor at the employers' and the courts' gates for similar protection, and that it offends "what many have believed to be the main thrust of liberalism in America, the primacy of individual rights."[289] Glazer has become a protagonist in the marshaling of public opinion against judicial enforcement of affirmative action programs. No longer seeking to secure racial equality, which he believes has been achieved with the outlawing of malevolent racial classifications, he looks benignly on the kinds of divisive occurrences that Blumer foresaw would muddy the waters of social problem resolution—in Glazer's words, to "the break in the civil rights coalition" and to the fact that spokesmen for leading Jewish groups—"The Anti-Defamation League of B'nai B'rith, The American Jewish Committee, The American Jewish Congress— are not happy with reverse discrimination."[290] Glazer recognizes that if "there is to be any halt or reversal in the development of practices of affirmative discrimination, then it will have to be because of court decisions."[291] However, he attributes such decisions not to the adoption or affirmation of a specific egalitarian or anti-egalitarian public philosophy, but rather to his hope that "dominant opinion on civil rights is no longer uniform, and is split on whether preferential employment on the basis of race and ethnic group is a proper response to discrimination and disadvantage."[292]

To understand the usage of racial classifications for any purpose, benign or malign, we place our discussion within the combined frameworks or symbolic interaction and the perspectives that define constitutional practice with respect to the Thirteenth and Fourteenth Amendments to the Constitution. Blumer is in the forefront of a significant proposal for social science, viz., that "objects (in their sense of meaning) must be seen as social creations—as being formed in and arising out of the process of definition and interpretation as this process takes place in the interaction of people."[293] Among the categories of objects subject to social creation are social objects themselves, including as one example of the socially creative process, the conceptualization whereby racial or ethnic classifications are formulated. Further, social objects like other "[o]bjects have no fixed status except as their meaning is sustained through indications and definitions that people make of the objects."[294] The fixing of the status of a social object is also a social act, fitting together the definitions of the social object, circumscribing the things classified together under a single heading, such that joint action with respect to it can take place. But such fixing of the status of any social object is not likely to be permanent. "Nothing is more apparent than that the objects in all categories can undergo change in their meaning."[295]

The classification of social objects occurs in the experiential world of the actors and, like the actors themselves, is subject to the vicissitudes of that world, including, especially in the matters of race and ethnicity, its political and judicial processes. In legislatures and courts of law meanings and classifications are established or undone, given or denied official recognition, and granted or refused legitimation. Such meanings and classifications are at one and the same time part of and the means employed to define, limit, and propel human action. When the joint collective actions in any society occur in the form of recurrent patterns, there exists a condition wherein the people "share common and pre-established meanings of what is expected in the action of [others] . . . and accordingly each . . . is able to guide his own behavior by such meanings."[296] Blumer understands that "it is just not true that the full expanse of life in a human society . . . is but an expression of pre-established forms of joint action."[297] Moreover, the apparent continuities of stable and repetitive actions are "as much a result of an interpretative process as is a new form of joint action . . . being developed for the first time."[298] Hence, social life is not a mere exhibition of abject creaturely obedience to "norms, values, social rules, and the like . . . [but] is subtended by a process of social interaction—a process that is necessary not only for their change but equally well for their retention in a fixed form."[299] Classifications, including racial classifications, are social constructions of a reality not being merely reacted to but being acted on—acted on for a purpose whose character, morality, and praxiology are themselves also part and product of the interactional process.

The institutionalization of the color line in Post–Civil War America is an instance of the imposition of an invidious hierarchical scheme of racial classification and relationships by white spokesmen who had already arrogated to themselves the power to define the nature and status of the black freedmen-and-women. Their conceptualizations derived from the system of slavery. Slavery had set forth the terms for the formulation of patterns of association that came to characterize black-white relations in and long after the Redemptionist Era. That era began with the federal government's acquiescence to "home rule" in the states of the former Confederacy; gave legitimacy to an emerging color line through the Supreme Court's reduction in applicability of the Civil Rights Acts and Civil War Amendments; and achieved racial caste institutionalization when all three branches of government disregarded the earlier promise to eradicate once and for all the badges and incidents of slavery.

Precisely because slavery was a condition of life and labor confined to the Negro people alone, their biological distinctiveness was given added importance when, as emancipated persons, they encountered whites. "Negro," thus, became a stigmatizing status because of the degradation of Africans and their descendants in slavery in the United States. This institutionalized degradation ceremony has been attested to by Wilbert E. Moore, who writes that

> The idea of racial inferiority certainly did not appear in colonial law with the introduction of Negroes, . . . [T]he legal determination and justification of who might be slaves developed slowly . . . [T]he legal conceptions, which had the practical effect of limiting slavery to Negroes, together with the process of pushing back the religious justification to the original heathenish condition of the Negro people, upon which the conversion of the individual slave had no bearing, were directly related to the idea that slavery rested upon an inherent inferiority of the enslaved.[300]

Because the alleged inferiority was said to be inherent, it was thought to be a fixed, ineradicable attribute of all members of the race—an attribute that took no account of the individual character and wide variations in skills, aptitudes, intelligence, interests, and orientations that actually existed among the people classified as belonging to the Negro race, or of the changes in these and other attributes that might occur in generations to come.

The race prejudice that developed in consequence of slavery is of the kind that is directed toward a conceptualized group and thus represents "a classification of individuals and . . . an abstract category inside of which we conceptually arrange individuals . . . The prejudice is manifested against a specific individual by identifying the individual with the conceptualized object and then directing towards him the attitude that one has toward the conceptualized object."[301] American race prejudice entailed adoption of a negative classification of the descendants of Africans such that they become a collective social object called Negroes; that classification fixed a seemingly unalterable image of inferiority on them, and this image, in turn, became a justification for widespread and variegated individual and institutional discriminatory treatment of them.

If American courts, Congress, and opinion leaders came to recognize that race prejudice consists in an institutionalized sense of invidious, hierarchical group position, that it owes its persistence and tenacity to having become embedded in the many, varied, organized, and proactive versions of the badges and incidents of Negro slavery, and that it expresses itself in applications to discrete individuals and concrete groups of persons classified as members of a discredited race, it would do much to dispose of the arguments against affirmative action. The latter depend on the following theses: That a color conscious but benign set of classifications militates against true equality by legitimating new inequities in the life chances of white ethnics; that affirmative action provides an unacceptable resolution of the black situation because it imposes "reverse discrimination"; and that admission and hiring programs based on affirmative action substitute race membership for the neutral meritocratic qualifications that should prevail in an open job market. Against these formidable objections it should be noted, first, that the meritocratic qualifications that are alleged to prevail do so within, and largely in accordance with, a color line that has been exposed as such in an essay by Blumer. Moreover, neither industrialization, urbanization, the introduction of a money economy, or the formalization of civil rights will inevitably break down traditional racial orders, nor will they make racist practices inefficient or unprofitable, or introduce a form of class unity that replaces and cuts through race solidarity.[302] The more difficult argument is that of just and equitable classification. Specifically: is a benign racial classification necessarily an instance of reverse discrimination? We think that it is not and that an explication that brings together the understandings of the classificatory process with that of the jurisprudential method for determining instances of prohibited inequality will show this to be the case.

The framers of the Thirteenth Amendment, according to the researches of Jacobus ten Broek,[303] clearly intended to relieve both enslaved and free black people in the United States from the entire complex of "burdens, badges and indicia" that radiated out from and beyond the institution of slavery. In their debates they were guided in great part by the tenets of the natural rights philosophy of the eighteenth century, a philosophy whose social and political relevance had declined so much in the twentieth century that Walter Lippmann took it upon himself to revive it as the basis for an ethically reconstructive public philosophy. The enactment of the Civil Rights Acts of 1866 and 1870 was declared by the Supreme Court to be proper legislative action in pursuit of eradicating the badges and incidents of slavery, but in 1883 a majority opinion restricted the applicable scope of those laws, declaring that, "It would be running the slavery argument into the ground to make it apply to every act of discrimination which a person may see fit to make as to . . . the people he will . . . deal with in . . . matters of intercourse or business." [304]

Twenty-three years later, the Court virtually emasculated the possible remedies available to blacks suffering from occupational discriminations by limiting whatever natural rights entitlements the "badges and incidents" phraseology had granted them to a prohibition on being enslaved. [305] It was not until 1968, in a case involving denial of home purchase to a black couple, that the Court overruled its decision in the 1906 case and reinstated and broadened the applicability of the Civil Rights Act of 1866 and the Thirteenth Amendment. [306] Justice Potter Stewart added to the Opinion his view that the 1866 Act "was designed to do just what its terms suggest: to prohibit all racial discrimination, whether or not under color of law, with respect to the rights enumerated therein . . ." [307]

Entitlement to employment, however, is not an enumerated right, and with the decline of natural rights philosophy as a guiding force, and its silence on the matter of making a living, there remains only a possibility that a revised public philosophy might establish job entitlement as a natural right. Walter Lippmann had proposed just such an enumeration at the peak of the Depression in 1934:

> I know that it is not the fashion to speak of the rights of man . . .
> All rights are, no doubt, ultimately a creation of the state and exist only where they are organized by the government. There are, however certain rights of the individual which . . . are provided

by the state . . . To these rights we must add . . . the right of access to remunerative work . . . A free collectivism would seek to guarantee at all times the opportunity to labor.[308]

Lippmann linked his proposal for a natural right to labor to a general social and economic program that would reconstruct American democracy through redressing "the balance of private actions by compensating public actions." Lippmann's scheme for a "compensated economy" clearly called for public regulation, but not ownership, of private enterprises and of the individual and corporate actions associated with them. It had become necessary, he believed, "to create collective power, to mobilize collective resources, and to work out technical procedures by means of which the modern state can balance, equalize, neutralize, offset, [and] correct the private judgments of individuals."[309] Little of Lippmann's original program was incorporated into United States policy; however, during World War II, the National Resources Planning Board proposed that full employment become the principal aim of postwar economic policy. The NRPB formulated an "Economic Bill of Rights," defining the "right to work usefully and creatively" as a basis for other proposed rights (income maintenance, education, housing, health insurance) appropriate to a "jural world order outlawing imperialism, old- or new fashioned." However, the federal Employment Act of 1946 did not enact a program espousing full employment, but rather continued the policy of the welfare state, tolerating an "acceptable" level of unemployment. As black Representative Augustus Hawkins would later observe, full employment had been redefined to mean "the highest level of politically tolerable unemployment" that Congress and the Executive would accept. Subsequent policy proposals have acquiesced in this limitation, in effect rejecting employment as a basic human right.[310]

Although Lippmann had not specifically directed his jobs proposals toward the solution of the race problem, legislation governing the hiring of minorities has become a significant feature of federal policy, especially after the passage of The Civil Rights Acts of 1964 evoked new attempts to bring about equality of economic opportunity.

The decline of natural rights philosophy elevated the importance of the promulgation, enforcement, and adjudication of regulations over persons, organizations, and institutions as a means of insuring that particular evils would be prevented and assuring that particular benefits would be equitably distributed. Special legislation, applying as it does to a particular class of persons or corporate bodies, necessarily entails the making of classifications in the very manner that symbolic interactionism generally describes, i.e., in relation to orienting action with respect to them. Such legislation is subject to invalidation as violative of The Equal Protections clause of the Fourteenth Amendment when specific claims are recognized by the Supreme Court: when the burdens or benefits that it imposes are said to be inequitably distributed; when petitioners from the group so classified successfully claim that the obligation imposed has an evil and prohibited intent, or that it does not reach the lawful intention that the legislators had in mind; when spokesmen for non-members of the classified group demonstrate to the Court's satisfaction that they have been improperly excluded and that the legislative category has been incorrectly circumscribed as far as achievement of its lawful public purpose is concerned; or when the purpose of the legislation is itself proven to be beyond or prohibited to the lawmaking powers of the congress.

It was the first and last of the above objections—specifically, that if the purpose of establishing and maintaining a racially segregated school system is to preserve white supremacy, it is a forbidden one; or, if it is to provide for the public school education to which every American is entitled, its segregated classification violates the public's interest in having its citizens equally educated—that the Supreme Court recognized in granting judicial relief to the black petitioners in *Brown vs. Board of Education of Topeka, Kansas,* in 1954.[311] However, in the debate over affirmative action and so-called reverse discrimination it is the identification and legitimacy of the public purpose served by a beneficial classification of blacks and other racial minorities that is at issue.

Affirmative action programs vary widely in their character and scope. Among those subjected to recent Supreme Court deliberations are: procedures whereby a fixed number of seats is set aside for members of disadvantaged minority applicants to a state university's medical school;[312] a collective bargaining agreement's reservation of fifty percent of the openings in an in-plant craft training program for black and Hispanic employees until such time as the percentage of minority craft workers would become commensurate with that of minorities in the local labor force;[313] a school district's collective bargaining agreement on layoffs under which seniority would be retained subject to the condition that at no time would there be a greater percentage of minority teachers laid off than the percentage of minority teachers employed at the time of the layoff;[314] a district court's race-conscious relief order to black and Hispanic victims of a major labor union's pattern of racial discrimination already held to be in violation of The Civil Rights Act of 1964;[315] and the city of Cleveland's consent decree providing race-conscious relief and other forms of affirmative action to black and Hispanic firefighters.[316] Common to all of these programs is the use of a beneficent racial and ethnic classification, a singling out of one or a specific set of groups for a putatively ameliorative public purpose. According to Nathan Glazer the official legitimation and activation of such classifications bring an "Orwellian nightmare" closer to realization: "New resentments are created; new turfs are to be protected; new angers arise; and one sees them on both sides of the line that divides protected and affected from nonprotected and nonaffected."[317] But, do the resentments, anger, and antipathies arise because an injustice is being foisted off on one segment of the American people as a remedy for racism, or because there is a widespread misunderstanding about the constitutional propriety of the racial and ethnic classifications that affirmative action programs make?

All classifications separate, and some, when activated, segregate. Blumer has pointed out that "Segregation is a primary process by which a human society develops an inner organization—an allocation of diverse elements into an articulated arrangement."[318] However, what becomes problematically significant is the segregative situation which monopolizes clearly identified and commonly valued benefits for one group at the expense of another. Where such monopolies prevail "The range of exclusions between racial groups is likely to be extensive." Moreover, "Where a sense of racial difference has been fused with a status difference, the inevitable tendency will be to extend the practice of exclusion along the array of relations."[319] Recognition that such monopolies are wrong but, having a long history, have become embedded in the social fabric at a number of crucial points in its organizational skein, might very well lead a reformist legislature, court, or private organization to adopt a dismantling procedure that assigns race-specific remedies to any or each of these points. Thus, Chief Justice Burger announced that although he and his fellow justices "recognize the need for careful judicial evaluation to assure that any congressional program that employs racial or ethnic criteria to accomplish the objective of remedying the present effects of past discrimination is narrowly tailored to the achievement of that goal . . . , we reject the contention that in the remedial context the Congress must act in a wholly 'color-blind' fashion."[320]

If a benign racial classification is within the purview of constitutional affirmation, what qualifications must it possess in order to pass successfully the test of judicial scrutiny? The answer has been supplied in Joseph Tussman's and Jacobus ten Broek's path-breaking analysis of procedures appropriate to Fourteenth Amendment review: "A reasonable classification is one which includes all who are similarly situated and none who are not . . . with respect to the purpose of the law."[321] Hence, a benign racial classification, aiming to remove the legacy of past race discrimination by encompassing only members of the victimized racial groups and excluding those who have not been similarly treated is not an instance of reverse discrimination, but rather a remedying benefit conferred on the one group that deserves the relief it will provide. The outraged feelings that Glazer seeks to warn us against might be assuaged by acceptance of the moral rectitude of the public purpose served by affirmative action programs coupled with a recognition that the classifications these programs make are directly and reasonably related to that purpose.

There remains the question of defining and justifying the purpose of affirmative action programs. Thus far we have suggested that their purpose is to eradicate the still lingering badges and incidents of slavery. That the drawing of a color bar across the entire range of occupations and professions is a major aspect of the legacy of slavery is something that melioristic social scientists might very well choose to investigate. Wilbert E. Moore pointed out as a result of his investigation of slavery that the "change of civil status from slavery to freedom without according [the freedmen] full civil rights had consequences [that are still] not resolved . . ." Moreover, having noted the introduction of "surreptitious servitude through peonage and gross economic discrimination against Negroes," he concluded that "the persistence of the marked economic and social disadvantages of American Negroes more than a hundred years after the abolition of slavery indicates the continuing effects of history on the present."[322] Ironically, Glazer, although he opposes legislative or judicial action designed to remove the effects of historically embedded racism,[323] provides a statement summarizing the latter as it became institutionalized in the years following the Civil War: "In the North . . . Negroes were present—they always had been—but they were so few and *so far down the social scale* that they were scarcely seen as a threat to anything. In the South, exclusivism was directed primarily against the Negroes, though Catholics and Jews came in for their share of prejudice, and, on occasion, violence. In the West, the Chinese and the Japanese were the main targets of a pervasive racism which included the Mexicans and the Indians."[324] Glazer means this statement to serve a different purpose—that of presaging his belief that the uneven extension of full citizenship to minorities in the United States is not pervaded by a ubiquitous racism but rather "by a steady expansion of the definition of those who may be included in it." Moreover, he wishes to establish the fact that the "dismantling of . . . [America's] system of prejudice and discrimination in law and custom began in the 1930s."[325] But designating the badges and incidents of slavery as a primary facilitator of this complex network of racism and xenophobia does no harm to his sanguine hypothesis; nor does his view of America's past necessarily preclude affirmative action from becoming a remedial part of the dismantling process that he so much admires.

The classifications employed by some of the affirmative action programs embrace other racial and ethnic groups in addition to the Negro. The medical school of the University of California at Davis sought to reserve a number of seats in its first year program for self-designated members of "disadvantaged minority groups," a classification that in practice embraced blacks, Chicanos, Asians, and American Indians; the United Steelworkers of America and the Kaiser Aluminum and Chemical Corporation established a percentage on their jointly administered craft training program affecting Hispanics and blacks; in the racial limitations on teacher layoffs the collective bargaining agreement with the Jackson [Michigan] Board of Education defined the protected minority teachers as black, American Indian, Oriental, and of Spanish descent; Cleveland's consent decree required it to take into account the number of black and Hispanic firefighters when making promotions in the city's fire department; and a sheet metal workers union local in New York City was required to institute a percentage admissions plan affecting non-whites, in practice referring to blacks and Hispanics. All of these classifications seem to be overinclusive with respect to an intent to eradicate the lingering effects of slavery. Moreover, they seem to invite claims for similar preferential treatment from the American descendants of European nationals who also experience occupational discrimination based on ethnic prejudices. However, a closer examination of these classifications suggests that a different interpretation is possible. If it could be established that the color-culture bar drawn against Asians, Amerinds, and Hispanics is a secondary effect of the racially organized system of black slavery, while the ethnic discriminations against European nationals arise from xenophobia of a different sort, then a benign classification affecting all of the legatees of slavery and excluding all those not affected by the prejudicial heritage of bondage would be consistent with the purpose originally intended by the Civil War Amendments and early Civil Rights Acts. Although the matter has not heretofore been considered in this way, we would like to suggest that there have been two heritages of discrimination institutionalized in this country—one stemming from slavery and its vestiges, radiating to engulf peoples considered to be the functional equivalents of blacks; the other arising out of Protestant American ethnocentrism and apprehension about the religion and the assimilability of certain classes of European nationals.

Blumer has emphasized that any theoretical approach to the analysis of race relations must take into account the several formational processes whereby such relations are transformed into an hierarchical order. Once one racial order has broken down, there emerges "a fluid, blurred, and variegated process of racial thrusts and accommodations." In turn, that process is often followed by "a positioning of racial groups as sovereign or quasi-sovereign peoples."[326] The several senses of group position that arise introduce a variation in the form and character of racial prejudice such that a "comparison of instances of racial prejudice shows that it may differ in intensity, in quality of feeling, [and, most important for the argument we are making here,] in the views by which it is supported, and in manifestation."[327] Blumer goes on to suggest that "There have been, historically three major areas of race relations in the United States—the contact with the native Indian population, the association of whites with Negroes, and the incorporation of a large number of ethnically diverse immigrant stocks into the developing American society."[328] He soon differentiates the historical situation further, distinguishing relationships that have developed affecting Japanese Americans, Chinese Americans, American Indians, Spanish-speaking people of the Southwest, Puerto Ricans and Filipinos.[329] However, despite many studies designed to explain racial relations, Blumer rightly complains about the failure in this field to develop a comprehensive theoretical framework consistent with empirical realities and taking account of the distinctive character of these relations.[330]

There is evidence to suggest that both the pre- and post-Civil War treatment of Asians, Amerinds, and Hispanics developed as adaptations from the system of black slavery or as an elaborative response to the white Anglo supremacy that that system has helped to legitimate. Herbert Hill has written with respect to the Sinophobic invective and occupational exlusions that organized labor and demagogic politicians proclaimed and put into practice against Chinese immigrants: "In part, this model of labor exploitation was derived from the earlier experience with a racially distinct slave labor force; in turn it provided a model that significantly influenced the treatment of blacks who were to be emancipated more than a decade later."[331] Political and labor union agitation against the Chinese in the decade after the Civil War was in great measure a surrogative activity, according to Alexander Saxton: In the hands of politicians and labor union agitators, the Chinese became hapless scapegoats for the emancipated blacks, who were temporarily protected by the short-lived Reconstruction policies.[332] It also seems to be the case that the slavocratic system of Southern agriculture was adapted to the recruitment, organization, and treatment of Asian, American Indian, and Mexican farm labor in California after such Confederate leaders as Joseph Le Conte and Ernest Hilgard became active in assisting the development of that region's agricultural economy.[333] According to the careful researches of Cletus E. Daniel, it was the powerlessness of the Chinese to resist the white farmowners' oppressive exploitation that made them attractive as a tractable labor force, and, after the Chinese had been driven from the fields by labor mobs[334] and exclusion legislation, made the Mexican bracero equally attractive and the Japanese fruit picker less desirable.[335] And, according to the agricultural historian, Donald J. Pisani, it was precisely the Japanese farm workers' effective challenge to the doctrine and practices of white supremacy in the fields that led white Californians to propose "measures to restrict Japanese immigration, segregate Japanese schoolchildren, and prohibit alien land ownership," and to seek ways to make the white Anglo-owned and operated family farm the unit of agriculture production in that state.[336] Underscoring the similarity of conditions of Mexican migrant laborers with that of black slaves, Paul S. Taylor, the most astute observer of the Hispanic-American work situation in America, noted, "Traditionally, the growing of cotton connoted mud, mules, and Negroes. Just so today the irrigation ditch stands for intensive agriculture, hand labor, and Mexicans."[337] California has been the significant racial frontier of America, the state where blacks, Asians, Mexicans, and indigenous Indians made contact, where the sense of group position that marks the institutionalized race prejudices against them was formulated under the auspices of white Anglo sovereignty.[338] Although the evidence presented above is insufficient to establish an unchallengeable case, it suggests that in the years just before and after the Civil War the ignominious badges of slavery were spread beyond their effects on the black population and pinned on to other non-white and some non-Anglo peoples. As Blumer once put the matter, "the color line was carried over from the old situations to the new situations—from the plantation to the factory, from the rural area to the city, from the old institutional settings to the new institutional settings."[339]

If this socio-historical hypothesis were to be accepted by Congress and the courts, it might entitle the present day legatees of the heritage of slavery to the kind of affirmative action relief that is recognized as proper for putting into practice the intentions of the framers of the Thirteenth Amendment and the Civil Rights Acts of 1866, 1870, 1875. At the same time, acceptance of this hypothesis about the limited spread of the effects of slavery would suggest that spokesmen for white ethnics, who insist that affirmative action procedures violate their rights under the equal protections clause of the Fourteenth Amendment, or who demand relief from an alleged discrimination imposed by their exclusion from the class of beneficiaries created by affirmative action decrees, have failed to realize that they are not entitled to the particular kind of relief provided. It is available to a strictly limited category comprised of legatees of slavery's badges and incidents. Although they might be eligible for relief from unlawfully imposed ethno-religious discriminations arising out of their membership in classes of persons proscribed as part of America's xenophobic heritage, their exclusion from the classification of persons who are inheritors of the burdens of slavery is not an instance of constitutionally prohibited under-inclusiveness, nor is it an example of reverse discrimination.

Students of race relations and advocates of racial reconstruction know that racial prejudices differ in their origin and in the ways they are justified. A theory of dual trajectories of institutionalized race prejudice not only contributes to an understanding of the complex origins of American racism but also facilitates acceptance of the varied and specific ways in which racial classifications might be preserved for beneficial rather than malign purposes.

There remains, however, the argument, made by social scientist opponents of affirmative action procedures and by some of the justices of the Supreme Court, that persons are entitled to relief under the promise of affirmative action or other provisions of the Civil Rights Acts only if it is demonstrated that they are victims of race discrimination in their specific life situations. There are two aspects to this objection. First, there is the thesis put forward by Thomas Sowell in several of his writings[340] that, because members of the several racial groups have responded to their particular oppressive situation with quite different strategies and enormously different outcomes, they do not deserve the same form of classificatory benefit. However, we know that the individual responses to a generalized condition of despised group position are many and varied and likely to yield an array of results, most of which are irrelevant to changing the fixed status of

the subordinate racial group itself.[341] There is the further and related, if obvious, point that those individuals who have somehow
overleaped the racist barriers that have held the rest of their racial
fellows back are not likely to appeal to the courts for aid.

Second, there is the thesis, enunciated most recently by
United States Supreme Court Justice Rehnquist,[342] that no court
should order a remedy utilizing racial preferences unless the minorities so benefited have been the "actual victims" of a particular
employer's racially discriminatory practices. Although the meaning of the term "actual victims" is unclear, it would appear to
require proof of a direct and immediate expression of racial
prejudice and/or discriminatory practice to be juridically acceptable. Such a requirement overlooks the complex and variegated
process of the construction and maintenance of a racially hierarchical order. The color bar can be drawn in such subtle ways—
the use of grandfather clauses to keep blacks from voting, or
Asians from joining the plumbers' craft association, are telling
examples—that neither its literal expression nor its visible effects
on generations of members of the proscribed group is extractable
from a context-free or historically uninformed reading of the employment record. Thus, it is quite possible that a discrepancy
might exist between the character of interpersonal relations among
members of different races employed at the same work site and
the continued operation of the color bar. Blumer observed that
"Whites may have, and do have, a wide and variable range of
feelings toward Negroes, from profound hostility to deep kindness and sympathy, yet adhere to the color line when and where
the social code requires its application."[343] He has also pointed
out that although "Much of the debarment of the Negro . . .
springs from feelings of dislike; additionally, much of it occurs
through a tacit collective recognition that it is 'not the thing
to do' to give him entrance to given posts . . ."[344] In light of
Blumer's strictures on the matter, a requirement that seekers of
the relief that affirmative action programs offer show that they
are actual victims of racial discrimination should insure that
whatever evidence is admitted be consistent with the rhetorical
subtleties of construction and the historical embeddedness of
practices that have gone into making and preserving the color-
culture.

RACE AND LABOR-MANAGEMENT
RELATIONS: POLITICAL REALISM
AND MORAL ORDER

Blumer's sociology of race and ethnic relations includes a
critique of the optimistic theories about the impact of industrialization on them. He points out that the claim that industrialization would bring about a social reorganization based on values of
universality and achievement is merely an unproved allegation.
Blumer insists that there is no historical evidence to demonstrate
that race would vanish as a social factor as industrialization pene-
trates deeper into the institutions of society. He goes on to point
out that many different and varied racial patterns could co-exist
with industrialization: industrialization does not necessarily and
as a matter of course undermine the traditional or established racial order. "In early industrialisation," Blumer notices, "the rational or secular perspective, which industrialism admittedly fosters and stresses, may compel an adherence to the racial system
rather than a departure from it . . . [The] *rational* operation of industrial enterprises which are introduced into a racially ordered
society may call for a deferential respect for the canons and sen-
sitivities of that racial order." And, Blumer added, "This observation is not a mere *a priori* speculation. It is supported by countless
instances of such decisions in the case of industrial enterprises in
the Southern region of the United States, in South Africa and in
certain colonial areas." Indeed, Blumer concluded on this point,
" . . . the rational imperative in industrial operations may function to maintain and reinforce the established racial order."[345]
Blumer's critiques of theories of industrialization and race
relations advance his perspective on a public philosophy that
would assure both freedom and equity. He observed that "the intrinsic structural requirements of industrialism need not, contrary to much *a priori* theorizing, force a rearrangement of the
relations set by the racial system."[346] Moreover, by the same
token, the introduction of rational industrial techniques did not
in and of themselves necessarily provoke racial tensions. Instead,
the "empirical evidence pertaining to this matter presents a very
varied picture." The assumption, so widespread in industrializa-

tion theories,—and, incidentally, we may add, in Marxist theories about the effect of capitalism on the formation of social classes, of which Blumer's argument is an implicit critique—that rationalization of production and increased geographic mobility will "open access in such a society to one another's occupations, lines of industrial endeavour, areas of entrepreneurial opportunities, and residential areas is not true." If industrialization occurs together with new racial contacts wherein relationships are at first vague and undefined, "they come to be defined quickly—defined under the overbridging sway of traditional views of the appropriate position of the races."[347]

Questions of equity in pluralistic mass societies involve more than a simple division of power and rights between a dominant and a subordinated group. Racial friction in multi-ethnic and racially structured industrial societies is more likely to occur, Blumer suggested, "at the points of contact between different subordinate racial groups" because in "the reshuffling which industrialisation induces, such subordinate groups may be brought into competition at scattered points in the industrial structure with resulting strain and discord." Pointing to such outbreaks of friction as those between Negroes and Mexicans in the United States and between Africans, Colored, and Indians in South Africa, and to the varied modes of accommodation that arise between industrial elites and the peoples brought into work for them, Blumer concluded "that members of the dominant and subordinate racial groups are not thrown into the competitive relationship that is presupposed by *a priori* theorising."[348]

Industrialization, Blumer insisted, had not and would not obliterate the significance of race and other irrationalities for modern societies. The much-vaunted effects of rationalization on racial prejudice, the supposedly beneficent consequences for racial discrimination that follow the introduction of a money economy, and the supposition that a fully established industrial society would necessarily tend to place workers and assign tasks in consideration of qualifications, efficiency and productivity have been powerful domain assumptions in economic and sociological theory, finding support in the writings of Marx,[349] Simmel,[350] and J. S. Mill.[351] More recently, they have been reasserted by William J. Wilson as factors producing a decline in the significance of race in contemporary America,[352] and by Annie Phizacklea and Robert

Miles as features modifying the development of class consciousness in Britain.[353] Blumer, on the other hand, rejects outright the thesis that the rationalization of economic relations will inevitably reduce the relevance of race for employers and workers.

A study of industrial history convinced Blumer that "the hiring and assignment of industrial workers from subordinate racial groups did not follow the postulates of industrialism." He went on to observe that " . . . members of such groups have not found entrance into managerial ranks; and entrepreneurs from such groups [have been] confronted by high walls barring them from exploiting opportunities lying in the province of the dominant group." To those who claimed that the "transfer of the lines of racial patterning to the industrial enterprise" was "merely a temporary stage in which the forces of industrialisation have not had opportunity to come to natural expression; [and that] with time, or in the long run, the industrial imperatives would gain ascendency, stripping the racial factor of any importance," Blumer replied, "We do not know how much time is needed to constitute the 'long-run'; certainly half a century of industrial experience in both South Africa and the South in the United States [has] brought no appreciable change in the position of the races in the industrial structure." On this point Blumer concluded that the "picture presented by industrialisation in a racially ordered society is that industrial imperatives accommodate themselves to the racial mould and continue to operate effectively within it."[354] If there is a set of factors that would disintegrate a racist social order, Blumer asserted, it would have to be found outside industrial imperatives. Precisely because the latter are likely to accommodate themselves to the traditional racial order, he insisted that there is no inevitable and unidirectional pattern of development following the onset of industrialisation. Each specific instance has its own intrinsic character and history; each would have to be analyzed and acted upon from the perspectives of the public philosophy that prevails and the interests and power relations that arise within the society.

Labor Conflicts
in a Post-Protestant Era

In his examination of labor management relations in the United States, Blumer went beyond the question of race relations and attempted to define a public philosophy that might guide the struggles between a variety of competing interest groups. Labor-management relations are part of the larger complex of issues that relate entrepreneurship to capital investment and both to the meaning of work. The latter, in turn, had been a central issue in Max Weber's analysis of *The Protestant Ethic and the Spirit of Capitalism*.[355] The elements stressed in Weber's work had entered the theory and practice of industrial relations as orientations toward problems of worker motivation, management-labor conflicts, the rights of workers, and the relations between workers and other groups in society. Some of these issues had also been addressed in Hugo Munsterberg's pioneering work on vocational tests and industrial morale, which in part drew on Weber's own empirical studies of factory workers.[356] They were given additional impetus in the Hawthorne studies that discovered that in twentieth-century America worker motivation arises less from Protestant ethics than from mundane social relations prevailing at the work site.[357] Work in a modern society seems to be guided more by social recognition and economic rewards than by a calling from God. Striving for grace through work has given way to searching for social, psychic, and economic security through labor—or by other means. The Calvinist-inspired separation of faith from works inadvertently led to a detachment of work from its salvational justification, especially after more general processes of secularization had set in. Thereafter, labor would seek its rewards within this world. Its rationale would seem to require a moral equivalent for Protestantism within a world that was moving further and further away from a single overarching faith.

The obverse side of the problem of worker motivation is that of worker dissatisfaction—i.e., what conditions might lead the worker to cease his efforts or subvert or sabotage the labor system? The strike had become an early focus of attention among sociologists in the United States because it seemed to herald a breakdown in the covenant that supposedly had united workers and employers in the joint effort of production.[358] Since the beginnings of industrialization, the factory has become a critical site at which men's moral and ethical obligations to each other and to God are put to the test.[359] From the point of view of the larger commonwealth, the strike seems to threaten the moral foundation of society: the social compact could not be sustained under conditions of conflict between employers and employees.[360] For this reason industrial sociologists and other melioristic reformers focused much of their attention on improving "human relations" in the factory.

Blumer's studies of entrepreneurial organizations, labor management struggles, the function and control of strikes, and the societal implications of industrial conflict broke out of the religiously-informed framework that had developed in academic industrial sociology—whose practitioners he regarded as "dreadfully naive with reference to the nature of industrial relations" and who employed "the stock of conventional ideas and modes of research . . . [that] are essentially hackneyed, unrealistic and uninspiring"[361]—and adumbrated a public philosophy appropriate to the realities of modern industrial conflicts. He pointed out that industrial relations proceeded according to their own inner logic, a logic that could not be fathomed by ideological directives, utopian hopes, cultural analyses, or such sociological conceptualizations as the status-conflict model, the study of long-term trends, application of the Harvard researchers' "human relations" approach, a quantification of attitudes, or the implementation of sociograms.[362]

The relations between workers and management in American industry, Blumer observes, are not interpersonal but collective, carried out through organizations representative, respectively, of workers and managers. Industrial relations, hence, can no longer be analyzed according to a "simple contract between a worker selling his labor and an employer purchasing that labor."

> That bare fundamental relation has been elaborated in our society
> [Blumer explains] into an extensive, diversified, complex and in-

direct network of relations in which the individual worker becomes an insignificant and inconspicuous figure . . . Relations between workers and management become primarily a matter of relations between organized groups.[363]

Industrial relations can properly be understood as relations between organized sectors of soceity. Precisely because they are "mobile, indirect and [of a] large dimensional character," Blumer likens industrial relations to "a vast, confused game evolving without the benefit of fixed rules and frequently without the benefit of any rules." Even their setting is unstable, "shifting and presenting itself in new forms," and putting "strains on the pattern of [the] game." The moves in the game are but "accommodative adjustments largely between organized parties." But, "the participants are far from satisfying their respective wishes and objectives in the temporal accommodations which they make to each other," and consequently put "constant pressure on their relations and [look with] an opportunistic readiness to change them." Hence Blumer concludes that "we deceive ourselves and perhaps engage in wishful thinking when we regard this shifting flow of relations in industry as temporary and transitory, to be followed by a shaking down of relationships into a permanent orderly system." So long as America remains a "dynamic, democratic, competitive society," the "mobile character of . . . [industrial] relations," together with their "degree of tension . . . rapidity of accommodations, and . . . shifts . . ." would continue.[364] Like race relations, those arising out of industrialization hold out no assurance of harmonious cessation or promise of ultimate resolution.

Blumer's perspective entails no assumption of a natural or inevitable relationship between capital and labor, nor any prophecy that capital and labor will eventually cooperate in a joint effort to build a good society. The human relations approach to industrial problems implicitly puts forward the idea that a covenanted brotherhood might emerge; its efforts are directed at enhancing or at least preventing the further fracture of that latent sense of brotherhood. However, from Blumer's perspective industrial fraternization is not likely; it is pointless to do nothing but wait until the day when its benefits might be realized. Because industrial relations are characterized by much fluidity and endemic conflict, labor and management are best understood as organized power groups, alternately competing and bargaining with each other, but not adhering to a strict code of ethical conduct while doing either.

In Blumer's view, labor-management conflicts are comprehensible as power relations because they occur within an arena wherein "people in pursuit of goals are thrown into opposition to one another, with sanctioned or allowable leeway in the forging of actions to achieve success in the face of such opposition, and where the pursuit is not made subservient to considerations of each other's welfare." [365] Power relations, "are set and guided by respective positions of effective strength, . . . marked by an opposition of interests, intentions, and goals . . . [and characterized by] scheming, maneuvering, the devising of strategy and tactics, and the marshaling and manipulation of resources." [366] The pattern of power relations that prevail in the labor-management sector also provides a model for understanding the character of a plural society—one in which almost all groups bargain and negotiate for what each regards as its fair share of social rewards and social participation. In such a society one may not assume the existence of a set of core social values, a progressive direction for history's conflicts, or a social compact governing the relations among the organized sectors of society. In Blumer's schema industrial and all other power relations are adversarial, and necessarily so, because each of the parties has opposed *interests*.

What Blumer refers to as "power action" is not conspicuous at the level of the union local in the United States, "particularly when local unions enjoy a high degree of autonomy," but it "comes to be pronounced . . . in the case of large international unions which have to function *as single entities* vis-a-vis large corporations, trade associations, and employer organizations." The "power psychology" prevalent here includes " . . . a lively scrutiny of the operating situation to ascertain what threats it holds, what obstacles it sets, what advantages it contains, and what exploitable facilities it yields." With such a psychology in operation among both labor unions and management organizations, "a conspicuous fluidity is introduced into their relations, . . . [p]olicies . . . become increasingly subject to compromise, tempering, and redirection under the impact of the passing array of newly

developing situations, . . . the relations between the parties become tenuous, shifting, and tentative as each views the other and
awaits developing action on the part of the other . . ." Moreover,
"there is an increasing tendency for the power struggle to move
over into the political arena."[367] Each party attempts to exploit
the political arena to gain its own ends: through legislation,
executive decisions, administrative actions, and the mobilization
of public opinion. Other groups in society are then vulnerable to
the pressures and manipulations of the vested interests.

The shift of this complex of power relationships to the political arena seems to call for the presence and authoritative guidance of a referee of a higher judge who can resolve the conflicts in
behalf of a higher public interest. In 1954, when the Keynesian welfare state was still in place, Blumer noted that the Taft-
Hartley law governing labor-management relations had posed
this question anew but not given it any new answer:

> This transferring of the power struggle between organized labor
> and management from the industial arena to the political arena
> marks a major transformation in their relations, with conse-
> quences which, while only dimly foreseen, will be momentous.[368]

Compulsory arbitration and mediation did not eliminate the industrial problem but only transferred it to another level. Such
political mechanisms could neither prevent a strike nor insure a
resolution of the basic conflict.

If the strike is seen as something other than an act of social
immorality or a breach of ethical conduct, there is still required
the imposition of an alternative ethical and moral code to adjudi-
cate conflicts in an industrial society. But the basis for a code of
public ethics and civil morality is problematical in societies like
the United States, characterized by a decline of religious consensus and a rise in the number and the variation in interests of organized groups. In the matter of industrial relations, the public interest is presumably activated in the action taken by governments
to referee contests between labor and management, but the mere
presence of a referee does not solve the problem of ethics except
at the procedural level, i.e., if both parties to a conflict accept the
rules of play that the referee introduces. In the process of exploring this dimension of the public interest, Blumer noticed another

distinction—that between a *legitimate* labor strike carried out for purposes consistent with the employees' interests in the job situation, and the *unwarranted withdrawal of labor's services* in order to serve some ulterior purpose.[369] Blumer's idea of a public philosophy requires the presence of an authority and a citizenry that can distinguish between legitimate and ulterior interests in behalf of the public good. However, because modern mass society is composed of a congeries of competing interests, the problem that seems most difficult to solve is where to locate the social source from which a disinterested group and a public-interested authority might arise. Blumer recognizes that the "line beyond which the public interest is seriously endangered is a matter of judgment and cannot be drawn precisely," and that there is required an "informed and competent judgment" that "justifies public alarm and calls for action."[370] However, Blumer insists, the crucial problem is that of simultaneously protecting both the public welfare and the rights of all parties to participate in the competition.[371] Although Blumer was not able to find an institutional arrangement whereby this cockpit of plural interests could be regulated so as to assure the triumph of the public interest over its adversaries or made to produce an institution embodying that interest, he provides hints and suggestions toward that end.

Moving labor-management or racial relations closer to legally codified procedures seems promising but, Blumer notes, this is not an unambiguous solution to this problem. Each party to an industrial or racial dispute has not only to satisfy its legitimate needs but also to respond to the pull of ancillary interests. The latter arise as side products of organization and expansion. The introduction of law into industrial and race relations is, thus, not likely to eliminate a resort to power practices nor to put an end to the quest for selfish ends. For example, Blumer cites occasions when management might initiate a deliberate policy of paternalism to forestall union organization or mitigate the adversarial character of employee-employer relations.[372] Or, to take another of his examples, labor might utilize a strike to satisfy extraneous interests, including exaction of personal tribute, acquisition of strategic advantage, advancement of political or ideological doctrines, or as a tactic in competiton with a rival. Still another kind of situation finds an employer exploiting a strike to create racial or ethnic divisions within the workforce, harm a competitor, or injure a rival union or a racial group within that union. Recourse to codified law does transfer the struggle between labor and management, or between the races, to the courts, but once there, each party might seek to bend the law in its own interests, whatever their relation to the public good.

The concept of public interest is usually linked to the detached role that the central government might play in resolving social conflicts and establishing the basis of a just and equitable political economy. During the decades when Blumer first formulated his ideas about social order the Keynesian doctrine was implemented, assigning to government the role of referee between labor and business and by extension, between all other interest groups. In that period, with business temporarily weakened by the depression and labor organized with the support of the Roosevelt administration, it appeared that the government did indeed represent the interest of society as a whole. Moreover, the New Deal seemed to evince a new interest in the amelioration of racial conflicts.[373] However, the compromise between labor and business that America's version of Keynesianism represented could succeed only so long as both parties would accept the government as a just and impartial referee. And the authority of racial refereeship could only be sustained if the government was invulnerable to accusations of white supremist leanings.

The existence of a public interest presumes a national consensus that is capable of overruling group interests that threatens it. In America such a national consensus has been achieved in times of extreme national crisis. One philosopher of the public interest, Joseph Tussman, has conceded that a severe threat to national security seems to be required before the nation can be goaded into accepting the priority of the claims of the public good.[374]

Blumer presents us with the problem of finding the locus of civic virtue in the modern state: the individual cannot be absolutely assured that the state will respond to public issues in accordance with the rules and ethics of justice. The modern state is too often a creature of interests and of fads and fashions; it lacks an overarching ethic, or interest, of its own—except survival. This was the point at which Max Weber had left the problem in his essay "Politics as a Vocation."[375] Weber had observed, "We are placed into various life-spheres, each of which is governed by different laws . . . Normally, Protestantism, however, absolutely legitimated the state as a divine institution and hence violence as a means . . . [But modern times are not normal; therefore] Whosoever contracts with violent means for whatever ends—and every politician does—is exposed to its specific consequences . . . After coming to power the following of a crusader usually degenerates very easily into a quite common stratum of spoilsmen. Whoever wants to engage in politics at all, and especially in politics as a vocation, has to realize these ethical paradoxes . . . Only he has the calling for politics who is sure that he shall not crumble when the world from his point of view is too stupid or too base for what he wants to offer." [376]

America's philosophical pragmatists, from whose outlook Blumer's perspective is descended, had always been interested in the moral groundings of their own society, especially after the religious authority of Puritanism had begun to lose its awesome power to inspire virtue. Two of Blumer's mentors, John Dewey [377] and George Herbert Mead, [378] had sought to invigorate a new civic consciousness by means of a public-spirited education and a broadened program of childhood socialization, but neither was able to locate a code of ethics in anything other than the processes whereby the self was developed. Each encouraged the formation of a social self whose fundamental obligation was to the larger community, but neither could assure America of its widespread appearance. Their program has recently been reintroduced by William M. Sullivan, who hopes to reconstruct an American public philosophy on the basis of a revived and truly social self, one attuned to the priority of civic virtue as a life-ideal; one that ensures that the maturation of the person occurs "within a context of interdependence and mutual concern." [379]

Blumer placed his stress on the inherently problematic character of the self in the modern world. He observed that although Mead had pointed out that the "generalized other is the chief position from which a human participant grasps and understands the social world inside of which he has to develop his conduct," he had not given social scientists any aid in knowing "how people construct their 'generalized others'" nor had he provided "a set of techniques which would enable people and scholars alike to improve their ability to take group roles." Further, neither Mead

nor any other theorist of human society had yet devised "an analytical account of how the developing social situation is to be
brought inside of the developing social act."[380] Blumer is also of
the opinion that a social scientist's proposal "to be the judge of
the beneficial or detrimental character of his [subject's] line of action . . . seems to fall outside of the domain of the scientific inquiry."[381] The self, no longer rooted in a faith, nor guided by a
set of fixed moral convictions, is beyond the evaluation of the social scientist but vulnerable to competing moral values. A variety
of interests might attach themselves to it, and the individual is
likely to adopt a different set of ethics to suit each situation.
Without an encompassing code of core values, and lacking assurance of other grounds for social consensus, there would seem
to be no basis for a public morality superior to that guided by the
many and varied self and group interests. A moral consensus
based on public opinion is not a solution because public opinion
is itself plural, reflecting the expression of competing values and
varying interests. The mass media contain the promise of breaking through the several public opinions and forging a mass consensus. However, as Blumer's analysis of mass society indicates,
consensus is transient and ephemeral and provides no unambiguous or unchanging standard to guide individual or institutional conduct.[382] Morality is, thence, placed in the middle stream
of action, where, presumably, it might be guided by whatever
ethics rise to the occasion. Nevertheless, as Blumer attempts to
show, it is possible to see a path to the public interest in the midst
of its less honorable competitors.

Although Blumer provides no assurance of the victory of
civic virtue over uncivil interests, his careful analysis of the actual
character of mass society suggests that there is room for the public good to find its representative and to be pursued. The public
consists not only of interest groups but also of the vast and shifting company of citizens who act as spectators of the interest conflicts that at any given moment occupy center stage in the political arena. As citizen-spectators that part of the public occupies a
unique position capable of exciting a disinterested interest, a perspective that, having no narrow interest of its own to protect, can
afford to adopt that of the general welfare. Such a perspective is
more likely to be evoked when the conflicting parties seek goals

that are injurious to the body politic or to the public good. Hence, when electric companies threaten the health and safety of the populace by proposing to use dangerous and uncontrollable sources of energy, when sanitation workers injure public health by refusing to pick up and dispose of refuse, or when municipal police go on strike leaving the civilian citizenry helpless to cope with crime, a powerful sense of the general public interest is likely to incite the people—or at least significant segments of the people—to corrective action. Like Tocqueville, who perceived that the predominant ethos of America was both egalitarian and commercial, Blumer conceives of the masses of Americans as self-interested. However, he allows for the possibility of a social and moral basis for civic virtue in the changing foundations of self-identification and the double life that each citizen lives as interested party and disinterested but active spectator.

A possible basis for official morality is also to be found in Blumer's writing. Much of socialization theory has emphasized the pattern whereby individuals come to define themselves in terms of their interests. It is not surprising, then, that the civic interest is perceived as chimerical, impossible of realization against the multiplicity of special and private interests. Yet, the central characteristic of mass society, its subjection to constant changes and to propelling individuals into new situations and different lines of conduct adds a corrective to the apparent mummification of society in its interests. The political arena, like the mass market in goods and the mass communications industry, offers greater opportunities for access than are found in more tightly stratified societies. Entrance into the public arena might sometimes have the effect of introducing an intrusion into the narrow-interest outlook of the new political participant. Whether as elected official, appointed civil servant, or member of the judiciary, the public servant by dint of his elevation into a new position in society, is subjected to new situations and different points of view wherein his old perspective might no longer serve to indicate the meaning or value of objects or to guide conduct. Under such conditions, the official's outlook is likely to change and to define issues in terms of new and different conceptions of interest, including that of the public interest. The many liberal decisions on First Amendment freedoms written by Supreme Court Justice Hugo L. Black, a sometime member of the Ku Klux Klan, are a fine example of such a conversion. Although it must be emphasized that Blumer's analysis does not promise the efflorescence of a public philosophy or a necessary intensification of interest in promoting the general welfare or enhancing the public good, it does perceive a society where these elementary forms of civic virtue have opportunity for emergence and room for maneuver.

Toward a Politically Realistic Public Philosophy

Blumer's analyses of mass society and of labor-management relations provide a key that might open the door to a more politically realistic public philosophy. However, at first glance, the character of mass society does not invite sanguinary prognoses. The pattern of power relations that Blumer has described as governing the resolution of labor-management disputes are but an instance of the competitive struggles characteristic of all interest groups in American Society, whether these be racial groups searching for rights, relief, jobs and space; religious groups struggling for jurisdiction over the salvation of souls; military groups fighting one another for additions to their budgets; businesses competing for shares of a market and profits; or educational institutions advertising aggressively for students, private contributions, and state subsidies. Such competitions are often carried out at political and juridical levels and occur at every level of these systems. So pervasive and relentless are these struggles for competitive advantage that at times the public good seems to have disappeared altogether and be represented by no one. Each competitor attempts to influence particular politicians, the outcome of elections, the content of law, the interpretation of legal procedures, and the focus of public opinion. Methods of gaining influence include not only the use of the mass media as instruments of communication, advertising, and propaganda, but also the many forms of bribery, fraud, and corruption commonly found modifying mass democratic politics. The legitimacy of the political order is then tied to those groups which succeed in their claims for advantage; the satisfaction of their greed becomes the sole support of the political order. Excluded groups may become so disenchanted that they withdraw their adherence to the mystique that grounds the fundamental societal *raison d'etre*, retreat into asocial isolation, seek entrance to another society, or mount a social movement to reform or revolutionize the one they inhabit. Under such a regime social structure has generated anomie.

When Blumer first examined the racial, industrial, and political order of America's mass society, he believed that the central government guided by the principles of the Keynesian welfare state could become the representative of the public good. Then, in the 1930s and during World War II, the nation appeared to confront the common problems of social reconstruction and defeat of a common enemy. These goals provided sufficient national purpose to overcome the countervailing ones advanced by special interest groups; the sense of national purpose sometimes appeared to transcend greed and to uplift the human spirit and often carried itself along on the belief that a job was to be done. Yet, even then those appearances were in part false. Governmental policies designed to promote the public good frequently excluded such groups as blacks, Appalachians, and Japanese Americans. Up to the early sixties the Keynesian welfare state concealed many corrosive elements: whatever inequities resulted from its operation seemed acceptable because in absolute terms each group could feel it had gained something relative to its own earlier position. Only when its utilitarian public philosophy—that sought the greatest good for the greatest number—could no longer hide the fact that blacks and other groups had been largely excluded from its efforts at redistributive justice would fundamental questions of equity be raised anew.

In the fifties and sixties almost all previously uninfluential groups became aware that they might participate in the political and litigational quest for what they regarded as their fair economic, cultural, and social share. These included not only the recently enfranchised and ethnically conscious racial and minority groups, but many others, representing virtually every conceivable interest from environmental preservation to economic restitution for past governmental actions; from sufferers of state negligence to claimants for tax exemption; from sexual deviants requesting redesignation as alternative life-style practitioners to pseudo-Oriental gurus demanding legal distribution of hallucinogenic drugs; from marchers demonstrating in behalf of gender equalization to antivivisectionists calling for a halt to medical experimentation on animals; from feminists supporting a mother's right to have an abortion to pro-life advocates insisting that the physically deformed and mentally incompetent be granted full rights to life, liberty, and the pursuit of happiness; from accusers of the law enforcement agencies' failure to do enough to prevent wife and child abuse to complainants that the courts are too vigilant in the prosecution of those who would commit a mercy killing. Awareness that status, class, and group position could be modified by political, legal, and judicial means became a salient part of common knowledge. The number of "vested interests" grew, and both the older established corporate structures and the newly forming advocates of social reconstruction felt that they must organize to insure their survival and advance their claims. The sheer increase in the number of players and their organizational effectiveness at both the political and juridical levels has resulted in a substantive change in the public political life of the United States. Blumer attended to this new development in his analysis of mass society.

MASS SOCIETY: BEYOND
THE SECULARIZATION PROCESS

Both Auguste Comte and Emile Durkheim defined secularization as the transference of religious values and sacred themes to the ever more mundane social order.[383] Although most American sociologists of the late nineteenth and early twentieth century put that definition to work in the development of their own discipline's epistemology and praxis,[384] and though certain later sociologists, e.g., Talcott Parsons[385] and Robert Bellah,[386] and the latter's followers, have employed a similar orientation in their understandings of theory construction and social reconstruction, a quite different process of secularization seems to have penetrated the American social order and deconstructed the lingering effects of its Protestant heritage: Much of institutional and individual life has been liberated from the constraints imposed by strict adherence to Pauline dictates, but in part as a result of this release, become confused, litigious, innovative, and questing. It is not the case that religion has been rejected altogether—America has not become an exemplar of the militantly atheistic society that Pierre-Joseph Proudhon hoped would succeed the *ancien regime*[387]—but, rather, that, as Protestantism's usefulness as a guide to public policy and private conduct approached marginal utility, its decline called forth three quite different responses: intellectual movements seeking to establish a substitute and superior civil religion; a fundamentalist resurgence hoping to recreate the original covenant and resacralize society in accordance with the precepts of old-time religion; and an unself-consciously nostalgic sociology of mass society, looking to criticize the new social organization in terms of all the traditions and unifying sentiments that it had abandoned. Tacitly rejecting the first and second and setting his own argument in direct opposition to the last-named response, Blumer has searched out the inherent integrity of the new social order and looked for the ethics of public conduct that its unique configurations of culture and institutional arrangements might inspire.[388]

Blumer's criticism of his colleagues points up the enormous extent to which they have devoted their efforts to counting the socio-cultural losses that mass society has supposedly permitted. By comparing the institutional units of mass society with their counterparts in earlier, traditional, and often enough, hypostasized social orders—e.g., carefully contrasting present-day family structures and functions, forms of government, judicial, education, economic, and religious systems, and structures of authority, morals, and beliefs with those of historical or even prehistorical societies—these sociologists "court disillusion and confusion." Such studies, Blumer contends, neither provide a comprehensive picture of the true character of mass society nor do they present an overview of the special features that distinguish it from other forms of human group association.

When sociologists and anthropologists employ paired dichotomies as constructs or typifications of older and present-day societies—Blumer has in mind such prominent formulations as "folk" and "urban"; "community" and "society"; "sacred" and "secular"; "*Gemeinschaft*" and "*Gesellschaft*"; "mechanical" and "organic"; "primary" and "secondary"; and "culture" and "civilization"—they tend to reify what in fact has not stood the test of empirical scrutiny. Moreover, these approaches with rare exception tend to skew discussions in behalf of the socially solidifying virtues of the older type and against the allegedly asocial and disorganizing vices of modern societies. By couching such discussions in nostalgic terms, these sociologists beg the question of a public philosophy for mass society, arguing in effect that only a restoration of the old regime will provide a socially secure American community. Thus, we would argue in illustration of Blumer's general criticism, that in the most recent variant of this conventional sociological theme, "getting saved from the sixties"[389] seems to call for a civil instauration of those "habits of the heart"[390] that once guided a virtuous community of redeemed or redeemable American souls.

When sociologists and other social thinkers designate present-day societies as "industrial" or "urban," they do little more than provide an abbreviation for the manifest equivocality buried in the meaning of those terms. Furthermore, they do not point to any way of comprehending or dealing with the tangled web of institutions that seems to describe social arrangements in a mass society. "Industrialization" and "urbanization" are terms that Blumer believes stand in for what are truly empty formulae. A mass society can be understood, he believes, in terms of its four central characteristics—massiveness, heterogeneous structure, openness to public life, and subjection to constant and rapid changes. If a public philosophy for mass society is to develop, his analysis seems to suggest, it will have to be built upon recognition of the political and social consequences of these features.

When Blumer came to analyze participation in the public life of American society—i.e., individual participation in elections, party memberships, and in contributing or responding to public opinion—he noticed how much the politically active citizenry resembled the movie audiences he had studied many years earlier. "The people who take part in public life," Blumer observed, "are drawn from all walks of life; they come from various professions, with varied status, from different localities, and belong to different organizations . . . [O]ne has only to think of the mass of moviegoers . . ." However, unlike the audiences at films, who more often than not are caught up in a solitary reverie after viewing the dramas on the screen, the participants in the public life of mass society constitute an "indeterminate, anonymous and unorganized group" which does "in fact really act." Their actions consist in "making choices: choosing products as a consumer at the market, choosing among mass media programs, choosing from among the array of suggestions, party policies, doctrines and candidates on the political battlefield." The mass in a modern democratic society is neither Marx's congeries of low status groups who act against their own class interests, nor is it Le Bon's milling and interstimulating crowd that undermines rational group interests; rather, it is a quasi-group that resides in a world whose most remarkable feature is the constancy of its changes. "The world of its actions is characterized by a series of mutually competitive models—products, blueprints, suggestions, themes, etc.—all clamoring for attention and espousal." Precisely because it must respond to the interminable changes endemic to mass society, the mass must remain open to all kinds of information and unconstrained by the shackles of traditional perspectives or debilitating ideologies.

A peculiar aspect of mass society is that its social formations are not necessarily confined to any bounded geographic or regional area; yet individuals and associations have quite varied access to information and quite disparate opportunities to exercise influence on public affairs or private matters. Despite spatial distance, the mass is brought closer together by means of advanced communication technologies. However, to the extent that the knowledge processed thereby is limited to the most common denominator of comprehension, it fails to communicate the specialized information that might be needed for forming a judgment. This in turn leads Blumer to the observation that "the various parts and sectors of a mass society tend to develop relatively independently." Each unit tends to discover and attempt to resolve its own problems, according to its own lights, and in relation to its own procedures and sense of applicable norms. Hence, it is not surprising that one investigation of modern corporate life has discovered that decision-making on difficult and important issues occurs within moral mazes, labyrinths of ethical confusion in which office intrigues, calculated deceptions, and strategic power plays are commonplace.[391] In general, Blumer points out, "large areas of mass society are typically prone to new sporadic developments, which bring to the most varied phases of group life new and unexpected situations to be tackled . . ." The single most significant difference between traditional and modern societies is "that the incentive, prerequisites and mechanics of continuous reshaping are the very essence of that melting pot which is mass society." Nevertheless, "mass society cannot realistically be regarded to be in the throes of dissolution."

In mass society an individual achieves a sense of limited and limiting identity through the definitions given to him and his situation by the ascriptive solidarities and the several institutional associations to which he or she refers. Such identities are sometimes ephemeral, sometimes fixed, sometimes fleeting. Each, however, provides an orientation to conduct that occurs in a society whose "natural state . . . [requires] continual adaptation to the fluctuating complex of factors with which it is consistently faced." The complex and mobile character of mass society tends to assure the defeat of the unaffiliated individual and to insure the formation and continuity of every form of at least potentially influential or protective human group association. Because the individual acquires only a segment of a whole human identity from any of these self-referencing groups, not only is there a high probability of personality disorganization, but also, and more significant for the problematics of the public philosophy, a severe threat to realization of that rational, enlightened, civic identity deemed necessary to the preservation of a democratic polity. The less than total individual, seemingly a creature of interest groups and ethnic sodalities, intersects with other beings similarly situated in the public arenas where their common concerns become matters for debate and decision. At the city, state and national levels, these common concerns are given expression through spokesmen for the organized interest groups. Such collectivities as these make possible what is beyond the reach of the individual citizen.

It is this novel form of representation in mass democratic society that gave birth to the lobbyist and to his function as a broker.[392] However, where originally the exercise of this function was thought to be an ethical violation of democratic process, it is now a practice without which its politics cannot be effective. Yet, the centrality of the lobbyist as a political figure is nowhere acknowledged either in America's formal political structures or in the basic constitutional and legal documents which uphold them. The lobbyist exists in a largely unregulated arena within which he or she brings clients and bought representatives together.

Up to now the lobbyist has been thought of as simply another functionary who in exchange for a fee performs a service. In the mass mind-set the lobbyist is thought of as a broker, who like the broker on the stock-market brings a buyer into contact with a seller. However, this analogical thinking is only partly justified. Where the stock-broker operates in a regulated market supervised up to 1933 by its own elected representatives and after that year by the Securities Exchange Commission, the lobbying industry remains unregulated either by an internal organization of its own or by an equivalent of the S.E.C. Under Federal regulations the lobbyist needs only to register as a representative of a special interest group or a foreign government. His fees are not regulated by law, the methods by which he influences legislators are not bound by ethical codes, and he is prepared to represent anyone, including enemies of the nation, criminals, the rich, the poor, or the privileged, without regard to the consequences for the public good that his actions might have. Under the terms of such a non-public philosophy, the client who is willing to pay the highest price—to buy the votes of legislators—plays a decisive role in defining public policy.

It is our contention that the political mechanism of lobbying cannot serve as a foundation for a public philosophy. Yet, as political realists we understand that the lobbyist serves a purpose in the modern democratic process. Congressional representation is based on place of residence, but most public issues are beyond local concern. The lobbyist represents interests that are based in the non-geographic organization of occupation, industry, class, status, race, ethnicity, education, etc. But precisely because the lobby role is central to the political process, it should be recognized as an integral part of mass democratic politics and of the American system of government. Formal recognition would entail regulation of the lobbying industry in a manner analogous to that of the stock market. Since the lobbyist would be recognized as a political actor, however, such regulation would have as its purpose the enhancement of the public good rather than of any special interests.

INDUSTRIAL CONFLICT RESOLUTION:
A MODEL FOR A PUBLIC PHILOSOPHY

Our remarks thus far lead to the following observations: modern society is likely to be characterized by constant and varied conflicts of interest. At best the differences that divide the inhabitants of the apparently permanently fractured American social order can be composed but not dissolved. Conflicts are, in the sense that Georg Simmel employed the term, *realistic,* that is, they arise less often out of the psychic disorders or wildly uncontrolled passions that sometimes block the deliberative faculties of an individual or a group than out of differences of opinion over the distribution of scarce values or things of value: money, status, opportunities, liberty of action, freedom of thought, etc. Given the probable permanence of these conflicts, together with a likelihood of social instability, numerous debates over equity and freedom, and an irregular reshuffling in the distribution of power, a public philosophy that is simultaneously faithful to the true character of its subject matter and to the ideals of democracy and equality would have to be one that countenances considerable amounts of social disruption at the same time that it permits such state interventions as would protect vital public interests. It is a public philosophy that encourages continuation of a free and competitive quest for the many conflict-evoking objectives that are ever-present, ever desired.

Blumer provides a model for such a public philosophy in his critique of the various proposals that have been put forward to solve the problems arising from industrial strife. Although other observers of labor-management conflicts have usually regarded the strike as either "a needless form of economic waste . . . , an interference with the natural and orderly operation of a wage and price system . . . , an unwarranted violation of property and personal rights . . . , a menace to the spirit and practice of cooperation which they believe should pervade a decent civilized life . . . , [or] an attack on the public or social order with far-reaching implications of danger to the institutions of orderly life,"[393] Blumer holds to the position that the strike is "natural to labor relations, and indeed that it plays a role which is indispensable to any effective system of labor relations."[394] Policies or programs that seek to eliminate strikes by eliminating the causes of strikes are "fanciful," Blumer asserts, resting on the fallacious presumptions that employer-employee conflicts are unrealistic, that their respective differences can always be composed by appealing to an inherent spirit of cooperation, and that it is possible to eliminate altogether the sense of adversarial opposition that describes the actual relations between labor and management.[395]

Nevertheless, Blumer holds that there are strikes that endanger the public interest, and he believes that when they occur, steps must be taken to control the situation and protect the public interest. As examples of strikes that might threaten vital and genuine public interests, he mentions a "strike in a large utility network, an extensive strike in the system of transportation or communication, a lasting strike in the production of vital raw products, a protracted national coal strike or national strike in the steel industry, [and] a continuing strike on the docks of an insular community."[396] However, although Blumer believes that "No government should forfeit its fundamental function of action to prevent injury to the public interest," and that any government "is freely justified to control the major strike that inflicts such injury," he does not believe that government action should take the form of abrogating labor's "right to strike."[397] Blumer would elevate the right to strike to a place alongside the other fundamental rights guaranteed to the American people: "This right [to strike] is not a mere incidental gratuity," he argues; rather, it is "basic to collective bargaining, basic to a structure wherein employees and employers may pursue . . . and adjust their interests." And, precisely because "of its fundamental importance to the vast industrial network of employer-employee relations, the right to strike has, or should have, the character of a public right."[398] The right to strike is a basic part of the public interest that deserves protection, but exercise of that right might move against the general welfare which the government is also pledged to protect. How, when they come into conflict with one another, can a government act to insure that neither the right to strike nor the public interest is abridged? In giving an answer to this knotty question, Blumer provides clues to a general public philosophy for modern mass society.

Blumer's analysis of public interest problems in labor-management relations entailed a critique of the chief means employed or proposed to control the injurious effects of strikes: imposition of a mandatory "cooling-off" period before a strike could begin; appointment of an independent fact-finding committee charged with the task of uncovering the exact character of the dispute, framing public opinion about it, and making recommendations for its resolution; compulsory arbitration; and government seizure and operation of a strike-bound enterprise. Of these, all but the last, government seizure—with respect to which Blumer proposed a carefully circumscribed approach—was found wanting. The requirement that ninety days must elapse before a called strike can begin, a provision of the Taft-Hartley Act, "rests on spurious and false premises"—i.e., it supposes that a strike is called as "a result of hot outbursts of temper" rather than after a careful and calculated decision on the part of labor's leaders—and only serves to postpone the strike.[399] A fact-finding committee is "inadequate to cope with the problem of the major strike" not only because the "issues as well as all pertinent facts are usually well established and known as a result of previous [union-employer] negotiations," but also because its mediating activity "has no authority to force agreement" and no assurance that the public opinion that its fact-filled report helps to shape will have an effect on the disputants.[400] Compulsory arbitration, designed to insure the general welfare against any injurious effects arising out of the disputing parties' refusal to resolve their differences, "blocks both parties from pursuing and protecting their own interests . . . [and thus] in principle . . . represents the antithesis of an effective system of employer-employee relations."[401]

There remains the proposal that when a vital public interest is at stake, the government should seize the enterprise in question and operate it *pro bono publico*. "Such seizure," Blumer observes, "is seemingly the capital weapon in insuring the safety of the community" and one with which Americans are familiar because of its use at critical moments during and immediately after the Second World War. However, Blumer enumerates the several options open to federal functionaries who seize a struck enterprise and evaluates them with respect to how well they serve the government's obligation to both secure the general public interest and protect the workers' right to strike. If, after seizure, the government decrees a settlement to the dispute, "laying down the terms as if it were an aribitrator," its action "is clearly contrary to the structure of collective bargaining"; if the government takes over the role and arrogates to itself the interests of either the employer or the employee and negotiates a settlement, it gives up its independent status as the representative of the public interest; finally, if the government enforces the contractural arrangements that prevailed before the strike began, its decision constitutes "a drastic interference with collective bargaining . . . [and upsets] the operating base of each of the parties toward the other." A strike, Blumer reminds us, "is clearly a contest of power, a matter of the extent to which each of the parties can stand the losses which the strike inflicts on it."[402] A seizure that modifies the power struggle by reducing the losses of one or both of the parties to the strike abridges the spirit as well as the substance of the workers' right to withhold their labor power. The precise character of a federal seizure, hence, will have to be reconceptualized if the comprehensive package of public interests is to be served by it.

Blumer proposes that a government seizure "be so arranged that the parties are put in essentially the position they would occupy if the strike were in actual progress." This means that even after the strike is brought to an end and the plant reopened by a government takeover, each of the disputants would have to dig into its own reserves in order to maintain, respectively, profits and salaries. This could be accomplished during the course of the seizure by the government imposing penalties on both parties "that would approximate the respective deprivations they would incur under the strike." In the matter of the workers, their wages could not be garnished so long as they continued to labor, but sums could be subtracted from the union's treasury based on a calculation of the loss of dues, reduction in union officers' compensation, and distribution of relief funds that would constitute organized labor's cost in a strike. Under such a policy, the government would retain its detached position at the same time that it acted in behalf of the total constellation of public interests. A seizure that kept production or distribution of goods or services going at the same time that it imposed on the disputing parties the costs that each would have incurred if the strike had continued would spur management and labor to hasten negotiations to compose their differences without interfering with the essentials of the collective bargaining process or abrogating the right to strike. A public philosophy to guide state action in the matter of industrial conflicts would permit a temporary and self-limiting federal seizure that, while stopping the kind of strike that threatens crucial public interests, would "allow for the play of the vital conditions of the strike." [403]

The state has an active but not unrestricted role to play according to the public philosophy appropriate to modern mass society. Its foremost duty is to protect and preserve the freedom of speech that is every person's civil liberty and to insure that in the incessant struggles for class advancement, status enhancement, and power to achieve those and related objectives, each individual has the opportunity to compete. The right to think, speak, read, and write as one pleases is not to be restricted to pleasant subject matters, deliberative discourse, or passionless advocacy; rather in welcoming any communicative intrusion into the public arena, the citizenry look forward to the innovative possibilities that are made manifest by such and willingly risk dealing with the dangerous nostrums and prejudiced opinions that a truly free society ought not stifle. The right to participate in every institution that affects or is affected by the general political economy entails not the imposition of equality of outcome, as the opponents of affirmative action policies insist, but rather the assurance that there will be competitors of every hue and every social background in each institutional setting. When medical schools assure admission to members of hitherto disadvantaged minority groups, when public schools, police, and fire departments seek out black, Hispanic, Amerind, and Asian recruits and assure them that the city's tardiness in implementing relief from the ignominious legacy that slavery had imposed on them will not be compounded by a color-and-culture-blind seniority and layoff system, and when industries and unions implement training programs for those members of the labor force who have been socially stigmatized and occupationally restricted because earlier industrial regimes had done nothing to obviate the vestiges of America's erstwhile system of involuntary servitude, they do not bring the general structure of competition in American society to an end, but modify it so as to insure that no one will be excluded from its trials and tribulations solely because of his color and all that that color entails. And, when the government carefully circumscribes its own interventions, insuring that society's general interest in liberty, equality, and the basic resources of life is not subverted by strikes, marches, demonstrations, and other popular or un-popular uprisings, it does so in accordance with a recognition that the public interest of a democratic mass society requires nei-ther nostalgia for a more traditional order nor imperative solu-tions to its conflicts. The momentum of life in modern society vacillates between the orderly and the unstable. The test of its public philosophy is how much it tolerates the ambiguity and allows for the freedom to innovate within the precarious bounda-ries of the *Lebenswelt*.

NOTES

The Problem of a Public Philosophy: A Sociological Perspective

1. William Graham Sumner, *Folkways: A Study of the Sociological Importance of Usages, Manners, Customs, Mores, and Morals,* (Boston: Ginn and Co., 1940. Originally published 1906), p. 78.

2. *Ibid.,* p. 98.

3. William Graham Sumner, "Foreword" to James Elbert Cutler, *Lynch-Law: An Investigation Into the History of Lynching in the United States,* (Montclair, N.J.: Patterson Smith, 1969. Originally published 1905), p. v.

4. Sumner, *Folkways . . . ,* p. 110–111.

5. William Graham Sumner, "The Conquest of the United States by Spain," *Yale Law Journal,* VIII (1899), pp. 168–193. Reprinted in *Essays of William Graham Sumner,* ed. by Albert G. Keller and Maurice R. Davie, (Hamden, Ct.: Archon Books, 1969), II, pp. 266–303.

6. William Graham Sumner, "The Bequests of the Nineteenth Century to the Twentieth," *The Yale Review,* XXII (1933), pp. 732–754. Reprinted in *Essays . . . , op. cit.,* I, pp. 208–235.

7. Sumner, *Folkways . . . , op. cit.,* p. 98.

8. William Graham Sumner, "The Influence of Commercial Crises on Opinions About Economic Doctrines," an address before the Free Trade Club, New York City, May 15, 1879. Reprinted in *Essays . . . , op. cit.,* II, pp. 44–66.

9. William Graham Sumner, "Discipline," undated. Reprinted in *Essays . . . , op. cit.,* I, pp. 24–25.

10. Howard Brotz, "Social Stratification and the Political Order," *The American Journal of Sociology,* LXIV (May, 1959), pp. 571–578; reprinted in Arnold Rose, ed., *Human Behavior and Social Processes: An Interactionist Approach,* (Boston: Houghton Mifflin Co., 1962), pp. 307–320. Quotation from p. 308.

11. Gunnar Myrdal, with the assistance of Richard Sterner and Arnold Rose, *An American Dilemma: The Negro Problem and Modern Democracy,* (New York: Harper and Brothers, 1944). For a critical assessment see Stanford M. Lyman, *The Black American in Sociological Thought: A Failure of Perspective,* (New York: G.P. Putnam's Sons, 1972), pp. 99–120.

12. Talcott Parsons, "Full Citizenship for the Negro American? A Sociological Problem," in Talcott Parsons and Kenneth B. Clark, eds., *The Negro American,* (Boston: Houghton Mifflin, 1966), pp. 709–754. For a critical assessment see Stanford M. Lyman, *The Black American in Sociological Thought: A Failure of Perspective, op. cit.,* pp. 145–170.

13. Seymour Martin Lipset, *The First New Nation: The United States in Historical and Comparative Perspective,* (New York: W.W. Norton, 1979), pp. 330–333. For a critical assessment see Stanford M. Lyman, "Legitimacy and Consensus in Lipset's America: From Washington to Watergate," *Social Research,* XLII (Winter, 1975), pp. 729–759.

14. Glenn Tinder, *Community: Reflections on a Tragic Ideal,* (Baton Rouge: Louisiana State University Press, 1980), p. 99.

15. See, e.g., Talcott Parsons, *The Social System,* (Glencoe: The Free Press, 1951); Paul F. Lazarsfeld, William H. Sewell, and Harold L. Wilensky, "Introduction" to their edition of *The Uses of Sociology,* (New York: Basic Books, Inc., 1967), pp. ix–xxxiii.

16. William Graham Sumner, "Democracy and Modern Problems," *The Independent,* March 28, 1889. Reprinted in *Essays . . . , op. cit.,* II, p. 234.

17. Sumner, "The Bequests . . . ," *Essays . . . , op. cit.,* I, p. 235.

18. These matters are covered extensively in Arthur J. Vidich and Stanford M. Lyman, *American Sociology: Worldly Rejections of Religion and Their Directions,* (New Haven: Yale University Press, 1985), pp. 53–194.

19. *Ibid.,* p. 16–19.

20. Luther Lee Bernard, "Henry Hughes, First American Sociologist," *Social Forces,* XV (December, 1936), pp. 154–174.

21. *The Positive Philosophy of Auguste Comte Freely Translated and Condensed by Harriet Martineau,* 2nd Edn. (London: Trubner and Co., Ludgate Hill, 1875), II, p. 120.

22. *Ibid.,* II, pp. 311–326.

23. Herbert Croly, *The Promise of American Life,* (New York: E.P. Dutton, 1963. Originally published 1909.), p. 369.

24. *Ibid.,* p. 368.

25. *Ibid.,* pp. 369–370.

26. *Ibid.,* pp. 389–390.

27. *Ibid.*, p. 431.

28. *Ibid.*, p. 436.

29. *Ibid.*, p. 441.

30. *Ibid.*, p. 440.

31. *Ibid.*, p. 441.

32. Henry Hughes, *A Treatise on Sociology, Theoretical and Practical,* (Philadelphia: Lippincott and Grambo, 1854; reprinted, New York: Negro Universities Press, 1968). See also *Selected Writings of Henry Hughes: Antebellum Southerner, Slavocrat, Sociologist,* ed. by Stanford M. Lyman, (Jackson: University Press of Mississippi, 1985).

33. Croly, *op cit.,* p. 396.

34. *Ibid.*, p. 81.

35. Joseph Le Conte, *The Race Problem in the South,* (New York: D. Appleton, 1892. Reprint, Miami: Mnemosyne, 1969).

36. Croly, *The Promise of American Life, op.cit.,* p. 396.

37. *Ibid.*, p. 409.

38. *Ibid.*, p. 410.

39. *Ibid.*, p. 412.

40. *Ibid.*, p. 414.

41. *Ibid.*, p. 417.

42. *Ibid.*, p. 426.

43. *Ibid.*, p. 424.

44. *Ibid.*, p. 428.

45. *Ibid.*, p. 429.

46. *Ibid.*, pp. 429–430.

47. Henry Hughes, *A Treatise on Sociology . . . op.cit.,* pp. 84–118, 161–206, 210–260, 286–292.

48. Croly, *The Promise of American Life, op.cit.,* pp. 430–431.

49. *Ibid.*, p. 454.

50. Lawrence M. Mead, *Beyond Entitlement: The Social Obligations of Citizenship,* (New York: The Free Press, 1986).

51. Lawrence M. Mead, *op.cit.,* p. 17.

52. *Ibid.*, p. 215. Emphasis in original.

53. *Ibid.*, p. 81.

54. *Ibid.*, p. 87.

55. *Ibid.*, p. 88.

56. See Stanford M. Lyman, "Henry Hughes and the Southern Foundations of American Sociology," in *Selected Writings of Henry Hughes . . . ,* p. 24.

57. Lawrence M. Mead, *op.cit.,* p. 88.

58. *Public Philosopher: Selected Letters of Walter Lippmann*, ed. by John Morton Blum (New York: Ticknor and Fields, 1985), p. 580.

59. Walter Lippmann, *Drift and Mastery: An Attempt to Diagnose the Current Unrest*, (New York: Mitchell Kennerley, 1914), pp. xvii–xviii.

60. Walter Lippmann, *Essays in the Public Philosophy*, (Boston: Little, Brown and Co., 1955), p. 147.

61. "The social scientist will acquire his dignity and his strength when he has worked out his method. He will do that by turning into opportunity the need among directing men of the Great Society for instruments of analysis by which an invisible and most stupendously difficult environment can be made intelligible." Walter Lippmann, *Public Opinion*, (New York: The Free Press, 1965. Originally pub. 1922), pp. 235–236.

62. " . . . [I]t is not necessary to choose between social control administered by the aggrandized state and a self-assertive individualism subject to no social control. That supposedly exclusive choice . . . overlooks entirely one of the oldest, best established, and most successful methods of social control in human experience. It is social control . . . by a common law which defines the reciprocal rights and duties of persons and invites them to enforce the law by proving their case in a court of law." Walter Lippmann, *An Inquiry into the Principles of the Good Society*, (Boston: Little, Brown and Co., 1937), pp. 265–266.

63. "The real law in the modern state is the multitude of little decisions made daily by millions of men. . . . The crucial difference between modern politics and that to which mankind has been accustomed is that the power to act and to compel obedience is almost never sufficiently centralized nowadays to be exercised by one will. The power is distributed and qualified so that power is exerted not by command but by interaction.

"The prime business of government, therefore, is not to direct the affairs of the community, but to harmonize the direction which the community gives to its affairs." Walter Lippmann, *A Preface to Morals*, (New York: The Macmillan Co., 1929), p. 275.

64. Walter Lippmann, "Notes for a Biography," *New Republic* LXIII (July 16, 1930), p. 250. Quoted in David W. Levy, *Herbert Croly of the New Republic: The Life and Thought of an American Progressive*. (Princeton: Princeton University Press, 1985), p. 135.

65. Lippmann, *Drift and Mastery, op.cit.*, p. 17.

66. See. W. I. Thomas, "Introductory," *Source Book for Social Ori-*

gins, (Boston: Richard G. Badger, 1909), pp. 3–28; and Frederick J. Teggart, *Theory of History,* (New Haven: Yale University Press, 1925), pp. 82–86, 107–149, 180–196.

67. Lippmann, *Public Opinion, op.cit.,* p. 233.

68. *Ibid.,* p. 234.

69. *Ibid.,* p. 236.

70. See Lester F. Ward, *Outlines of Sociology,* (New York: The Macmillan Co., 1913), pp. 262–294. For the Ogburn-Merriam proposal, see "A Review of Findings By The President's Research Committee on Social Trends," *Recent Social Trends in the United States: Report of the President's Research Committee on Social Trends,* (New York: McGraw-Hill Book Co., 1933), pp. lxx–lxxv. For a discussion of the implications of such proposals for the development of sociology in America, see Vidich and Lyman, *American Sociology . . . , op.cit.,* pp. 20–35, 137–150.

71. Lippmann, *An Inquiry into the Principles of the Good Society, op. cit.,* pp. 30–31.

72. *Ibid.,* p. 32.

73. *Ibid.,* p. 33.

74. Quoted in Edward Hallett Carr, *The Twenty Years' Crisis, 1919–1939: An Introduction to the Study of International Relations,* (New York: Harper Torchbooks, 1964. Orig. pub. 1939), p. 24.

75. Lippmann, *Public Opinion, op.cit.,* p. 40.

76. *Ibid.,* p. 58.

77. *Ibid.,* pp. 54–55.

78. *Ibid.,* p. 44.

79. *Ibid.,* p. 55.

80. *Ibid.,* p. 61.

81. Munsterberg (1863–1916) had developed an early version of the lie detector, contributed to the rise of personnel testing, written achievement tests, and proposed mass studies of industrial workers. A lasting contribution was his posthumously published study of films, *The Film-A Psychological Study: The Silent Photoplay in 1916,* (New York: Dover, 1970. Originally published in 1916.) For the impact of his work on sociology, see Vidich and Lyman, *American Sociology, op.cit.,* pp. 87–104.

82. Lippmann to John Collier, March 22, 1915. *Public Philosopher: Selected Letters of Walter Lippmann, op.cit.,* p. 26. For the social significance of Griffith's film see Bosley Crowther, "The Birth of *Birth of a Nation,*" in *Black Films and Film-Makers: A Comprehensive Anthology*

From Stereotype to Superhero, ed. by Lindsay Patterson, (New York: Dodd, Mead & Co., 1975), pp. 75–83; Richard A. Maynard, *The Black Man on Film: Racial Stereotyping,* (Rochelle Park, N.J.: Hayden Book Co., 1974), pp. 25–40; Thomas Cripps, *Slow Fade to Black: The Negro in American Film, 1900–1942,* (New York: Oxford University Press, 1977), pp. 41–69; William K. Everson, *American Silent Film,* (New York: Oxford University Press, 1977), pp. 72–89; Richard Schickel, *D. W. Griffith: An American Life,* (New York: Simon and Schuster-A Touchstone Book, 1984), pp. 212–302.

83. Lippmann, *Public Opinion, op.cit.,* p. 61.

84. *Ibid.,* p. 106.

85. *Ibid.,* p. 216.

86. Lippmann to Oliver Wendell Holmes, Jr., *Public Philosopher: Selected Letters of Walter Lippmann, op.cit.,* pp. 132–133.

87. Lippmann, *Public Opinion, op.cit.,* p. 203. Lippmann seems to have been unaware of Max Weber's observations on the matter at the Frankfurt Congress of sociologists in 1910. See Max Weber, "Towards a Sociology of the Press," tr. by Hanno Hardt, *Journal of Communication,* XXVI (Summer, 1976), reprinted in Hanno Hardt, *Social Theories of the Press: Early German and American Perspectives,* (Beverly Hills: Sage Publications, 1979), pp. 174–185.

88. *Ibid.,* p. 202.

89. Lippmann, *Public Opinion, op.cit.,* p. 219.

90. *Ibid.,* pp. 229–230.

91. *Ibid.,* p. 230.

92. Sumner, *Folkways . . . , op.cit.,* pp. 47–48.

93. Sumner, "The Bequests of the Nineteenth Century to the Twentieth," in *Essays . . . , op.cit.,* pp. 233–234.

94. Sumner, *Folkways . . . , op.cit.,* pp. 50–51.

95. Lippmann, *Public Opinion,* p. 230.

96. *Public Philosopher: Selected Letters of Walter Lippmann, op.cit.,* p. 580.

97. Lippmann, *Essays in the Public Philosophy, op.cit.,* p. 42.

98. *Ibid.,* p. 43.

99. Quoted from a letter from Lippmann to Helen Armstrong in John Morton Blum, "Introduction," *Public Philosopher: Selected Letters of Walter Lippmann, op.cit.,* p. xiii.

100. Lippmann to Lawrence J. Henderson, October 27, 1922 in *Ibid.,* p. 149. The letter, addressed to one of the founders of Harvard's program in industrial sociology and a member of the Harvard committee

on the admission of Jews, may not have been sent. See Ronald Steel, *Walter Lippmann and the American Century,* (Boston: Little, Brown and Co., 1980), p. 613 n. 13.

101. Steel, *op.cit.,* pp. 186–196.

102. *Ibid.,* pp. 187–194.

103. See two essays by Randolph Bourne, "Trans-National America" and "The Jew and Trans-National America," in his *War and the Intellectuals: Collected Essays, 1915–1919,* ed. by Carl Resek (New York: Harper Torchbooks, 1964), pp. 107–123, 124–133.

104. Horace Kallen, *Culture and Democracy in the United States: Studies in the Group Psychology of the American Peoples,* (New York: Boni and Liveright, 1924; Reprint, New York: Arno Press, 1970).

105. Ellsworth Faris, "If I Were a Jew", in his *The Nature of Human Nature and Other Essays in Social Psychology,* (New York: McGraw-Hill Company, 1937; Reprint, Dubuque, Ia.: Brown Reprints, 1971), pp. 350–353.

106. Walter Lippmann, *U.S. War Aims,* (Boston: Little, Brown and Co., 1944), pp. 208–210.

107. Steel, *op.cit.,* pp. 453–454.

108. The following is from Walter Lippmann, "Introductory Note," in Carl Sandburg, *The Chicago Race Riots, July, 1919,* (New York: Harcourt, Brace and Howe, 1919; reprint, Harcourt, Brace, and World, 1969), pp. xix–xxi.

109. Walter Lippmann in the *New York Herald Tribune,* December 18, 1941. Quoted in Gordan Prange, *Pearl Harbor: The Verdict of History,* (New York: McGraw Hill, 1986), pp. 4–5.

110. Lippmann in *The Washington Post,* February 12, 1942. Quoted in Peter Irons, *Justice at War: The Story of the Japanese American Internment Cases,* (New York: Oxford University Press, 1983), p. 60.

111. Lippmann to Francis Biddle, February 20, 1942. *Public Philosopher: Selected Letters of Walter Lippmann, op,cit.,* p. 415.

112. Steel, *op.cit.,* p. 394.

113. See Jacobus ten Broek, Edward N. Barnhart and Floyd Matson, *Prejudice, War and the Constitution,* Japanese Evacuation and Resettlement Studies, vol. III, (Berkeley University of California Press, 1954). Among those removed from the West Coast at this time was Tamotsu Shibutani, later to be Herbert Blumer's student at the University of Chicago. Shibutani utilized the experience to inform his study of rumor in times of crisis, *Improvised News: A Sociological Study of Rumor,* (Indianapolis: The Bobbs-Merrill Co., 1966) and his subsequent term of

service in the United States armed forces to document *The Derelicts of Company K: A Sociological Study of Demoralization*, (Berkeley: University of California Press, 1978).

114. *Public Philosopher: Selected Letters of Walter Lippmann*, *op.cit.*, p. 617.

115. Lippmann, *Essays in the Public Philosophy*, *op.cit.*, p. 123, 124.

116. *Ibid.*, p. 140.

117. Charles de Montesquieu, *The Spirit of the Laws*, Bk. XI, 3. Quoted in Lippmann, *Essays in the Public Philosophy*, *op.cit.*, p. 144.

118. William James, *A Pluralistic Universe*. In *Essays in Radical Empiricism and A Pluralistic Universe*. Quoted in Lippmann, *Essays in the Public Philosophy*, *op.cit.*, p. 144.

119. Lippmann, *Essays in the Public Philosophy*, *op.cit.*, p. 146.

120. *Ibid.*, p. 179.

121. *Ibid.*, p. 181.

122. *loc.cit.*

123. Herbert Blumer, "Social Attitudes and Non–Symbolic Interaction," *Journal of Educational Sociology*, IX (May, 1936), p. 517.

124. Lippmann, *Essays in the Public Philosophy*, *op.cit.*, p. 133.

125. *Ibid.*, p. 129.

126. *Ibid.*, p. 128.

127. *Ibid.*, p. 129.

128. Edward de Grazia and Roger R. Newman, *Banned Films: Movies, Censors, and the First Amendment*, (New York: R.R. Bowker Co., 1982), pp. 9, 5.

129. Hugo Munsterberg, *The Film-A Psychological Study: The Silent Photoplay in 1916*, *op.cit.*

130. See e.g., Helen MacGill Hughes, *News and the Human Interest Story*, (Chicago: University of Chicago Press, 1940).

131. Benjamin B. Hampton, *History of the American Film Industry From Its Beginnings to 1931*, (New York: Dover Publications, 1970. Originally published in 1931), pp. 297–299.

132. Edward Alsworth Ross, "What the Films are Doing to Young America," *World Drift* (New York: Century, 1928), p. 179.

133. Garth Jowett, *Film: The Democratic Art*, (Boston: Little, Brown & Co., 1976), pp. 220, 231, n. 48.

134. Herbert Blumer, *Movies and Conduct*, (New York: Macmillan, 1933), Herbert Blumer and Philip M. Hauser, *Movies, Delinquency, and Crime*, (New York: Macmillan, 1933).

135. I. C. Jarvie, *Movies and Society,* (New York: Basic Books, 1970), pp. 325–326.

136. For an example of present-day misunderstanding of Blumer's studies, see Robert H. Lauer and Warren H. Handel, *Social Psychology: The Theory and Application of Symbolic Interaction,* (Boston: Houghton Mifflin Co., 1977), pp. 323–324. At the time of their publication, Blumer's findings were distorted to support the censorious interests of the Payne Fund in a journalistic summary, *Our Movies Made Children* by Henry James Forman (New York: Macmillan, 1933). After Forman's book was given the official imprimatur of the Motion Picture Research Council and endorsed by the research project's executive director, Dr. W. W. Charters, a leading social psychologist, Kimball Young, complained about Forman's selective attention to the more sensational examples and protested that his book had done social psychology, education, and sociology a disservice. Moreover, he predicted that Forman's version of Blumer's studies would awaken a "wave of sentiment against the movies." Kimball Young, "Review of the Payne Fund Studies," *American Journal of Sociology* XL (September, 1935), p. 255. See also Jowett, *op.cit.,* pp. 220–225.

137. Herbert Blumer, "Collective Behavior," in Alfred M. Lee, ed., *New Outline of the Principles of Sociology,* (New York: Barnes and Noble, 1951), pp. 186–187.

138. Herbert Blumer and Philip M. Hauser, *Movies, Delinquency, and Crime, op.cit.,* p. 46.

139. Herbert Blumer, "Moulding of Mass Behavior Through the Motion Picture," *Publications of the American Sociological Society,* XXIX (August, 1935), pp. 119, 124.

140. Blumer, *Movies and Conduct, op.cit.,* p. 197.

141. *Ibid.,* pp. 198, 199.

142. W. I. Thomas, "Introductory," *Source Book for Social Origins,* pp. 3–26.

143. Alfred Schutz, "Some Structures of the Life-World," in I. Schutz, ed., *Alfred Schutz—Collected Papers III: Studies in Phenomenological Philosophy.* (The Hague: Martinus Nijhoff, 1966), pp. 116–132.

144. Frederick Teggart, *Theory and Processes of History,* (Berkeley: University of California Press, 1941), pp. 149–150, 196–197, 242–296, 307–312.

145. Blumer, *Movies and Conduct, op.cit.,* p. 194.

146. Blumer, "Moulding of Mass Behavior . . . ," *op.cit.,* p. 126.

147. *loc.cit.*

148. *loc.cit.*

149. *loc.cit.*

150. Blumer, "Moulding of Mass Behavior . . . ," *op.cit.*, pp. 126–127.

151. *Ibid.*, p. 126.

152. *Ibid.*, p. 127. Emphasis in original.

153. Lippmann, *Public Opinion, op.cit.*, pp. 211–213.

154. Lippmann, *Essays in the Public Philosophy, op.cit.*, p. 20.

155. *Ibid.*, p. 42.

156. Herbert Blumer, "Collective Behavior," *op.cit.*, p. 191.

157. *Ibid.*, p. 192.

158. *Ibid.*, p. 190.

159. *Ibid.*, p. 192.

160. *Ibid.*, p. 191.

161. *Ibid.*, p. 192.

162. *Ibid.*, p. 193.

163. *loc.cit.*

164. Herbert Blumer, "Public Opinion and Public Opinion Polling," *American Sociological Review*, XIII (October, 1948), pp. 542–549.

165. Herbert Blumer, "Rejoinder to Professors Woodward and Newcomb," *American Sociological Review*, XIII (October, 1948), p. 554.

166. Herbert Blumer, "Suggestions for the Study of Mass-Media Effects," in *American Voting Behavior*, ed. by E. Burdick and A. J. Brodbeck, (Glencoe, Ill.: The Free Press, 1959), pp. 202, 205.

167. Blumer, "Collective Behavior," *op.cit.*, p. 192.

168. *Ibid.*, p. 193.

169. *loc.cit.*

170. Herbert Blumer, "Morale," in William Fielding Ogburn, ed., *American Society in Wartime*. (Chicago: University of Chicago Press, 1943), p. 207.

171. The following draws on information about Parsons's activities before and during World War II in William Buxton, *Talcott Parsons and the Capitalist Nation-State*, (Toronto: University of Toronto Press, 1985), pp. 76–116. Unless cited otherwise, Parsons's statements are quoted from his unpublished "Memorandum for Council for Democracy," written in 1940 and partially reproduced in Buxton's book.

172. Letter to Edith Nourse Rogers, January 23, 1941. Quoted in Buxton, *op.cit.*, p. 102.

173. Parsons to Edward Hartshorne, August 29, 1941. Quoted in Buxton, *op.cit.*, p. 104.

174. Talcott Parsons, "Propaganda and Social Control," *Psychiatry* V, Fourth Quarter (1942), pp. 551–572. Reprinted in *Idem, Essays in Sociological Theory,* revised edition, (New York: The Free Press, 1964), p. 166.

175. *Ibid.,* p. 159.

176. Lippmann, *Public Opinion, op.cit.,* p. 153.

177. Lippmann, *Essays in the Public Philosophy, op.cit.,* p. 23.

178. *Ibid.,* p. 23.

179. *loc.cit.*

180. *Ibid.,* p. 24.

181. *Ibid.,* p. 25.

182. Blumer, "Collective Behavior," *op.cit.,* p. 209.

183. Blumer, "Morale," *op.cit.,* p. 211.

184. *Ibid.,* p. 214.

185. *Ibid.,* p. 218.

186. *Ibid.,* p. 219.

187. *Ibid.,* p. 220.

188. *Ibid.,* p. 229.

189. *Ibid.,* p. 223.

190. *loc.cit.*

191. *loc.cit.*

192. *Ibid.,* p. 223.

193. *Ibid.,* pp. 222–223.

194. *Ibid.,* p. 223.

195. *loc.cit.*

196. *loc.cit.*

197. *Ibid.,*p. 226

198. *Ibid.,* p. 228.

199. *loc.cit.*

200. *Ibid.,* pp. 228–229.

201. *Ibid.,* p. 229.

202. *Ibid.,* p. 230.

203. Talcott Parsons, "Full Citizenship for the Negro American? A Sociological Problem," *op. cit.,* pp. 709–754.

204. Robert E. Park, "Our Racial Frontier on the Pacific," *Survey Graphic* LVI (May 1, 1926), pp. 192–196. For critiques of this formulation see Seymour Martin Lipset, "Changing Social Status and Preju-

dice: The Race Theories of a Pioneering American Sociologist," *Commentary* IX (May, 1950), pp. 475–479; and two works by Stanford M. Lyman: "The Race Relations Cycle of Robert E. Park" *Pacific Sociological Review*, XI (Spring, 1968), pp. 16–22; *The Black American in Sociological Thought: A Failure of Perspective, op.cit.*, pp. 22–70.

205. T. W. Adorno, Else Frenkel-Brunswick, Daniel J. Levinson, and R. Nevitt Sanford, *The Authoritarian Personality*, (New York: Harper and Row, 1950). See also the chapter on "Prejudice" in *Aspects of Sociology* by the Frankfurt Institute for Social Research, (Boston: Beacon Press, 1972), pp. 169–181.

206. Herbert Blumer, "Sociological Implications of the Thought of George Herbert Mead," *American Journal of Sociology*, LXXI (March, 1966), p. 536.

207. Herbert Blumer, "Symbolic Interaction and the Idea of Social System" *Revue Internationale de Sociologie*, XI: 1–2 (1975), p. 5.

208. *Ibid.*, p. 9.

209. Herbert Blumer, "Group Tension and Interest Organization," *Proceedings of the Second Annual Meeting of the Industrial Relations Research Association*, (1949), p. 152.

210. Blumer, "Symbolic Interaction and the Idea of Social System," *op.cit.*, p. 7.

211. Herbert Blumer and Troy Duster, "Theories of Race and Social Action," in *Sociological Theories: Race and Colonialism*, (Paris: United Nations Educational, Scientific and Cultural Organization, 1980), p. 232.

212. Herbert Blumer, "Research on Racial Relations: The United States of America," *International Social Science Bulletin*, X:3 (1958), p. 405.

213. Blumer and Duster, *op.cit.*, p. 233.

214. Blumer, "Research on Racial Relations . . .", p. 405.

215. *Ibid.*, p. 432.

216. *Ibid.*, p. 435.

217. Blumer and Duster, *op.cit.*, p. 211–221.

218. *Ibid.*, p. 228.

219. *Ibid.*, p. 229. Emphasis in original.

220. *Ibid.*, p. 230.

221. *Ibid.*, p. 233.

222. *loc.cit.*

223. Here we have drawn upon Herbert Blumer, "Social Structure and Power Conflict," in Arthur Kornhauser, Robert Dubin, and Arthur

M. Ross, eds., *Industrial Conflict,* (New York: McGraw Hill, 1954), pp. 232–239.

224. See Lewis M. Killian, "Herbert Blumer's Contributions to Race Relations," in Tamotsu Shibutani, ed., *Human Nature and Collective Behavior: Papers in Honor of Herbert Blumer,* (Englewood Cliffs: Prentice-Hall, 1970), p. 189.

225. Herbert Blumer, "Social Problems as Collective Behavior," *Social Problems,* XVIII (Winter, 1971), p. 299.

226. Blumer and Duster, *op.cit.,* p. 234.

227. Blumer, "Social Problems . . . ," *op.cit.,* p. 303.

228. *loc.cit.*

229. Blumer and Duster, *op.cit.,* p. 234.

230. Blumer, "Social Problems . . . ," *op.cit.,* pp. 303–304.

231. *Ibid.,* p. 304.

232. Cf. Herbert Blumer, "The Nature of Race Prejudice," *Social Processes in Hawaii,* V (1939), p. 11 with Blumer, "Reflections on Theory of Race Relations," in Andrew W. Lind, *Race Relations in World Perspectives,* (Honolulu: University of Hawaii Press, 1955), p. 18.

233. Blumer, "Reflections on Theory of Race Relations," *op.cit.,* pp. 14, 17.

234. *loc.cit.*

235. *Ibid.,* p. 18.

236. Herbert Blumer, "Industrialisation and Race Relations," in Guy Hunter, ed., *Industrialisation and Race Relations,* (London: Oxford University Press, 1965), pp. 220–253.

237. Herbert Blumer, "Social Science and the Desegregation Process," *Annals of the American Academy of Political and Social Science,* CCCIV (March, 1956), p. 141.

238. *loc.cit.*

239. *Ibid.,* p. 142.

240. *loc.cit.*

241. *loc.cit.*

242. *Ibid.,* pp. 142–143. Emphasis on original.

243. *Ibid.,* p. 143.

244. Herbert Blumer, "The Future of the Color Line," in John McKinney and Edgar T. Thompson, eds., *The South in Continuity and Change,* (Durham: Duke University Press, 1965), pp. 322–336.

245. Blumer, "Social Problems . . . ," *op.cit.,* pp. 304–305.

246. See Nathan Glazer, *Affirmative Discrimination: Ethnic Inequality*

and Public Policy, (New York: Basic Books, 1975); and *Ethnic Dilemmas, 1964–1982,* (Cambridge: Harvard University Press, 1983), pp. 159–232.

247. See Thomas Sowell, *Civil Rights: Rhetoric or Reality,* (New York: William Morrow and Co., 1984), pp. 13–90, 109–140.

248. Blumer, "The Future of the Color Line," *op.cit.,* p. 323.

249. *Ibid.,* p. 322.

250. Ethnographic and sociological investigations employing the color line concept have noted its operation in the North as well as the South. See Ray Stannard Baker, *Following the Color Line: American Negro Citizenship in the Progressive Era,* (New York: Harper Torchbooks, 1964. Originally published in 1908), pp. 26–150; St. Clair Drake and Horace R. Cayton, *Black Metropolis: A Study of Negro Life in a Northern City,* (New York: Harper Torchbooks 1962. Originally published in 1945), I, pp. 99–286; August Meier and Elliott Rudwick, *Along the Color Line: Explorations in the Black Experience,* (Urbana: University of Illinois Press, 1976).

251. Blumer, "The Future of the Color Line," *op.cit.,* p. 328.

252. *loc.cit.*

253. *loc.cit.*

254. *loc.cit.*

255. *loc.cit.* Emphasis in original.

256. *Ibid.,* p. 330.

257. *loc.cit.*

258. *Ibid.,* p. 331.

259. *Ibid.,* pp. 331–332.

260. *Ibid.,* p. 332.

261. *Ibid.,* p. 334.

262. *Ibid.,* p. 332.

263. *loc.cit.*

264. *loc.cit.*

265. *Ibid.,* p. 334.

266. *Ibid.,* pp. 332–333.

267. *Ibid.,* p. 334.

268. *loc.cit.*

269. Herbert Blumer, "Race Prejudice as a Sense of Group Position," *Pacific Sociological Review,* I (Spring, 1958), pp. 3–7.

270. Blumer, "The Nature of Race Prejudice," *op.cit.,* pp. 15–18.

271. See, e.g., David Brion Davis, "Slavery and the American Mind," in Harry P. Owens, ed., *Perspectives and Irony in American Slavery,* (Jackson: University Press of Mississippi, 1976), pp. 51–69.

272. Blumer, "Reflections on Theory of Race Relations," *op.cit.*, p. 12.

273. Blumer, "Race Prejudice as a Sense of Group Position," *op.cit.*, pp. 3–4.

274. Blumer, "The Nature of Race Prejudice," *op.cit.*, p. 11.

275. Blumer, "The Future of the Color Line," *op.cit.*, pp. 322–336.

276. Blumer, "Industrialisation and Race Relations," *op.cit.*, pp. 231–246.

277. Blumer, "The Nature of Race Prejudice," *op.cit.*, pp. 19–20; "Race Prejudice as a Sense of Group Position," *op.cit.*, pp. 6–7.

278. Winthrop D. Jordan, *White Over Black: American Attitudes Toward the Negro, 1550–1812*, (Chapel Hill: University of North Carolina Press, 1968), p. 374.

279. Jacobus ten Broek, *The Antislavery Origins of the Fourteenth Amendment*, (Berkeley: University of California Press, 1951), p. 148.

280. A rich, varied and polarized literature has arisen on the matter. In addition to the works of Nathan Glazer and Thomas Sowell discussed *infra*, among works that might be consulted to comprehend the character, framework and issues involved see: John E. Fleming, Gerald R. Gill, David H. Swinton, *The Case for Affirmative Action for Blacks in Higher Education*, (Washington, D.C.: Howard University Press, 1978); Gerald R. Gill, *The Meanness Mania: The Changed Mood*, (Washington, D.C.: Howard University Press, 1980; Marshall Cohen, Thomas Nagel, and Thomas Scanlon, eds., *Equality and Preferential Treatment: A Philosophy and Public Affairs Reader*, (Princeton: Princeton University Press, 1977); three works by Ronald Dworkin, *Taking Rights Seriously*, (Cambridge: Harvard University Press, 1978), pp. 150–205, 223–239; *A Matter of Principle*, (Cambridge: Harvard University Press, 1985), pp. 205–213, 293–334; *Law's Empire*, (Cambridge: The Belknap Press of Harvard University Press, 1986), pp. 381–399; Alan H. Goldman, *Justice and Reverse Discrimination*, (Princeton: Princeton University Press, 1979); Barry R. Gross, ed., *Reverse Discrimination*, (Buffalo: Prometheus Books, 1977); Robert K. Fullinwider, *The Reverse Discrimination Controversy: A Moral and Legal Analysis*, (Totowa: Rowman and Littlefield, 1980); John C. Livingston, *Fair Game? Inequality and Affirmative Action*, (San Francisco: W.H. Freeman and Co. 1979). British philosophers and social scientists have also contributed studies: Brian Wilson, ed., *Education, Equality and Society*, (New York: Harper and Row, 1975); and two works by Antony Flew: *Sociology, Equality and Education: Philosophical Essays in Defense of a Variety of Differences*, (New York: Harper and Row,

1976); and *The Politics of Procrustes: Contradictions of Enforced Equality,* (Buffalo: Prometheus Books, 1981). A definitive defense of affirmative action with a sustained reply to its opponents will be found in Herbert Hill, "Race, Ethnicity and Organized Labor: The Opposition to Affirmative Action," *New Politics,* n.s., I:2 (Winter, 1987), pp. 31–82.

The dispute over the unconstitutional affirmative action procedure established by the medical school of the University of California at Davis has evoked a number of analyses and critiques: Allan P. Sindler, *Bakke, DeFunis, and Minority Admissions: The Quest for Equal Opportunity,* (New York: Longman, 1978); United States Commission on Civil Rights, *Toward an Understanding of Bakke,* Clearinghouse Publication 58 (Washington, D.C.: U.S. Government Printing Office, May, 1979); Joel Dreyfuss and Charles Laurence III, *The Bakke Case: The Politics of Equality,* (New York: Harcourt, Brace, Jovanovich, 1979); J. Harvie Wilkinson III, *From Brown to Bakke: The Supreme Court and School Integration, 1954–1978,* (New York: Oxford University Press, 1979); Terry Eastland and William J. Bennett, *Counting By Race: Equality from the Founding Fathers to Bakke and Weber,* (New York: Basic Books, 1979); Timothy J. O'Neill, *Bakke and the Politics of Equality: Friends and Foes in the Classroom of Litigation,* (Middletown, Ct.: Wesleyan University Press, 1985).

281. Blumer and Duster, *op.cit.,* p. 233.

282. *New Negro Alliance vs. Grocery Company,* 303 U.S. 552 (1938). Reprinted in Joseph Tussman, ed., *The Supreme Court on Racial Discrimination,* (New York: Oxford University Press, 1963), pp. 233–239.

283. *Hughes vs. Superior Court of California,* 339 U.S. 460 (1950) in Tussman, *op.cit.,* pp. 262–267.

284. *Ibid.,* p. 263.

285. *Ibid.,* p. 264.

286. *loc.cit.*

287. *loc.cit.*

288. John Marshall Harlan, "Dissent," in *Civil Rights Cases* 109 U.S. 3 (1883). Reprinted in Stanley I. Kutler, *The Supreme Court and the Constitution: Readings in American Constitutional History,* 3d edn. (New York: W. W. Norton, 1984), pp. 204–205.

289. Glazer, *Ethnic Dilemmas . . . , op.cit.,* pp. 176–177.

290. *Ibid.,* pp. 180–181.

291. *Ibid.,* p. 181.

292. *loc.cit.*

293. Herbert Blumer, "The Methodological Position of Symbolic

Interactionism," Chapter 1 of his *Symbolic Interactionism,* (Englewood Cliffs: Prentice-Hall, 1969), pp. 11–12.

294. *Ibid.,* p. 12.

295. *loc.cit.*

296. *Ibid.,* p. 17.

297. *Ibid.,* p. 18.

298. *loc.cit.*

299. *Ibid.,* p. 18–19.

300. Wilbert E. Moore, *American Negro Slavery and Abolition: A Sociological Study,* (New York: The Third Press, 1971), pp. 85–86.

301. Blumer, "The Nature of Race Prejudice," *op.cit.,* pp. 12–13.

302. See the following essays by Blumer: "The Study of Urbanization and Industrialization: Methodological Deficiencies," *Boletim de Centro Latinos de Pesquisas em Ciencias Sociais,* II (May, 1959), pp. 17–34; "Early Industrialization and the Laboring Class," *The Sociological Quarterly,* I (January, 1960), pp. 5–14; "Industrialization and the Traditional Order," *Sociology and Social Research,* XLVIII (January, 1964), pp. 129–138; "Industrialisation and Race Relations," *op.cit.,* pp. 220–253.

303. ten Broek, *op.cit.,* pp. 149–151.

304. *The Civil Rights Cases,* 109 U.S. 3 (1883).

305. *Hodges versus United States,* 203 U.S. 1 (1906). For the details of this and related cases see Loren Miller, *The Petitioners: The Story of the Supreme Court of the United States and the Negro,* (New York: Pantheon Books, 1966), pp. 185–198.

306. For a comprehensive discussion see Herbert Hill, *Black Labor and the American Legal System, I: Race, Work and the Law,* (Washington, D.C.: The Bureau of National Affairs, Inc., 1977), pp. 63–92.

307. *Jones vs. Mayer,* 392 U.S. 409 at 436 (1968).

308. Walter Lippmann, *The Method of Freedom,* (New York: The Macmillan Co., 1934, pp. 107, 110.

309. *Ibid.,* pp. 46–50.

310. The foregoing draws on Bertram Gross, "Rethinking Full Employment, I," *The Nation,* CCXLIV (January 17, 1987), pp. 44–48.

311. 247 U.S. 483 (1954).

312. *Regents of the University of California vs. Bakke,* 438 U.S. 265 (1978).

313. *United Steelworkers of America, AFL-CIO-CLC vs. Brian F. Weber et.al.,* 443 U.S. 193 (1979).

314. *Wygant et. al. vs. Jackson Board of Education* 476 U.S. 90 L Ed. 2nd 260, 106 S.Ct. (1986).

315. *Local 28 of the Sheet Metal Workers International Association and Local 28 Joint Apprenticeship Committee vs. Equal Employment Opportunity Commission et.al.*, No. 84–1656 (1986).

316. *Local Number 93, International Association of Firefighters, AFL-CIO, CLC vs. City of Cleveland*, No. 84–1999 (1986).

317. Nathan Glazer, *Affirmative Discrimination: Ethnic Inequality and Public Policy, op.cit.*, pp. 75–76.

318. Blumer, "Social Science and the Desegregation Process," *op.cit.*, p. 137.

319. *Ibid.*, pp. 139–140.

320. *Fullilove vs. Klutznick*, 448 U.S. 448 (1980). Reprinted in Stanley I. Kutler, ed., *The Supreme Court and the Constitution: Readings in American Constitutional History, op.cit.*, pp. 699, 700.

321. Joseph Tussman and Jacobus ten Broek, "The Equal Protection of the Laws," *California Law Review*, XXXVII (September, 1949), pp. 345–346.

322. Moore, *op.cit.*, p. 170.

323. Glazer, *Affirmative Discrimination . . . , op.cit.*, pp. 68–73.

324. *Ibid.*, pp. 20–21. Emphasis supplied.

325. *Ibid.*, pp. 6–7, 21.

326. Blumer, "Reflections on Theory of Race Relations," *op.cit.*, p. 14.

327. Blumer, "The Nature of Race Prejudice," *op.cit.*, p. 11.

328. Blumer, "Research on Racial Relations: The United States of America," *op.cit.*, p. 403.

329. *Ibid.*, pp. 410–413.

330. *Ibid.*, pp. 429–438.

331. Herbert Hill, "Anti-Oriental Agitation and the Rise of Working-Class Racism," *Transaction: Social Science and Modern Society*, X (January–February, 1973), p. 44.

332. Alexander Saxton, *The Indispensable Enemy: Labor and the Anti-Chinese Movement in California*, (Berkeley: University of California Press, 1971).

333. See Stanford M. Lyman, "Henry Hughes and the Southern Foundations of American Sociology," in his edition of *Selected Writings of Henry Hughes: Antebellum Southerner, Slavocrat, Sociologist, op.cit.*, pp. 55–56.

334. On the eviction of Chinese laborers from California's farms, see Carey McWilliams, *Factories in the Fields: The Story of Migratory Farm*

Labor in California, (Boston: Little, Brown and Co., 1939), pp. 66–80.

335. Cletus E. Daniel, *Bitter Harvest: A History of California Farm-workers, 1870–1941,* (Ithaca: Cornell University Press, 1981), pp. 66–67, 73–76, 82–83.

336. Donald J. Pisani, *From the Family Farm to Agribusiness: The Irrigation Crusade in California and the West, 1850–1931,* (Berkeley: University of California Press, 1984), p. 442.

337. Paul S. Taylor, "Mexicans North of the Rio Grande," *Survey Graphic,* XIX (May, 1931). Reprinted in his anthology, *On the Ground in the Thirties,* (Salt Lake City: Peregrine Smith Books, 1983), p. 1.

338. See Arthur J. Vidich and Stanford M. Lyman, *American Sociology . . . , op.cit.,* pp. 242–248.

339. Blumer, "The Future of the Color Line," *op.cit.,* p. 324.

340. See Thomas Sowell, *Ethnic America: A History,* (New York: Basic Books, 1981), pp. 223–224; *Pink and Brown People and Other Controversial Essays,* (Stanford: Hoover Institution Press, 1981), pp. 4–5, 8–9, 10–18, 23–25; *Markets and Minorities,* (New York: Basic Books, 1981), pp. 19–33; *The Economics and Politics of Race: An International Perspective* (New York: William Morrow, 1983), pp. 29, 131–132, 159–167, 185–202; *Civil Rights: Rhetoric or Reality, op.cit.* pp. 37–61, 73–90, 109–123, 130–140; *A Conflict of Visions: Ideological Origins of Political Struggles,* (New York: William Morrow, 1987), pp. 93–99, 123–125, 200–203, 230.

341. Blumer, "The Future of the Color Line," *op.cit.,* pp. 322–323; "Research on Racial Relations . . . ," *op.cit.,* pp. 427–435.

342. "Dissent," *Local 28 of the Sheet Metal Workers International Association and Local 28, Joint Apprenticeship Committee vs. Equal Employment Opportunity Commission et. al.* No. 84–1656. Decided July 2, 1986.

343. Blumer, "The Future of the Color Line," *op.cit.,* p. 323.

344. *Ibid.,* p. 331.

345. Herbert Blumer, "Industrialisation and Race Relations," pp. 232–283.

346. *Ibid.,* p. 234.

347. *Ibid.,* p. 236.

348. *loc.cit.*

349. Karl Marx, *Early Texts,* trans. and ed. by David McLellan, (Oxford: Basil Blackwell, 1972), pp. 178–183.

350. Georg Simmel, "A Chapter in the Philosophy of Value," tr. by Albion W. Small, *American Journal of Sociology,* V (March, 1900), esp.

pp. 577–578 and *idem, The Philosophy of Money,* tr. by Tom Bottomore and David Frisby, (London: Routledge and Kegan Paul, 1978), pp. 131–203, 343–354, 409–428.

351. John Stuart Mill, *A Logical Critique of Sociology,* ed. by Ronald Fletcher, (London: Michael Joseph Ltd., 1971), pp. 215–296.

352. William J. Wilson, *The Declining Significance of Race,* (Chicago: University of Chicago Press, 1978).

353. Annie Phizacklea and Robert Miles, *Labour and Racism,* (London: Routledge and Kegan Paul, 1980), esp. pp. 127–232.

354. Blumer, "Industrialisation and Race Relations," *op.cit.,* pp. 235–239.

355. Trans. by Talcott Parsons (New York: Charles Scribner's Sons, 1930).

356. See Vidich and Lyman, *American Sociology, op.cit.,* pp. 87–94.

357. See F. J. Roethlisberger and William J. Dickson with the assistance and collaboration of Harold A. Wright, *Management and the Worker: An Account of a Research Program Conducted by the Western Electric Company, Hawthorne Works, Chicago,* (Cambridge: Harvard University Press, 1966. Orig. pub. 1939); F. J. Roethlisberger, *Management and Morale,* (Cambridge: Harvard University Press, 1965. Orig. pub. 1941); George Homans, *The Human Group,* (New York: Harcourt, Brace and Co., 1950), pp. 369–399; George Caspar Homans, *Coming to My Senses: The Autobiography of a Sociologist,* (New Brunswick, N.J.: Transaction Books, 1984, 1986), pp. 135–166; and Richard C. S. Trahair, *The Humanist Temper: The Life and Work of Elton Mayo,* (New Brunswick, N.J.: Transaction Books, 1984), pp. 225–270.

358. See, e.g., Robert E. Park, *The Crowd and the Public and Other Essays,* trans. by Charlotte Elsner, ed. by Henry Elsner, Jr., (Chicago: University of Chicago Press, 1972), pp. 47–48, 90–92.

359. See Richard T. Ely, *Studies in the Evolution of Industrial Society,* (Port Washington: Kennikat Press, 1971. Orig. Pub. 1903), II, pp. 426–486; *Idem, The Labor Movement in America,* (New York: Arno Press and The New York Times, 1969. Orig. Pub. 1886), pp. 295–332.

360. Ernest T. Hiller, *The Strike: A Study in Collective Action,* (New York: Arno Press and The New York Times, 1969. Orig. Pub. 1928), esp. pp. 266–277.

361. Herbert Blumer, "Sociological Theory in Industrial Relations," *American Sociological Review,* XII (June, 1947), p. 272.

362. *Ibid.,* pp. 274–276.

363. *Ibid.,* p. 272.

364. *Ibid.*, p. 277.

365. Herbert Blumer, "Social Structure and Power Conflict," in Arthur Kornhauser, Robert Dubin, and Arthur M. Ross, eds., *Industrial Conflict, op.cit.,* pp. 234–235.

366. *Ibid.*, p. 235.

367. *Ibid.*, pp. 237–239.

368. *Ibid.*, p. 239.

369. Herbert Blumer, *The Rationale of Labor-Management Relations,* Rio Piedras, Puerto Rico: Labor Relations Institute, University of Puerto Rico, 1958), pp. 21–36.

370. *Ibid.*, pp. 41–42.

371. *Ibid.*, pp. 43–55.

372. Herbert Blumer, "Paternalism in Industry," *Social Processes in Hawaii,* XV (1951), pp. 26–31.

373. See, e.g., James C. Cobb and Michael V. Namorato, eds., *The New Deal and the South,* (Jackson: University Press of Mississippi, 1984).

374. Joseph Tussman, *Obligation and the Body Politic,* (New York: Oxford University Press, 1960), pp. 107–109.

375. Max Weber, "Politics as a Vocation," *From Max Weber: Essays in Sociology,* trans. and ed. by H. H. Gerth and C. Wright Mills, (New York: Oxford University Press, 1946), pp. 77–128.

376. *Ibid.*, pp. 123–128.

377. See John Dewey, *The Public and Its Problems,* (New York: Henry Holt and Co., 1927), pp. 197–199, 206–213. *Idem, The Philosophy of John Dewey,* ed. by John J. McDermott, (Chicago: University of Chicago Press, 1973, 1981), pp. 397–420, 454–493, 575–597, 620–678, 712–723; *Idem, Characters and Events: Popular Essays in Social and Political Philosophy,* ed. by Joseph Ratner, (New York: Octagon Books, 1970), II, pp. 447–478, 493–503, 645–649, 709–856.

378. George Herbert Mead, *Selected Writings,* ed. by Andrew J. Reck (Indianapolis: Bobbs-Merrill Co., 1964), pp. 3–5, 82–93, 114–170, 248–293, 392–408.

379. William M. Sullivan, *Reconstructing Public Philosophy,* (Berkeley: University of California Press, 1982), p. 168.

380. Herbert Blumer, "George Herbert Mead," in Buford Rhea, ed., *The Future of the Sociological Classics,* (London: George Allen and Unwin, 1981), pp. 166–167, 168–169.

381. Thomas J. Morrione and Harvey A. Farberman, "Conversation with Herbert Blumer: II," *Symbolic Interactionism,* IV (Fall, 1981), p. 277.

382. Herbert Blumer, "Über das Konzept der Massengesellschaft," tr. by Dorly Frey and Heinz Otto Luthe, in *Militanter Humanismus: Von den Aufgaben der modernen Soziologie,* herausgegeben von Alphons Silbermann (Frankfurt am Main: S. Fischer Verlag, 1966), pp. 19–37.

383. See Richard Vernon, *Citizenship and Order: Studies in French Political Thought,* (Toronto: University of Toronto Press, 1986), pp. 125–230.

384. Vidich and Lyman, *American Sociology . . . , op.cit.,* pp. 53–86, 105–194.

385. Talcott Parsons, "The Symbolic Environment of Modern Economies," *Social Research,* XLVI (1979), pp. 436–453.

386. Robert N. Bellah, *The Broken Covenant: American Civil Religion in Time of Trial,* (New York: Seabury, 1975).

387. Vernon, *op.cit.,* p. 215.

388. Unless otherwise indicated, the quotations from Blumer that follow are English translations from his essay, "Über das Konzept der Massengesellschaft," German tr. by Dorly Frey and Heinz Otto Luthe, in Alphons Silbermann, ed., *Militanter Humanismus: Von den Aufgaben der modernen Soziologie, op.cit.,* pp. 19–37.

389. Cf. Steven M. Tipton, *Getting Saved from the Sixties: Moral Meaning in Conversion and Cultural Change,* (Berkeley: University of California Press, 1982).

390. Robert N. Bellah, Richard Madsen, William M. Sullivan, Ann Swidler, and Steven M. Tipton, *Habits of the Heart: Individualism and Commitment in American Life,* (Berkeley, University of California Press, 1985).

391. Robert Jackall, *Moral Mazes: The World of Corporate Managers,* (New York: Oxford University Press, 1988).

392. See Joseph Bensman and Arthur J. Vidich, *American Society: The Welfare State and Beyond,* rev'd. edn. (South Hadley, Mass.: Bergin and Garvey Publishers, 1987), pp. 30, 85, 106–109.

393. Blumer, *The Rationale of Labor-Management Relations, op.cit.,* p. 37.

394. *Ibid.,* p. 38.

395. *Ibid.,* p. 39.

396. *Ibid.,* p. 42.

397. *Ibid.,* p. 43.

398. *loc.cit.*

399. *Ibid.,* pp. 44–45.

400. *Ibid.*, pp. 45–46.
401. *Ibid.*, pp. 46–47.
402. *Ibid.*, pp. 47–50.
403. *Ibid.*, pp. 52–55.

Selected Works of
Herbert Blumer

*Read before the annual meeting of the American Sociological Society, New York City, December 28–30, 1947.

Public Opinion
and Public Opinion Polling*

This paper presents some observations on public opinion and on public opinion polling as currently performed. It is hoped that these observations will provoke the discussion for which, I understand, this meeting has been arranged. The observations are not along the line of what seems to be the chief preoccupation of students of public opinion polling, to wit, the internal improvement of their technique. Instead, the observations are designed to invite attention to whether public opinion polling actually deals with public opinion.

The first observations which I wish to make are in the nature of a prelude. They come from a mere logical scrutiny of public opinion polling as an alleged form of scientific investigation. What I note is the inability of public opinion polling to isolate "public opinion" as an abstract or generic concept which could thereby become the focal point for the formation of a system of propositions. It would seem needless to point out that in an avowed scientific enterprise seeking to study a class of empirical items and to develop a series of generalizations about that class it is necessary to identify the class. Such identification enables discrimination between the instances which fall within the class and those which do not. In this manner, the generic character of the object of study becomes delineated. When the generic object of study is distinguishable, it becomes possible to focus study on that object and thus to learn progressively more about that object. In this way the ground is prepared for cumulative generalizations or propositions relative to the generic object of investigation.

As far as I can judge, the current study of public opinion by polling ignores the simple logical point which has just been made. This can be seen through three observations. First, there is no effort, seemingly, to try to identify or to isolate public opinion as an object; we are not given any criteria which characterize or distinguish public opinion and thus we are not able to say that a given empirical instance falls within the class of public opinion and some other empirical instance falls outside of the class of public opinion. Second, there is an absence, as far as I can determine, of using specific studies to test a general proposition about public opinion; this suggests that the students are not studying a generic object. This suggestion is supported by the third observation—a paucity, if not a complete absence, of generalizations about public opinion despite the voluminous amount of polling studies of public opinion. It must be concluded, in my judgment, that current public opinion polling has not succeeded in isolating public opinion as a generic object of study.

It may be argued that the isolation of a generic object, especially in the realm of human behavior, is a goal rather than an initial point of departure—and that consequently the present inability to identify public opinion as a generic object is not damning to current public opinion polling. This should be admitted. However, what impresses me is the apparent absence of effort or sincere interest on the part of students of public opinion polling to move in the direction of identifying the object which they are supposedly seeking to study, to record, and to measure. I believe it is fair to say that those trying to study public opinion by polling are so wedded to their technique and so preoccupied with the improvement of their technique that they shunt aside the vital question of whether their technique is suited to the study of what they are ostensibly seeking to study. Their work is largely merely making application of their technique. They are not concerned with independent analysis of the nature of public opinion in order to judge whether the application of their technique fits that nature.

A few words are in order here on an approach that consciously excuses itself from any consideration of such a problem. I refer to the narrow operationalist position that public opinion consists of what public opinion polls poll. Here, curiously, the findings resulting from an operation, or use of an instrument, are regarded as constituting the object of study instead of being some contributory addition to knowledge of the object of study. The operation ceases to be a guided procedure on behalf of an object of inquiry; instead the operation determines intrinsically its own objective. I do not care to consider here the profound logical and psychological difficulties that attend the effort to develop systematic knowledge through a procedure which is not a form of directed inquiry. All that I wish to note is that the results of narrow operationalism, as above specified, merely leave untouched the question of what the results mean. Not having a conceptual point of reference the results are merely disparate findings. It is logically possible, of course, to use such findings to develop a conceptualization. I fail to see anything being done in this direction by those who subscribe to the narrow operationalist position in the use of public opinion polls. What is logically unpardonable on the part of those who take the narrow operationalist position is for them to hold either wittingly or unwittingly that their investigations are a study of public opinion as this term is conceived in our ordinary discourse. Having rejected as unnecessary the task of characterizing the object of inquiry for the purpose of seeing whether the inquiry is suited to the object of inquiry, it is gratuitous and unwarranted to presume that after all the inquiry is a study of the object which one refuses to characterize. Such a form of trying to eat one's cake and have it too needs no further comment.

The foregoing series of logical observations has been made merely to stress the absence of consideration of a generic object by those engaged in public opinion polling. Apparently, it is by virtue of this absence of consideration that they are obtuse to the functional nature of public opinion in our society and to questions of whether their technique is suited to this functional nature. In this paper I intend to judge the suitability of public opinion polling as a means of studying public opinion. This shall be done from the standpoint of what we know of public opinion in our society.

Admittedly, we do not know a great deal about public opinion. However, we know something. We know enough about public opinion from empirical observations to form a few reasonably reliable judgments about its nature and mode of functioning. In addition, we can make some reasonably secure inferences about the structure and functioning of our society and about collective behavior within our society. This combined body of knowledge derived partly from direct empirical observation and partly from reasonable inference can serve appropriately as means of judging and assessing current public opinion polling as a device for studying public opinion.

Indeed, the features that I wish to note about public opinion and its setting are so obvious and commonplace that I almost blush to call them to the attention of this audience. I would not do so were it not painfully clear that the students of current public opinion polling ignore them either wittingly or unwittingly in their whole research procedure. I shall indicate by number the features to be noted.

1. Public opinion must obviously be recognized as having its setting in a society and as being a function of that society in operation. This means, patently, that public opinion gets its form from the social framework in which it moves and from the social processes in play in that framework; also that the function and role of public opinion is determined by the part it plays in the operation of the society. If public opinion is to be studied in any realistic sense its depiction must be faithful to its empirical character. I do not wish to be redundant but I find it necessary to say that the empirical character of public opinion is represented by its composition and manner of functioning as a part of a society in operation.

2. As every sociologist ought to know and as every intelligent layman does know, a society has an organization. It is not a mere aggregation of disparate individuals. A human society is composed of diverse kinds of functional groups. In our American society illustrative instances of functional groups are a corporation, a trade association, a labor union, an ethnic group, a farmer's organization. To a major extent our total collective life is made up of the actions and acts of such groups. These groups are oriented in different directions because of special interests. These groups differ in terms of their strategic position in the society and in terms of opportunities to act. Accordingly, they differ in terms of prestige and power. As functional groups, that is to say as groups acting individually in some corporate or unitary sense, such groups necessarily have to have some organization—some leadership, some policy makers, some individuals who speak on behalf of the group, and some individuals who take the initiative in acting on behalf of the group.

3. Such functional groups, when they act, have to act through the channels which are available in the society. If the fate

of the proposed acts depends on the decisions of individuals or groups who are located at strategic points in the channels of action, then influence and pressure is brought to bear directly or indirectly on such individuals or groups who make the decisions. I take it that this realistic feature of the operation of our American society requires little explication. If an action embodying the interests of a functional group such as a farmers' organization depends for its realization on decisions of Congressmen or a bureau or a set of administrators, then efforts on behalf of that action will seek to influence such Congressmen, bureau, or administrators. Since in every society to some degree, and in our American society to a large degree, there are individuals, committees, boards, legislators, administrators, and executives who have to make the decisions affecting the outcome of the actions of functional groups, such key people become the object of direct and indirect influence or pressure.

4. The key individuals referred to who have to make the crucial decisions are almost inevitably confronted with the necessity of *assessing* the various influences, claims, demands, urgings, and pressures that are brought to bear on them. Insofar as they are responsive and responsible they are bound to make such an assessment in the process of arriving at their decisions. Here I want to make the trite remark that in making their assessment these key individuals take into account what they judge to be worthy of being taken into account.

5. The above points give a crude but essential realistic picture of certain important ways in which our society operates. The fifth feature I wish to note is that public opinion is formed and expressed in large measure through these ways of societal operation. This point requires a little elaboration. The formation of public opinion occurs as a function of a society in operation. I state the matter in that way to stress that the formation of public opinion does not occur through an interaction of disparate individuals who share equally in the process. Instead the formation of public opinion reflects the functional composition and organization of society. The formation of public opinion occurs in large measure through the interaction of groups. I mean nothing esoteric by this last remark. I merely refer to the common occurrence of the leaders or officials of a functional group taking a stand on behalf of the group with reference to an issue and voic-

ing explicitly or implicitly this stand on behalf of the group. Much of the interaction through which public opinion is formed is through the clash of these group views and positions. In no sense does such a group view imply that it is held in equal manner and in equal degree by all of the members of the group. Many of the members of the group may subscribe to the view without understanding it, many may be indifferent about it, many may share the view only in part, and many may actually not share the view but still not rebel against the representatives of the group who express the view. Nevertheless the view, as indicated, may be introduced into the forum of discussion as the view of the group and may be reacted to as such. To bring out this point in another way, one need merely note that in the more outstanding expressions of view on an issue, the individuals almost always speak either explicitly or implicitly as representatives of groups. I would repeat that in any realistic sense the diversified interaction which gives rise to public opinion is in large measure between functional groups and not merely between disparate individuals.

I think that it is also very clear that in the process of forming public opinion, individuals are not alike in influence nor are groups that are equal numerically in membership alike in influence. This is so evident as not to require elaboration. It is enough merely to point out that differences in prestige, position, and influence that characterize groups and individuals in the functional organizations of a society are brought into play in the formation of public opinon.

The picture of a series of groups and individuals of significantly different influence interacting in the formation of public opinion holds true equally well with reference to the expression of public opinion. By expression of public opinion I mean bringing the public opinion to bear on those who have to act in response to public opinion. This expression is not in the form of a parade or array of the views of disparate individuals, in an open forum. Where the views are voiced in open forum they are likely, as has been indicated, to be in one way or another the expression of group views. But in addition to the voicing of views in the open forum, the expression of public opinion is in the form of direct influence on those who are to act in response to public opinion. Through such means as letters, telegrams, petitions, resolutions, lobbies, delegations, and personal meetings interested groups and individuals bring their views and positions to bear on the key persons who have to make the decisions. I am not concerned with whether such forms of expressing public opinion should occur; I merely wish to emphasize that in any realistic consideration of public opinion it must be recognized that such means of expressing public opinion do occur. A society which has to act will use the channels of action that it has in its structure.

6. The last feature of public opinion that I wish to note is that in *any realistic sense* public opinion consists of the pattern of the diverse views and positions on the issue *that come to the individuals who have to act in response to the public opinion*. Public opinion which was a mere display, or which was terminal in its very expression, or which never came to the attention of those who have to act on public opinion would be impotent and meaningless as far as affecting the action or operation of society is concerned. Insofar as public opinion is *effective* on societal action it becomes so only by entering into the purview of whosoever, like legislators, executives, administrators, and policy makers, have to act on public opinion. To me this proposition is self-evident. If it be granted, the character of public opinion in terms of meaningful operation must be sought in the array of views and positions which enter into the consideration of those who have to take action on public opinion.

It is important to note that the individual who has to act on public opinion has to *assess* the public opinion as it comes to his attention, because of the very fact that this public opinion comes to him in the form of diverse views and usually opposed views. Insofar as he is responsive to public opinion he has to weigh the respective views. How this assessment is made is an obscure matter. But one generalization even though trite, can be made safely, to wit, that the individual takes into account different views only to the extent to which such views count. And views count pretty much on the basis of how the individual judges the "backing" of the views and the implication of the backing. It is in this sense, again, that the organization of the society with its differentiation of prestige and power enters into the character of public opinion. As was explained above, the key person who has to act on public opinion is usually subject to a variety of presentations, importunities, demands, criticisms, and suggestions that come to him through the various channels in the communicative structure of society. Unless one wishes to conjure in his imagination a very fanciful society he must admit that the servant of public opinion is forced to make an assessment of the expressions of public opinion that come to his attention and that in this assessment consideration is given to expressions only to the extent to which they are judged to "count."

The foregoing six features are, I believe, trite but faithful points about public opinion as it functions in our society. They may serve as a background for the examination of public opinion polling. I may state here that in this discussion I am not concerning myself with the problem of whether the individual opinions one gets through the polling interview are reasonably valid. My discussion, instead, is concerned with the question of the value of poll findings even if one makes the dubious assumption that the individual opinions that are secured are valid.

In my judgment the inherent deficiency of public opinion polling, certainly as currently done, is contained in its sampling procedure. Its current sampling procedure forces a treatment of society as if society were only an aggregation of disparate individuals. Public opinion, in turn, is regarded as being a quantitative distribution of individual opinions. This way of treating society and this way of viewing public opinion must be regarded as markedly unrealistic. The best way I can bring this out is by making continuous reference to the common sense empirical observations of public opinion that were noted previously. We do not know at all whether individuals in the sample represent that portion of structured society that is participating in the formation of public opinion on a given issue. That the sample will catch a number of them, or even a larger number of them, is very likely. But, as far as I am able to determine, there is no way in current public opinion polling to know much about this. Certainly the mere fact that the interviewee either gives or does not give an opinion does not tell you whether he is participating in the formation of public opinion as it is being built up functionally in the society. More important, assuming that the sample catches the individuals who are participating in the formation of the given public opinion, no information is given of their part in this process. One cannot identify from the sample or from the replies of those constituting the sample the social niche of the individual in that portion of the social structure in which the public opinion is being formed. Such information is not given in the conventional items of age, sex, occupation, economic status, educational containment or class status. These are rarely the marks of significant functional position in the formation of public opinion on a given issue. We do not know from the conventional kind of sample or from the responses of the interviewee what influence, if any, he has in the formation or expression of public opinion. We do not know whether he has a following or whether he doesn't. We do not know whether or not he is speaking on behalf of a group or groups or whether he even belongs to functional groups interested in the issue. If he does, perchance, express the views of some such functional group, we don't know whether or not that group is busily at work in the channels of society to give vigorous expression to their point of view. We do not even know whether he, as an individual, is translating his opinion into what I have termed previously "effective public opinion."

In short, we know essentially nothing of the individual in the sample with reference to the significance of him or of his opinion in the public opinion that is being built up or which is expressing itself functionally in the operation of society. We do not know whether the individual has the position of an archbishop or an itinerant laborer; whether he belongs to a powerful group taking a vigorous stand on the issue or whether he is a detached recluse with no membership in a functional group; whether he is bringing his opinion to bear in some fashion at strategic points in the operation of society or whether it is isolated and socially impotent. We do not know what role, if any, any individual in the sample plays in the formation of the public opinion on which he is questioned, and we do not know what part, if any, his opinion as given has in the functional public opinion which exists with reference to the issue.

What has just been said with reference to the individual component of the public opinion poll applies collectively to the total findings. The collective findings have no assurance of depicting public opinion on a given issue because these findings ignore the framework and the functional operation of the public opinion. If this is not clear from what has already been said, I would like to point out the enormous difficulty that occurs when one seeks to assess the findings of a public opinion poll in terms of the organization of society with which an administrator, legislator, executive, or similarly placed person has to contend. As I have stated earlier such an individual who is presumably responsive to public opinion has to assess public opinion as it comes to his attention in terms of the functional organization of society to which he is responsive. He has to view that society in terms of groups of divergent influence; in terms of organizations with different degrees of power; in terms of individuals with followings; in terms of indifferent people—all, in other words, in terms of what and who counts in his part of the social world. This type of assessment which is called for in the instance of an organized society in operation is well-nigh impossible to make in the case of the findings of public opinion polls. We are unable to answer such questions as the following: how much power and influence is possessed by those who have the favorable opinion or the unfavorable opinion; who are these people who have the opinion; whom do they represent; how well organized are they; what groups do they belong to that are stirring around on the scene and that are likely to continue to do so; are those people who have the given opinion very much concerned about their opinion; are they going to get busy and do something about it; are they going to get vociferous, militant, and troublesome; are they in the position to influence powerful groups and individuals *who are known;* does the opinion represent a studied policy of significant organizations which will persist and who are likely to remember; is the opinion an ephemeral or momentary view which people will quickly forget? These sample questions show how markedly difficult it is to assess the results of public opinion polling from the standpoint of the things that have to be taken into account in working in an organized society. This difficulty, in turn, signifies that current public opinion polling gives an inaccurate and unrealistic picture of public opinion because of the failure to catch opinions as they are organized and as they operate in a functioning society.

What I have said will appear to many as distinctly invalid on the ground that public opinion polling has *demonstrated* that it can and does detect public opinion faithfully, by virtue of its marked success in predicting election returns. This contention needs to be investigated carefully, particularly since in most circles polling, wherever applied, is regarded as intrinsically valid because of its rather spectacular success in predicting elections. What I think needs to be noted is that the casting of ballots is distinctly an action of separate individuals wherein a ballot cast by another individual has exactly the same weight as a ballot cast by another individual. In this proper sense, and in the sense of real action, voters constitute a population of disparate individuals, each of whom has equal weight to the others. Consequently, the sampling procedure which is based on a population of disparate individuals is eminently suited to securing a picture of what the voting is likely to be. However, to regard the successful use of polling in this area as proof of its automatic validity when applied to an area where people do not act as equally weighted disparate individuals begs the very question under consideration. I would repeat that the formation and expression of public opinion giving rise to effective public opinion is not an action of a population of disparate individuals having equal weight but is a function of a structured society, differentiated into a network of different kinds of groups and individuals having differential weight and influence and occupying different strategic positions. Accordingly, to my mind, the success attending polling in the prediction of elections gives no validity to the method as a means of studying, recording or measuring public opinion as it forms and functions in our society.

There is a very important contention in this connection which has to be considered. The contention can be stated as follows:

> An election by public ballot is in itself an expression of public opinion—and, furthermore, it is an effective and decisive expression of public opinion. It is, in fact, the ultimate expression of public opinion and thus it represents the proper norm of the expression of public opinion. In the election by ballot each voter, in accordance with the basic principles of democracy, has his say as a citizen and has equal worth to every other citizen in casting his ballot. If election by ballot be recognized as the genuine referendum in which true public opinion comes to expression, then the preeminence of current public opinion polling as the device for recording and measuring public opinion is established. For, public opinion polling with its current form of sampling has demonstrated that it can predict reliably and effectively the results of the election. Accordingly, public opinion polling, in itself, can be

used as a type of referendum to record and measure the true opinion of the public on issues in the instances of which the public does not go to the election polls. Thus, public opinion polling yields a more reliable and accurate picture of public opinion than is represented by the confused, indefinite, slanted, and favor-ridden expressions of opinion that come ordinarily to the legislator, administrator, or executive who has to act on public opinion. The public opinion poll tells us where people stand. It gives us the *vox populi*.

My remarks with reference to this contention will be brief. It should be evident on analysis that the contention is actually a normative plea and not a defense of polling as a method of study of public opinion as such public opinion functions in our society. The contention proposes that public opinion be construed in a particular way, to wit, that public opinion *ought to be* an aggregation of the opinions of a cross section of the population rather than what it is in the actual functioning of society. To my mind it is highly questionable whether in the day by day operation of our society public opinion ought to be of the nature posited by the public opinion poll. Many appropriate questions could be raised about how and to what extent public opinion is expressed at the election polls, and, more important, whether it would be possible or even advisable for public opinion, in the form of an aggregation of equally weighted individual opinions, to function meaningfully in a society with a diversified organization. However, such questions need not be raised here. It is sufficient to note that if one seeks to justify polling as a method of studying public opinion on the ground that the composition of public opinion *ought to be* different than what it is, he is not establishing the validity of the method for the study of the empirical world as it is. Instead, he is hanging on the coat-tails of a dubious proposal for social reform.[1]

In this paper I have presented criticisms of "public opinion polling" as a method for the recording and measurement of pub-

---

[1] I refer to such a program as dubious because I believe the much needed improvement of public opinion in our society should be in the process by which public opinion organically functions, i.e., by arousing, organizing, and effectively directing the opinion of people who appreciate that they have an interest in a given issue. A reliance, instead, on a mere "referendum" by an undifferentiated mass, having great segments of indifferences and nonparticipation, is un-

lic opinion. These criticisms have centered around the distortion that stems from the use of a sample in the form of an aggregation of disparate individuals having equal weight. These criticisms should not be misinterpreted to mean that such a sampling procedure is invalid wherever applied or that wherever polling makes use of such a sampling procedure such polling is intrinsically invalid. Clearly, the criticism applies when such a sampling procedure is used to study a matter whose composition is an organization of interacting parts instead of being merely an aggregation of individuals. Where the matter which one is studying is an aggregation of individual units then the application of the sampling procedure spoken of is clearly in order. I make this banal statement only to call attention to the fact that there are obviously many matters about human beings and their conduct that have just this character of being an aggregation of individuals or a congeries of individual actions. Many demographic matters are of this nature. Also, many actions of human beings in a society are of this nature—such as casting ballots, purchasing tooth paste, going to motion picture shows, and reading newspapers. Such actions, which I like to think of as mass actions of individuals in contrast to organized actions of groups, lend themselves readily to the type of sampling that we have in current public opinion polling. In fact, it is the existence of such mass actions of individuals which explains, in my judgment, the successful use in consumer research of sampling such as is employed in public opinion polling. What I find questionable, and what this paper criticizes, is the use of such sampling with its implicit imagery and logic in the study of a matter which, like the process of public opinion, functions as a moving organization of interconnected parts.

The last item I wish to consider briefly refers to the interesting and seemingly baffling question of how one should or can sample an object matter which is a complicated system of interacting parts having differential influence in the total operation. Perhaps the question in itself is absurd. At various times I have

---

likely to offer a desirable public opinion. At the best, in my judgment, such a "referendum" could operate as a corrective supplement and not as a substitute. The important question concerning the directions in which public opinion might secure its much needed improvement is, of course, outside the scope of this paper.

asked different experts in sampling how one would sample an organic structure. With a single exception these individuals looked at me askance as if the question were idiotic. But the problem, I think, remains even though I find it difficult to state. In human society, particularly in modern society, we are confronted with intricate complexes of moving relations which are roughly recognizable as systems, even though loose systems. Such a loose system is too complicated, too encumbered in detail and too fast moving to be described in any one of its given "cycles" of operation adequately and faithfully. Yet unless we merely want to speculate about it we have to dip into it in some manner in order to understand what is happening in the given cycle of operation in which we are interested. Thus, using the public opinion process in our society as an illustration we are able to make a rough characterization as to how it functions in the case, let us say, of a national issue. However, if we want to know how it functions in the case of a *given* national issue, we are at a loss to make an adequate description because of the complexity and quick movement of the cycle of its operation. So, to know what is going on, particularly to know what is likely to go on in the latter stages, we have to dip in here and there. The problems of where to dip in, how to dip in, and how far to dip in are what I have in mind in speaking of sampling an organic structure.

I suppose, as one of my friends has pointed out, that the answer to the problem requires the formulation of a model. We have no such model in the instance of public opinion as it operates in our society. My own hunch is that such a model should be constructed, if it can be at all, by working backwards instead of by working forward. That is, we ought to begin with those who have to act on public opinion and move backwards along the lines of the various expressions of public opinion that come to their attention, tracing these expressions backward through their own various channels and in doing so, noting the chief channels, the key points of importance, and the way in which any given expression has come to develop and pick up an organized backing out of what initially must have been a relatively amorphous condition. Perhaps, such a model, if it could be worked out, would allow the development of a realistic method of sampling in place of what seems to me to be the highly artificial method of sampling used in current public opinion polling.

Morale

THE STATE OF THE PROBLEM

Modern war has made morale a consideration of primary importance. The formation of huge conscript armies in place of professional, mercenary, or volunteer forces has compelled attention to the so-called spiritual factor. There is need of developing among conscript soldiery a spirit to fill the place of what is otherwise accomplished by habit, interest, and wish. The appearance of so-called total warfare has led to a similar concern. The enlistment of all citizens in the war effort and the subordination of their institutions to this enterprise set a problem of developing allegiance, of implanting convictions, and of establishing a new outlook. The development of "psychological warfare" has further spotlighted the problem of morale. The use of propaganda, doctored news, falsified information, rumor, and deceptive publicity to arouse dissension and to undermine faith has now become a familiar story. Before such aggressive and insinuating attacks warring nations find it necessary to bulwark the allegiance and determination of their citizenry.

It is such characteristic features of modern war which have set the problem of morale and made it a matter of conspicuous concern. While military leaders throughout history have been somewhat cognizant of a problem of morale, the problem, until recent times, has been casual and not of much conscious interest. This has been due likely to the fact that in most collective undertakings the formation of morale is spontaneous, and the requisite devices for its guidance are contained in the natural ways of living of the group. The primitive tribe, the religious sect, the band of fighters, the small professional army—all develop naturally the spirit of unity and the fortification of effort essential to their tasks. There is little occasion for morale to become a pressing problem. In our modern life the setting is markedly different; it is that of a large aggregate society whose members have distant and remote relations and possess different values and problems. In such a society people do not have the same purpose and the intimate sense of mutual support that make morale a spontaneous matter in a common group or natural community.

The introduction of a huge enterprise such as a war effort in a modern society is confronted with such a setting. It is a problem of forming collective conduct among individuated people in new, unusual, and artificial relations without the benefit of the inspiration and control of a congenial group. This task involves the development of favorable attitudes and sentiments, of outlooks and points of view, of a spirit of mutual purpose, and of co-operation.

The interest in the topic of morale, as we all know, has become widespread. The term has become popular and loaded with honorific meaning. Accordingly, it has been appropriated by different people for amazingly diverse purposes and used to justify countless proposals which their authors regarded as beneficial. This has operated to make the term vague and confused—a vagueness and confusion which have carried over into the academic and scientific fields. Workers in the psychological and social sciences have been particularly eager to employ the term. Seemingly, they have been content to start with a specious and obvious notion of it and then to develop conceptions suitable to their interests and biases. The result has been to make its meaning and understanding confused and to lead to a variety of amazing proposals as to how morale should be established. The situation has been sufficiently bad to make a number of students altogether suspicious of the "scientific" value of the idea of morale and resolved to have nothing to do with it.

The picture, on one hand, of the importance of the conditions which have set the problem of morale and, on the other, of the confused notions of morale makes it necessary to try to clarify the term. This I propose to do in a rather lengthy consideration of the nature of morale.

THE NATURE OF MORALE

My purpose is to discuss the rudimentary yet fundamental features of group morale—morale as an organization of collective intention rather than as a form of experience in the individual. One can get a clear understanding of its character by analyzing the simple circumstance or condition in which it arises. This circumstance is that in which a group is striving to realize a collective goal. The goal may be that of surviving in the face of catastrophe like a defeat in battle, a pestilence, or a severe impairment of food supply; it may be that of attaining conquest over some territory or peoples; it may be that of a realization of a reform or revolutionary program; it may be that of being successful in some expedition. Indeed, the circumstance occasioning morale exists whenever any group of human beings undertakes to engage in some enterprise. Nations at war, armies, religious sects, reform movements, revolutionary movements, political parties, exploring expeditions, a band of mountain climbers, a corps of scientific workers, football teams, a hunting expedition, a group of children making a boat—these are just a few of countless group enterprises in which morale has its natural setting.

In reflecting on the generic situation of group morale, namely, a collective enterprise, one can see clearly two fundamental features: the relation of the group toward its goal and the relation of the members of the group to one another. The ability of a group to realize an objective or goal depends on the intensity of its inclination toward that goal and on its capacity of sticking together as a group. Morale centers around these two features. Where morale is high, there is a persistence in carrying out the task of the group and a willingness to stick together on behalf of the group cause. Morale is poor when there is little attachment to the goal and where there is no effective willingness toward joint undertaking. Morale is undermined when adherence to the goal is lessened, as through disheartenment, and where there is a break in the spirit of cooperation, as through dissension. These two features of intention and co-operation may be readily translated into the moral traits which bulk so large in the current thinking on morale. Corresponding to the effort on behalf of the goal are such traits as determination, courage, stubbornness, fortitude, will to persist, stoutheartedness, and the refusal to quit. Corresponding to the mutual relations of the members are qualities of allegiance, loyalty, spirit of co-operation, camaraderie, and fellowship.

It should be noted that these two fundamental factors—group intention and co-operation—do not exist as items separate from each other. They are intimately related, with each dependent on the other and each fortifying the other. If the members of a group develop a collective goal which is highly valued, they become much more disposed to camaraderie and fellowship. Conversely, if the members have a strong feeling of common identification, and sense in one another congeniality and a readiness to mutual aid, there are imparted extra significance and value to the goal. This reciprocal relation between common goal and fellow-feeling brings out the important point that group morale is a collective product and that it is shared. It is a collective product in the sense that it arises from the response of persons to one another and to symbols of one another; the image which the members have of the group goal is dependent on the way in which the goal is pictured to them by the actions and expressions of one another. It is shared in that it is formed out of mutual stimulation and reinforcement. *Group morale exists as a disposition to act together toward a goal.*

This statement of group morale in terms of its two fundamental features of purpose and co-operation is simple and is essentially a truism. Yet it provides us with the fundamental ideas necessary for the understanding of morale and for the analysis of particular forms of morale. In the light of it, it is possible to note a number of things on which there is much confused thinking.

First, it should be realized that morale can be organized around very different collective goals—around aims that embody very different conceptions of life and widely diverse sets of ideals. Morale can be very high in groups whose objectives impress us as bizarre, superstitious, idiotic, or immoral. A religious sect, such as the Millerites in the face of ridicule, contempt, and persecution may persist in the preparation for the millennial day when they may ascend to heaven in white robes. The Fuzzy-Wuzzies with their primitive spears and bows and arrows may hurl themselves in suicidal effort into devastating rifle fire. A band of pirates may plunge into a campaign of murder, destruction, and pillage with the highest of morale. The peoples of a dictatorship may sacrifice life, property, and individual independence most readily and retain a staunch purpose. It is erroneous to believe that morale presupposes that people possess a noble doctrine, a highly moral philosophy, or a code of Christian ethics. Similarly, it is faulty to believe that good morale requires a certain kind of moral person. Morale, in a collective undertaking, may be high among all types and levels of people—the good, the bad, the arrogant, the humble, the depraved, the cultured, the illiterate, the intelligent, the stupid, the learned, and the ignorant. For all that is basically necessary for morale is that the people in a group have a goal which they value highly and seek eagerly and a sense of mutual support in their effort to attain it.

Next it may be noted that morale exists with reference to a particular collective enterprise—with reference to the particular group task. There is, it is true, some sense in speaking of what Hocking aptly terms a "morale of being"[1]—a general state of readiness of a people to begin with spirit a wide range of undertakings. This is akin to the physical tone of the body in a healthy athlete; in the group it is present in the form of a tradition to accomplish things and of a customary practice of energetic action. Despite the significance of such a general readiness to morale, it is nevertheless true that the morale of people is contingent on the particular way in which they view the goal of an undertaking. The same group may have high morale for one kind of enterprise and a very weak morale for a different kind of undertaking. In war effort the group may act with strong morale; in the reorganization of a peacetime society it may have markedly poor morale. This is no more than saying that people will act together with vigor and determination when "their heart" is in the enterprise. This point is painfully simple but needs to be appreciated.

In the light of it we must realize that *any* people, irrespective of race, nationality, economic condition, or state of culture, may have high morale if the collective enterprise to which they are committed enlists completely their hopes, fervent wishes, and aspirations. The primitives in the African jungles, the peons in a

---

[1] William Hocking, "The Nature of Morale," *American Journal of Sociology,* XLVII, No. 3 (November, 1941), 302–20.

plantation economy, the slaves in a rigid caste order, the proletariat of the slums, any nationality—Italian, Poles, Danes,
Frenchmen—any race, or any religious people may develop high
morale in some particular undertaking. The same group of people
may show amazing morale in one situation; in another it may be
devoid of morale.

Another commonplace point that follows from the discussion so far is that morale is a product of experience. It is indeed
rare for a group to form almost spontaneously a collective goal
charged with high value and to develop instantaneously a sense
of mutual support among its members. Some crises, such as an
immoral attack, may quickly arouse such a disposition. Usually,
however, the group has to build up its goal, forming an image of
its position and of its task out of continuing experience. It is a
process of growth and learning, of changed views and assess-
ments of the group aim, of transformation of the conceptions
which the people have of themselves with reference to the collective undertaking. People usually have to form and re-form their
images of the goal, discover and rediscover their group, develop
and redevelop their allegiance. The line of experience may be
long and it may be bitter. High morale, in the form of a fixity of
purpose and an abiding sense of unity, is forged out of a complicated process of definition and redefinition of goal, of evaluation
and revaluation of event, until there is a common understanding
imbedded in the feelings and images of the people. Morale is not
something already made, merely to be pumped into people. It is
not, as Hocking points out, something that is manufactured in
the psychological workshop. It is not induced by the mere application of so-called psychological laws apart from experience in
the collective enterprise. The most conspicuous cases of morale
in history have occurred without the benefit of psychologists.

The historical background of the people, the kind of events
in their experience, the way in which these events are interpreted,
the singularity of their goal, of their interests, intentions, and
self-conceptions—all point to the uniqueness of the structure of
morale in different situations. We may note this in the significant
difference between the morale structures in present-day China,
Japan, Soviet Russia, Germany, and England. Such a commonplace point needs to be mentioned in the face of current notions

that morale is something to be produced by a series of techniques, tricks, and formulas.

Finally, passing reference should be made to the often mentioned point that the test of morale is the ability of the group to meet adverse circumstance. The strength of morale is indicated by the disposition to persist in the face of setbacks, arduous circumstances, reverses, and defeats. A collective enterprise moving along without difficulty or opposition requires no high order of morale. And, incidentally, sampling of a group in such a condition may easily yield a fallacious picture of the state and degree of morale. An estimation of the morale of a group in advance of the test of adversity should be in terms of factors that refer to persistent effort, something, incidentally, not easily accomplished by so-called morale tests now popular among psychologists. We might bear in mind the comment of Wellington on the Battle of Waterloo: "The French and English soldiers were equally brave at Waterloo; the English were brave five minutes longer."

INADEQUATE VIEWS OF MORALE

Realizing that morale exists in the disposition of a group to act together toward a goal and that its vigor depends on how vitally the goal is framed, we can consider a number of current views of morale and recommendations for its formation which seem inadequate.

First of all, we should note that it is distinctly conceivable, although unlikely, that a collective enterprise, with even the huge dimensions of winning a national war, may be carried on effectively with a minimum of morale. A group, such as a nation, may have an equipment fully adequate for the task, an efficient organization, and a trained and skilful personnel. The participation of the people in such an enterprise may occur as a matter of course. It may be brought about by force or coercion, by mere habituation to assigned tasks, or by matter-of-fact obedience. In such an efficiently organized effort there may be little need for the group to be strongly animated by a common goal or to feel keenly any participation in mutual effort. The features of technological organization and efficient skills, of equipment and strength, *may* lessen dependency on morale.

Conversely, one should realize that a group with a high morale may fail in a collective task because of the absence of equipment, techniques and skills, or numbers. The disintegration of primitive tribes in the face of European aggression presents a pathetic panorama of such instances. Consequently, while the importance of morale in group undertakings is self-evident, one should view it in proper perspective and realize that it may not be effective under certain conditions and that under other conditions it may not be required.

One of the most widespread and least considerate conceptions of morale is the idea that morale results from a surcease from strain and labor. The view is that the spirit of people is kept high if they are provided with entertainment, amusement, and the facilities of relaxation. The arrangement for shows, theatrical performances, dance bands, reading material, athletic contests, dances, and socials ranks high, as we all know, in current efforts to establish morale. The ordinary morale officer in the armed services, I suspect, thinks primarily in terms of these things in carrying out his task. The view is prominent likewise in efforts to form civilian morale. Without minimizing the value of relaxation and fun for mental balance, or the way in which the efforts to provide them may give an impression of the interest of other people in one's welfare, it is clear that they do not meet what is crucial in group morale. This crucial feature is the formation of a highly valued goal. Such efforts characteristically are not directed to such a purpose.

Another view very much in the forefront of thinking and effort today is that morale is to be achieved through the formation of individual character. The belief is that if individuals have courage, faith, determination, and self-confidence, a high morale will automatically emerge in the group. Hence there is resort to exhortation, sermonizing, and education to inculcate such moral virtues in individuals. Again, it seems that such efforts, however commendable ethically, miss what is essential in morale. Individuals may be brave, determined, and self-confident and yet have little interest in or desire for a given collective goal. Under such circumstances they would have slight morale. The formation of an inspired goal in the case of a group may lead to courage, faith, and determination on the part of individuals; there is no evidence and no reason to believe that such traits in individuals will lead to an inspired group goal.

Still another idea of morale widely current these days in both lay and professional circles is that it comes in *adjusting* people to their life-situations and circumstances. If effective and happy adjustment is secured, morale is established. With this view morale effort becomes a matter of removing grievances, softening hardships, and establishing happy social relations. The faith in adjustment as the means to morale is perhaps most conspicuous in persons dealing with maladjusted people—as in social workers—but it is also prominent in other groups. In the case of this view I wish to note, again, a failure to touch what is central in collective morale. It is easy to conceive of a group of well-adjusted individuals hopelessly weak in morale in a given collective undertaking. If the individuals have little heart in the undertaking, their condition of happy adjustment is of little value. Adjustment is not the gateway to collective moral. The converse is much more likely to be true. People animated strongly by a common aim have an impressive way of enduring hardship and bearing grievance. Individual discomfort recedes before strong collective purpose.

The same point applies to another prominent notion of morale, namely, the view that morale is formed through a program of mental hygiene. This view is pronounced among psychiatrists and has become popular through the efforts of some psychiatrists to give "expert" recommendations on the formation of morale. In brief, the view is that morale is achieved if people are prepared to cope with anxiety and to avoid panic. Those who propose this view seem to hold before their eyes a picture such as the bombing of London or the flight of the French before the German armies. What is essential, it is felt, is to maintain a clear head and a poise of feeling. However plausible and sensible this view may seem, it does not deal with what is central in morale. A group of sane and mentally well-balanced individuals has no guaranty of developing morale. Their preparation for anxiety and panic is not the means of developing a strongly determined goal. It is rather the existence of such a goal which is the most effective preventative of anxiety and panic.

If space permitted, there might be added discussion of other current views of morale such as that it is to be achieved through rigorous discipline, through the development of a spirit of toughness, through the development of good leadership, through the stimulation of hatred, and through the generation of emotional enthusiasm. All these views, it seems to me, suffer from the same general type of confusion—in taking resultant and concomitant features of morale as central and in believing that the formation of these features will create morale. Instead, I would turn to the simple and truistic statement made earlier—that morale is the disposition of a group to act together toward a collective goal and that accordingly its strength depends on how the goal is conceived, on the feelings and interests developed around it, and on the mutual support which the members sense in one another. If the goal is vital and the sense of mutual effort strong, morale is high. It is not necessary for the people to have a clear understanding of the value of their goal—all that is necessary is that they sense or feel its importance. It seems clear that the development of morale centers around the process of defining and forming the goal and around the cultivation of the sense of common effort. The judgment and assessment of morale should be made in terms of this picture.

FORMS OF MORALE

If we view morale from the standpoint of the way in which the group has come to frame the goal of its undertaking, it is possible to distinguish several significant forms. There are three forms that merit discussion.

The first is where the goal is of rational expedience and hence where its achievement is of practical necessity. The demands of a situation may be such as to compel a group of people to stick steadfastly to a common aim because of practical necessity. The bands of pioneers threading their way across the hazardous plains illustrate this form of morale. The defense by crew and passengers on a ship against an attack by pirates was a common instance of this type of morale. A village, community, people, or nation endangered by aggressive attack of outsiders develops usually this kind of morale. Their goal is forced on them by the necessities of their situation; their consecration of effort to it is caused by practical expediency. This kind of morale occurs chiefly in groups whose collective enterprise is one of defense. But it is to be found also in other kinds of situations, as in the case of professional groups whose code requires them to persist in certain tasks despite unfavorable and adverse conditions. Doctors, soldiers, firemen, nurses, bandits, policemen, sailors, and miners may carry out a hazardous collective undertaking solely because its performance is conceived by them as something that has to be done. These various instances suggest, then, that the goal is one of practical necessity. The fact that the goal has a practical or expedient character does not mean that the morale need be low or feeble. If the goal is regarded as of high necessity, the intention and determination of the group to attain it may be very firm, and the sense of mutual responsibility in this task may be great.

This form of morale has its own unique character, and its formation is through means quite different from those in the other two forms of morale which I will shortly discuss. Where it is necessary to form practical morale consciously, it has to be done by making clear to people their situation and interpreting their common position and duty in such a way that the task is viewed as one of practical necessity. The beating of tom-toms, the resort to stratagems, the reliance on emotional appeals, and the evocation of religious sanctions are essentially irrelevant. Instead, the method is one of intelligent interpretation.

This form of morale has the advantage of not suffering from illusion. However, certain disadvantageous features should be noted. It is lacking in the dynamic impulsion that comes when the goal has a transcendental character. Further, the morale is likely to decay when the practical necessity of the goal is no longer felt, or if the successful attainment of the goal seems increasingly certain.

A second form of morale which can be distinguished develops around a romantic goal. The goal is colored with a variety of emotional and imaginative qualities which make it appealing, magnetic, and glorious. These qualities may stand for such diverse things as gain, loot, booty, riches, prestige, power, adventure, achievement, a new position in society, or a new social order. The El Dorado in the case of bands of Spanish adventurers, the recapture of the Holy Land in the case of the Crusaders, the prospect of loot in the case of predatory nomads, the prospect of power and glory in the instance of a band of political adventurers, the picture of international prestige and influence in a nationalistic movement, and the vision of a millennial order in the case of revolutionary movements—such are instances of romantic goals.

It is clear that the morale developed in such collective enterprises is significantly different from that where the goal is of practical necessity. It occurs usually in expansionist and aggressive collective enterprises. Because the goal stands for new achievement, the spirit of people is enlivened. They form a new, elevated conception of themselves or reaffirm previous exalted self-conceptions. The goal acquires a transcendental nature and yields a dynamic impulsion. In the development of the romantic goal or in the formation of the kind of morale that corresponds to it there is a legitimate place for myth creation and illusory coloration. The goal must be overvalued in the sense of having a character which numbs people to practical consequences and to ordinary private judgments. In deliberate effort to form such a kind of morale, emphasis must be given to the depiction of the romantic certainties and opportunities of the future—not to the practical necessities of the present.

The third and perhaps the most vital form of morale arises when the goal is sacred. The goal represents the primary as well as the ultimate value in life; its achievement becomes a matter of irrevocable duty and of divine injunction. As one would suspect, this type of morale is to be found most noticeably in the case of religious sects and movements. From the early Christian bands down to the contemporary Jehovah's Witnesses there have been innumerable instances of sectarian groups showing the most dogged persistence in the face of ridicule, punishment, hardship, deprivation, assault, and loss of life. This attachment to a sacred objective may be found also in the case of certain reform movements—more frequently in the case of revolutionary parties. It may arise in other groups—even in a national or racial people. Apparently, it is the type of morale in present-day Japan.

The rudiments of morale where the goal is sacred are easily

discernible. They exist in the form of a set of convictions and a set of myths. Since the goal is sacred, people have a conviction of its supreme rectitude which renders them impervious to critical reflection upon its character or value. Since the goal is sensed as supremely perfect and accordingly in harmony with the true nature of the universe, people are convinced that its attainment is inevitable. Obstacles, delays, reversals, defeats, and frustrations become merely the occasion for renewed effort just because ultimate success is bound to occur. Finally, there is the conviction of being intrusted with a sacred mission. Because of the supreme value of the goal, because of the divine sanction which it implies, the people attached to the goal feel a sacred responsibility for its realization. They have a cause. They feel themselves to be a select group, especially chosen to execute a transcendental mission. With such convictions and self-conceptions a group is likely to develop an amazing determination in its quest and a striking cohesion in its ranks.

It is clear that the development of the sacred goal and the formation of morale corresponding to it are different from that of the practical goal or the romantic goal. The method is fundamentally the reaffirmation of myths and the fortification of a fixed conception which the people have of their destiny.

These three types of morale—the practical, the romantic, and the sacred—seem to me to be the fundamental forms. In any given instance of collective enterprise all three types may be present, with different people in the group framing the goal in different ways. However, it is almost certain that one of the types will be dominant—dominant to the point of being almost exclusive.

It should be realized that each type requires a special soil in which to grow—a soil set by the traditional background of the people, their customary practice and their current position. To seek to foster one of these forms of morale in an unfavorable setting is likely to be fruitless. The methods of cultivating practical morale are likely to be disintegrative in a group which is nurturing a romantic or sacred goal. The methods of romantic and sacred morale are likely to fall flat in a group organized around a goal of essential expediency.

In the light of this discussion we can turn to some consideration of morale in the United States in the present war.

MORALE IN AMERICA

Morale in this country in the present war seems clearly to be of the first type which I have considered—that which is organized around a goal of practical necessity.

The background for our morale was none too propitious. The unfavorable circumstances are still vivid in our memory and so will require little more than mere mention. The organization of our national life on the basis of interest groups exerting constant and numerous pressures would not suggest an easy formation of a joint goal and spirit of co-operation. The existence of conflicts between races, between the native population and minority groups, between labor and industrialists, between various economy blocs, between political groupings, and between alignments on New Deal legislation suggests an unfavorable prospect. The disillusionment following in the wake of the first World War, the presence of a substantial pacifistic philosophy, especially in youths, and the vigorous presentation of a traditional isolationist position were not encouraging factors. The fact that participating in the war had become a bitter issue of the first magnitude indicates further the peculiar background out of which morale would have to be formed. There was practically nothing in the situation that would favor the formation of a romantic or sacred goal. However, the attack on Pearl Harbor following upon an increasing apprehension and suspicion of Axis intentions definitely set our war effort as a matter of practical necessity.

This, I think, represents the state of American attitude and the temper of American feeling with reference to our war effort. We are in the war, and necessity requires us to win it. The typical view is, "Let's get it over with." It is about the only common view and feeling among American people, and it points to a goal of essential expediency. The winning of the war is a terminal end. The effort to get the American people to view this goal in a romantic or sacred way has been markedly unfruitful. The evidence is all too convincing that the American people do not hearken to the urgings that the war should be won to establish a new order of life or to extend and materialize an ideal philosophy. They are not animated by the sense of a cause, of engaging in a crusade, of carrying out a sacred mission; or of affirming new conceptions of themselves in terms of glory, prestige, power, or esteemed position. Scattered voices, to be sure, speak out for such sacred or romantic conceptions, and individuals, here and there, envision such goals. But their views do not seem to represent the way in which the American people sense and feel their objective. For them the winning of the war is a necessary job that has to be done.

In characterizing American morale in this way, there is no impugning of the genuine character of patriotic sentiment. Indeed, it is because of the high value placed on the nation, on what it stands for, and on what it implies in individual life that the winning of the war becomes a matter of practical necessity. There is no question as to the existence of a sense of duty and of a willingness of co-operation. Morale organized around a goal of essential expediency has these features. This type of morale, as suggested in previous remarks, may be exceedingly firm: the spirit of determination may be profound and the spirit of co-operation may be unquestioned. The only point which I wish to stress is that the collective enterprise is organized primarily on the principle of essential and reasoned necessity, and adjustment is made to it chiefly on this basis.

This principle indicates the framework in which morale is formed in this country and sets the line along which conscious efforts to foster morale must move. Fundamentally, the task is that of sustaining the realization that the winning of the war is a necessity and of making and keeping *clear* what is jointly required for this purpose. The generation of emotional enthusiasm, the weaving of a veil of sublimity around the enterprise, the cultivation of myths, or the glorification of gains to be achieved may serve accessory uses, but they do not represent, in my judgment, the central line along which our morale is being formed.

With this understanding of the type of our morale and the principle around which it centers, we can turn to a series of questions, of which the first will be: What is the state of our morale?

The answer to this question is obviously a matter of judgment. So far there are no devices that measure precisely the disposition of people to act together toward a given collective goal. We can only judge this as reasonably as possible.

As we approach this problem it is important to realize a point suggested earlier—that it is possible for a collective enterprise, even of huge dimensions, to be carried on with a minimum of intense attachment to a goal or heightened spirit of co-operation. This may be true in a measure in our country—I do not say that it is true. It is conceivable that our equipment, skills, organization, size, and power are providing a momentum that is carrying on the collective effort without much demand on collective determination or collective support. It is possible, though highly doubtful, that the war might be fought through to a successful conclusion without a high order of morale among people in general. I mention this merely to indicate that the efficiency of collective effort, while it usually points to high morale, is no necessary sign of it. There is always an amount of habituation in a collective enterprise—a participation in the swing of things that is naturally given, and taken for granted, without implying strong collective determination.

Accordingly, the successful carrying-on of joint activity and the signs or indices thereof need not betoken a high order of morale. Purchase of government bonds, liberal contributions to charitable enterprises serving the war, obedience to draft legislation, acceptance of rationing and other restrictions, acceptance of high taxation, increased production and increased conservation—all these are undeniable signs of efficient group functioning but not necessarily of high morale. I wish to be painfully clear here. I do not mean that such activities imply hypocrisy but merely that in themselves they are no certain indication of a strong collective intention to achieve a goal. Nor, as is shortly to be explained, is a deficiency in such activities, under certain circumstances, a sign of low morale.

The real test of morale, as asserted before, is the ability to persist in effort in the face of obstacle and adversity. The demonstrated willingness of the people to endure hardships, suffer deprivations, make sacrfices, and assimilate reversals and still persist in their effort is the true sign of morale. The extent to which the various activities mentioned above—purchase of bonds, etc.—represent significant deprivations and sacrifices, I am not able to judge. Further, it is not possible to say with certainty how willingly the American people would undergo more profound and vital sacrifices as in the case of a lengthy war, or serious defeats of our armed forces, or dubious prospects of victory. Personally, I believe that morale would be high, just as I believe that the various forms of war participation mentioned above do point to a good morale.

I believe this to be so because of the type of morale which we have—that centering around a goal of practical necessity. Much of the indicatory action mentioned—purchase of bonds, acceptance of rationing restrictions, response to draft rules, increased industrial production, etc.—may have occurred as a result of emotional enthusiasm or as mere acquiescence in a collective program. It seems, however, to have arisen much more from a feeling and understanding that it was required in the war effort. It is conceived of, and accepted, in terms of a practical action *necessary* for the winning of the war. Where such realization is made clear there seems to have been successful response. Where demands made on the citizenry are not clearly understood by them as genuinely essential to the war effort, there may be dilatory and unsatisfactory response. It is in this sense that a deficiency of certain kinds of activities such as bond purchase or rationing may indicate not low morale but instead an inability to relate these actions to the sense of required need. My impression is that our people generally respond wholeheartedly to a major demand made of them when its essential necessity to the winning of the war is made clear. I should expect this in view of the generic type of our morale. I suspect that increasing deprivation or adversity would be taken in stride just because of the likelihood that they would yield a more vivid sense of *needed* behavior in the war effort.

To the extent that the appreciation of the necessity of certain actions for the achievement of the goal is not vivid, one may expect a certain amount of opposition, or token adherence, or compromising on the extent of participation. I think that most of us are familiar with this at different points in our own personal lives. We see it in minor evasions of rationing, in the tempering of contributions, and so forth. Without an imminent sense of the practical demands made by the war effort such behavior is not unexpected or to be taken too seriously as signs of poor morale. It is too much to expect people to have an omnipresent sense of the demands required for the winning of the war. There are areas of public life, accordingly, where desired action has to be guided and secured by law and regulation.

Ultimately, the genuine indications of poor morale where it is organized around a goal of practical necessity are clear: an unwillingness on the part of given people to understand what is required of them by the war necessity or, in the face of such an understanding, a refusal to act on the basis of it. Such unwillingness and refusal indicate a divided group, a rejection of the goal of the group enterprise, the absence of co-operative feeling. An inertia, a reluctance, a hesitation, or a failure to act in a required way must be identified as arising from a refusal to understand the importance of what is asked or a refusal to act on such an understanding, before being taken as a sign of poor morale.

In the light of these ideas we can consider briefly some of the things that are regarded usually as the danger spots in our morale situation. One of them is our alien and minority groups: Italians, Germans, Japanese, East Europeans, and Negroes. A full discussion of the position, attitudes, and conduct of such peoples in this country would have to be lengthy. There is no need of it in this paper. Such peoples on the whole have not endangered our morale. Rather, in many ways we have refused them the full co-operation which they have been willing to give; or we have failed to make clear the importance to them of our winning the war and to grant them an opportunity commensurate to this importance. Despite such a degree of failure, such peoples have co-operated and, as far as I can judge, have never constituted any significant threat.

There has been much concern over how American people would respond to deprivation in the form of rationing, economic dislocation, and taxation. This has been and still is regarded as a source of danger to morale. The evidence from our experience so far is that satisfactory acceptance and adjustment are readily made, once the need of such actions is clearly recognized. I would expect this to be true in the future.

A third danger is presumed to spring from foreign propaganda. This likewise seems to be of little significance. The evidence is quite clear that foreign short-wave broadcasts are listened to by relatively few people, many of whom are animated chiefly by curiosity. Such broadcasts have been declared by some individuals to be the source of rumors and malicious assertions subsequently to be planted in our population by enemy agents. Despite persistent search and interest, I have not been able to get any convincing evidence which would bear out this contention. As far as I can judge, foreign propaganda has not seriously threatened our morale.

A more serious apprehension arises in the case of interest politics and in the operation of strong pressure groups. The picture of the continuing struggles between labor, farmer, and industrialist is disquieting. Strikes, opposition to labor regulation, question of parity prices, pressure for special-interest legislation, the effort to revoke previously enacted laws of welfare, with attendant charge, countercharge, and propaganda, suggest a picture such as Hitler had in mind when he wrote of being able to induce dissension and revolution in this country whenever he wished. Yet, there seems to be no doubt that each major interest and bloc are committed to the winning of the war. The major difficulties seem to arise from a suspicion that one group or the other is seeking to use the war situation to its own advantage— that the winning of the war is to implement a gain by one group at the expense of others. Where such suspicion is absent, cooperation seems to be readily secured. When events occasion a vivid reaffirmation of the need of winning the war, conflict between interest groups seems to subside.

Finally, many thoughtful students are disquieted by the picture of a sizable heterogeneous group suspected to be lukewarm, with attitudes tinged by political bitterness and personal enmity and intrenched in the possession of a significant press. It is felt that this group, keystoned by certain powerful newspapers, is ready to sabotage the war effort when opportunity arises for the satisfaction of personal, clique, and "circle" aims. That there is a certain ground for this apprehension may be true. It seems clear, however, that such a group is controllable by a general attitude in this country of winning the war, that such a group, itself, voices such an endeavor, and that in perilous circumstance where necessity becomes imminent attachment to the war goal would become greater.

In short, it would seem on the whole that American people are united on the basis of winning the war. Their morale remains high and their unity stable to the extent that they believe one another to be seeking this end. The threat to morale seems to arise primarily in suspicions on the part of various groups that others are using the war for special purposes or plan to do so. In a way

American morale seems to be in the nature of a *modus operandi* in the face of a crucial need—threats of the violation of such a relation seem to be the chief source of danger to morale.

In my closing remarks I would like to make some general observations. A morale, such as ours, which is formed around a goal of expedient necessity, implies the suspension of previous aims and values rather than their transformation. The aims and values of individual citizens and special groups are subordinated or shelved. The common expression "for the duration" is more than a convenient circumlocution. It is highly symbolic of our psychology. It signifies the thought and expectation of roughly resuming from the point of interruption occasioned by the war. Under such a psychology tensions, conflicts, and cross-strivings are held in abeyance or in check—they are not resolved. Such a condition is to be expected in collective effort directed to a goal of practical necessity and need not be incompatible with a strong morale. However, to the extent that the goal loses its character of essential need, tensions and conflicts may reappear. If the winning of the war comes to be regarded increasingly as certain, as inevitable on the basis of the effort and organization made, there is likely to be a relaxing of felt need and a resurgence of inner conflict and struggle. Such is a danger likely to be encountered by our country. The condition is one wherein victory and success do not lead, as is often asserted, to increased morale. In the study of many groups whose morale has been of the practical sort my impression is that morale has been strengthened by victory up to the point where ultimate achievement is sensed as uncertain; beyond that point continued success, while not leading necessarily to distintegration of collective effort, is likely to lessen the intensity of the morale.

A further thought refers to the post-war situation. In it our morale may be low or nonexistent. By this I mean that we may not be able to form a collective goal of reconstruction which will command a high order of determined effort and co-operative spirit. The existence of a high morale in the war effort is no sign of the retention of such morale in a different undertaking.

My final remark is a sketchy one referring to the transformation of the morale of a people. It should be clear that morale may change as experience leads to a redefinition of the goal. The change may be great enough to transform the fundamental type of morale. It is possible for practical, romantic, and sacred goals to change into one another—but such a transformation requires profound and unusual experience. Whether the shifts, travail, and intensity of our war experience may induce a change in our type of morale, as they have in certain other nations, cannot be foretold. But the possibility should be mentioned. The emergence of a romantic or sacred goal in our country embodying a new dynamic ideal would have profound consequences for the world order after the war.

BIBLIOGRAPHY

American Journal of Sociology, "National Morale," Vol. XLVII, No. 3 (November, 1941).

Annals of the American Academy of Political Science, July, 1941, and March, 1942.

Farago, L. *German Psychological Warfare.* New York, 1941.

Gillespie, Robert D. *Psychological Effects of War on Citizen and Soldier.* New York, 1942.

Hall, G. Stanley. *Morale: The Supreme Standard of Life and Conduct.* New York, 1920.

Hocking, William E. *Morale and Its Enemies.* New Haven, 1918.

Taylor, Edmund. *The Strategy of Terror.* Boston, 1940.

Watson, G. B. (ed.). *Civilian Morale.* Boston, 1942.

The Nature of Race Prejudice

When one views the recent and present relations between races in different parts of the world he must necessarily be impressed by the magnitude, the tenacity, and the apparent spontaneity of racial prejudice. That it is exceedingly common can scarcely be denied. That it may persist as a chronic attitude over decades of time can be shown by several instances. That it may emerge immediately in new contacts between races can be easily documented, especially in the contacts of whites with other ethnic groups. Indeed, so impressive is its extensiveness, persistency, and apparent spontaneity that many students regard it as inevitable. They believe that it arises from some simple biological tendency—such as an innate aversion of race to race—which is bound to express itself and to dominate race relations.

Interestingly enough, the actual facts of race relations force us to adopt a very different view. For, frequently, racial prejudice may not appear in racial contacts; if present, it may disappear; or, although present, it may not dominate the relations. Instead of thinking of racial prejudice as an invariant and simple matter it must be viewed as a highly variable and complex phenomenon. This is shown, first of all, by the markedly differing character of race relations themselves. There are many instances where members of divergent races may associate in the most amiable and free fashion, intermarrying and erecting no ethnic barriers between them. In other instances there may prevail rigid racial exclusion supported by intense attitudes of discrimination.

Between these extremes there may be other forms of association. Further, the history of any fairly prolonged association between any two ethnic groups usually does not show the continuous existence of any fixed or invariant relation. Instead the association and the attitudes which sustain it usually pass through a variety of forms. The markedly differing and variable nature of race relations should make it clear that racial prejudice is not inevitable or bound to dominate the relations. Even though it be very common and very tenacious it must be recognized as merely one form of ethnic relation. It must or may not be present; and even where present, it usually arises inside of a temporal sequence of relations.

Even more important is the realization that racial prejudice is highly variable itself. Instead of always having the same form, nature, and intensity, it may differ a great deal from time to time and from place to place. A comparison of instances of racial prejudice shows that it may differ in intensity, in quality of feeling, in the views by which it is supported, and in manifestation. The prejudice of the American southerner toward the Negro may be great, but it is recognized by many as being less than that of the South African white toward his colored neighbors. The attitude of prejudice of the gentile toward the Jew has varied in intensity and form from locality to locality and from time to time. Ethnic prejudice may be bitter in one situation and mild in another. The fact that we generally speak of an increase or decrease of prejudice points to its variability. Thus, while prejudice is very real and obtrusive, and while it is permissible to treat it as a type phenomenon, recognition must be taken of its changeable and differing character.

The fact that prejudice is not a constant accompaniment of race relations, and that it is variable in its nature, indicates that it is a product of certain kinds of situations and experiences. Two problems are immediately suggested: (1) what are the situations which give rise to racial prejudice, and (2) what experiences account for the variation in its nature and form. Before discussing these two problems it is advisable to consider briefly the nature of race prejudice and point out some of the features by which it is usually identified.

Race prejudice always exists as a group prejudice directed against another group. This means two important things: (1) it exists as a collective or shared attitude, and (2) it is directed toward a *conceptualized group* or abstract category. Each of these two features requires some explanation. Race prejudice is a collective or shared attitude in the sense that it is held by a number of people, who stimulate one another in the expression of the attitude. Through this form of interaction they build up, sustain, and reinforce the attitude in one another. Through conversation, through the observation of one another's actions, through relating one's experiences, through the expression of one's feelings and emotions before others, through circulating tales, stories and myths, the members of an ethnic group come to build up a common or collectively shared attitude. This shared character of the attitude of racial prejudice raises the interesting question as to how far the attitude is shaped by the intertransmission of experience rather than by direct contact with the group toward which the attitude is directed. All that needs to be indicated here is that its character will differ in accordance with what enters into these collective experiences.

In speaking of race prejudice as directed toward a "conceptualized group" or abstract category, all that is meant is that the object toward which it is directed represents a classification of individuals and so is an abstract category inside of which we conceptually arrange individuals. For example, we may speak of prejudice against the Jew, the Negro or the Oriental; in these cases, the Jew, the Negro, and the Oriental stand respectively for certain large classifications or categories in which we conceptually arrange people. The prejudice exists as an attitude toward the classification or is built up around the conceptualized object which stands for the classification. Or, paradoxically, we may say that the prejudice exists as an attitude toward what is logically an abstraction.[1] The prejudice is manifested against a specific individual by identifying the individual with the conceptualized object and then directing towards him the attitude that one has toward the conceptualized object. Thus one may identify an individual as being *a* Negro, and thus be led to direct towards him the attitude that one has toward *the* Negro. If a Negro successfully disguises himself (as by wearing a turban which gives him the appearance of being a Hindu) so that he is not detected or classified as a Negro, he will escape the attitude which is held toward the Negro. Perhaps all this is obvious; but it is important to recognize that racial prejudice is directed toward a conceptualized object, and that individuals come to bear the brunt of this preju-

[1] This point is of considerable importance because where the oldest of a group attitude is an abstraction it is possible to build up toward it very weird and extreme notions which may vary widely from the facts of concrete experience.

dice to the extent to which they are identified with the conceptualized object.

The two features which we have just discussed—the fact that the attitude is a product of collective experience, and that it is directed toward a conceptualized object—are intimately interrelated. Generally we may say (a) that the content of the collective experience determines the form and nature of the conceptualized object, and (b) that the conceptualized object becomes a framework inside of which collective experience may take place. Let us explain each of these two statements. With reference to the first statement it should be pointed out, first of all, that the content of collective experience of one group will determine what classifications they will make of other peoples and so what conceptualized objects they will build up. This gives to the conceptualized objects a somewhat arbitrary character. Thus the American gentile will ordinarily have a concept of the Jew which takes no recognition of the keen conceptual differentiations that the Jews are liable to make among themselves, such as between Spanish Jews, German Jews, Russian Jews, or Polish Jews. Or the American white may conceive the Negro as consisting of individuals who have any trace of Negro ancestry, whereas what the Frenchman means by the Negro is likely to be a very much narrower group. Many other instances could be given; but the illustrations will suffice to show that the particular classifications which are made or which are selected out may vary considerably. The variation seems to be due to the differences of group experience. Not only is the form of the conceptualized object determined by collective experience but the way in which the object is conceived is determined by this experience. This should be self-evident. Southern whites with their experiences during slavery and following the civil war formed a conception of the Negro which was necessarily different from that developed by the whites in Brazil, where the line of experience was significantly different.

While the conceptualized object is formed, shaped, and colored by the experiences of the group, it is equally true that the conceptualized object orders, directs, and constrains the experiences of the group. So we come to explain statement (b) mentioned above. When a concept of an ethnic group is formed and that group is conceived in a certain way, the concept and the conception will influence to a large extent the kind of experiences that people will have in their association with members of that ethnic group. They will subject this association to the form and framework that is laid down by their concept and conceptions of the ethnic group; accordingly, the kind of experiences they have with members of another ethnic group is largely coerced by this framework. The southern white in his contact with a Negro acts toward him on the basis of a pretty fixed conception that he has of him, expects from him a certain kind of behavior, is sensitized to perceive certain actions, is prepared to interpret these actions in well-defined ways, and is ready to respond emotionally in a fixed manner. This will suggest how the conceptualized object which is had of a race may largely predetermine the collective experiences that come from association with members of that race. Reasons will be given later to suggest why this predetermination of experience by the conceptualized object may become rigid and extreme, and under what conditions it may be slight and malleable. Here it is sufficient merely to point out that collective experience and conceptualization interact to control one another, and to suggest that this mutual control may become so tight that they become essentially one, or their natures identical.

The experiences of ethnic group A with ethnic group B, built up as they are largely in terms of the interaction inside of group A, will reflect themselves in the conception which group A has of group B; this conception will largely control the nature of the experiences which the members of group A have with group B, and the way in which they digest these experiences in their interaction with one another. The history of race prejudice is a history of the interaction between concept and experience. This is what is involved, then, in the statement that race prejudice is a case of prejudice of one group against another group.[2]

It is time now to consider what is peculiar to the attitude of racial prejudice—what distinguishes it from other kinds of racial attitudes. The usual tendency is to regard this attitude as simple

[2]It is clear that whether an indivdiual generalizes his distasteful or thwarting experiences into an attitude of prejudice against a group depends largely on the presence of conceptualized objects in his culture. An American white may have highly distasteful experiences with one or several red-headed people: he is very unlikely to develop an attitude of prejudice against the "red-head," because in American culture there is no conceptualization of the "red-head" which would encourage this. The same kind of experiences with Negroes might easily lead

or unitary, as if it were made up of a single feeling such as dislike or hatred. Such a view, however, is impossible and cannot be squared with facts. Admittedly, the chief feeling in racial prejudice is usually a feeling of dislike or an impulse of aversion; but it is a mistake to regard such a feeling or impulse as the only one, or even necessarily always the main one. Instead, racial prejudice is made up of a variety of feelings and impulses which in different situations enter into the attitude in differing combinations and differing proportions. Hatred, dislike, resentment, distrust, envy, fear, feelings of obligation, possessive impulses, secret curiosities, sexual interests, destructive impulses, guilt—these are some of the feelings and impulses which may enter into racial prejudice and which in their different combinations give it a differing character. Some of these feelings and impulses may be vivid and easily identified; others are obscure; and still others may be present without their presence being realized. We are forced, I think, to realize that the attitude of racial prejudice is constituted and sustained by a variety of impulses and feelings, and that it gets its peculiar complexion from the peculiar nature of these impulses and feelings. In this way we can account for the differences in racial prejudice that have already been mentioned. The impulses and feelings that come to be embodied in a given instance of racial prejudice have been induced and shaped by the past and present experiences of the given ethnic group. From this point of view we can regard race prejudice as a medium for the expression of various feelings and impulses, some of which may be the consequence of experiences that have no reference to the group against which the prejudice is manifested.

The complexity of the constituent and sustaining elements of an attitude of race prejudice makes it difficult to explain exhaustively the experiences and situations that give rise to racial prejudice. Yet, certain of the more important lines of origin can be pointed out. One of them, undoubtedly, is the general ethno-

---

him to form a prejudiced attitude against the Negro: in this instance the form of conceptualization would easily permit and justify such a generalization of experience. Further, even if one does develop an attitude of prejudice against a conceptualized group built up out of his own experience it is likely to be weak and ineffective unless shared by his fellows. One is largely sustained in his attitude by the reinforcement which he gets from his fellows.

centrism of groups, showing itself in some aversion to strange and peculiar ways of living, and in a feeling of the inherent superiority of one's own group. There seems to be little doubt that many actions of a strange and alien group may appear uncouth and sometimes repulsive and lead to the formation of an unfavorable impression which may come to be built up into a collective attitude. Such an attitude because it springs from the perception of actions which seem to be offensive and occasionally disgusting may get rooted in the antipathies of people. In addition the general feeling of the superiority of one's own group leads easily to the tendency to disparage other groups, to discriminate against them, and to take advantage of them. There seems to be little doubt that ethnocentrism, in these two phases, is a primitive tendency of group life; as such it must be reckoned with as a nucleus around which an attitude of racial prejudice may develop. And the greater the ethnocentrism, the greater is the likelihood that it may lead to group prejudice. Something of this is to be seen in the frequency with which racial prejudice appears among expanding imperialistic peoples.

Yet, however important ethnocentrism may be as a factor in racial prejudice, it does not seem to be the decisive factor. Of more importance is what amounts to a primitive tribal tendency in the form of fear of an attack, of displacement, or of annihilation. This is suggested by the nature of the situations where racial prejudice is usually most pronounced and serious. Racial prejudice is usually most acute in a social situation which has the following characteristics.

1. The two ethnic groups live together in some degree. The subordinate ethnic group is accepted to some extent, in the sense that it is associated with and depended upon by the dominant ethnic group. The relation between the two groups may be one of mere accommodation or symbiosis, but in any event, the two groups live together inside of a common territory as parts of a unitary society.

2. The acceptance of the subordinate ethnic group, however, is limited and involves various kinds of exclusion and discrimination. There are certain privileges and opportunities which its members arc regarded as not being entitled to. In this sense, the subordinate ethnic group is assigned to an inferior status or, as is frequently said, it is expected to keep to a certain place.

3. The dominant ethnic group has a fear that the subordinate group is not keeping to its place but threatens to claim the opportunities and privileges from which it has been excluded. As such, it is sensed and felt as a threat to the status, security, and welfare of the dominant ethnic group.

It is in a social situation with these three features that racial prejudice seems to have its primary setting. As the saying goes, as long as the subordinate ethnic group keeps to its place, prejudice toward it is at a minimum. Indications of getting out of its place are felt by the dominant ethnic group as an attack and invoke primitive feelings of tribal protection and preservation. Some of the areas of exclusion have a particularly strong symbolic significance, so that entrance into such areas is an especially acute sign of what is felt to be unwarranted and dangerous aggression and attack. Unaccustomed economic competition ranks high here; also entrance into the more intimate sphere of exclusion. What adds peculiarity to this feeling of being attacked is the fact that the dominant and subordinate ethnic groups, as mentioned above, are usually living together. This means that the attack seems to come from an "inner enemy;" the resulting apprehension seems to be of peculiar complexity—more abiding, more perplexing, more worrisome and more unstable. The fact that the threatening group must be accepted yields an anomalous and instable character to the feelings of apprehension.

The greater the threat which is *felt,* the greater is likely to be the prejudice. The size of the subordinate ethnic group, its degree of militancy, its degree of clannishness, and the extent of its claims are factors which are likely to determine the extent of the threat. On the side of the dominant ethnic group, the degree of ethnocentrism, the degree of tribal solidarity, the rigidity of the idea of its own status, and the tightness of the lines of exclusion which it lays down are factors which increase the likelihood of its construing actions as an attack upon it.

The foregoing discussion should make clear the general character of racial prejudice and the lines along which it is formed. If ethnic contacts are attended by feelings of ethnocentrism, and if the ethnic group in the dominant position feels that its common status is insecure and is under the threat of an attack by a subordinate ethnic group, prejudice seems to be the inevitable result. Ethnocentrism helps to set and sustain patterns of social exclusion. Failure to observe these patterns by the excluded group are felt as threats and attacks to tribal status, security, and welfare. Feelings of aversion, fear, and hostility—all more or less in a state of suspension—seems to be the result.

It cannot be too strongly emphasized that the formation of racial prejudice is not an immediate or inevitable matter but that, instead, it is a product of collective experience, and is dependent upon the extent to which this collective experience fits the conditions which have been specified. The initial conditions of ethnic contact may or may not be conducive to the development of racial prejudice; if the framework of ethnocentrism is not laid down along ethnic lines, racial prejudice is not likely to get started. (As in the case of the early expansion of Mohammedanism which, while involving extensive ethnic contacts, was organized on the basis of *religious* ethnocentrism and gave rise to religious prejudices. Further, the incidents of experience in the association between ethnic groups may or may not lead a dominant group to feel that it is being threatened.

When specific instances of racial prejudice are traced through it will usually be found that the prejudice has followed upon a series of experiences or incidents which are resented by a dominant ethnic group and construed as affronts, unwarranted aggressions and attacks—usually as signs of a possibly more abiding and more threatening attack. The history of race prejudice could be written (and would have to be written) in terms of such incidents, especially the more exciting ones. For it is such incidents that stir people, arouse feelings, and initiate that interchange of experience that we can speak of metaphorically as a process of collective digestion. Such collective experiences yield the new meaning and content that become fused into the "conceptualized object" which the one ethnic group has made of the other. Since these collective experiences are an outgrowth of primitive and deep seated feelings, it is not surprising that the conceptualized object becomes emotional and fixed in nature, and that in acquiring such a form it exercises a coercive control over subsequent collective experience.[3] A social situation favoring (and attended

---

[3]It should be realized that an attitude of racial prejudice, once formed, is transportable. It may be brought into a situation where it has not previously existed; or communicated to those whose own experiences have not given rise

by) a run of incidents, especially of a critical nature, which make a dominant ethnic group *feel* that its position is being jeopardized and its security seriously threatened easily conduces to tenacious racial prejudice. A very powerful complex of feelings and sentiments may develop, under the influence of collective experience, and become fused into the conceptualized image of an ethnic group.[4]

It is not surprising that the attitude of racial prejudice should become deeper embedded in the individual as the collective feeling becomes more intense and the conceptualized object more emotionally forbidding. It may even get deeply rooted in the individual's antipathies so that the individual's organism rebels at even the thought of entering into certain kinds of relations—especially intimate touch relations—with members of the other ethnic group. Such antipathies seem to be in the nature of strong defense reactions which seem *to be symbolic* of the collective feelings of exclusiveness and fear of invasion. Indeed, although it might seem incredible, the primitive feeling of tribal preservation may become transferred to the antipathies so that some of them become more important than existence itself. The Southern whites would probably prefer the thought of annihilation to the thought of their women becoming the consorts of Negroes.

The analysis of racial prejudice which has been made should throw some light on the viciousness of behavior in which racial prejudice may at times express itself, and on the ease with which it may become a scapegoat mechanism. Since the attitude of

---

to it. In this way, racial prejudice may occur in situations which do not have the features which we have been discussing.

[4]It is appropriate to note that the conditions that give rise to prejudice may likewise give rise to prejudice in other kinds of groups. Many instances are provided in American history, especially in the case of European immigrant groups. Usually, such groups were regarded as inferior by the native whites: their effort to improve their economic and social position was frequently regarded as undue encroachment and as a threat pressing themselves in discrimination and occasionally in violence. What is of crucial significance in such instances, as students have frequently noted, is that members of such a group which is incurring prejudice, in not being ethnically distinct, may avoid much prejudice and move into other groups. Group prejudice is difficult to maintain under such conditions. Where prejudice arises against people who are racially distinct and recognizable, the prejudice is more persistent and less easily escaped. This seems to be the chief reason for the greater tenacity of race prejudice as against other forms of group prejudice.

prejudice is rooted in a primitive feeling of tribal preservation and may, under the influence of historical experience, become highly symbolical of such a tribal position, it is not surprising that in response to a critical incident, it might express itself in vicious and brutal behavior. Deep rooted fears, restrained and simmering hatreds, strong defense feelings, and strongly felt antipathies may all gain an expression at such a time. Indeed, many other feelings and impulses which enter into the structure of the attitude—especially the more unconscious ones—may gain expression at this time. (It is well to remember, as stated previously, that a variety of impulses and feelings may enter into the attitude of racial prejudice as a result of the collective experiences of the group.)

Light is also thrown on the ease with which racial prejudice may become a scapegoat mechanism. Mention has already been made of the fact that the interexchanging of experience between members of an ethnic group may be more influential in the formation of their attitude than actual experience with the group toward which prejudice is developed. This makes ample room for the development of myths and for the focusing on a given race of feelings that have nothing intrinsically to do with it. In this way the attitude toward an ethnic group may come to be the carrier of feelings and impulses aroused in other areas of experience. This can be done with special ease in the case of race prejudice, since the ethnic group is sensed as an "inner enemy," as a more or less persistent threat to vital security and existence. At times of critical distress, disturbance, or calamity it is easy to hold it responsible for the insecurity and woes that are experienced.

Before ending the discussion, some attention may be given to the interesting problem of the breaking down of racial prejudice. First of all, it should be noted again that racial prejudice is not inevitable in ethnic contacts. Racial prejudice may not even appear; or if it does appear, it may not take root; or, if it does take root, it may not grow. All depends upon the nature of the social situation and upon the incidents which occur; for these will influence the collective experience of the group and the resulting conceptualizing of the racial object. In the association of races, first of all, it is quite possible for people to classify one another on other bases than that of ethnic makeup in making their important group differentiations. In this event, the important group opposi-

tions may easily cut across ethnic lines. This is to be seen historically in religious movements, in nationality opposition, and in
some present day radical movements. Indeed, it might be declared that the widespread racial prejudice that exists in the world
today is but a historical accident; that it is an expression of a historical epoch in which there is present at the same time heightened
ethnocentrism on the part of groups that happen to be *ethnically
distinct,* and a vast increase in contacts between such groups. Racial prejudice seems to have followed definitely in the swing toward modern nationalistic expansion. It may happen in the future, as it has at times in the past, that ethnic makeup will be of
little meaning in the important group classifications that people
make of one another, and consequently in the "tribal units" with
which they identify themselves.

Where racial prejudice already exists, its disappearance or
mitigation seems to turn on the condition that the subordinate
ethnic group is no longer felt as a threat. This may be brought
about in a number of ways. The subordinate ethnic group may
keep fastly to an assigned status or to what the dominant group
regards as its proper place; hence it is no longer felt as a threat. Or
the subordinate group may retire into a segregated position, reducing its contacts with the dominant group, and building up a
bilateral society. Both of these adjustments have gone on, and are
going on today, in different parts of the world; but they seem to
be only temporary appeasements—under modern conditions of
communication and contact such adjustments can scarcely be expected to solidify or endure. The other way by which the subordinate group is no longer felt as a threat is by the dominant group
changing its conceptualization of the subordinate groups, so that
the group no longer is regarded as offensive and unacceptable. To
the extent to which the group is regarded as acceptable and as-
similable, to this extent it ceases to be regarded as a threat. Where
the acceptance is full, the meaning of the original ethnic classification has disappeared.

Modern intentional efforts to break down racial prejudice
are usually always along this third line, that is they try to change
the *idea* which people of one race have toward another. We see
this effort in the case of some churches, some educational agencies, and some humanitarian groups and individuals, all of whom

try to point out the injustice and absurdity of a prevailing view of racial prejudice. The importance of such efforts is not to be minimized, but it is questionable whether they do have or can have much influence where racial prejudice is pronounced, or where the "conceptualized racial object" is strongly set. For the prejudice is certain to be rooted in the antipathies; and these do not change easily even though it be shown that the conceptualization is false and unjustifiable. Efforts to have members of different races appreciate their common human character by entering into personal contact are likely to be more fruitful; for where people have an opportunity to identify themselves with one another and to learn each other's personal experiences, a collective conceptualization is difficult to maintain. But even such efforts are limited in possibility and run counter again to antipathies. Any profound change in antipathies is likely to come only as a result of a new body of collective experience built up either around new issues in which the ethnic factor is of no import, or based on a shift in the social scene (such as an extensive population change) in which races are brought into new forms of interdependency.

In closing this paper I wish merely to note that no discussion has been given in it to the topic of counter-prejudice—the defensive prejudice of the subordinate ethnic group against the dominant one. In many ways this counter-prejudice is more complicated, interesting and important than direct racial prejudice. It has been little studied.

Race Prejudice as
a Sense of Group Position*

In this paper I am proposing an approach to the study of race prejudice quite different from that which dominates contemporary scholarly thought on this topic. My thesis is that race prejudice exists basically in a sense of group position rather than in a set of feelings which members of one racial group have toward the members of another racial group. This different way of viewing race prejudice shifts study and analysis from a preoccupation with feelings as lodged in individuals to a concern with the relationship of racial groups. It also shifts scholarly treatment away from individual lines of experience and focuses interest on the collective process by which a racial group comes to define and redefine another racial group. Such shifts, I believe, will yield a more realistic and penetrating understanding of race prejudice.

There can be little question that the rather vast literature on race prejudice is dominated by the idea that such prejudice exists fundamentally as a feeling or set of feelings lodged in the individual. It is usually depicted as consisting of feelings such as antipathy, hostility, hatred, intolerance, and aggressiveness. Accordingly, the task of scientific inquiry becomes two-fold. On one hand, there is a need to identify the feelings which make up race prejudice—to see how they fit together and how they are supported by other psychological elements, such as mythical beliefs. On the other hand, there is need of showing how the feeling complex has come into being. Thus, some scholars trace the complex feelings back chiefly to innate dispositions; some trace it to personality composition, such as authoritarian personality; and others regard the feelings of prejudice as being formed through social experience. However different may be the contentions re-

*Read at the dedication of the Robert E. Park Building, Fisk University, March, 1955.

garding the makeup of racial prejudice and the way in which it may come into existence, these contentions are alike in locating prejudice in the realm of individual feeling. This fact is clearly true in the work of psychologists, psychiatrists, and social psychologists, and it tends to be predominantly the case in the work of sociologists.

Unfortunately, this customary way of viewing race prejudice overlooks and obscures the fact that race prejudice is fundamentally a matter of relationship between racial groups. A little reflective thought should make this very clear. Race prejudice presupposes, necessarily, that racially prejudiced individuals think of themselves as belonging to a given racial group. It means, also, that they assign to other racial groups those against whom they are prejudiced. Thus, logically and actually, a scheme of racial identification is necessary as a framework for racial prejudice. Moreover, such identification involves the formation of an image or a conception of one's own racial group and of another racial group, inevitably in terms of the relationship of such groups. To fail to see that racial prejudice is a matter (a) of the racial identification made of oneself and of others, and (b) of the way in which the identified groups are conceived in relation to each other is to miss what is logically and actually basic. One should keep forever in mind that people have to come to identify themselves as belonging to a racial group; such identification is not spontaneous or inevitable but is a result of experience. Further, one must realize that the kind of picture which a racial group forms of itself and the kind of picture which it may form of others are similarly products of experience. Hence, such pictures are variable, just as the lines of experience which produce them are variable.

The body of feelings which scholars, today, are so inclined to regard as constituting the substance of race prejudice is actually a resultant of the way in which given racial groups conceive of themselves and of others. A basic understanding of race prejudice must be sought in the process by which racial groups form images of themselves and of others. This process, as I hope to show, is fundamentally *a collective process*. It operates chiefly through the public media in which individuals who are accepted as the spokesmen of a racial group characterize publicly another racial group. To characterize another racial group is, by opposition, to define one's own group. This is equivalent to placing the two groups in relation to each other or defining their positions vis-à-vis each other. It is the *sense of social position* emerging from this collective process of characterization which provides the basis of race prejudice. The following discussion will consider important facets of this matter.

I would like to begin by discussing several of the important feelings that enter into race prejudice. This discussion will reveal how fundamentally racial feelings point to and depend on a positional arrangement of the racial groups. In this discussion I will confine myself to such feelings in the case of a dominant racial group.

There are four basic types of feeling that seem to be always present in race prejudice in the dominant group. They are (1) a feeling of superiority, (2) a feeling that the subordinate race is intrinsically different and alien, (3) a feeling of proprietary claim to certain areas of privilege and advantage, and (4) a fear and suspicion that the subordinate race harbors designs on the prerogatives of the dominant race. A few words about each of these four feelings will suffice.

In race prejudice there is a self-assured feeling on the part of the dominant racial group of being naturally superior or better. This is commonly shown in a disparagement of the qualities of the subordinate racial group. Condemnatory or debasing traits, such as laziness, dishonesty, greediness, unreliability, stupidity, deceit and immorality, are usually imputed to it. The second feeling, that the subordinate race is an alien and fundamentally different stock, is likewise always present. "They are not of our kind" is a common way in which this is likely to be expressed. It is this feeling that reflects, justifies, and promotes the social exclusion of the subordinate racial group. The combination of these two feelings of superiority and of distinctiveness can easily give rise to feelings of aversion and even antipathy. But in themselves they do not form prejudice. We have to introduce the third and fourth types of feeling.

The third feeling, the sense of proprietary claim, is of crucial importance. It is the feeling on the part of the dominant group of being entitled to either exclusive or prior rights in many important areas of life. The range of such exclusive or prior claims may be wide, covering: the ownership of property such as choice lands and sites; the right to certain jobs, occupations, or professions; the claim to certain kinds of industry or lines of business; the claim to certain positions of control and decision-making as in government and law; the right to exclusive membership in given institutions such as schools, churches and recreational institutions; the claim to certain positions of social prestige and to the display of the symbols and accoutrements of these positions; and the claim to certain areas of intimacy and privacy. The feeling of such proprietary claims is exceedingly strong in race prejudice. Again, however, this feeling even in combination with the feeling of superiority and the feeling of distinctiveness does not explain race prejudice. These three feelings are present frequently in societies showing no prejudice, as in certain forms of feudalism, in caste relations, in societies of chiefs and commoners, and under many settled relations of conquerors and conquered. Where claims are solidified into a structure which is accepted or respected by all, there seems to be no group prejudice.

The remaining feeling essential to race prejudice is a fear or apprehension that the subordinate racial group is threatening, or will threaten, the position of the dominant group. Thus, acts or suspected acts that are interpreted as an attack on the natural superiority of the dominant group, or an intrusion into their sphere of group exclusiveness, or an encroachment on their area of proprietary claim are crucial in arousing and fashioning race prejudice. These acts mean "getting out of place."

It should be clear that these four basic feelings of race prejudice definitely refer to a positional arrangement of the racial groups. The feeling of superiority places the subordinate people *below;* the feeling of alienation places them *beyond;* the feeling of proprietary claim excludes them from the prerogatives of position; and the fear of encroachment is an emotional recoil from the endangering of group position. As these features suggest, the positional relation of the two racial groups is crucial in race prejudice. The dominant group is not concerned with the subordinate group as such but it is deeply concerned with its position vis-à-vis the subordinate group. This is epitomized in the key and universal expression that a given race is all right in "its place." The sense of group position is the very heart of the relation of the dominant to the subordinate group. It supplies the dominant group with its framework of perception, its standard of judgment, its patterns of sensitivity, and its emotional proclivities.

It is important to recognize that this sense of group position transcends the feelings of the individual members of the dominant group, giving such members a common orientation that is not otherwise to be found in separate feelings and views. There is likely to be considerable difference between the ways in which the individual members of the dominant group think and feel about the subordinate group. Some may feel bitter and hostile, with strong antipathies, with an exalted sense of superiority and with a lot of spite; others may have charitable and protective feelings, marked by a sense of piety and tinctured by benevolence; others may be condescending and reflect mild contempt; and others may be disposed to politeness and considerateness with no feelings of truculence. These are only a few of many different patterns of feeling to be found among members of the dominant racial group. What gives a common dimension to them is a sense of the social position of their group. Whether the members be humane or callous, cultured or unlettered, liberal or reactionary, powerful or impotent, arrogant or humble, rich or poor, honorable or dishonorable—all are led by virtue of sharing the sense of group position to similar individual positions.

The sense of group position is a general kind of orientation. It is a general feeling without being reducible to specific feelings such as hatred, hostility, or antipathy. It is also a general understanding without being composed of any set of specific beliefs. On the social psychological side it cannot be equated to a sense of social status as ordinarily conceived, for it refers not merely to vertical positioning but to many other lines of position independent of the vertical dimension. Sociologically it is not a mere reflection of the objective relations between racial groups. Rather, it stands for "what ought to be" rather than for "what is." It is a sense of where the two racial groups *belong*.

In its own way, the sense of group position is a norm and imperative—indeed, a very powerful one. It guides, incites, cows, and coerces. It should be borne in mind that this sense of group position stands for and involves a fundamental kind of group affiliation for the members of the dominant racial group. To the extent that they recognize or feel themselves as belonging to that group they will automatically come under the influence of the sense of position held by that group. Thus, even though given individual members may have personal views and feelings different from the sense of group position, they will have to conjure with the sense of group position held by their racial group. If the sense of position is strong, to act contrary to it is to risk a feeling of self-alienation and to face the possibility of ostracism. I am trying to suggest, accordingly, that the locus of race prejudice is not in the area of individual feeling but in the definition of the respective positions of the racial groups.

The source of race prejudice lies in a felt challenge to this sense of group position. The challenge, one must recognize, may come in many different ways. It may be in the form of an affront to feelings of group superiority; it may be in the form of attempts at familiarity or transgressing the boundary line of group exclusiveness; it may be in the form of encroachment at countless points of proprietary claim; it may be a challenge to power and privilege; it may take the form of economic competition. Race prejudice is a defensive reaction to such challenging of the sense of group position. It consists of the disturbed feelings, usually of marked hostility, that are thereby aroused. As such, race prejudice is a protective device. It functions, however shortsightedly, to preserve the integrity and the position of the dominant group.

It is crucially important to recognize that the sense of group position is not a mere summation of the feelings of position such as might be developed independently by separate individuals as they come to compare themselves with given individuals of the subordinate race. The sense of group position refers to the position of group to group, not to that of individual to individual. Thus, vis-à-vis the subordinate racial group the unlettered individual with low status in the dominant racial group has a sense of group position common to that of the elite of his group. By virtue of sharing this sense of position; such an individual, despite his low status, feels that members of the subordinate group, however distinguished and accomplished, are somehow inferior, alien, and properly restricted in the area of claims. He forms his conception as a representative of the dominant group; he treats individual members of the subordinate group as representative of that group.

An analysis of how the sense of group position is formed

should start with a clear recognition that it is an historical product. It is set originally by conditions of initial contact. Prestige,
power, possession of skill, numbers, original self-conceptions,
aims, designs, and opportunities are a few of the factors that may
fashion the original sense of group position. Subsequent experience in the relation of the two racial groups, especially in the area
of claims, opportunities, and advantages, may mould the sense of
group position in many diverse ways. Further, the sense of group
position may be intensified or weakened, brought to sharp focus
or dulled. It may be deeply entrenched and tenaciously resist
change for long periods of time. Or it may never take root. It
may undergo quick growth and vigorous expansion, or it may
dwindle away through slow-moving erosion. It may be firm or
soft, acute or dull, continuous or intermittent. In short, viewed
comparatively, the sense of group position is very variable.

However variable its particular career, the sense of group
position is clearly formed by a running process in which the
dominant racial group is led to define and redefine the subordinate racial group and the relations between them. There are two
important aspects of this process of definition that I wish to
single out for consideration.

First, the process of definition occurs obviously through
complex interaction and communication between the members
of the dominant group. Leaders, prestige bearers, officials, group
agents, dominant individuals, and ordinary laymen present to
one another characterizations of the subordinate group and express their feelings and ideas on the relations. Through talk,
tales, stories, gossip, anecdotes, messages, pronouncements,
news accounts, orations, sermons, preachments, and the like,
definitions are presented and feelings are expressed. In this usually vast and complex interaction separate views run against one
another, influence one another, modify each other, incite one another and fuse together in new forms. Correspondingly, feelings
which are expressed meet, stimulate each other, feed on each
other, intensify each other, and emerge in new patterns. Currents
of view and currents of feeling come into being, sweeping along
to positions of dominance and serving as polar points for the organization of thought and sentiment. If the interaction becomes
increasingly circular and reinforcing, devoid of serious inner opposition, such currents grow, fuse, and become strengthened. It

is through such a process that a collective image of the subordinate group is formed and a sense of group position is set. The evidence of such a process is glaring when one reviews the history of any racial arrangements marked by prejudice.

Such a complex process of mutual interaction with its different lines and degrees of formation gives the lie to the many schemes which would lodge the cause of race prejudice in the makeup of the individual—whether in the form of innate disposition, constitutional makeup, personality structure, or direct personal experience with members of the other race. The collective image and feelings in race prejudice are forged out of a complicated social process in which the individual is himself shaped and organized. The scheme, so popular today, which would trace race prejudice to a so-called authoritarian personality shows a grievous misunderstanding of the simple essentials of the collective process that leads to a sense of group position.

The second important aspect of the process of group definition is that it is necessarily concerned with *an abstract image* of the subordinate racial group. The subordinate racial group is defined as if it were an entity or whole. This entity or whole—like the Negro race, or the Japanese, or the Jews—is necessarily an abstraction, never coming within the perception of any of the senses. While actual encounters are with individuals, the picture formed of the racial group is necessarily of a vast entity which spreads out far beyond such individuals and transcends experience with such individuals. The implications of the fact that the collective image is of an abstract group are of crucial significance. I would like to note four of these implications.

First, the building of the image of the abstract group takes place in the area of the remote and not of the near. It is not the experience with concrete individuals in daily association that gives rise to the definitions of the extended, abstract group. Such immediate experience is usually regulated and orderly. Even where such immediate experience is disrupted the new definitions which are formed are limited to the individuals involved. The collective image of the abstract group grows up not by generalizing from experiences gained in close, first-hand contacts but through the transcending characterizations that are made of the group as an entity. Thus, one must seek the central stream of definition in those areas where the dominant group as such is characterizing the subordinate group as such. This occurs in the "public arena" wherein the spokesmen appear as representatives and agents of the dominant group. The extended public arena is constituted by such things as legislative assemblies, public meetings, conventions, the press, and the printed word. What goes on in this public arena attracts the attention of large numbers of the dominant group and is felt as the voice and action of the group as such.

Second, the definitions that are forged in the public arena center, obviously, above matters that are felt to be of major importance. Thus, we are led to recognize the crucial role of the "big event" in developing a conception of the subordinate racial group. The event that seems momentous, that touches deep sentiments, that seems to raise fundamental questions about relations, and that awakens strong feelings of identification with one's racial group is the kind of event that is central in the formation of the racial image. Here, again, we note the relative unimportance of the huge bulk of experiences coming from daily contact with individuals of the subordinate group. It is the events seemingly loaded with great collective significance that are the focal points of the public discussion. The definition of these events is chiefly responsible for the development of a racial image and of the sense of group position. When this public discussion takes the form of a denunciation of the subordinate racial group, signifying that it is unfit and a threat, the discussion becomes particularly potent in shaping the sense of social position.

Third, the major influence in public discussion is exercised by individuals and groups who have the public ear and who are felt to have standing, prestige, authority, and power. Intellectual and social elites, public figures of prominence, and leaders of powerful organizations are likely to be the key figures in the formation of the sense of group position and in the characterization of the subordinate group. It is well to note this in view of the not infrequent tendency of students to regard race prejudice as growing out of the multiplicity of experiences and attitudes of the bulk of the people.

Fourth, we also need to perceive the appreciable opportunity that is given to strong interest groups in directing the lines of discussion and setting the interpretations that arise in such discussion. Their self-interest may dictate the kind of position they wish the dominant racial group to enjoy. It may be a position which enables them to retain certain advantages or, even more, to gain still greater advantages. Hence, they may be vigorous in seeking to manufacture events to attract public attention and to set lines of issue in such a way as to predetermine interpretations favorable to their interests. The role of strongly organized groups seeking to further special interest is usually central in the formation of collective images of abstract groups. Historical records of major instances of race relations, as in our South, or in South Africa, or in Europe in the case of the Jew, or on the West Coast in the case of the Japanese show the formidable part played by interest groups in defining the subordinate racial group.

I conclude this highly condensed paper with two further observations that may throw additional light on the relation of the sense of group position to race prejudice. Race prejudice becomes entrenched and tenacious to the extent the prevailing social order is rooted in the sense of social position. This has been true of the historic South in our country. In such a social order race prejudice tends to become chronic and impermeable to change. In other places the social order may be affected only to a limited extent by the sense of group position held by the dominant racial group. This I think has been true usually in the case of anti-Semitism in Europe and this country. Under these conditions the sense of group position tends to be weaker and more vulnerable. In turn, race prejudice has a much more variable and intermittent career, usually becoming pronounced only as a consequence of grave disorganizing events that allow for the formation of a scapegoat.

This leads me to my final observation which in a measure is an indirect summary. The sense of group position dissolves and race prejudice declines when the process of running definition does not keep abreast of major shifts in the social order. When events touching on relations are not treated as "big events" and hence do not set crucial issues in the arena of public discussion; or when the elite leaders or spokesmen do not define such big events vehemently or adversely, or where they define them in the direction of racial harmony; or when there is a paucity of strong interest groups seeking to build up a strong adverse image for special advantage—under such conditions the sense of group position recedes and race prejudice declines.

The clear implication of my discussion is that the proper and the fruitful area in which race prejudice should be studied is the collective process through which a sense of group position is formed. Race prejudice has a history, and the history is collective. To seek, instead, to understand it or to handle it in the arena of individual feeling and of individual experience seems to me to be clearly misdirected.

BIBLIOGRAPHY

Allport, Gordon. *The Nature of Prejudice*. Boston: The Beacon Press, 1954.

Blumer, Herbert. "The Nature of Race Prejudice," *Social Process in Hawaii*, V (June, 1939), 11-20.

Cash, W. J. *The Mind of the South*. New York: Alfred A. Knopf, 1941.

Faris, Ellsworth. "The Natural History of Prejudice," in *The Nature of Human Nature*. New York: McGraw-Hill, 1937. Chap. XXXII.

Park, Robert E. *Race and Culture*. Glencoe, Illinois: The Free Press, 1950.

Ten Broek, Jacobus, et al. *Prejudice, War and the Constitution*. Berkeley: University of California Press, 1954.

The Future of the Color Line

My approach to the topic of the changing relations between Negroes and whites in the American South is from the standpoint of the common concept of the "color line." This is an exceedingly apt and discerning term which helps to pinpoint what is crucial in the relation of the two racial groups. The term does not cover all of the ways in which Negroes and whites meet nor does it refer to all of the important relations between their respective institutions and modes of life. Instead, it singles out a central dimension of their interconnection—a dimension along which the "racial problem" lies and is formed. The distinction is of considerable importance. Extensive changes may take place in broad areas of the relationship of the two racial groups without appreciable effect on the color line; this may be seen, for example, in the preservation of the color line in the face of the profound transformations wrought by industrialization or by demographic change. It is a mistake to construe the broad social changes which are taking place in institutional areas in the South as necessarily portending some notable transformation in the basic relationship of the two racial groups. Change in this basic relationship must be sought, instead, in what happens to the color line.

The ostensible meaning of the color line is clear. It is a line which separates whites and Negroes, assigning to each a different position in the social order and attaching to each position a differential set of rights, privileges, and arenas of action. It defines the approach of each racial group to the other, it limits the degree of access to each other, and it outlines respective modes of conduct toward each other. The color line stems from a collective sense held by whites that Negroes as a racial group do not qualify for equal status, and that because of their racial difference Negroes have no claim to being accepted socially. Thus, the color line expresses and sustains the social positions of the two groups along two fundamental dimensions—an axis of dominance and subordination, and an axis of inclusion and exclusion.

Three important features of the color line should be noted. First, it represents a positioning of whites and Negroes as abstract or generalized groups; it comes into play when members of the two races meet each other not on an individual basis but as representatives of their respective groups. It is only when the encounters between whites and Negroes are controlled by an identification of their respective racial membership that the color line is set. Second, the color line is a collective definition of social position and not a mere expression of individual feelings and beliefs. Whites may have, and do have, a wide and variable range of feelings toward Negroes, from profound hostility to deep kindness and sympathy, yet adhere to the color line when and where the social code requires its application. The sense of group position is the central ingredient in the color line. Third, as a metaphor, the color line is not appropriately represented by a single, sharply drawn line but appears rather as a series of ramparts, like the "Maginot Line," extending from outer breastworks to inner bastions. Outer portions of it may, so to speak, be given up only to hold steadfast to inner citadels. We will have occasion in the subsequent discussion to indicate the relevance of these three points to the present and imminent changes in race relations in the South.

It is well to keep in mind that the color line has grown up as a primary basis for the organization of southern life. The color line was forged through many generations of critical experience in which the self-identity and survival of the whites as a given kind of group were at stake. The collective definition or social code elaborated from this experience came to be deeply embedded in the mores. The color line came to be felt by whites as natural, proper, and sacred, and as such to be zealously guarded against trespass by Negroes and preserved from disrespect by whites.

It is also desirable to keep in mind the impotent position of southern Negroes under the historic relationship with whites. The color line forced into being among them a posture of concealment of strong feelings of resentment and bitterness. The color line stood fundamentally for a denigration of Negroes as inferior and a rejection of them as alien. Yet it was not wise for Negroes to express before whites their feelings as they experienced affronts, indignities, and the various forms of exploitation which went with their inferior and impotent status. It was precisely this area of feelings, and of the sentiments and thoughts built up in it, that was typically unknown to southern whites under the operation of the color line. This condition, even more than the separation of the races into two communities with disparate areas of interaction and universes of discourse, was the major bar to communication and understanding between the two racial groups.

The foregoing remarks provide a suitable background for considering the present and proximate status of the color line. The color line in the South is under considerable attack. It is undergoing transformation, although so far more in a symbolic than in an actual sense. The attack, to re-employ our previous metaphor, is taking place chiefly at the outer battlements; it has scarcely entered into the intermediate fortifications, and of course has not touched inner citadels. It is currently being waged chiefly at certain points in the public area of civil rights; only rarely has it begun to enter the crucial area of economic position, and it is remote from the inner field of private association. How widespread will be the attack, how deeply it will penetrate and with what degree of success depends on a variety of forces, some currently in operation and some on the horizon. I wish to direct my discussion to this latter matter.

The initial forces which have operated to bring about changes in the color line can scarcely be thought of as having arisen indigenously from the cultural and social structure of the South. The powerful and deeply embedded code of the color line plus the impotency of the southern Negro have effectively prevented this from happening. It is commonly thought that the rather profound social transformation undergone by the South during the last few decades under the impact of industrialization, agricultural changes, demographic changes, educational advancement, and similar developments is responsible for undermining the color line. The evidence gives little support for this view. It appears, instead, that in this transformation the color line was carried over from the old situations to the new situations—from the plantation to the factory, from the rural area to the city, from the old institutional settings to the new institutional settings. The Negro was subjected to essentially the same subordination and exclusion. In the new industrial structure the Negro, as of old, was confined to low-status jobs; in the cities he had the poorest housing and other facilities; and he continued to be barred from white institutions and allocated to a separate world of association. The color line persisted with vigor, changing in form as it adapted to new conditions such as the use of the automobile, but preserving essentially intact the social positions of the two racial groups. This characterization should not be construed as denying such developments as the scattered formation of new liberal attitudes among southern whites, the emergence here and there of outstanding spokesmen of such attitudes, and the activity of an occasional southern organization seeking to ameliorate racial tensions. Insofar as such developments were able to exercise influence, their effect was more in the direction of improving conditions on the Negro side of the color line or of softening the harshness of treatment in the case of infractions of the color line, than in changing the color line itself. To these observations one should add that Negro residents in the South, individually and collectively, were negligible in initiating attacks on the color line. While their resentments and dissatisfactions with the color line were extensive and acute, the impotency and insecurity of their position restrained them from challenging the color line.

The import of these observations is to call attention to the fundamental fact that the significant agents of change of the color line have been located outside of the arena of southern life. We easily see this as we identify the more conspicuous ones which through law, administrative decree, judicial determination, policy, and action have exerted direct and indirect pressure to change the color line. Thus, we think of (a) the federal government in its many divisions—administrative acts of the executive branch, desegregation decisions in the armed services, judicial interpretation by the federal courts, legislation by Congress, and enforcement acts by appropriate federal agencies; (b) the policies and posture of a host of national organizations and institutions such as churches, educational associations, labor unions, and profes-

212 Selected Works of Herbert Blumer

sional associations espousing stands contrary to different features of the color line; (c) national media of communication—periodicals, the press, television, and radio—presenting definitions which challenged the color line in different ways; (d) national political parties which through their platforms staked out official aims which, even though semiceremonial, were in conflict with the color line; and (3) a variety of national action groups, such as the NAACP, spearheading frontal attacks on the color line.

This identification of the major forces which are in play highlights a matter of central importance for an understanding of what is happening to the color line in the South. It is that changes in the color line are an expression and result of *the increasing incorporation of the South into the life of the nation.* This may seem to be a trite observation, scarcely worthy of mention. Yet it goes, I think, to the very heart of the problem of the color line in the South. It calls our attention to several facts. It points out that the change of the color line is both a consequence and a part of a massive movement toward national integration and not a result of scattered and disparate ines of regional activity. The pressures on the color line are not to be thought of as the machinations of questionable officials high in the circles of the federal government, or as incitement by outside agitators, or as the misguided efforts of innocent but uninformed northerners. Instead, the pressures are those of bringing the South increasingly within the body of laws, standards, principles, policies, and institutional arrangements which prevail generally in the nation. One may easily fail to see this fundamental fact when one views singly such events as a decision of a federal court, or a resolution of a religious conference, or the efforts of a team of outsiders to register Negroes on voter rolls in a southern county. However, these events, like a large number of congruent happenings, are but the manifestations of a vast process of embracing the South within a national pattern.

All sections of the nation are becoming increasingly welded into a large polity and entity under the play of such forces as increasing economic interdependency, mobility of people, extension of communication, the dissemination of sanctioned professional standards, the growth of national organizations and the elevation of their importance, the interlocking of institutions on a national basis, and the growth of federal direction and control.

The South is already caught up in this massive movement of national integration. There are no tenable grounds for assuming that the South will halt, or be able to halt, this process of its increasing incorporation into national life. It is this perspective which provides us with solid grounds for forming a judgment on the status of the color line in the South in the proximate future.

The incorporation of the South into the national pattern will bear heavily on it in the case of the color line, especially in the Deep South where the color line is most rigidly set. Unquestionably, intense resistance will be offered to making accommodations to the national pattern of Negro-white relations since such accommodations strike, especially in their symbolic character, against the sense of identity and social position which the white group has forged in its historic past. Yet, however bitter and lingering may be the resistance, however dramatic may be acts of opposition at this or that part, however fearsome may be acts of violence and counterviolence, and however contrived the resort to evasion and token accommodation, the resistance can scarcely be viewed as likely to be successful in the face of the ponderous process of incorporation which is in play. We may expect far more, not less, pressure to bring the area of Negro-white relations in the South under the laws and standards of the nation. The South is being edged bit by bit in this direction. There is nothing on the horizon to suggest that this movement will not continue and indeed pick up increasing momentum.

The recognition that the South is being brought abreast of the rest of the nation leads to a significant conclusion, namely, that the fate of the color line in the South will depend increasingly on what happens to Negro-white relations in the nation as a whole. The gaining by southern Negroes of the rights which they enjoy generally elsewhere in the nation—even though this is and will be a strenuous and dramatic struggle in itself—is but an initial stage of the much larger shifting of the social positions of Negroes and whites in the nation. To understand the destiny of the color line in the South, it is necessary to view it from the larger perspective of what is happening to the alignment of Negroes and whites generally in the nation. The problem of Negro-white relations is becoming more and more a nation-wide problem and less and less a problem localized in a given geographical area. To understand the fate of the color line in the South, we must accordingly shift the forces of analysis to this broader arena of Negro-white relations in which the course of the future lies.

The discussion should begin with the recognition that a color line exists not only in the South but in all sections of the nation. In the North and West it is drawn differently from the manner characteristic of the traditional South; nevertheless, it is present extensively and set profoundly. It expresses the fact that in these sections the two racial groups occupy different social positions along the axes of dominance-subordination and exclusion-inclusion. Historically in these sections Negroes were barred, by tacit agreement if not by law, from equal access to many parts of the public arena; they were restricted predominantly to the lower levels of industrial occupation; they were scarcely ever allowed to enter the area of white management; they were subjected to strong residential separation; and they were excluded generally from private circles of white association. That, in comparison to the South, there was less exploitation of them, less hostile attacks on them, less overt denigration of them, and much less conventional "prejudice" shown toward them, does not alter the fact that a strong color line has been drawn against them. Northern and western whites have been much less aware of their color line and much less sensitive about it, but Negroes have felt its impact keenly.

Today Negroes are engaged in a struggle throughout the nation against their subordinate position—not merely in the South toward which dramatic events have focused attention. At present this struggle is taking place primarily in the outer band of the color line, seeking to gain what is customarily referred to as "civil rights," that is to say, to remove the segregated position of Negroes *in the public arena*. What is sought, chiefly, are such rights as free access to public accommodations and public institutions, the enjoyment of the franchise, the equal protection of laws, and equal rights as consumers. Since these rights stem from the legal status of Negroes as citizens and since the exercise of such rights has become a national imperative under the play of the huge forces which are welding the nation into a polity and entity, there is full reason to believe, as previously mentioned, that the rights will be gained. This has already happened in given regions of the North and West. That this will happen generally throughout the nation, even though at a much slower pace in the South, is the reasonable, indeed certain, prospect of the future.

The acquisition of civil rights by Negroes in the South will thus have two stages, so to speak—first, being brought abreast of the general level of enjoyment of such rights as exists elsewhere in the nation, and then sharing in the further struggle to extend those rights that is occurring on a national basis. This assertion may seem blithe in view of the bitter resistance and formidable obstacles set up in the South, particularly in the Deep South, against granting Negroes the round of civil rights which they enjoy elsewhere in the nation. Yet, as I have remarked, the major forces of our epoch are working steadily to weave the South into the national pattern. The border states are already being detached from what was previously a much larger isolated region and this same movement toward national incorporation is clearly at work in the states in the Deep South. The very fact that the resistance in such states to granting civil rights has become such a pronounced matter of *national* concern is itself indicative of the broad movement which is in play to bring the South inside of national patterns. It is this movement, and not the separate acts of resistance to it, which spells out the future of the color line in the South. The movement derives its momentum from the shaping forces of the contemporary age; the acts of resistance, however much they stimulate each other, gain their sustenance from a weakening traditional structure. The maintenance of the color line as it existed traditionally in the South would require a retention of the previous condition of regional isolation of the South in its social, organization, and legal life. This isolation is breaking down and all signs indicate that it will break down much more rapidly in the future. Despite a lag, especially in rural regions, in extending to Negroes the rights of citizenship under the laws of the land and the standards of the nation, the course of the movement is clear.

It is a serious mistake, however, to regard the achievement by Negroes of civil rights, as presently defined, as equivalent to removing the color line. Whites are generally disposed, it is true, to view the matter in this way. They believe that if Negroes can vote, enter into politics, eat in any restaurant, go to any theater, ride on any public conveyance, have access to any hospital, attend any public function, enroll in any public school, apply for any job, and freely enter government employment, in short enjoy the ostensible rights of citizenship, the color line will have disappeared. However, the area of civil rights constitutes only a part, even though a highly significant part, of the larger region from which the Negro has been barred by the color line. The contested area of civil rights is, as previously stated, but the outer band of the color line. Inside of it lies the crucial area of economic subordination and opportunity restriction—an area of debarment of Negroes which is exceedingly tough because it is highly complicated by private and quasi-private property rights, managerial rights, and organizational rights. Still further inside of the color line are the varied circles of private association from which the Negro is grossly excluded. Thus, the successful achievement of civil rights merely peels off, so to speak, the outer layer of the color line. By itself, it does not alter significantly the social positions of the two racial groups. It raises somewhat the position of the Negro on the dominance-subordination axis but leaves this axis of relationship essentially intact. Its effect on the inclusion-exclusion axis is negligible.

That the satisfaction of demands for civil rights will neither dissolve the color line nor lessen the struggle waged against it can be appreciated further by recognizing how the struggle for civil rights has intensified racial consciousness. Such intensification of racial consciousness has been particularly pronounced in the case of the Negro. The struggle has released, aroused, and mobilized the feelings of bitterness and resentment which Negroes experience as a result of their objectionable social position. Their attitudes, even though largely concealed, have hardened against the whites as a group—against "the Man." Evidence of this may be seen in their increased militancy, in their disparagement of "Uncle Tom" types in their own ranks, in the pressure on their leaders to take a more decisive and militant posture, and in an increasing suspicion of whites extending even to liberal sympathizers. The struggle for civil rights is leading Negroes to a renewed assessment of their disadvantaged social status, bringing into sharper focus the illegality and injustice of their social position, making them chafe under the seeming insensitivity of whites to their plight, and with their increased sense of common identity making them writhe with bitterness over publicized instances of wanton indignity and cruelty occurring in the resistance of whites. They have become increasingly sensitive and touchy with regard to the posture and intentions of whites. To sum up, we are presented with the seemingly anomalous situation in which the struggle for civil rights, even as it moves ahead toward achievement, intensifies the Negro's sense of his disadvantaged position and reinforces his feelings that white society is lined up against him.

We may expect, then, a continuation of assault on the color line but it will shift, as it is now shifting, to a different and inner band. This band, as suggested previously, consists of the barriers confronting the Negro in his efforts to improve his economic lot. These barriers are extensive, varied, and formidable. To specify them is to recite the obvious—the difficulties of the Negro in getting employment, his assignment to lower paying jobs, the ceilings placed on his movements upward in the job structure, his difficulties in entering the areas of management, especially middle and upper management, his difficulties in gaining the training necessary to qualify for higher level jobs, and the formidable restrictions placed on him in the field of private entrepreneurship. Much of the debarment of the Negro, represented by such barriers, springs from feelings of dislike; additionally, much of it occurs through a tacit collective recognition that it is "not the thing to do" to give him entrance to given posts; and part of it results from a lack among Negroes of the training and experience needed to qualify for given posts. Whatever be the causes—and they are indeed complex and intertwined—this general area of debarment of the Negro is extensive, solidly structured, and deeply set. It constitutes a much more formidable part of the color line than is represented by the debarment of the Negro from the exercise of civil rights in the public arena.

What are the prospects of a change in this important part of the color line? We are witnessing today a large variety of scattered efforts to penetrate or remove the barriers which confine the Negro to an inferior economic position and to a sphere of markedly limited opportunity. They take such forms as pressure for fair employment legislation, widening of civil service to negroes, administrative acts by branches of the federal government on behalf of equal opportunities in employment, greater admission of Negroes to labor unions, scattered voluntary efforts by large business corporations to increase the number of Negro employees and to open higher positions to them, direct demands by Negro groups supported by picketing and boycotts, inauguration of programs of vocational training, development of opportunity programs for Negro youth, and improvement of public education for Negro children. Without discounting the noticeable effects, here and there, of such efforts one must conclude that they have done comparatively little to improve the economic and opportunity base of Negroes in American society. As of the present they are more than offset by two prodigious developments taking place in the life of the Negro. These are, first, the well known demographic movement which is massing Negroes in the deteriorated or deteriorating areas of our large cities, and, second, the technological changes which are closing the doors to conventional fields of Negro employment. To recite the disabilities that flow from each of these two developments would require a lengthy chapter. It is sufficient to state that the combination of the two is producing a vast urban Negro proletariat with a high incidence of unemployment, with no secure foothold in the occupational structure, with restricted opportunities to escape or rise, and largely shut off from white society. The formation of such an urban Negro proletariat is currently proceeding at a pace which far outstrips the totality of the scattered remedial efforts referred to above.

It is not easy to determine or assess how the formation of this urban Negro proletariat will affect the color line. The formation is a new element in the positioning of the two races; its probable effects on their relationship are obscure. Certain conditions and ingredients of the new urban Negro population can be noted. It is an ecologically segregated and socially ingrown community; it is a poor and underprivileged group; it is marked by considerable community and family disorganization; it suffers a considerable loss of its better trained and economically successful members through migration; and its economic sights and hopes are low. This set of conditions might suggest that the urban Negro, like many underprivileged groups in history, would settle into, and accept, an inferior even though miserable position. But we have to recognize another set of conditions in the new urban Negro community—free discussion and movement within it, an increasing sensitivity of Negroes in it to their plight, a placing of the blame for this plight on white society and hence a generation of increased bitterness toward whites, a stronger disposition to fight back, a fuller appreciation of their civic rights and a greater readiness to use them, a conduciveness to agitation and to formation of protest movements, and the possession of strategic political power. These conditions point to the probability that the urban Negro proletariat, unlike Negroes at the bottom of the social and economic ladder in the past, will not humbly accept this position but be poised to protest and rebel in some fashion. Such a posture introduces great uncertainty as to the status of the color line in the proximate future. The great unknowns are whether the urban Negro proletariat will be mobilized to act with some concert on behalf of a cause, whether its great political potential will be effectively used, and whether the larger white society will be led to undertake a massive program for the improvement of the position of the urban Negro.

A few words should be said about the latter possibility. It is obvious that national attention is increasingly being drawn to the situation of the urban Negro. A number of separate lines of great concern converge on this situation. Let us take note of them. In itself the general concern today with the increasingly pressing question of Negro-white relations leads more and more to the urban setting of these relations. The mounting concern with unemployment in our society, especially as a result of automation, focuses on the urban Negro since he is the chief sufferer from it. The looming concern with urban slums and urban renewal comes to be largely centered on the urban Negro. The mounting problem of delinquency and crime and the growing efforts to cope with the problem direct major concern to the urban Negro. The huge problems which have arisen to confront public education in our large cities, highlighted by the questions of drop-outs, discipline, and de facto segregation, bring the urban Negro centrally into the focus of attention. The augmenting financial difficulties of large cities in providing the services demanded of them have made the position of the Negro a matter of central municipal concern. And, finally, the growing political power of the urban Negro on the municipal, state, and federal levels evokes an order of political responsiveness that makes the urban Negro community an object of sensitive consequence. Given these formidable lines of concern, each of which is likely to increase in magnitude, it is well conceivable that a massive attack will have to be made, chiefly under federal auspices, to improve the economic and community position of the urban Negro.[1] Such an attack would arise less from racial considerations and more from the dictates of national interest.

If such a massive attack is not made and if conditions among urban Negroes are allowed to continue as they are now developing, the prospects are indeed high that discord and overt strife will be persistent marks of the color line. There is no conceivable likelihood that a social code would or could be developed to hold the disparate social positions of the two racial groups in an orderly relation such as was achieved under the color line now breaking down. If, in contrast, a massive attack is undertaken that raises significantly the economic position of the Negro, opens to him all doors in the occupational structure, makes available to him the level of training and preparation to enter such doors, and allows him free residential movement, this would be basically equivalent to eliminating the color line in the intemediate area in which it is now most massively entrenched.

The South will not escape, of course, the struggle that will center on the area of economic position and social opportunity of the urban Negro. The significant signs point to the preponderant likelihood that the struggle will be national in sweep and in character. The major battlegrounds—to use this expression—will be chiefly in the large cities of the North and West, in the headquarters of national organizations, and in the seats of government, particularly the federal government. But the South will be brought into the pattern that emerges and develops on the national scene. What this pattern may be, as foregoing remarks suggest, is a matter of pronounced conjecture. That there will be struggle is certain, since Negroes will be too aroused to accept an economic and social status of such disability and since, out of its own interests, the nation cannot ignore the problems that converge on a depressed urban Negro proletariat. The forces that may be brought

---

[1] Since this article was written (December, 1963), the federal government has shown an increasing interest in such a move, especially in its prospective anti-poverty program.

into play in the struggle are far too lacking in shape to fore-shadow the outcome of the struggle. The future of the color line in this intermediate band remains a highly problematic matter.

There remains for consideration the question of the status and fate of what was previously referred to as the inner citadel of the color line. This position of the color line must be recognized as very different from the outer layers represented respectively by denial of civil rights in the public arena and by exclusion of Negroes from economic and social opportunity. This "inner" line of separation is drawn along the inclusion–exclusion axis of the relationship between the two racial groups. It arises from a feeling that the Negro is alien and different and thus needs to be distinguished from those parts of the color line that reflect a sense that the Negro is inferior or subordinate. Its presence can be noted most clearly among whites who are willing to accept Negroes as having equal social status yet who are not disposed to admit them into intimate and private circles, represented by social sets, cliques, private clubs, friendship sets, family circles, courtship, and marriage. Even though this line of exclusion is woven into the lines of separation that stem from a sense of different status posi-tion and is obscured by these other lines of separation, it is un-questionably of powerful influence and of great import in the structure of the color line. It comes to vivid expression in that ultimate emotional shibboleth, "Do you want your daughter to marry a Negro?"

Despite its important place in the color line this form of ex-clusion has largely escaped scholarly study. We know little about it, analytically. But some observations are in order. First, it seems reasonable to expect it to decline in influence were the status posi-tions of the two racial groups in American society to become equalized; however, even in this event there are no grounds to ex-pect it to disappear. Second, it lies outside of the formal controls of a society; it is a matter of personal attitude and thus falls inside of the area of individual determination. Edicts, decrees, and laws cannot direct this line of separation as they may do in the case of other parts of the color line; it is peculiarly immune to outer as-sault. The two foregoing observations call attention to the fact that an erasing of the color line in the area of civil rights and in the area of economic position and social opportunity does not signify its elimination in this inner band. Third, it is entirely conceivable that even in a situation of equal social status the Negro group would accommodate to exclusion as a separate racial group—as, indeed, Jews have done in large measure. Such an accommodative relation is fully tenable without being a source of tension and discord in a social order.

Social Science
and the Desegregation Process

This paper undertakes to analyze segregation as a social process. Subsequently, consideration is given to the problem of desegregation and to the general lines along which programs of desegregation must move. Our concern is primarily with racial desegregation.

Segregation is continuously at work in all human societies as a natural, unguided, and unwitting process. It takes the form of a diverse and chiefly undesigned operation which sets apart groups of people inside of a larger, embracing society. This setting apart may result from practices of exclusion employed by one group against others, or by voluntary withdrawal on the part of given groups, or by the operation of natural forces which place individuals in different localities or different social spheres. The result of this undesigned process is to form disparate groups. Each group is relatively homogeneous. Each constitutes the arena for the bulk of the associations and experiences of its members. Each is limited in access to the life of other groups. Each is denied, accordingly, the special privileges granted by other groups to their members. Segregation is a primary means by which a human society develops an inner organization—an allocation of diverse elements into an articulated arrangement.

NATURE OF SEGREGATION

Sociologists have been concerned with two chief manifestations of this natural process of segregation. These are (1) the formation of diversified areas of residence, chiefly in large cities, and (2) the exclusion exercised by human groups in accepting members and in granting privileges. A brief consideration of these two forms of segregation will be helpful.

Ecological studies of the residential distribution of people, particularly in large cities, show a pattern of distinguishable areas. Each area tends to be distinctive in terms of the people who inhabit it, the kind of local institutions lodged in it, and the general round of life of its people. Such areas are familiar to us in the case of "black belts," "little Italies," and other ethnic areas; they are also noted in the case of slums, workingmen areas, homeless-men areas, apartment-house areas, "gold coasts," and rooming-house areas.

The formation of such differentiated areas, while not un-affected by deliberate governmental policy, is primarily a natural and spontaneous process. They are the product roughly of three kinds of forces: (1) neutral forces, such as level of income and ac-cessibility to places of work; (2) forces of attraction, such as wishing to live among people with whom one identifies oneself; and (3) forces of rejection, as when people are found unaccept-able or unsuitable as residents in given areas. This process of eco-logical differentiation, operating without any over-all conscious design, promotes the formation of separate social worlds, guides and fosters separate areas of association, and restricts participa-tion in the life of outside groups. In our modern complex world this natural process of ecological allocation has become a primary medium and cause of segregation.

The study of human group life reveals clearly another line of segregation in the form of the exclusion exercised by one group against members of other groups. Such exclusion is indigenous in human societies. Every group having a sense of identity and some kind of purpose exercises some measure of control over membership in its body and over access to the privileges which its life affords. Whether it be a family, a social club, a clique, a group of friends, a business organization, a professional society, a labor union, a church, or a self-conscious neighborhood, the group necessarily recognizes certain criteria of membership and rejects those who are deemed not to meet such criteria. Similarly, it does not grant to outsiders the particular rights and privileges open to its membership. It is only because such group exclusion is so rarely challenged that we fail to realize how basic and exten-sive it is in the life of human societies. If groups could not draw lines and exercise control over accessibility to their ranks and their privileges, their existence would be intrinsically doomed and group life would be chaotic. In this legitimate sense there is in play in every human society a continuous process of preserving group domains and of excluding outsiders from ingress into such domains. Quite obviously, this process of exclusion has the effect of allocating people into separate groups, of confining them to such groups, and of establishing barriers to their free participation in each other's group life.

These few remarks call attention to the fact that a twofold process of segregation is continuously at work in modern society. This process is natural, spontaneous, and inevitable. It is essential, in the form of group exclusion, to the existence of all human societies; in the form of ecological differentiation it is essential to the existence of modern, urbanized societies. One can say, rhetorically, that the process of segregation in one or the other form is accepted, employed, and condoned by all human societies.

SEGREGATION AS A SOCIAL PROBLEM

It is evident, immediately, that when we speak of segregation as a social problem, as a condition to be prevented or overcome, we are not referring to the total process of segregation. We refer instead only to special instances which have been challenged. Such challenges arise in the form of a claim to the right of being accepted into a group or sharing the privileges which the group denies through its act of exclusion. It is evident that the claim arises and has validity only through the application of the standards of a larger inclusive group, such as an embracing political society with legal rights of citizenship or a transcending moral community with a set of ethical expectations. Given lines or instances of group exclusion become suspect only when they contravene political or moral rights. Since this constitutes the heart of the *problem* of segregation, a few further words of elaboration are in order.

Every human group may be regarded as having properly an

area of private rights—chiefly in the form of deciding whom to allow to become members and to enjoy the privileges which the group life is able to provide. As suggested above, the group possession of such areas of private right is sanctioned in every society irrespective of wide differences in the nature of the rights and in the gratifications which their exercise yields. Discrimination arises when a given line of private right is defined legally or morally as a public right and the group does not accept the definition. The continuing exercise of the private right at the expense of a given group having legal or moral claims to the privileges is what constitutes segregation as a social problem. Thus segregation, as a problem, arises in the wake of the application of moral or legal definitions which stake out claims where none existed previously. Many forms of group exclusion may have a legitimate acceptance and status only to be defined later as contravening public rights. Since in our changing modern world new legal and moral definitions are readily applied to varieties of established group exclusions, we may expect new problems of segregation to arise.

In locating the problem of segregation in a clash between established group exclusion and a legal or moral claim to the privileges protected by the exclusion we can identify the lines of force affecting the outcome of the clash. On the one hand, note has to be taken of how deeply set is the practice of group exclusion and how effective is the apparatus for maintaining the practice. On the other hand, attention must be given to the authority attending the moral or legal claim and, again, to the effectiveness of the apparatus available to implement the claim. These observations set a broad framework inside of which a more detailed analysis can be undertaken.

THE SEGREGATING GROUP

To understand segregation it is necessary to see its position in the life of the segregating group. Almost always the practices of exclusion or rejection which it involves have grown up naturally in the life experiences of the group. Through these life experiences the group has come to develop a social position, a sense of identity, and a conception of itself in the light of which the practice of exclusion appears natural and proper. As a natural part of the social order the practice comes to be embedded in feelings and convictions and to be justified logically by a set of reasons whose validity is self-evident. Also, the practice is usually legitimated and bulwarked by the endorsement given by institutional authorities within the group; as the spokesmen of the group their official approval places a stamp of truth and virtue on the practice. Further, as a customary practice the exclusion feeds, so to speak, on itself; its continuous routine occurrence becomes an affirmation of its validity. As each member of the group gives expression to the practice in voice and deed, he reinforces in other members the value which all of them are disposed to attach to the practice. Sustained by these various sources of strength and sanction the established practice of group exclusion tends to be a firm part of the way of life.

This general process which imparts toughness and fixity to established practices of group exclusion is usually intensified in cases of racial segregation. The reasons for this are fairly clear. The recognition of racial or physical difference sustains and intensifies the sense of social or status difference which may have happened to develop between racial groups. The observable physical difference reinforces and rivets the feeling of the dominant racial group that the subordinate racial group is alien and not of its kind. Similarly, the feeling of superiority in the dominant group derives a greater measure of natural validity by virtue of the ability to note biological differences between the two groups. Thus, the feeling of racial difference adds tenacity to the practices of exclusion.

We need to note, also, that the range of exclusions between racial groups is likely to be extensive. They meet each other not in a restricted or specialized way, as in the case of the relation of journeymen to apprentices, but over a wide area of diverse association. Where a sense of racial difference has been fused with a sense of status difference, the inevitable tendency will be to extend the practice of exclusion along the array of relations. Since each line of exclusion symbolizes to the dominant group its social position, all its established lines of exclusion hang together and sustain each other.

In a further continuation of our background remarks we wish to point out that patterns of racial exclusion may decline and wither away as naturally and unwittingly as they come into existence and grow. Any number of developments may interfere with the conditions and processes that cause and sustain such patterns. The social positions of the two racial groups may be shifted by changes in wealth, education, achievement, and prowess. The dominant group may change its conception of itself and of the subordinate group. Members of two racial groups may be forced through sheer expediency to associate in ways contrary to established lines of exclusion, as under varying conditions of complex industrial life. The dominant racial group may lose much of its identity through the mobility of its members and through their intermingling with other people who are not accustomed to draw the usual lines of exclusion: in this way practices of exclusion do not get the affirmation that comes otherwise from their regular and unquestioned repetition. The spokesmen and institutional leaders of the dominant group may come to appraise the established exclusions in new and different ways; to speak with a divided voice is to fragment the standing of the practices. Such occurrences as these may undermine in a natural and undesigned way established patterns of racial exclusion, without the benefit of organized efforts to eradicate them. The significance of a natural and unwitting disintegration of established patterns of racial exclusion is pronounced. It is doubtful if deliberate efforts to break down given forms of exclusion in a firmly established racial order can succeed without the operation of a prior or a concurrent process of their natural undermining.

DESEGREGATION

We can now consider the problem of desegregation. We are interested in considering the general problem of how practices of racial exclusion which are challenged as morally improper or illegal are eliminated through conscious policy and deliberate action. In other words we deal with desegregation not as a natural and unwitting process but as a directed effort to displace an established form of racial exclusion. In this latter form the problem of desegregation is thrown on a different plane. It is not a task of eliminating or reversing the process which led to segregation but rather of arresting or immobilizing its end operation.

To be sure, much—indeed most—of scholarly thought in current psychological and social science presumes that racial desegregation is to be achieved by the elimination or changing of the process which brings segregation into being. This process is usually given a four-step temporal sequence: (1) conditions which implant (2) attitudes of racial prejudice which (3) lead to racial discrimination which (4) results in a condition of segregation. It is thus reasoned that to eliminate segregation one has to eliminate discrimination; to eliminate discrimination one has to change the attitudes which bring it about; and, usually, to change the attitudes one has to correct the conditions that cause them.

Such a formulation is markedly unsuited to success in conscious efforts at racial desegration. It implies, essentially, a destruction of a tightly interwoven and solid social structure. This can be appreciated by bearing in mind that a given form of racial exclusion is a customary adjustment which has evolved naturally out of given lines of historic experience; that it reflects the actual social positions occupied by the racial groups in their social order; that it expresses the fundamental conception which the dominant racial group has of itself and of the subordinate group; that it carries the virtue and the validity of authoritative endorsement; that it gains continuous affirmation through the daily reinforcement which members of the dominant group give to one another's feelings and convictions; and that it is an interlinked part of a system of racial exclusion. To try to eliminate the given practice of racial exclusion by altering the network of conditions which bring it about and sustain it is a task of formidable magnitude. To try to eliminate the practice by changing one phase or part of the network—as in the effort to inculcate attitudes of racial tolerance—is to ignore the complicated structure which sustains the phase or part. The attempt to achieve racial desegregation by a correction of the process which brings segregation about represents a highly unpromising line of action.

The alternative is to block the process from achieving its end result. This is done by controlling the decisions of the main functionaries who carry a given form of racial segregation into actual execution. It is important to recognize that in any given kind of racial segregation there are strategically placed individuals or small groups who set the policies and issue the orders without which the given practice of segregation could not be maintained. School boards, superintendents of education, real estate boards, realtors, hotel owners and managers, medical boards, hospital superintendents, and directors of recreational systems are a very few examples. All work through a system of subordinates who in carrying out orders and understood policies sustain in practice the given form of racial segregation. Thus, control of the decisions of the chief functionaries responsible for the actual operation of the practice of segregation offers a direct means of arresting or immobilizing that practice. To put the point in terms of a theory of social action we can say that it is not essential in efforts to change human conduct to alter, on the part of individuals, the feelings and attitudes behind that conduct, or, on the part of the group, the collective values, claims, and expectations which sustain the conduct. Feelings and attitudes, values and expectations, have *to gain expression* in conduct; the apparatus essential to such expression is, itself, vulnerable and offers pivotal points for arresting the end expression. Contemporary social and psychological science is backward in coming to see and appreciate this picture.

ROLE OF FUNCTIONARIES

To exert effective influence on the decisions of centrally placed functionaries in the operating pattern of segregation it is necessary to use the weight of transcending prestige, authority, and power. The functionaries, as members of the dominant racial group, are highly likely to share the feelings and values of that group toward the given form of exclusion, or else to respond to the expectations and pressures of that group. For them to make decisions that are opposed to the feelings and expectations of the dominant group it is necessary for them to be constrained and supported by a transcending group having prestige or power.

Basically, the outcome of the struggle to achieve racial desegregation through conscious effort depends on what influences the central functionaries have to take into account in making their decisions. If the conscious effort takes the form of an educational campaign to change the views of the members of the dominant racial group or a campaign of moral exhortation to change their feelings, the functionaries are essentially well protected. They need merely, so to speak, await the outcome of such effort; they are subjected to no special pressure to change their customary lines of decision and are not forced in juxtaposition to their own group. Parenthetically, this is another reason for the relative ineffectiveness of attempts to achieve racial desegregation through general educational and moral campaigns.

A different setting is formed if the conscious efforts at desegregation are along lines which force functionaries to take cognizance of solicitations, demands, and pressures made on them to carry out a different line of decision. Such influences, if attended by any degree of weight, have the effect, psychologically, of detaching the functionaries from their group and of leading them to weigh such influences over against the views and expectations of their racial group. This is the kind of setting that is brought into being by the enactment and application of laws against segregation or by the imposition of regulations and expectations against segregation by leaders of associations and institutions in which the functionaries are in some measure incorporated. The functionaries have to take account of these demands and to form their decisions with some regard to the demands. In a genuine sense the functionary is an exposed target. This is the basic fact which structures the struggle toward deliberate racial desegregation. It also provides the opportunity for adroit advancement even where the dominant racial group is solidly opposed in feeling to a given line of desegregation.

ROLE OF ORGANIZATIONS

Recognizing the pivotal position of the decisions of functionaries, we easily see the important role of organizational pressure and support. The dominant group in a racial community, to a man, may have strong feelings of opposition to a given form of desegregation, yet be lacking in organizations to mobilize such opposition and convert it into action. Under such conditions, even though sharing the feelings of the dominant group the functionary may readily bow to the outside demands and pressures, particularly if these are backed up by weighty organizational support. Conversely, a functionary sympathetic to desegregation may be effectively deterred, not necessarily by the attitudes held by the members of the dominant racial group but by organizations among them that bespeak trouble. There is no need to spell out other possible combinations. The central point is clear. The carrying through as well as the blocking of deliberate desegregation depends on mobilizing and focusing influence and power on central functionaries. This calls, in the case of either side, for the development of organizatonal strength. The vehicle of procedure is strategical maneuvering, designed to marshal and utilize the potentials of power and prestige available in the given situation. Such potentials are almost certain to vary from situation to situation, thus calling for different tactical operations on local scenes.

It should be observed that in this contest, so to speak, to affect the decisions of the central functionaries, the advantage in the long run is in the hands of the side which is able to capitalize on the prestige and strength of the transcending group. Agencies seeking to achieve racial desegration have a particularly strong strategic weapon (it is not always seen or used) in focusing on the validity of *applying* the transcending legal or moral standard. This makes it unnecessary to challenge or impugn the feelings and attitudes of the functionary toward the subordinate racial group, or to try to change such feelings and attitudes. It makes it unnecessary, further, to argue the merits or the validity of the legal or moral standard. Instead, the approach to the functionary can appropriately be made in terms of the validity and need of *applying* the standard. This provides the opportunity of shifting the contest from a question of a struggle between the racial groups to a question of obedience to the transcending legal or moral standards. Since such standards carry implicitly the dictates of obedience, one is provided with a line along which to press the case which can largely avoid the issue of racial dispute. It may be added that this line becomes the most effective basis on which to build up organizational strength in acting toward central functionaries, for it offers opportunities of enlisting a support inside the dominant racial group that would be lost on the straight issue of racial struggle.

CONCLUSIONS

A few remarks should be made, in closing, on the relation of conscious or designed racial desegregation to natural and unwitting racial desegregation. There can be no question that the former acts back on and abets the latter. Where given programs of racial desegregation succeed, they weaken the support of other established forms of segregation. They interfere with the routine, repetitive affirmation of lines of racial exclusion. Further, in allowing the members of the racial groups to associate as equals in the new situation they lay the groundwork for acting toward one another on a human and personal basis rather than on a basis of membership in racial groups. Deliberate desegregation enters, thus, into a cyclical and reciprocal relation with natural desegregation.

The Rationale of
Labor–Management Relations

The three lectures which I am to give will deal with the general topics of disputes in the relations between employers and employees. I shall be concerned particularly with the problem of the labor strike and with the important question of how this problem may be handled.

In treating these matters I find it necessary to begin with a discussion of the fundamental character of labor-management relations. Without knowledge of the basic way in which labor and management are related it is not possible to speak intelligently on labor disputes or on control of strikes. Accordingly, my initial lecture is devoted to an analysis of the underlying premises of the relations between employers and employees, especially when these relations involve the organization of employees in labor unions.

In beginning this analysis we must respect the extensive differences to be found in the forms of relationship between employers and employees. The variation is very impressive. Allow me to refer to a few of the many lines of difference. We may note the difference in the size of the working units, the difference in the forms of ownership, the difference in the form of the working force, and the difference in the pattern of interest of employers in employees. Working units may vary in size from single employees as in the case of farm hands in some agricultural areas to large aggregations of workers in huge factories as in the case of the River Rouge plant of the Ford Motor Company. Ownership varies widely; the single employer who works with his employees; the small employer who is strictly a manager; large scale private ownership with the owners exercising management; corporate ownership with the owners in an absentee status; ownership by the State, and ownership by the employees. The working force may vary in many directions, from skilled to unskilled employees, from homogeneous to heterogeneous working groups, from permanent to transient workers and from employees with traditions of industrial experience to those lacking such experience. The interests of employers may be those of a kinsman in his kinfolk, those of paternalism, those of impersonality in an aggregation of mere working "hands," those of legal regard for contractual relations, and those of profound respect for a powerful organization of workers. There are many other dimensions of difference in the relationship between employers and employees. Indeed the forms of such relationship over the world and in past history are so profusely different as to suggest the impossibility of reducing them to any orderly or common pattern.

Yet, careful reflection does point to something that is common and intrinsic to these diverse forms, something that I regard as fundamental to the relations of employers and employees. This basic and common condition is constituted by the logic of the interests of employers and employees, of management and workers. The intrinsic nature of the employer-employee relationship is to set and cultivate common interest among those in the employer or managerial role. Similarly, the logical position of employees inclines them to a body of common interests. Each of these two sets of interests which stem naturally from the given position in the employer-employee relationship differs from the other. It is necessary to understand the nature of these basic interests respectively of employers and employees in order to understand labor-management relations.

Amid all of the different forms of ownership or types of management one may note clearly two basic interests that are common to the employer role. One of these centers around the need of directing the working force; the other around the need of operating the given employer enterprise in a profitable manner. These two needs are intrinsic and inescapable. They necessarily become charges on management, i.e., on those executing the employer role. Let me spell this out.

In all employment situations there is need of exercising direction of the work of those who are employed. Work assignments have to be laid out, rules established for the performance of the work, authoritative direction exercised over those engaging in the work, and some modicum of discipline imposed on them to secure proper work performance. These are tasks that are required in every work situation involving an employer and employees. They have to be performed irrespective of the many different forms which ownership and management may take in widely diverse industrial situations. It does not matter whether the employer or manager is a single individual or a huge corporation, a kinsman or a stranger, a private enterprise or a state controlled enterprise, or whether the employer is paternalistic, benevolently minded, democratically inclined, impersonal, or ruthlessly exploitative. In all instances this given managerial function has to be carried out. The performance of this function belongs, by definition, to some type of management. Corresponding to the need to manage is, of course, the right to manage. The exercise of this right, the protection of it, and the furthering of it are of necessary concern to management wherever it may be. They constitute and represent an intrinsic logical core of the role of the employer as he or any of his agents carry on an employer-employee relationship.

Alongside of this basic interest in directing the working arrangement there is another fundamental and inescapable interest that belongs to management. This second interest is to manage the given industrial enterprise profitably. It is clear that the survival and hence the existence of the industrial enterprise—whatever it may be—must depend on its profitable operation. An industry whose costs of operation, over time, exceed the return from such operation would of course be doomed to extinction. The only qualification to this statement is the ability to call on an available fund of reserves or to enjoy some form of subsidization to cover the losses of operation. Such types of aid can be only limited in industrial activity, whatever its form. They are atypical—no economy can allow any significant amount of continuing operation at a loss. The need of operating the employer enterprise profitably holds true regardless of the type of economy, of ownership, or of social setting. Whether in a simple and primitive barter of handicraft economy or a highly industrialized manufacturing economy; whether under private, state, or employees ownership; or whether in a familial, paternalistic, capitalistic, socialistic, or cooperative setting, the given industrial enterprise has to be operated so that its costs do not exceed its returns. The impact of these observations should be clear; namely, that management has a charge placed on it everywhere to operate profitably, to strive to maintain the solvency of the enterprise, however that solvency be calculated. We need to note that this charge is a logical and intrinsic element in the role of industrial management, whatever be the form of the industrial relationship.

I submit, then, that among all the variegated forms of employer-employee relations employers have two fundamental needs which are indigenous to their position. These needs become interests. At times some employers may be indifferent to these interests or indeed flout them. But such luxury can be only rare and infrequent. To surrender these interests in any continuous sense would lead the affected industrial enterprise to extinction. In effect, it would constitute managerial suicide. The very needs of survival of their enterprise require employers to respect and pursue the two interests which are indigenous to their role.

Now, we must note that employees, on their side, likewise have a set of interests that stem from the intrinsic nature of their role. These interests center in the job or position which they fill as employees. There are four major lines of concern to which employees are sensitized by virtue of their position. One is the remuneration of their labor, since such remuneration is likely to set the framework for their social existence. The dependency on remuneration lays employees open to a concern about the continuity, the security and the availability of employment. A third obvious line of concern is with regard to the conditions under which they work. Finally, we may note that employees will have some regard for themselves, some concern about self-respect in the face of the managerial direction to which they are subject. Admittedly, there is pronounced variation in the extent to which employees in different industrial situations may have these concerns. In some instances, particularly in stable primitive economies, the concerns are so remote as to suggest that they do not exist; however that they are present, even though in latent form, becomes evident when changes threaten customary arrangements along any of the four specified lines. Making the fullest allowance for the differences in the extent and the acuteness of these four concerns in different employment situations, we must recognize that they are built into the employee role. They constitute a body of interests that are indigenous to the role.

We should note the differences in the ways employers and employees become cognizant of their respective interests and define them, and the extent to which they become attached to their interests. Their interests as employers or employees may be interwoven with a variety of outside interests which have no logical connection with the employment situation but which are brought inside of the employer-employee relationship. Thus, employers in some settings show only the bare minimum of concern about profitable operation or the direction of employees necessary to keep the enterprise going; since the enterprise may move along under the impetus of customary routine the two central interests of employers may indeed be negligible. Correspondingly, employees in stable and integrated communal life may have no occasion to be concerned with their employment position. Further, employers may develop strong concerns for their interests while their employees may lag way behind in a concern for their employee interests. The reverse relationship is much more infrequent but occurs on occasion in a startling fashion. Usually, a strong and devoted attention by one party to its interests seems to exercise a pressure on the other party to do likewise. The most important observation to be made is that increasing industrial sophistication leads to a cleaner cut attachment to interests; with maturity and professionalization groups become more singularly concerned with their interests. The growth of industrial society brings the interests of employers and employees into sharper focus for each of them.

Despite the variety of settings, the fundamental way in which employer-employee relations must be viewed is in terms of the basic interests which are intrinsic to their respective positions. On one hand, to repeat, employers or managers are concerned with the profitable operation of business enterprises and with the need of directing the necessary operations; on the other hand, employees are concerned with employment, remuneration, condition of work, and treatment consonant with their self-regard. These two sets of interests, however they may be defined, provide the common foundation for relations between workers and management. They also supply the key to understanding the basic difficulties to be found in the relations of employers and employees.

It is important to recognize that these two sets of interests orient their holders in different directions. This different orientation lays a basic for conflict and opposition—a matter which I shall develop later. Of more importance at this point in my discussion is that neither employers nor employees can genuinely serve each other's interests and still remain faithful to the demands of their respective roles. Management cannot represent the interests of the employees without sacrificing in some degree the functions for which it exists. Similarly, workers cannot assume the functions of management without restricting their interests as employees. I wish to elaborate this point because of its critical significance in labor-management relations.

Management cannot represent the interests of workers because its role requires it to be management-centered. Its conduct of the business enterprise must aim to keep the enterprise on a profitable basis and to direct the working force in the various ways required for its operation. These must be its primary and its ultimate consideration. With its eyes on these aims, it must necessarily place the interests of the workers in a position of lesser or secondary importance. This becomes evident—if evidence is needed—when the interests of management and those of employees come into conflict. If the profitable operation of the enterprise requires a reduction in the labor force or a curtailment of wages, or if the direction of the work requires the workers to perform disagreeable or onerous tasks management will act to meet these requirements. It will not—and I add should not—sacrifice such needs of operation out of consideration for the wishes and welfare of the workers who will be affected adversely. Regardless of how benevolently inclined management may be towards its workers, regardless of how sincerely it may wish to act in the welfare of its workers, it cannot allow such considerations to take dominance over its built-in tasks of operating the enterprise and operating it profitably.

Many students would wish to qualify what I have said, by declaring that only under capitalistic enterprise or entrepreneurship is management incapable of representing the interests of workers. Such students would assert that in such types of industrial economy management would necessarily ignore the interests of workers or relegate such interests to a minor position. They would hold, however, that this would not be true under a socialistic structure of industry, or in a cooperative enterprise, or in worker-owned enterprise. In such instances, they believe, management could genuinely represent the interests of the workers.

Since my point is that management, wherever it be, is necessarily committed to the unavoidable function of management it will be helpful to look into those situations where presumably management would be indirect or direct agents of the workers. A little reflection should make it clear that even in such situations management cannot give priority to the interests of the workers. For whether owned by the worker-State, or the cooperative, or by the workers themselves, there must be management—and the management has to keep its eyes fixed on solvent operation and effective direction of the working force. Thus, in contemporary worker-States, like that of Soviet Russia, the management of industrial enterprises is juxtaposed to the workers in the enterprises. Working rules must be established, hours fixed, work quotas set, wages established, assignments given, and work supervised. These provide abundant sources of dissatisfaction and grievances among employees. Further, all of these phases of operation are covered by a need to have the industry operate profitably, i.e., yield returns equivalent to or in excess of costs. This financial and accounting requirement removes, further, the possibility of the management of Soviet industrial enterprises acting primarily in behalf of the interests of workers. Short shrift would be made of managers who betrayed their managerial charge by doing so.

The same picture is seen in the case of worker-owned enterprises. Paradoxically the management of such enterprises even though directly chosen by the workers and frequently consisting of workers themselves, have to carry out the two basic requirements of the managerial role. They have to direct, and they have to guide the enterprise in a profitable manner. This lays the basis for a cleavage between the workers in the role of managers and workers in the role of employees. This cleavage may be slight in the small industrial enterprise that is owned by the workers. In the large worker-owned enterprises it becomes pronounced. This condition was illustrated nicely in a humorous incident a few years ago in the case of the American Cast Iron Pipe Company, a large worker-owned company in Birmingham, Alabama. Like any industrial plant this factory had to have a management. The management had to operate like good managements do—keep an eye on costs, set up efficient operations, assign work, maintain quality in performance, require good output, and exercise discipline. The workers found themselves subject to the same general round of direction, supervision, and control by "bosses" that occur under private ownership. Indeed, a substantial number of the workers—mind you, the owners of the company—found their position as employees so unsatisfactory *vis-a-vis* their management that they initiated serious efforts to organize a union in the plant. One of the workers was asked to explain this anomalous behavior of trying to organize a union against their own company. His quoted answer is most interesting: "Sure, this is my plant, but somebody has to protect my rights as a downtrodden working stiff against my privileges as a bloated capitalistic stockholder." We see neatly revealed this dichotomy between worker interests and management interests.

The foregoing discussion is sufficient, I hope, to make clear that in carrying out its necessary functions management cannot genuinely represent and protect the interests of workers. The reverse relation holds true in a comparable manner. In pursuing their legitimate interests, workers cannot be genuinely faithful to the interests of management. As employees they cannot be in the role of management; to assume that role they have to step out of their employee role and subjugate the interests embedded in that role. As employees their concerns are logically employee centered, not management centered.

Thus, the logical structure of the employer-employee relationship contains two fundamental roles, each carrying different functions and a set of distinct interests. Each set of interests is legitimate and each makes a proper claim on the occupants of the given role. Managers who are indifferent to the effective and profitable direction of the enterprises with which they are entrusted are poor managers, wherever they be; employees who have no concern in the nature and conditions of their employment are obviously guiding themselves by the definition of some alien role. Since the roles and attendant interests are distinct and different the occupants of neither role can act on behalf of the interests of the other role without making some sacrifice of the interest implied in their own role. Such sacrifices may and do occur, but usually only within narrow limits. Marked departures from the interests set by their role are sporadic, and result from extraordinary conditions. Under competitive conditions such marked departures imperil either the life of the enterprise or the well being of the workers. The import of these observations is the redundant proposition that employers and employees have to represent their respective interests—neither can do a good job in representing the interests of the other.

The representation of their respective interests is admittedly unequal as between employers and employees unless the employees can act collectively. The employee, as a separate individual, is in no effective position to protect and further the interests that inhere in his employee role. The employer has the authority to determine who is to be employed and how the work is to be performed. In the face of this power the individual worker is in a weak position to defend or advance his interests, unless perchance his specific labor is irreplaceable. I need not recount the history of individual bargaining in industry. It is an unambiguous story of the essential impotency of the individual worker to act effectively on behalf of his employee interests. This condition, of course, provides the general reason for the origin and development of the labor movement and for the formation of labor unions. Concerted action by employees on behalf of their interests is the only means whereby employee interests get an operating anchorage. The rise of labor unions, however their formation may be enmeshed in the peculiarities of local conditions, is a natural outcome of the inability of employees as individuals to protect the interests of their role.

When employees are able to act collectively the relation between the interests of employees and those of employers is brought into clearer focus. The union is a structural arrangement which allows employee interests to come to the fore, to come to an expression which has to be dealt with. The union-management relationship is thus the means of bringing out in relief the implicit feature of the employer-employees relationship. The picture which is thus revealed is one of conflict between interests at divergent and shifting points, requiring recurrent accommodation. Since the conflict and accommodation of divergent interests is the heart of the problem of labor relations, I wish to extend my discussion of it.

Conflicts develop naturally between employers and employees as each group pursues its own interests. The interests operate for each of the two parties as general directing perspectives that sweep over the multitude of concrete matters—wage rates, work assignments, working rules, disciplinary acts, etc.—that enter into the relations between the two parties. Many of these concrete matters occasion no conflict of interests, that is to say that neither of the two parties regards its interests as involved in the matters at the particular time, or as being affected adversely by the prospective actions for which the matters stand. Other matters, as conceived by the parties at the given time, become occasions for disagreement and dispute.

This characterization is trite, yet important. It calls attention to the fact that conflict between employers and employees is not all-inclusive and continuous—it is rather selective, spotty, and shifting. Instead of the occupants of employer and employee roles being locked continuously in opposition across the full band of their relationships, opposition occurs at scattered and shifting points in accordance with how the parties define the application of their interests. Industrial conflict does not issue relentlessly from a fixed and pathological strain in the social structure (as is implied, for example, in the Marxian doctrine), but arises at changing points as the industrial parties pursue their interests.

Yet we should not blink our eyes to the fact that there is a real difference between the interests of employers and employees. As I have sought to point out in my discussion, this difference is built into their respective roles in the industrial relationship. It is a natural difference and not one that stems from a pathological structure of a diseased condition in the industrial area of life. Because it belongs naturally to the logical texture of the employer-employee relationship, to ignore it or to gloss over it can be only misleading in any conscientious effort to analyze the problem of industrial disputes. There are many widely held and strongly held views which rest on the premise that differences between employers and employees are pathological, that they stem from abnormal and alien conditions, and hence that industrial peace is to be achieved by the elimination of these allegedly abnormal and alien conditions. The most conspicuous of these views is that known as the "Human Relations in Industry" approach. It premises a natural and indigenous condition of cooperation in industrial enterprise since both employers and employees have to enter into joint action to produce the products of that enterprise. Thus, it presumes that any friction, any disagreement or any dispute represents a departure from the intrinsic cooperative character of the enterprise and signifies the play of some alien and unnatural influence. However ethically commendable it may be, the premise underlying this approach grossly distorts the basic nature of the employer-employee relationship. Differences in interest do exist between the roles of employer and employee.

The fundamental explanation of industrial conflict lies in these differences in interest as they come to expression in given concrete matters in the industrial relationship. In a consonant manner, the effective handling of such conflicts must be sought along the line of adjusting these differences, not in trying to eliminate basic interests. What is clearly called for are workable means of adjusting the differences in the views and positions of employer and employee, that is, arriving at a proposal which each of the parties finds acceptable under the prevailing circumstances. Let me point out here that collective bargaining, unquestionably the most valuable contribution to the labor relations problem, is precisely a mechanism for the accommodation of interest. Collective bargaining presupposes conflicts in interest, differences in demands and positions; it is a means of enabling the parties to achieve workable arrangements. It typifies the process of accommodation that is basic to a satisfactory employer-employee relationship.

My treatment of the nature and role of the interests of employers and employees must be rounded by a discussion of outside interests which may enter to confuse, engulf, distort, and pervert the legitimate interests of employers and employees. The intrusion of such outside interests which have no natural or logical relevancy to the employer-employee relationship complicates and hinders that relationship. In forming a clear understanding of the problem of labor relations it is advisable to identify and consider the more important forms of such intrusion. I shall deal with those which enter through the labor union, those that enter through management, and those that enter through the State.

The union may be a source of alien interests that confuse or complicate the employer-employee relationship. One should recognize, first of all, that a labor union comes to establish interests of its own aside from the interests of the employees that it represents. Once established, a union has a need of surviving, of entrenching its existence and, as occasion provides, of expanding its size and power. Leaders and an operating personnel may become dependent on their union for their income and livelihood. In the direction and operation of the union the interests of this group may take precedence over the interests of the workers. The variance between the two sets of interests is generally small since the union usually is led to promote the interests of the workers. However, a union may follow other interests. Thus, in becoming institutionalized and being given a respectable position in the community, a union may be dulled in its responsiveness to the interests of employees. Or a union may become an instrument for personal or political aims of its leaders. Or it may become a vehicle of a movement with a radical, a religious, or a political ideology. In such ways a union may be turned to the pursuit of interests which diverge from interests stemming from the employees' role. The insertion of such interests into the bargaining arena blurs and hinders employee-employer relations.

On its side management may be a similar point of entree for interests alien to the employer-employee relationship. An effort may be made to inculcate employees and union personnel with managerial values or ideologies. Management may strive to weave a paternalistic fabric around the employees and put itself in the position of protector and representative of their interests. It may seek to mould the employees along the line of political or social philosophies. These are suggestions of the ways in which management swerves from or goes beyond its strict managerial interests. Again, the insertion of such outside interests muddies the employer-employee relationship.

Finally, the State may intrude into the employer-employee relationship in such a way as to prevent the interests in that relationship from getting expression or accommodation. Instead of setting a legal framework which would facilitate such expression and accommodation the State may seek to determine what these relations should be. As in Soviet Russia, it may impose its own interests, dictating the acts of both management and employees. Or the State may rig the framework in favor of the interests of one of the parties at the expense of the other. Or it may take into its own hands the settling of the disagreements and disputes of the parties. In such ways, the State may direct the interest of employers or employees, arrest their expression, infuse them with political concerns that do not stem naturally from the employer-employee relationship, or substitute its own interests for those of the parties. Such intrusions confuse, pervert, or submerge natural relations between employers and employees.

The import of my remarks on the entrance of alien interests into the employer-employee relationship should be clear. The grafting of such alien interests onto the relationship should not conceal a recognition of the basic and natural character of that relationship. This basic character is that of two sets of interests, logically implicated in the roles, which in being applied to concrete matters give rise at divergent points to disagreements and disputes. The handling of these disputes becomes a problem of adjusting interests at these given points. This is the framework inside of which the problem of the labor strike should be placed.

THE NATURE AND FUNCTION
OF THE LABOR STRIKE

No aspect of employer-employee relations excites more interest, arouses more feeling, and generates stronger attitudes than the labor strike. Because people view it so readily in terms of feeling and conviction they easily misconstrue its place and its function. Since the strike plays a decisive role in labor relations it requires careful and detached analysis.

We may start with some reference to the general public attitude toward the strike. By and large the outside community feels the labor strike to be improper and indeed pernicious. It is easy to understand why. For one thing, the strike seems to be a clear source of economic loss. Wages are lost, profits are lost and production is lost. There seems to be no sense in such economic waste, particularly since the waste, like misused time, appears to be unrecoverable. Such a judgment based on simple economic considerations enters into the general community attitude towards the labor strike. Along with it there is likely to be some sentimental concern over the suffering believed to accompany the economic losses of the strike—some feeling over the plight of the families of the workers on strike, or over the loss of profits, or over the interference with the local industry dependent on worker income, or over the inconveniences which the strike may occasion in the community. In addition, the strike appears to many as a form of moral irresponsibility, an inexcusable failure on the part of management and labor to work out their difficulties. Usually, one or the other of the parties is suspected or felt to be the culprit whose unreasonableness, arrogance, greed, and lack of public virtue has brought the strike into being. The feeling is that if the miscreant party would only act with proper moral decency and with a sense of public responsibility, there would be no occasion for the strike. Finally, most outsiders sense that the labor strike is a challenge and threat to public order. The employees stay away from work and seem thus to attack property rights; they put up picket lines or engage in other acts to discourage or prevent other people from a right to work; they may become unruly and disorderly, engage in violence, injure people, damage property, and get in conflict with police. Such actions appear to be on the fringe, if not in the center, of illegal behavior and to symbolize an attack on the principle of normal and orderly social relations.

From such sources is built the general community image of the labor strike. The labor strike is viewed as something harmful, something that is out of place in normal, orderly life, and as something that should not be. As happens with things that are regarded as morally out-of-key the strike is viewed as an abnormal occurrence for which there is no justification and no need. This attitude—which I think is widespread and deeply entrenched—flows over into two directions worthy of note. One is that taken by scholars who believe that labor strikes arise from hidden pathological conditions; for them, the task is set to discover these causes so that with such knowledge one may eliminate the strike. The other direction is a call by the public for the prevention of strikes; if need be, by government action.

Against this popular view of the labor strike as something wrong and out-of-place I wish to contend that the labor strike is indispensable for proper and effective labor-management relations. Instead of bespeaking an alien and pathological background, the labor strike arises naturally out of the intrinsic nature of employer-employee relations. Instead of undermining or disintegrating such relations the labor strike serves to establish and maintain such relations. The elimination of the labor strike would destroy effective and wholesome labor relations. Oddly, the labor strike constitutes the cornerstone of any solid edifice of management-labor relations. This is what I wish now to explain.

The explanation should begin with a reminder of what is basic to the employer-employee relationship, namely the two sets of differently oriented interests which that relationship logically brings into being. To review this matter briefly, let me state that both management and workers are obviously needed in every employer-employee relation. The position of management requires management to be concerned with the direction of operations and with the profitable conduct of such operations. These are inescapable functions and proper functions. The interests built up by management around these functions are legitimate. On their side, the employees have a natural and proper concern about such vital things to them as their wages, the security of their employment, the condition of their work, and their self-respect in how they are being directed. These are a legitimate set of interests. Neither employers nor employees are equipped to serve each other's interests; i.e., to direct their own participation in the industrial enterprise in terms of the interests of the other. Employers are in no position to conduct the enterprise solely or chiefly to serve the vital interests of the workers; to renounce their interests in directing work and in profitable operation would be to imperil the enterprise. In turn, workers are unsuited to follow solely or chiefly the interests of management and to renounce concern in the vital conditions of their employment. Each of the two parties is alone suited to attend to and care for its respective interests. However, employees can serve their interests effectively only if they can act together. The individual employee, by himself, is clearly impotent to exercise effective control over his employee interests; the organization of employees is the essential means to the safeguarding of such interests. Such organization of employees, when it becomes formalized, becomes a labor union. As the agency of the workers, the union has as its chief function the protection and advancement of the employee interests.

Now what is clearly needed in employer-employee relations is some apparatus which will permit employers and employees to pursue their respective interests and still to get along together in an effective working relationship. An apparatus to do this is called for because of the fact that the interest of employers and those of employees are not naturally complementary. Instead they are likely to come into opposition and conflict at different points in the complex areas in which they meet. If workers want more wages, that is their interest; management has to view such a demand in terms of its interests. There may be opposition. If management wants a 48-hour work week and the workers want a 40-hour week, then there is a point of opposition. Similar instances of disagreement may arise to a host of matters—work assignments, seniority claims, disciplinary actions, and so forth. If the two parties are to get along together—and obviously such joint action is indispensable—there must be some reconciliation of their different wishes and demands, some accommodation of the different positions set by their respective interests. If the interests of the two parties are accorded the expression which their legitimacy warrants, the necessary apparatus for the accommodation of their interests is an arrangement that will allow for mutual discussion and negotiation of their conflicting demands. This, of course, is what collective bargaining does.

With this picture as a background we may now turn to the strike. There are clearly three reasons why the strike, in the sense of the right to strike, is essential to effective labor-management relations. First, it is a device which is frequently needed in the organizing of workers; second, it serves as a protection to the maintenance of the labor union; and third it is indispensable to the structure of collective bargaining. I wish to spell out each of these three ways by which the instrument of the strike plays a vital and necessary role in labor-management relations.

Unless laws provide an orderly procedure whereby workers may organize and gain recognition by their employer, the right to strike is indispensable. Today so many countries have laws which protect such organization and recognition that we are likely to undervalue the significance of the organizational strike. Yet in earlier times in such countries and still in many places today the strike was or is an essential instrument in enabling the workers to gain recognition as a collective bargaining unit. If a group of workers banding together in some kind of union is told by management, "We want nothing to do with you," what is the group to do? If it is to gain some kind of acceptance by management its only recourse is to force management to give that acceptance. The strike, either through use or the threat of use, is the means par excellence of gaining recognition. In serving to gain for workers an acceptance which is otherwise denied, the labor strike lays the foundation for an employer-employee relationship wherein each party may pursue and safeguard its own interests. The thousands of times in which the strike or the threat of its use has brought about such a relationship makes clear the vital role of the labor strike. To prohibit the strike, without some lawful alternative which safeguards organization and recognition, is to deprive employees of an essential means of following their interests. If we grant that logically the interests of workers are legitimate, and that a satisfactory employer-employee relationship must allow both parties to pursue their interests, then the organizational strike must be seen as vital and necessary.

In a very similar way the labor strike must be seen as a necessary instrument for the maintenance of the labor union. The possibility of using the strike is a major means whereby unions can gain assurance of continuing to exist after being formed. To appreciate the full significance of this point it is necessary to recognize the uncertain and risky position of the labor union. The fact that many labor unions are strong and deeply entrenched should not mislead us into a belief that the maintenance or survival of labor unions is a self-assured matter. I wish to discuss this matter at a little length.

The most important observation is that the labor union is not essential to the operation of the industrial enterprise. While the enterprise cannot function without management and workers, it can get along without the organization of the workers. This places the union in an anomalous position. In contrast to management and workers, the union as the third party to the industrial relationship has to create its position and establish its claim to participation. Even though the labor union performs an essential function as the medium for the pursuit of worker interests, it is logically an ouside party. Not having an indigenous position in the industrial relationship it has to be alert to and contend with forces which threaten to undermine its acceptance. Threats to its position and existence come from many quarters. I wish to comment briefly on the more important sources of menace to the union.

The chief source is the general attitude of management and employers toward unions in their plants. This attitude reflects the recognition that the union is an outside entity and not needed for the operation of the plant. It is rare, extremely rare, to find a management that believes the union to be essential to the operation of its business. Indeed, with scarce exceptions, managements believe that they could do a better job in operating their businesses if they did not have unions on their hands. Given a free choice managements would preponderantly elect to run their businesses without unions. This typical and pervading view by management that it doesn't need the union and really doesn't want the union is a running potential threat to the union's existence. Another source of insecurity to the union is set by the possibility of being raided by rival unions. Without some kind of guaranteed protection of its area of jurisdiction a union, unless overwhelmingly strong, is exposed to a threat of encroachment by some new or existing union. A third recurring source of threat to the union lies in the feelings of employees toward their union. Employees may become indifferent to their union, feel little sense of obligation to it, and give little spontaneous support to it. Finally, the union is likely to encounter an atmosphere of rejection on the part of the general community and its chief institutions.

In the face of such sources of threat to its existence and security the labor union is compelled to develop and maintain strength. The strike becomes a major weapon in affording assurance to the union that it will be able to exist. What is important is not the use of this weapon but the fact that the weapon is available for use. To prohibit or outlaw the strike without providing protection to the security of unions would seriously endanger their existence and their ability to function as the agent for the expression and safeguarding of worker-interests.

It should be clear from this discussion that unless laws provide and protect union recognition and union security, the strike is indispensable for the formation and maintenance of labor unions. If it be granted that employees alone are qualified to pursue their interests and that this can be done effectively only through their collective organization, then it is evident that the strike is a vital foundation to the employee wall of the labor-management structure.

But even more significant is the value of the strike in enabling employers and employees to adjust their interests. Here, again, what is important is the availability of the strike for use rather than its actual employment. It must be borne in mind that the association of employers and employees gives rise to many shifting points of disagreement as each of the two parties pursues its interests. Effective relations make imperative some means of enabling the parties to adjust these differences. Collective bargaining is the means by which this may be accomplished. It is the device which enables both parties to pursue their interests and at the same time to adjust their interests. In the last analysis collective bargaining depends on the right of the employees to strike. Without this right the employees would lose their leverage in getting management to bargain; i.e., make a serious effort to meet the demands advanced by the employees on behalf of their interests. Management might elect in negotiations to reject any and all demands proposed by the employees. What is the union, as the bargaining agent, to do in such a situation? How is it to get the management to give serious consideration to its proposals? Without the right to strike the union would be helpless; management would steadfastly refuse to make any concessions since there would be no coercion or penalty which it would incur because of the refusal. Mind you, I am not suggesting that the management which refuses to entertain union demands is acting evilly; indeed, the safeguarding of its interests could lead it to reject legitimately all union proposals. If the union had no recourse other than to accept the refusal it would obviously be in no position to safeguard the equally legitimate interests of the employees. Under these conditions collective bargaining would become a mockery—there would be no decisive reason why management should strive to work out anything with the union. It is the right of the employees to strike which in the last analysis provides the leverage necessary to make collective bargaining work. With that right the employees are put into a position whereby they can force management to give consideration to the proposals which are advanced. The strike is the ultimate reserve weapon. The thought or suggestion of its use is potent in inducing management to consider seriously what the employees believe their interests require. To ban the strike would undercut the institution of collective bargaining. It would remove a major pressure on the parties to achieve the "meeting of minds" for which collective bargaining exists.

That the strike has the effect of making collective bargaining work is readily observed by anyone with much familiarity with collective bargaining negotiations. It is easy in collective bargaining for negotiations to go on and on, with management showing no wish or inclination to grant any demand, even in part. From its point of view management may be acting very sincerely since, let it be recognized, any concession which management makes is not, strictly speaking, to its managerial interests. The protraction of negotiations as a result of this disinclination to make any concessions can easily lead to an impasse. It is of interest to note how quickly negotiations speed up and how readily the parties strive to work out some kind of agreement when there is a serious threat of a strike. It is the strike, hovering in the background, which in the last analysis, supplies the force necessary to make collective bargaining work.

I trust that I have made clear that the strike, especially in the form of the right to strike, is an essential and key element in any satisfactory structure of employee-employer relations. Programs which would seek to handle the problem of the strike by eliminating the right to strike seriously misunderstand the logic and rationale of employer-employee relations. Such programs would destroy the foundations of an arrangement whereby management and employees in pursuit of their respective legitimate interests are able to adjust the differences which inevitably arise between them. To banish the right to strike would result in the suppression of the interests of workers, as we see for example in Soviet Russia, and block the "meeting of minds" essential to satisfactory employer-employee relations.

The recognition of the value of the strike should not mean of course that no steps should be taken to reduce the likelihood of strikes. This is a different problem—indeed a proper problem. It is a matter of good common sense to try to reduce the occasion for the strike. From what I have said it is clear that much can be done to remove the major conditions which foster the rise of the strike. The three main inducing conditions of which I have spoken suggest lines of remedial action. First, if lawful provisions exist whereby employees can freely organize and gain due recognition as a bargaining unit, there is little need for the organizing strike. The wisdom of such provisions is attested by the labor acts enacted in a number of the more advanced industrial nations. Second, if unions are given substantial security their reliance on the strike for purposes of survival is greatly removed. Legal provisions which assure a union its membership and dues for a designated period and which give it protection in its area of jurisdiction do much to offset the insecurity that inclines unions to the use of the strike. Third, the improvement of collective bargaining procedures can do much to curb the remaining major source of the strike. Paradoxically, the mere availability of the strike in collective bargaining is probably the major condition militating against the need of using it; this availability should be kept unimpaired. But in a broader sense any condition or contrivance which contributes to the free expression and serious consideration of worker complaints and demands reduces the likelihood of the strike. Among such means we may note a procedure within plant operations which permits the orderly presentation and serious treatment of grievances; an understanding to avoid in bargaining sessions the use of provocative emotional symbols; a studious policy of refraining from derogatory personal references; and the cultivation of sincere effort to reach agreement. Obviously the likelihood of resorting to the strike may be lessened if the parties show mutual respect in their bargaining and strike honestly to achieve some accommodation of their differences.

However, despite all such efforts to remove the occasion for the use of the strike, its employment may be very much in order. Even though a union may be well organized and free from threats to its security and even though the collective bargaining machinery may be working very adequately the occasion and, indeed, need for the strike may exist. The situation in which this condition occurs is clear. A union may advance legitimate demands. The management with equal legitimacy may reject the demands as untenable from its point of view. Negotiations on the demands may be honest and thorough without the union believing that it could sincerely modify or withdraw its demands and without the management believing that it could grant the demands in whole or part. If in the face of this impasse the union is willing to pay the price of a strike and the company, similarly, is willing to incur the penalty of the strike, the resort to the strike is natural and healthy. It is natural in arising from a genuine opposition of interest. It is healthy in that it is the means of establishing a workable relation between the parties on an issue on which they are otherwise hopelessly at odds. One should not lose sight of the fact that the strike may serve genuinely to end a conflict or to compose a difference which defies resolution by the parties in any other way. Let me illustrate the point with a single instance, the strike, a few years ago, of the United Steelworkers against the steel companies over the issue of pensions. From the point of view of employee interests the Union believed that their demand for a more satisfactory pension system was proper and wholesome. The steel companies believed with equal sincerity that there was no place in the operation of its plants for the increased costs of the requested pension system. Full and, I think, honest discussions between the parties did nothing to dislodge either from its point of view. One cannot say that either party was wrong or unjustified in its position. Yet obviously some kind of accommodation of their differing interests had to be achieved. The parties had to get along with each other in some kind of workable relation on this momentous issue. In the given instance each party regarded its interests to be sufficiently important to stand the costs of a strike. The strike became, then, the decisive means of composing a disagreement that could not be resolved by any alternative procedures in the hands of the two parties.

We should recognize, accordingly, that the labor strike plays a legitimate and indeed salutary role in the adjustment of the interests of labor and management. It serves not only to buttress the proper functioning of collective bargaining, as I have explained earlier, but becomes also a real part of the process by which in given crucial situations, the parties work out their relations to each other so that they can get along in the actual running of the industry.

I have sought in the foregoing discussion to make clear the place and the function of the strike in employer-employee relations. An analysis of the logical character of the relationship between the two parties points to the need of the pursuit and the accommodation of the legitimate interests which both parties have in their relationship. The labor strike must be recognized as intrinsic to the satisfactory flow of their relations—partially in aiding employees to form and maintain a collective organization, partially in exerting a force to compel the parties to bargain seriously, and partially in enabling them to resolve crucial differences that cannot be composed through negotiation.

A recognition of the need and vital role of the strike in labor-management relations should not blind us to the fact that the strike may be misused and abused. I wish to conclude my remarks with a brief discussion of the kinds of strikes which do not really belong in the labor-management picture. These are strikes which do not stem from the interests set by the logical nature of the employer-employee relationship but arise instead from alien interests that are introduced into that relationship. Let me refer to some of the more usual forms in which the strike may be used to satisfy extraneous interests. Some union officials may use the strike, or the threat of it, to exact personal tribute—a practice which has been not uncommon in the building trades. Or some officials may use the strike for personal political advantages. Or the strike may be employed to advance a political or social doctrine aiming to change the social order rather than to adjust differences in the employee-employer relationship. Or the strike may be used as a retributive weapon, merely to inflict injury on a hated management. Or, it may be used in connivance with an employer to harm or eliminate a rival employer. It should be noted that employers may likewise make use of the strike for purposes that are foreign to the employee-employer relationship. The employer may provoke a strike to aid or harm some union officials or some faction in the internal politics of the union. Or an employer may connive with the union to strike a competing employer to damage or ruin his business. Or, similarly, such connivance may be made with one union to use the strike to undermine or destroy another union.

Obviously, there are many ways in which the strike may be misused to further aims that have nothing to do with the legitimate interests of employees and employers in their relationship. Such strikes are not healthy. Steps to prevent or eliminate such illegitimate strikes are very much in order. However, great care must be taken in such efforts not to destroy or impair the foundations of legitimate strikes. It would be a serious mistake in coping with improper strikes to adopt a program which would eliminate or curb the right to use the legitimate strike. The result would be to undermine the foundations of the relationship needed to serve the interests of both employers and employees.

CONTROL OF THE LABOR STRIKE

What is the problem of the labor strike? Why should the labor strike be controlled? How can the labor strike be controlled? These are the questions which I wish to discuss in this lecture.

Much confusion and misunderstanding are to be found in the ways in which the labor strike is thought to constitute a problem. It is necessary to cut through the confusion and locate the problem as clearly as possible.

Many people, including scholars and students of labor relations, regard the labor strike as being intrinsically wrong and as unnecessary. Some of them, particularly economists, view the strike as a needless form of economic waste and as an interference with the natural and orderly operation of a wage and price system. Others regard the strike as an unwarranted violation of property and personal rights. Others treat it as an attack on the public or social order with far-reaching implications of danger to the institutions of orderly life. Still others regard the strike as a menace to the spirit and practice of cooperation which they believe should pervade a decent civilized life. Regardless of how they differ in their premises, all of these people have a common belief that the labor strike, *per se,* is the problem. For them, the labor strike has no natural or justifiable place in human group life. Their position, accordingly, is that the labor strike as such should be eliminated.

This common view, in my judgment, reflects a serious misunderstanding of the place and role of the labor strike in employer-employee relations. It needs to be corrected. I find it advisable to remind you that the strike is natural to labor relations, and indeed that it plays a role which is indispensable to any effective system of labor relations. An effective system of labor relations, in my mind, is one in which both employers and employees are free to pursue the interests which arise logically from their respective roles in the employment context. The pursuit of these interests leads to shifting points of disagreement between them. These differences need to be composed by a process, such as collective bargaining, which permits the parties to develop some kind of workable agreement. The labor strike plays an essential part in this process: by aiding in the formation and maintenance of the labor organization, without which employees are not able to pursue their interests; by exercising a pressure on the parties to strive seriously to compose their differences; and by enabling the resolution of crucial differences that resist solution through negotiation. While the value of the strike comes mainly from its availability rather than from its use, there are many occasions when its employment contributes in a salutary fashion to the resolution of differences which cannot be composed in any other way.

These observations, which I have developed in my preceding lectures, should make it clear that the strike, particularly the right to strike, is essential to an effective system of labor relations. To ban the strike would be to deny to employees the right and opportunity to pursue the interests which intrinsically exist for them in their employee role; it would implant in the structure of employer-employee relations an enduring source of tensions— a tension which under propitious circumstances would be sure to break forth. In superimposing on employee-employer relations an artificial framework which is not consonant with their logical character the prohibition of the strike would lead to an unhealthy situation. We must judge in the same way the well motivated intention to eliminate the labor strike *per se,* by removing the presumed causes of the strike. Here again, we must note that this approach misunderstands the basic character of employer-employee relations and hence misconstrues the nature and place of the labor strike. While much can and should be done to reduce the occasions for resorting to the strike, to try to eliminate the "cause" of the strike would be to undertake a ridiculous task. As I have sought to show, the labor strike is an integral part of the logical structure of employer-employee relations. To render the strike, as such, unnecessary presumes the possibility of eliminating all opposition or conflict between the interests of employers and employees, or of guaranteeing that these two parties would inevitably compose their differences through peaceful discussion. These two premises are fanciful. They belie both the logical nature of the roles of employer and employee and the realistic character of human behavior.

If we do not regard the labor strike, *per se,* as a problem, where, then, does the problem lie? Many would say the problem exists in the improper use of the strike. Certainly, as I have mentioned in the preceding lecture, the strike may be misused and abused. It may be employed, for instance, to further the personal interests of union leaders, to advance social and political doctrines, to inflict injury in a spirit of revenge, to incite and use the inner political struggles of a union, or at the instigation of management to eliminate business competition. Like any social weapon the labor strike may be used for purposes other than that for which it is intended. Its purpose in the employer-employee relationship is to reconcile conflicts between the interests which the two parties have in that relationship. To use the strike on behalf of interests that are logically alien to that relationship is a misuse.

Unquestionably, the misuse of the labor strike constitutes a problem but not a serious problem. Figures are not available, of course, on the extent of such misuse. My impression is that improper strikes form only a slight fraction of labor strikes. With only infrequent exceptions labor strikes are nailed down to specific and designatable issues that clearly stem from the employer-employee relationship. On occasion such issues may serve as a cover to hidden purposes, but even in these instances the issues have independent sense and legitimacy in terms of the employer-employee relationship. Preponderantly, labor strikes are held to a framework of legitimate employee interests. It is interesting to note that even union racketeers, or union leaders strongly committed to a political doctrine, are forced to fit the direction of their union inside of acceptable union practice. The coercion to do so increases with the stabilization and social acceptance of unions in the community. In short, there are a set of checks which prevent or limit the disposition to misuse the labor strike—checks in the form of what the workers expect of the specific strike, the relative ease of determining whether the strike is "phony", the views and attitudes of other unions, and even the usual laws against fraud and corruption. Undoubtedly, improper strikes occur and call for efforts to prevent them. But such strikes are relatively few and sporadic and represent a minor tangent to the main stream of labor strikes. They do not constitute the main problem of the labor strike.

If the labor strike, as such, is not legitimately a problem, and if the misuse of the labor strike is only a limited problem, we may ask again, "In what manner is the labor strike a problem?" The answer is clear. The labor strike becomes a problem when it inflicts appreciable harm on the community, depriving people of food and vital services, or endangering the survival of the community as in the case of disaster or war it justifies public alarm and calls for action. The line beyond which the public interest is seriously endangered is a matter of judgment and cannot be drawn precisely. But even though this line be fuzzy and subject to a latitude of uncertainty the labor strike becomes unquestionably a problem when in informed and competent judgment it threatens the public welfare.

Now it should be clear that the overwhelming majority of strikes do not endanger the public interest. They impose no harm or only insignificant harm on the community. In the usual strike the only people who are affected adversely are the parties themselves. The strikes are essentially private affairs which while of great importance to the parties do not have serious consequences to the public. Even in the bigger and longer strikes the public is likely to be only inconvenienced or subject to bearable discomforts; the public is not endangered or the functioning of the social order threatened. By any reasonable rule one would have to admit that labor strikes, by and large, do not set any significant problem for the community. While efforts are always in order to remove the occasion for strikes, the proponderant majority of labor strikes does not loom up as anything serious for community life.

However, as I have said, there is the occasional major strike which may be judged to threaten the public interest in a vital and genuine manner. The strike in a large utility network, an extensive strike in the system of transportation or communication, a lasting strike in the production of vital raw products, a protracted national coal strike or national strike in the steel industry, a continuing strike on the docks of an insular community—these are the kinds of strikes which may seriously threaten the public interest. They are the only kinds of labor strikes which constitute any real problem to society. On the assumption that a strike of this kind genuinely affects or threatens to affect seriously the public interest the community is justified in endeavoring to control the strike. This is the problem of control I wish to discuss.

It is important to understand the nature of this problem. To view it as a mere matter of protecting the public welfare is inadequate. To be sure, such protection is obviously needed. No government should forfeit its fundamental function of acting to prevent injury to the public interest. The government is freely justified to control the major strike that inflicts such injury. However, we should not lose sight of the importance of the right to strike. This right is not a mere incidental gratuity. Instead, as I have sought to explain previously, the right to strike is basic to collective bargaining, basic to a structure wherein employees and employers may pursue their interests and adjust their interests. Because of its fundamental importance to the vast industrial network of employer-employee relations, the right to strike has, or should have, the character of a public right. In our own nation this right is part of the law of the land. Thus, in dealing with the problem of the major strike there is need of recognizing the presence of two basic principles and rights—that of protecting the public interest and of striking. To act on the basis of solely one of them and to ignore or undercut the other constitutes a real danger. The paradoxical task of preserving both principles in efforts to control the major strikes constitutes the crucial problem. Before suggesting the lines along which this might be done, it may be helpful to discuss the chief means which are currently used or proposed to deal with the major strike that endangers the public interest.

The first of these means of which I wish to speak is legislation prohibiting the strike for a specified period of time. This is what the well-known Taft-Hartley Act seeks to do. Such legislation presumes, apparently, that the major strike results from faulty bargaining between the parties, especially in the form of aroused tempers that block reasonable negotiations. What is needed, it is contended, is a "cooling-off" period during which the parties can regain composure and resume negotiations in the reasonable spirit that is conducive to the solution of their difficulties. This manner of meeting the major strike is obviously defective. It rests on spurious and false premises. Major strikes are rarely a result of hot outbursts of temper. A major strike for a union is a formidable affair with weighty risks and many grave consequences. Usually, a union will hesitate a long time before committing itself to a major strike. The decision of a union to resort to a major strike ordinarily has a lengthy background of searching analysis, evaluation, and judgment. The same kind of weighty considerations lie behind the decision of management not to make the concession which might forestall the strike. These crucial decisions of both parties result from cool calculations and are not the product of momentary gusts of passion. We need to note also that, usually, serious collective bargaining is not wanting in the case of the major strikes. The specific issues from which the major strike springs are usually discussed at length by the parties. These observations suggest that a "cooling-off" period has little relevance. Its effect is to postpone the strike, not to resolve the issues that produce the strike.

A second device widely recommended and frequently used to head off the major strike is the appointment of a "fact-finding" committee—an impartial outside agency which is to collect and reveal the essential facts in the case of the issues in dispute, make or suggest recommendations, and help to set a framework of public opinion. By bringing the essential facts to light and giving them reasonable interpretation the fact-finding committee, it is felt, serves to focus a kind of moral pressure upon the parties to come to an agreement.

In my judgement the fact-finding committee is distinctly inadequate to cope with the problem of the major strike. Let us review its professed as well as its unofficial functions. It is very doubtful whether it is able to make any contributions in the finding of facts. The issues as well as all pertinent facts are usually well established and known as a result of previous negotiations. Their interpretation along the line of recommendations is usually also set, especially if there have been efforts at mediation. The fact-finding committee may undertake, unofficially, mediation of its own. If undertaken its only advantage comes from the greater prestige of the committee. Yet, like the mediator the fact-finding committee has no authority to force agreement. Hence, its mediatory influence is likely to be little in the face of the strong positions that the parties have usually reached in the case of the major strike. Similarly, while the work of the fact-finding committee may shape public opinion considerably, this carries with it no assurance that the parties will bow to this opinion. In short, as has been shown in many instances, the device of the fact-finding committee is not able to control the major strike. Its occasional success in heading off a major strike does not mean that it is equipped to prevent such strikes. It has no power to handle the strike which occurs despite its efforts. Since the problem of the major strike exists not in the strikes which are forestalled but in those which occur it is clear that the fact-finding committee is not the reliable means for the control of the major strike.

Another type of solution which is frequently proposed and seriously entertained is the use of compulsory arbitration. The line of reasoning behind this proposed solution is simple, clear, and superficially compelling. The argument is that if the parties still remain apart after exhaustive bargaining the matter should be taken out of their hands. The welfare of the community should be protected from their stubborn refusal to resolve their dispute. Accordingly, the settlement of their dispute should be entrusted to an impartial and competent person or board and the parties should be required to abide by the decision of this outside agency. However reasonable such a procedure may appear on its surface, a little reflection shows that it cuts the roots of the structure of collective bargaining. In depriving the parties of the right to settle their own dispute compulsory arbitration in effect blocks both parties from pursuing and protecting their own interests. Thus, in principle, compulsory arbitration represents the antithesis of an effective system of employer-employee relations. It stands for the imposition of an outside scheme on such relations—the dictation of such relations by a third party which does not represent the interests of either of the two primary parties. Many advocates of compulsory arbitration would contend that in being limited to the few situations where a major strike cannot be prevented, compulsory arbitration would exercise little influence on the full structure of collective bargaining. This is a deceptive position. To implant compulsory arbitration at the point of the major strike is to give it the strongest foothold in the structure of employer-employee relations. The greater expectation is that it would spread from this crucial vantage point. It would constitute a constant jeopardy to the structure of collective bargaining in being the model for the control of the most pronounced and weighty industrial disputes. A device which is so basically contrary to the character of effective employer-employee relations cannot be regarded as a suitable way of meeting the problem of the major strike.

The remaining device which I wish to consider is governmental seizure of the given industrial enterprise to assure its continual operation. Such seizure is seemingly the capital weapon in insuring the safety of the community. It is the ultimate resort if other devices fail. It is the quickest means if immediate control of the major strike is necessary. It is both an emergency measure and a final measure. As such it has established itself as the only reliable or assured means of protecting the public interest. We are familiar with its use in the United States during the second World War and at critical points in the post war period. Because it has become, apparently, the only reasonably certain measure of control of the major strike it is important to analyze it in some detail.

We may assume that governmental seizure is adequate to protect the public interest against the danger that is set by the major strike. This phase of the problem need not be discussed. The important question is what effect does governmental seizure have on the employer-employee relationship? May I remind you here of the point made previously, namely that control of the major strike sets the interesting and crucial problem of reconciling two basic principles—the protection of the public interest and the protection of the right to strike. It is clear that as used so far governmental seizure makes no place for the latter principle or what it stands for. By forbidding employees the right to strike the government interferes with the process of collective bargaining at one of its most vital points. The government is put in a peculiar and anomalous position with regard to the employer-employee relationship. It is interesting to see what it may do. For one thing it may decree a settlement of the dispute, laying down the terms as if it were an arbitrator. Such a line of action, of course, is clearly contrary to the structure of collective bargaining. For another thing, the government may step into the role of the employer and negotiate a settlement of the dispute underlying the major strike. This, of course, is to abrogate to itself the interests of the employer which, of course, it does not have. I am not interested at the moment in the legality of such unsurpation—I merely wish to point out that the government, acting out of its own interests, is not a fit representative of the interests of the employer. Nor can it represent the interests of the employees. To put itself in the role of either of the parties or to act on behalf of the interests of either party is of course to contradict the essential nature of collective bargaining.

The third and most usual position of the government under the seizure is merely to retain the status quo. Under governmental direction the enterprise continues to operate as previously. The workers and the management serve under the terms of their prior arrangement, in short under terms that are in dispute between them. The two parties are expected and encouraged to continue their negotiations while the enterprise is operating under the control of the government. Superficially, once more, this arrangement seems to be sensible and fair since on the one hand it protects the public interest in providing for the operation of the enterprise and on the other hand it does not interfere with collective bargaining or with the opportunity of the parties to resolve their own difficulties. Actually the seizure is a drastic interference with collective bargaining in upsetting the operating base of each of the parties toward the other.

Because of its crucial significance I wish to spell out this point. As explained in earlier remarks the strike is an integral part of the collective bargaining process in two noteworthy ways. First, the threat of its use serves as a pressure on the parties to strive to reach agreement on their difficulties. Second, failing this, the strike becomes a medium for resolving their dispute. In this latter role the strike is clearly a contest of power, a matter of the extent to which each of the parties can stand the losses which the strike inflicts on it. It is the willingness or unwillingness to endure the losses which provides the basis for the resolution of the strike and of the disputed matters out of which the strike arose. That resolution remains in the hands of the parties on the basis of their pursuit of their respective interests.

A governmental seizure which sets and maintains the status-quo has the effect, first of all, of seriously weakening the influence which the strike would exert in forcing the parties to reach an agreement. In this type of seizure the workers receive their wages, the managing personnel receive their salaries, the employers receive their profits, the union receives its dues, and the union officials receive their compensation. Since the flow of operations and the benefits yielded to each party by that flow are essentially unimpaired the parties suffer no pressure from these vital sources to work out a solution to their differences. Thus, there is removed the compelling kind of force which is so influential under collective bargaining in getting the parties to settle their difficulties. The status-quo seizure must be recognized, accordingly, as a serious interference with the collective bargaining process. It undermines that process at one of its most crucial points in lifting the concrete and vital pressures that otherwise would operate to impel the parties toward agreement.

Of even greater significance is the fact that the status-quo seizure seriously upsets the relative strength of the two parties in whatever bargaining goes on under the seizure. The seizure obviously tilts the scale in favor of the party that stands to gain from the status-quo. The position of that party is fortified by the seizure. It need do no more than wait out the seizure and make no concessions from its stand on the disputed issues. The other party is obviously placed at a disadvantage in the bargaining. It is forced to abide by the status-quo even though its interests impel it to a change in the status-quo. Further, the prohibition of the strike deprives it of the strength which it would otherwise have in the bargaining. It must be evident that the status-quo seizure interferes with the collective bargaining process in fortifying one party and weakening the other in the power which they may bring to their collective bargaining.

All of these observations show that governmental seizure in its current forms is marked by serious deficiencies. While such seizure satisfies the need for protecting the public interest it contradicts and jeopardizes the principles underlying collective bargaining. Many scholars would regard this contradiction as inevitable, as bound to occur because of the prohibition of the strike. Yet I think that it will be clear on further reflection that the condition is not inevitable. Instead it calls for a re-analysis of the problem—an analysis designed to achieve a seizure arrangement in which the right to safeguard the public interest does not eliminate or bar the benefits which the right to strike allows. Thus, while the act of seizure necessarily forbids the strike the seizure should be so arranged that the parties are put in essentially the position they would occupy if the strike were in actual progress. This is the direction along which the solution of the problem should be sought. I would like to advance my thoughts along this line.

Clearly, there are two crucial features that make the strike important and effective as an instrument in resolving the differences between the parties. The first of these is the deprivations it causes for each of the parties. With the cessation of operations management loses profits, continues to incur sizeable maintenance costs, and has its market disorganized. Employees lose wages, the union loses dues, and union officials suffer losses in salary. Each of the parties is forced to dig into reserves. Such deprivations provide the pressures that push the parties toward a settlement. The second feature is that the strike becomes a contest of power—the comparative ability and willingness of each of the parties to stand its deprivations. This relative position of power of the two parties sets the framework of the settlement. Accordingly, the respective power of the parties in the strike situation is a crucial part of the collective bargaining process.

These commonplace observations suggest the kind of conditions which should prevail under the seizure. The guiding principles are clear: the parties should be required to settle their own dispute; they should be subject, as far as practical, to the same deprivations which they would incur in the actual strike; the respective power of the parties should not be upset or materially changed by the seizure. In other words, as far as is practicable, the same compelling conditions should exist under the state of seizure that the parties would be subject to in the actual strike situation.

Admittedly it would not be possible to match these conditions exactly. Obviously, under seizure the workers would earn their wages and the industrial enterprise retain its market. However, it seems to me, that certain penalties could be imposed on the parties that would approximate the respective deprivations they would incur under the strike. The approximation would at least be in areas where the parties are most sensitive and accordingly most impelled to settle their dispute. Thus, under the seizure the government could exact a directing charge against the enterprise equivalent to a combination of the profits earned under seizure and the maintenance costs that would have to be borne by management if the enterprise were not operating. In the strike situation, of course, the management would suffer the loss of profits and the expenses of maintenance. So we have here what is a good approximation of the major deprivation imposed on management by an actual strike.

The approximation of the major deprivation in the case of the workers and their union would have to be made in a more round-about manner. One could not obviously make any charge against the wages of the workers since such wages are earnings for work performed. However, charges could be made against the financial resources of the union roughly equivalent to the inroad on such resources in the actual strike situation. In the case of a strike the union receives no dues; it is usually required to supply relief funds; and its own officials usually have to take marked reductions in their salaries. The calculation of these combined sums would vary according to the industry; yet a fair calculation could be made, and covered in some multiple of the dues of the members, apportioned by days. The treasury of the union (including the locals) is the vulnerable point of the union, especially the large union that is likely to be involved in a major strike. To exact a running charge against the union treasury under the seizure would have the same compelling effect on the union that is exercised on management by the charge against the industry.

This is not the place to discuss the legal problems involved in the financial charges on the industry and the union. Competent legal counsels inform me that there is a reasonable framework in American law to provide for their possibility. A seizure of the union corresponding to the seizure of the industry may be required. This would not be out of place when we recognize the union as an integral part of the operating structure of the industry.

We can easily see the effects of such financial charges under seizure. The parties would be hurt in the vital spots that spur them on to action in the strike situation; neither of them would find their position under seizure to be tolerable. Both would experience a formidable pressure to settle their differences—the pressure that comes otherwise from the strike situation. The prohibition of the strike would not deprive the parties of the power or disability which the right to strike entails. The government could maintain the detached position which it should have of not interfering with collective bargaining and not tilting the scales on behalf of either party. It is not hard to imagine that the dispute would be settled more quickly than by the actual strike. It is not hard to foresee that both parties, mutually, would strive to avoid a seizure that would inflict such deprivations. Neither management nor the union would favor this kind of seizure—a fact which bespeaks its crucial possibilities.

It is in this type of seizure that I believe we have the effective means to the control of the major strike. As I have said earlier, the problem of the labor strike exists genuinely only in the case of the strike which endangers the public interest. What is needed for its control is a device which while protecting the public interest will not undermine the structure of collective bargaining. A form of seizure which while prohibiting the strike will allow for the play of the vital conditions of the strike is the answer.

Industrialization and Problems of Social Disorder

The industrialization of a society is generally regarded as a period of stress, disorganization, and disorder. Discontent among workers, unrest in the general population, feelings of alienation among dislocated people, the development of new and unsatisfied aspirations, congestion and unsatisfactory living conditions in industrial towns, disorganization of the family and of the native community, conflict between workers and management, labor agitation, the development of radical doctrines, the rise of protest movements, and intense political struggles—such are the kinds of disturbed and disorderly conditions commonly associated with early industrialization. Because of their dramatic character, because of the grave problems that they set, because they signify a society in the throes of reorganization, these disturbing conditions have aroused and captured the interest of scholars.

These happenings can be designated as a distinct area of social effects of early industrialization. These social effects are different from the new social forms brought about by industrialization. They are also different from the changes which industrialization is presumed to cause in the traditional order. Instead, they constitute a different array of happenings—happenings of stress arising from the breakdown of the settled order of life of pre-industrial societies and from efforts to achieve new schemes of living.

Scholars have regarded industrialization as a powerful process which results in disorganization and disorder and which, accordingly, is responsible for their occurrence. Industrialization is assigned the role of an agent which brings about these specific transitional happenings. This is apparent in the questions posed for scholarly study and in the propositions presented as the knowledge in this area. Scholars ask such questions as what kind of disruptive setting for workers does early industrialization introduce into the new industrial establishments; what is the condition of the working class or industrial proletariat to which industrialization gives rise; what is the nature of the industrial conflicts which industrialization brings into being; how does the family and the village become disorganized under the impact of industrialization; what are the urban problems to which industrialization gives rise; and what kinds of radical movements and protest activities does industrialization lead to. The propositions and interpretations advanced by scholars of early industrialization are even more decisive in terms of the causality assigned to industrialization in this area of events. The literature is full of assertions that early industrialization produces a discontented working class; forms a dispossessed and rootless industrial proletariat; instigates family and community disorganization; fosters a state of anomie; induces agitation, strikes, and riots; leads to radicalism and rebelliousness; and results in revolutionary and protest movements.

This monograph attempts to analyze the role of industrialization in the social disturbances and disorders which it allegedly brings about. I shall endeavor, first, to spell out more fully the considerations which have led scholars to regard industrialization as the agent of such social disturbances and disorders. Next, I shall point out the considerable variability of these happenings under early industrialization. Finally, I will explain the shortcomings and fallacies of using industrialization to account for such events when they do occur.

THE ALLEGED ROLE OF INDUSTRIALIZATION IN PRODUCING SOCIAL DISORDER

An examination of the literature reveals a confused and unsystematic picture of thought with regard to how industrialization brings about the conditions of social disturbance and disorder attributed to it. For the most part the picture consists merely of assertions and not of analyses—direct declarations that early industrialization leads to various forms of turmoil and upheaval instead of accounts of how it is supposed to bring about these consequences. Many scholars start with an unquestioned premise that the industrialization of societies leads naturally to disorganization and disorder. Guided by this premise they do little more than pick out certain kinds of disturbances or disorderly outbreaks and attribute them almost automatically to the play of the industrializing process. Rarely are efforts made through empirical study to show how the industrializing process brings about these consequences. If there is need to account for such connections, resort is usually made to convenient conventional explanations or to an ad hoc importation of psychological doctrines—such as that frustration leads inevitably to aggression. Such ready-made explanations or plausible psychological doctrines are used to shore up the naturalness and inevitability of the social consequences attributed to industrialization.

It is possible to piece together from the miscellany of studies, assertions, and explanations a composite picture which is fairly systematic and serviceable. The bare outline of this picture is as follows. There are three fundamental ways in which industrialization brings about a condition of social disorganization: (1) by introducing a strange and discordant framework to which people have to adjust; (2) by disintegrating the traditional order; and (3) by releasing sets of new forces which are disruptive. The condition of social disorganization is manifested in (a) a variety of disturbed feelings or psychological disorders, (b) a disruption of groups and institutions, and (c) a variety of more or less violent expressions of protest. Let us now examine more closely each of the above items.

Setting of an alien scene

Scholars in general believe and many of them declare that industrialization introduces a life arrangement which is strange, unfamiliar and disturbing to people in a preindustrial society. This life arrangement embraces the new industrial establishments in which people have to work, the new industrial communities in which they have to live, the new kind of home life in which they have to engage, the new social groups which they have to face, the new direction of interests which they have to undertake, the new forms of monetary and contractual relations in which they have to enter, the new array of merchandise which they covet and attempt to possess, and the new mode of life made possible by cash income. The rearrangement of life along these diverse lines is alien to customary routines, opposed to established habit and taste, contrary to what is expected of others and of oneself, adverse to regularized family and personal organization, and antagonistic to traditional values. Accordingly, the new framework of life appears as a form of cultural shock, disquieting people, arousing distaste and repugnance, awakening vain hopes and unrealistic wishes, and causing dissatisfaction and discontent.

There is no need to spell out this general view in detail for each of the major lines along which the new and strange industrial arrangement appears. However, for purposes of better comprehension, it is useful to present a fuller picture of it in the case of two of these lines.

I will consider first the instance of the factory milieu. The working milieu in the new industrial establishments is declared to be strange and forbidding. In it, it is argued, the workers have no status, no property or tools, no independence, no customary work rights, and little sense of personal dignity. They are forced to adjust to unfamiliar and onerous work rhythms—fixed working hours, mandatory work assignments, steady pace of work, and the repetitive performance of monotonous work tasks. They are forced to bow to a strange and harsh system of discipline in which they have no say, and which they are not privileged to resist. In their work they are required to associate with mere acquaintances or with strangers, frequently from a different ethnic, cultural, or geographic background, with whom they share no communal feelings. In the face of these new and alienating conditions of work the workers are said to become insecure, discontented, and disaffected.

As a second instance, let us consider the new setting in the industrial communities in which the workers have to live. These communities are usually held to be urban communities. The conventional picture that is presented is that the workers and their families are thrown into congested areas and quarters, with poor housing, inadequate sanitation, inferior municipal services, and faulty school and service facilities. They are separated from kinfolk and fellow villagers, and are required to live side by side with strangers of different backgrounds. Their association with one another is remote, impersonal and secondary in nature. They are confronted with forms of city life which are unfamiliar and puzzling. Their old institutions are not at hand and the new institutions are strange and uninviting. They are compelled to rely on outside services and facilities which are scarcely known to them. They stand in awe before a vague yet powerful officialdom and bureaucracy whose ways are mysterious and forbidding. Confronted with this array of strange and repelling conditions of life, the workers become insecure and their families become disorganized.

If we add to these accounts of the factory milieu and of the industrial community comparable accounts of the new environment represented by other items such as the separation of work from the home, the formation of new budgetary practices, involvement in the intricacies of monetary and contractual relations, the problems and use of cash income, and the need of entering into new group relations, we have a seemingly formidable picture of the alien world which industrialization introduces. This world is seen as disconcerting, usually repelling, and a source of uncertainty and anxiety. To thrust a preindustrial people into this world is to subject them to cultural shock and to induce psychological and social instability among them.

Such is the theme which one finds running through the literature. Industrialization is thought of as introducing an alien social arrangement which is contrary to what preindustrial people are accustomed. In having to fit their lives to this arrangement and meet its demands people are thrown into a state of insecurity, anxiety, and hostility.

Disintegration of the traditional order

A second major way by which industrialization is declared to bring about social disturbance and disorder is by disrupting the traditional order of life. Scholars attribute great weight to this factor. The predominant belief of scholars is that industrialization operates to undermine and disrupt the established order of life. The general consequence of such disintegration is to detach people from their customary social positions, to confuse the norms by which they guide their behavior, to shatter the values by which they hold themselves in line, and to weaken the control exercised over them by others. In these ways, individuals are alienated from a secure framework of group life and, correspondingly, traditional society is broken up. In being alienated, individuals become insecure, develop anxieties and hostilities, and become instable. In being broken up, societies become demoralized and disorganized. Thus, through its disintegrating effects on the traditional order, industrialization is held responsible for individual and social disorganization.

There are a number of important ways by which the process of industrialization is declared to remove individuals in a preindustrial society from their established social positions and social roles. One of them is the displacement of individuals from the economic pursuits on which they depend, as in the case of handicraft workers who are unable to meet the competition of machine-made goods. Another is the initiation of sizable migratory movements, as people are drawn from field and village to industrial centers. Still another is the fostering of the physical mobility that is set by an impersonal labor market with its insecurity of employment and the likelihood of frequent shifts in jobs. All of these developments remove the individual from his customary social position inside of his original community. As a result he loses the sense of support given by others, feels alienated from the world in which he lives, and feels insecure in having to depend on his own resources.

Concomitant with this weakening of personal organization, the individual suffers disturbance in the social rules and values on which he had relied. Industrialization undermines traditional systems of norms and values. This is done chiefly in three ways. First, as a secularizing force it raises doubts about the validity of canons which govern customary village and community life; traditional responsibility to kinfolk and neighbors is weakened and traditional deference to institutional authority figures is lessened. Next, through the emphasis which it places on contractual relations, industrialization breaks down systems of paternalistic relations and feudal allegiance; others no longer have the obligation of taking care of the person and, correspondingly, the individual loses the security that comes from the assurance that others have this responsibility. Finally, industrialization disrupts established forms of mutual assistance as they have existed in the traditional communities; the individual is forced to rely on himself in directing his activities and forging his career.

In addition to disrupting the established social positions of people and undermining basic social values, early industrialization breaks down traditional social controls. In being separated from their local communities, individuals are removed in large measure from the demands and expectations that are ordinarily imposed on them by kinfolk, neighbors, and the agents of local institutions. Thus, deviations from customary conduct are much easier and irregularities in behavior escape the restraints which otherwise would curb them. The breakdown of such systems of traditional control fosters and abets social disorganization.

In disrupting traditional life in such ways as these, industrialization is seen as ushering in a general state of personal and social disorganization.

Release of new social forces

Early industrialization is presented as bringing about personal and social disorganization through the cultivation and release of expectations and demands for a new kind of life. Early industrialization is commonly viewed as engendering wishes for emancipation on the part of women, desires for greater freedom on the part of youth, general wants for a better standard of material living, interests in pursuing wealth and profit, a seeking for higher social status, an elevation of personal ambition, a nursing of new hopes and aspirations, and a disdain for many of the old ways of living. These new kinds of generalized demands on life, as they arise in different segments of the population, induce a state of social ferment. They signify both a dissatisfaction with the current way of life and a turning away from traditional life as a cure for that dissatisfaction. Instead, they point to a different order of life to be sought in the future. Such demands represent discontent and a striving for something new and better. Both the discontent and the groping provoke disturbance and disorder.

The literature presents only a fragmentary picture of how industrialization is supposed to bring into existence these new generalized demands. That industrialization produces them is assumed more than it is demonstrated. At best we find piece-meal declarations, with large areas between them left unexplained. Typical of such piece-meal declarations are the following: The entry of women into industrial occupations, their earning of a cash income paid into their own hands, and the breakdown of traditional family control are regarded as conditions of their initial independence and sources of their desire for greater emancipation. The same conditions are advanced as an explanation of how industrialization fosters the emancipation of youth. The formation of new material wants is linked to the new forms of manufactured merchandise and products placed on the market. Incitation to the improvement of social status is tied to the greater opportunities for occupational advancement in an industrial structure of employment. The greater freedom permitted by monetary and contractual relations is thought to promote the desire for individual regulation of goals and career. The earning of cash income from industry and the prospects of ways of increasing this income are believed to promote a striving for profit and wealth. The initial release from traditional forms of control is regarded as leading to a quest for greater freedom and for means which will enable individuals to organize their own lives more effectively. These illustrative instances are sketchy but they typify what one finds in the literature where an effort has been made to pin the different kinds of new wishes and hopes specifically to industrialization. In general, scholars have not sought to trace in any careful or systematic way how the process of industrialization, itself, gives rise to the various sets of new generalized demands on life which industrialization is declared to bring into being. However, there is no question that scholars generally regard industrialization as inducing and releasing such forces. Nor is there any doubt that they view these forces as powerful factors in leading to social disturbance and disorder during periods of early industrialization.

To summarize briefly the three lines of influence we have been considering, industrialization is thought to lay the basis for social disturbance and disorder by introducing an alien and unfamiliar pattern of life, by disrupting the traditional order of life, and by releasing new social forces. To complete the picture, we now have to consider the nature and significance of the social disturbance and disorder induced by industrialization.

Psychological disorder

Industrialization is commonly regarded as inducing and fostering feelings or psychological states that lead to disturbance and disorder. These feelings may range from something as vague as uneasiness to something as pointed as hostility. They cover such diverse psychological states as insecurity, anxiety, anomie, loss of purpose, unrest, dissatisfaction, discontent, rebelliousness and hatred. These feelings are regarded as natural products of the three lines of disorganizing influence which industrialization exerts on the life of preindustrial societies. The introduction of a new industrial scene with its strange and discordant features, the undermining of traditional institutions, and the release of new sets of desires and aspirations—all combine to engender insecurity, anxiety, dissatisfaction, and hostility.

These feelings signify that the individuals and collectivities who hold them have become alienated or psychologically separated from the prevailing order of life. They do not feel at home in it and do not derive from it the satisfactions which they seek. Consequently, they are sensitized and oriented to reject it, either in whole or in part. Their resentment may be suppressed and hidden, smoldering in anxiety and bitterness. Or it may break forth in various forms of overt conduct. Individuals may seek solace by resorting to alcohol or licentious behavior. Or they may take flight in religious behavior, frequently in the form of ecstatic and secretive rites. Or, instead, the overt expression may take the form of attacks on the traditional order. Or the feelings may be channelized into movements which seek to transform the prevailing order of life. Whatever the direction they may take, such feelings indicate a state of disturbance and instability on the part of individuals; at the same time, they constitute threats to the stability and continuity of the prevailing social arrangements. It is particularly important to note that people who are in the grip of such feelings are open to agitation, proselytizing, demogoguery, charismatic appeals, or mutual excitation to outbreaks in behavior. For many students this susceptibility explains many of the unusual forms of behavior found in periods of early industrialization—fads, cults, strikes, riots, demonstrations, flouting of law and order, emergence of radical doctrines, militant social movements, and attacks on established institutions.

Social disorganization

Social disorganization refers to an inability of a social unit to mobilize itself so as to execute the function or functions which it is required to perform. The "disorganization" does not exist in the failure to execute the function; it exists in the inability of the social unit to mobilize itself to act as an entity in seeking to execute the function. Thus, social disorganization manifests itself in a confusion or conflict of goals, or in a similar confusion or conflict in policy with regard to how to act toward a given goal, or in an inability to achieve the coordination of activities needed to act as an entity on a given policy. These manifestations signify that the acting unit—whether it be a family, an institution, an army, a government, a segment of society, or a society—itself has broken down or fallen apart in the face of the task or function which it is required to perform. The sign of deep disorganization as against transitory disorganization is the inability to regain the capacity to act as a unit vis-a-vis necessary functions and tasks. In this latter case social disorganization is chronic.

Starting with this minimal definition we can consider how social disorganization is brought about by industrialization in the broad unit of society. It should be noted, first, that the disturbed feelings which we have been considering have their counterpart in the state of the prevailing social order. The various feelings such as insecurity, anxiety, and discontent signify that individuals and groups holding them are alienated from the social order. Turning this statement around we can say that the presence of such feelings means that the prevailing social order no longer commands a full measure of natural acceptance and allegiance. To this extent, the traditional order has uncertain anchorage and is disposed to instability. Thus, in the execution of its tasks, especially in the face of serious problems and crises, a society may not gain the obedience and acceptance that are required; hence it enters into a condition of disorganization.

Industrialization is thought additionally to produce social disorganization by disrupting and weakening two of the major mechanisms on which a society depends for maintaining cohesion and exercising effective control. These are the system of traditional authority and the system of traditional values. Industrialization is viewed as undercutting traditional authority as it exists in the family, in village and tribal organization, in the position of dominant social classes, in the roles of institutional agents, and in the status of prestige groups. Similarly, industrialization is seen as undermining traditional values such as respect for established positions and rights, deference and obedience to authority figures, and readiness to carry out customary responsibilities. This weakening of traditional authority and traditional values means social action is less likely along the established lines used by the society in carrying out its functions. To this extent the society is less likely to act as a concerted unit.

A further major way in which industrialization induces social disorganization is in bringing into being a variety of groups and individuals who by necessity struggle for positions or for achievement of new goals. Such aggressive groups are represented by industrial owners, labor organizations, manufacturing associations and a variety of interest groups that grow up around the new industrial system. Aggressive individuals are represented by entrepreneurs, aggressive owners, ambitious workmen, and aspiring labor leaders. We need to note two things of importance in the case of such groups and individuals. First, as new kinds of groups and new types of individuals, they have no established social niches, and their activities are not defined and regularized by the traditional order. In this sense, the groups and individuals are relatively free and autonomous. Second, the goals pursued by such groups and individuals are new and out of keeping with the traditional order; the society has no developed apparatus to regulate or control such pursuits. The result is that these groups and individuals in pursuing their objectives readily enter into conflict with one another and with traditional groups and types of individuals. The arena of such conflicts may spread into traditional institutions themselves, such as the government, the polity, the church, and the army. Gates are opened to opportunism, political adventuring, and sheer power play. The established society may not be able to contain these new forms of conflict or to direct them into regularized channels. In this event, the society incurs disorganization in the form of a decreasing capacity to act as a concerted unit.

The foregoing brief discussion indicates the ways in which a preindustrial society is thought to become disorganized under the impact of industrialization. By failing to retain the natural allegiance of its members, by a weakening of its primary mechanisms of control (the system of authority and system of values), and by the emergence of new areas of conflict, the society loses capacity to act in a concerted fashion.

Many students see such social disorganization in a variety of conditions and phenomena that draw attention in periods of early industrialization. They note such things as a weakening in family discipline, desertion, separation of mates, delinquency, crime, the rise of urban problems, breakdown of municipal facilities, labor agitation, strikes, militant labor movements, emergence of radical doctrines, corruption in government, use of positions for personal enrichment, opportunism, power play, and formation of revolutionary movements.

Protest reactions

This area of social disturbance, more than others, has attracted the attention of scholars interested in the social effects of early industrialization. The term has come to be used to cover a range of disturbances, such as absenteeism, shirking on the job, sabotage of work, strikes, riots, labor agitation, the formation of militant labor unions, the formation of orgiastic religious cults, and emergence of radical and revolutionary movements. Most scholars do not seek to explain how these disturbances are tied to industrialization; they merely regard them as part of the general condition of disorganization brought about by industrialization. Other scholars, however, are more specific in that they regard these disturbances as alternative forms of protest. In their view, industrialization arouses insecurity and discontent—feelings of the sort we have considered above in the section on psychological disorder. These feelings are fundamentally feelings of protest. The feelings press for release. One form of release may be mild as in the case of a high rate of absenteeism, or in the frequent quitting of jobs. A more vigorous form of expression is in sabotage, riots, and strikes. A compensatory type of release takes the form of a retreat to ecstatic religious cults. Finally, the most violent and lasting kind of expression is in the form of radical or revolutionary movements. Given underlying feelings of protest, many scholars assert, one or another of these alternative types of expression will occur. It is in this way that early industrialization is regarded as responsible for the more or less violent social disturbances that occur during periods of its operation.

ASSESSMENT OF INDUSTRIALIZATION AS A SOURCE OF SOCIAL DISORDER

The preceding views present the familiar picture of industrialization as an agent of determinate social change. However plausible and convincing this conventional picture of the influence of early industrialization may seem to be, it must be rejected as intrinsically false. A careful analysis of the problem and of the evidence compels one to recognize that the process of industrialization is indifferent and neutral with regard to social disorganization and disorder which follow in its wake. One cannot find in the character of the industrializing process anything which necessarily produces, presages, or explains social disturbance as a consequence of its operation. The following discussion is designed to make this clear.

Preliminary observations

There is nothing approaching a constant relation between early industrialization on one hand and social disorganization and disorder on the other. A scrutiny of a variety of separate instances of early industrialization yields a picture of great difference in the presence and extent of disorganization and disorder. This is especially true if one makes the comparison on the level of local industrial communities. One will find communities under early industrialization in which workers and residents are satisfied, in which there are none of the usual signs of disorganization, and in which there are no indications of protest activities. This is particularly likely to be true if the new industries are placed in already established small communities. Aside from the instances in which early industrialization is unattended by disorganization and disorder, other instances show pronounced differences in the extent and expression of disturbance and disorder. Conspicuous variation is to be seen in such items as breakdown of family discipline, delinquency, strikes, labor agitation, rioting, radicalism, unrestrained political struggles, and revolutionary movements. It is evident that social disorganization and disorder are in no sense uniform and constant among instances of early industrialization. Disorganization and disorder may vary from being extensive and severe to being absent.

It is the writer's impression that the high connection which scholars believe to exist between early industrialization and social disorganization derives from three considerations. The first is that scholars have been more attracted to instances of early industrialization where disorganization and disorder were pronounced; such instances are usually dramatic and serious, and thus readily invite study. Second, scholars are likely to be concerned with early industrialization on a national or regional basis, thus being prone to overlook what occurs on the local community level. Third, scholars are likely to deal with early industrialization in later periods of its operation and hence are likely to bypass attention to it in its initial stages. For these reasons their ideas concerning the connection of early industrialization with disorganization and disorder seem to be derived from a body of selected instances.

In periods of early industrialization there are likely to be in play many forces, apart from the industrializing process, which promote social disorganization and social disorder. One should bear in mind that areas undergoing industrialization are usually brought into varied lines of contact with the outside world. Foreign products may enter the market. Visitors may enter the area. Representatives of foreign companies, institutions, agencies, missions, and professional bodies may come in. Local people, in turn, may travel abroad, work abroad, or study abroad. Communication with the outside world may increase. Wire services, motion pictures, radio programs, and magazines may play into the region. Trade relations may diversify contacts with the outside world. The need and effort of the country to establish political relations in the wider world becomes a matter of importance. One can say correctly that a region or country undergoing industrialization is at the same time being incorporated in the outside and more advanced world. The doors are thus opened to the entrance of many modernizing influences which implant new ideas, arouse new wishes and aspirations, and stimulate people to adopt or follow foreign models. Such modernizing influences may lead people to develop wishes for new comforts, standards of a higher level of living, wishes for higher wages, a desire for the education of children, a demand for adequate public and social services, a wish to exercise control over conditions of work, a wish to improve one's social status, a desire to have the rights enjoyed by similar groups abroad, and a favorable regard for imported political and social doctrines which offer prospects of a better life. Much of the psychological disorder which we have discussed earlier in this chapter is rooted in new pictures of rights, of privileges, and of a more appealing order of life than that offered by nonindustrial factors. In addition to the entry of such disrupting forces from the outside world, internal developments of a nonindustrial nature may be potent in inducing disorganization and disorder. Such developments as rural impoverishment, agricultural crises, excessive population growth, migratory movements, urbanization, nationalism, acute and exhausting political struggles, and especially fiscal difficulties of the central government can be major sources of disorganization. They occur with considerable frequency in preindustrial societies undergoing industrialization.

Students who are inclined to regard early industrialization as an agent of social disorganization rarely endeavor to separate industrialization from these other kinds of factors and conditions which produce disorganization. They are prone to attribute to the industrializing process whatever disorganization is seen to occur during the period of industrialization. This can be a source of extraordinary error and confusion. As I have sought to suggest, early industrialization is likely to be a period of stress in which many kinds of nonindustrial influences from abroad and from within are in play to disrupt prevailing life and social arrangements. Scholars should be on guard against the common tendency to attribute to the industrializing process the effects of such nonindustrial influences. Such caution is particularly in order today when many so-called underdeveloped regions are caught in the throes of social disorganization even though they are not being industrialized. Frequently they show the same kinds of disturbances and disorder which are commonly attributed to industrialization in comparable regions undergoing industrialization.

There is a marked variation in what industrialization introduces into the life of preindustrial societies. In terms of the milieu and the system of internal governance in industrial establishments, for example, conspicuous differences exist in what may be introduced at this point. Managers may have a free hand in setting wages and hours of work, or they may be subject to legislation which fixes minimum wages and maximum hours of work. Management may be unrestricted in the exercise of disciplinary authority, or it may be hemmed in by legislative rules or by contractual regulations. Management may follow harsh and inconsiderate labor practices or be guided by an enlightened and benevolent labor policy. The factory may be old, dirty, dark and unhygienic; or it may be modern, clean, pleasant and sanitary. Management may be indifferent as how foremen or supervisors train new workers, or it may have thoughtfully designed programs of training. Castelike barriers and ceilings may be imposed on upward progression, or free opportunities may exist for promotion. Workers may be denied any voice in their conditions of work, or they may possess and use a formal or informal grievance procedure. Enough has been said to indicate that the milieux of the new industrial establishments, including schemes of governance, vary greatly. They are in no sense intrinsically unnatural, menacing and harsh; to the contrary, they may be pleasant, interesting and inviting. In view of the different forms which the industrial pattern may take in factories and working establishments, one should be very careful in assuming that the pattern has a natural character that is conducive to disorganization. The same observation can be made about the makeup of the industrializing process at its other major points of entry. Differences of a similar magnitude, even though of a different order, can be seen at each of the points. Viewed in terms of what it introduces, industrialization speaks with many different tongues. Recognition of the varying forms which the industrializing process may take should give pause to scholars who regard it as naturally leading to disorganization.

The people on whom the industrializing process impinges meet it with schemes of interpretation which shape their responses to it. Their position is not that of passive organisms who are coerced into fixed lines of action by an inherent stimulus quality of what is presented to them. Instead, they define the presentations in terms of their preestablished ideas, compare them with other areas of their experience, and are influenced by suggestions and definitions given by their associates. Accordingly, interpretations and responses dependent on various perspectives may vary greatly in the face of the same kind of situation. In the case of the working situation in the factory or new industrial establishment, workers under early industrialization may differ greatly in the schemes which they use to judge and evaluate their work situation. They may view their work situation as novel and exciting, as providing a source of much needed money, as offering possibilities for personal and family advancement, as being onerous but to be endured for other purposes—or as being exploitative, as being marked by unfair discrimination, and as denying opportunities for improving one's lot. Such schemes of interpretation do not spring from the objective nature of the work situation. Instead, they come from other sources, such as traditional ideas that antedate industrial employment, a comparison with previous work experiences, a comparison with the lot of other types of workers, ideas from the outside world, and the definitions provided by one's fellows. Thus, the same kind of work situation may induce discontent in one region, indifference in a second region, and eager acceptance in a third. The possibility must be borne in mind that people may approach the various situations set by early industrialization with widely differing schemes of interpretation. What may provoke anxiety, discontent, and hostility in some people may induce a different set of feelings in others.

The remainder of our preliminary observations will refer to social disorganization, viewed in terms of the ability of the acting social unit to mobilize itself for concerted action. What is important, accordingly, are not the disturbing problems which the acting unit encounters or the strains and disruptions which it experiences. Instead, the importance lies in how the acting unit copes with the problems and disruptions. If the acting unit can maintain an ability to act in a concerted and organized way it is not disorganized, however pressing and acute the changes which it is undergoing may be. This observation applies to a society as an acting unit. If a society, so to speak, recognizes its problems, devises clear and consistent policies for dealing with them, implements the policies firmly and decisively, and keeps dissident tendencies under control, it is not disorganized, however grave the problems and however much change the society may undergo. It is a gross error to identify disorganization with change, even with drastic change. Instead, the heart of social disorganization is the inability to cope with change.

This point should be kept in mind when dealing with early industrialization. To seek or to see disorganization in the changes which take place or in the problems which arise is to move in the wrong direction. Instead, disorganization should be sought and perceived in the state of the social machinery which exists for concerted action and control. A society may become disorganized in the face of few problems or minor crises; contrariwise, a society faced with many problems and major crises may escape disorganization by virtue of being able to act concertedly and decisively with regard to those problems. Thus, in the case of early industrialization, disorganization does not exist in the removal of productive functions from the family, or in the separation of the nuclear family from the extended family, or in migration to congested urban areas, or in unsatisfactory conditions of work, or in severing individuals from a paternalistic or feudal system, or in differences in interest between labor and management, or in the rise of new sets of wishes and aspirations. These may set occasions for disorganization but are not its substance. Instead, whether or not disorganizaton occurs depends on how the family deals with the removal of its productive functions, how the nuclear family mobilizes itself when removed from the extended family, how migrants work out adjustments to urban living, how workers organize themselves in the face of unsatisfactory working conditions, how individuals address the opportunities for greater freedom as well as the loss of support from others, how the local and central governments attack the new social problems which face them. In each of these instances the *how* is not given by the particular situation which sets the need for action. Its explanation must be sought elsewhere, predominantly in the state of the resources which allow for the mobilization of action. Scholars concerned with disorganization under early industrialization will be misled by preoccupation with the changes, problems and crises which may arise. Of more crucial importance are the facilities, the means, and the will to deal with changes, problems, and crises.

The foregoing observations help to bring proper perspec-

288 Selected Works of Herbert Blumer

tive to the problem of the relation of early industrialization to social disorganization and disorder. Scholars need to bear in mind
that there is nothing approaching a constant relation between
early industrialization and social disorganization, that many factors other than the industrializing process may operate to induce
disorganization, that the industrializing process is markedly uneven in the nature of the situations which it introduces, that the
experience of people in the face of these situations depends on
how the people define or interpret the situations, and that disorganization should be viewed not in terms of changes in life and
structure but in terms of capacity to deal with such changes. With
these observations in mind we can now undertake an analysis of
the role of early industrialization in relation to social disorganization and disorder.

Relation of early industrialization
to disorganization and disorder

Our problem is whether early industrialization introduces
or brings about changes of such a nature that disorganization and
disorder are natural consequences.

As we have seen, industrialization is regarded as producing
changes of this character in three ways: (1) introducing new
life situations which are strange, bewildering, and distasteful;
(2) disrupting the traditional order; and (3) arousing new sets of
generalized demands for new arrangements of life. These three
forms of change lead to a state of social disorganization. The state
of disorganization manifests itself in various kinds of disorder. I
shall now examine critically each of the three alleged sources of
social disorganization.

Introduction of alien situations

The contention is that early industrialization introduces a variety of new situations in which people have to fit, such as factory
life, urban residence, contractual relationships, use of money,
availability of new merchandise, and greater freedom. These new
situations are held to be unfamiliar, confusing, and frequently

harsh. Hence, they are thought to arouse insecurity, anxiety, and hostility.

There are several reasons why this contention is not tenable. In the first place, the situations which are introduced need not have a character conducive to feelings of insecurity, anxiety, and hostility. The situations introduced by early industrialization are not uniform. They may range from being repelling to being inviting; they may be chronically strange or they may be adjusted to quickly; they may be harsh and forbidding or they may be gratifying and attractive. In factories, for example, labor policy may be harsh or considerate, discipline may be extreme or tempered, physical conditions may be pleasant or distasteful, new workers may be carefully trained or left to struggle by themselves, the pace of work may be moderate or extreme, workers may be given opportunities for advancement or held in dead-level positions, workers may be subject to autocratic authority or exercise some voice in their conditions of work, and wages may have no bottom or have minimums set by legislation or labor agreement. Appreciable variations exist in the nature of factory life under early industrialization. There is nothing in the industrializing process which requires that the factory situation be uniform under early industrialization, or that it have the negative character assumed by some. The same observation applies to the other situations which industrialization is declared to introduce. The conditions of residence in industrial centers may vary greatly. The general scheme of contractual arrangements may be on a straight "business-like" basis or permeated with chicanery, hedging, or power abuse. The amount of available money, the value which it carries, and the lines of its use may vary significantly in different situations. These comments are sufficient to underscore the point that early industrialization does not introduce situations which have a uniform social or psychological makeup. Nor is there anything in the industrializing process which requires them to approximate such a uniform makeup.

Of much more importance than the makeup of the situations introduced by the industrializing process is the way in which the situations are interpreted and defined by the people who have to act in them. The definition and not the situation is crucial. It is the definition which determines the response. The situation does not set the definition; instead, the definition comes from what the people bring to the situation. Thus, the situations supposedly introduced by industrialization may be viewed and responded to in different ways. A type of factory situation which seems unbearable to workers in one region may be accepted with eagerness by workers in another region. What seems to be an intolerably low wage scale to the new industrial workers in one place may seem munificent to workers elsewhere who come from a background of impoverishment. Living conditions in congested urban quarters may be repelling in one instance but found satisfactory in another instance by people whose conditions of previous rural residence were even worse. It is sufficient to say that under conditions of early industrialization, people may welcome changes in their routines, be glad to move to industrial centers, accept work in industrial establishments with eagerness, relish the opportunities of urban life, enjoy the possibilities of freedom, and adjust to their new situations without appreciable strain. The point of these observations is that the nature of the situations introduced by industrialization, and the experience of people in such situations are set by the way in which the situations are defined by them. The so-called objective makeup of the situation does not determine the definition of it.

These observations should make it clear that there is no warrant to accept the contention that early industrialization naturally introduces a set of situations generating insecurity, anxiety, resentment, and hostility. The variations in what is introduced should, in themselves, cause the scholar to take pause. But beyond this, we need to know how people are prepared to interpret and meet the situation with which they are confronted. This latter form of knowledge lies outside of the domain of the industrializing process. A full knowledge of the industrializing process does not tell us the nature of the interpretations which people bring to the situations. The industrializing process is neutral and indifferent to these interpretations.

Disintegration of the traditional order

This is the chief way by which early industrialization is thought to induce social disorganization. The major lines of disintegration are the breakdown of the extended family, the under-mining of the village and rural community, the disruption of systems of authority, the crumbling of systems of paternalistic and feudal relations, the destruction of traditional values, and the overtaxing of the facilities of municipal and central governments. These lines of disintegration are tied to a variety of features of the industrializing process—the separation of economic production from the family and village, the migration of workers and their families to industrial centers, mobility in employment, urban growth, the expansion of contractual relations, and the availability and use of money. The resulting state of social disorganization takes the form of a detachment of individuals from regularized positions and orbits of life, the breakdown of traditional ways of controlling them, and the inability of institutions to function in customary ways. The state of disorganization is reflected in various social problems such as divorce, desertion, breakdown of family discipline, delinquency, crime, urban disorder, decay of the village and the rural community, and various kinds of protest behavior.

The response of the traditional order to the industrializing process, however, need not be disruptive, but may take other forms. Consequently, the contention which we are considering rests on a considerable amount of question begging. But let us forego this point. Let us also pass by the very relevant question as to whether factors other than industrialization are responsible for the indicated lines of disintegration. Let us, in other words, grant the dubious assumption that the industrializing process by itself removes productive functions from the family and village, initiates migration of workers and their families to industrial centers, places them in congested urban residence, puts workers in an impersonal labor market, removes them from prior systems of paternalistic, tribal, or feudal relations, and thrusts them into a system of contractual and monetary relations. The crucial question is whether these changes lead naturally to disorganization.

The honest answer to the question is that they need not do so. The changes obviously set situations which have to be met. But the changes do not indicate or determine *how* they are to be met. Alternative possibilities of great significance exist in the case of each of the changes. One does not know the direction which will be taken by the reorganizing actions in the case of any of the changes. Thus, the shift in productive functions from the home to the factory may strengthen the family by placing it in a better economic position and permitting parents to devote more attention to the welfare of their children. The migration of people from villages and farms may relieve pressure and distress in such areas. Migrants and their families may find urban conditions of residence to be an improvement over previous conditions of residence with better opportunities for a less arduous life, for the education of children, and for an elevation of status. Detachment from the extended family may result in a strengthening of the nuclear family, just because it is thrown on its own resources. Adjustments to mobility of employment may be taken in stride as thousands of cases of worker families show. Detachment from paternalistic, feudal, or tribal systems may be a relief from distasteful restraints and an opportunity for forge one's own pursuit of a better life. Participation in a fuller system of contractual and monetary relations may be a means of organizing careers on a more hopeful and solid basis.

These few observations should make it clear that divergent responses may be made to changes which industrialization occasions in the traditional order. The responses may range from drastic disorganization to vital remobilization, with many intermediate forms. The industrializing process does not determine or account for the given form taken by the response. A knowledge of the industrializing process may be helpful in spotting the points in traditional life which are subject to change; yet it does not provide a foresight as to how the change is to be met or handled. It may indicate that artisans and handicraftsmen are displaced from traditional employment; it does not indicate how they will reorganize their lives in the face of such displacement. It may indicate that economic production is removed from the home; it does not tell us how the family adjusts to this removal. It may indicate that workers and their families move from their local communities; it does not tell us what is the effect of this on the local communities. It may indicate the detachment of the nuclear family from the extended family; it does not indicate what happens to the nuclear family. It may indicate that workers and their families are going to reside in urban communities; it does not tell us how they will meet conditions of urban life. It may indicate that workers will be subject to mobility in employment; it does not indicate how this will affect their lives. It may indicate a detachment of industrial workers from paternalistic and tribal systems; it does not tell us how workers will respond to this detachment. It may indicate that workers are thrown into a nexus of contractual and monetary relations; it does not tell us how they will reorganize their lives in this nexus. It may tell us that traditional forms of authority are weakened; it does not tell what may emerge to replace this authority, nor how effective it may be. It may indicate a change in traditional values; it does not tell us what may be the character and efficiency of the new schemes which are used in their place.

In short, the industrializing process does not tell us whether the changes which it *may* induce in the traditional order will be disorganizing. It is neutral, indeterminate and indifferent to this possibility. The scholar who assumes that because change or dislocation is introduced into the traditional order by industrialization, such change or dislocation is disorganizing in character, rests his case on an untenable premise.

Release of new social forces

This contention is that early industrialization generates a series of new demands on life, such as the wish by women for emancipation, the desire of youth for greater freedom, a general desire for superior living comforts, a search for higher social status, and an elevation of ambition and aspiration. These demands signify dissatisfaction with current conditions and they constitute strivings for new social arrangements. The pressure they occasion is held to result in disorganization.

There are a number of important reasons why this contention should not be accepted. First, early industrialization may occur without being accompanied by such demands. This seems to have been true in the case of early industrialization in Great Britain and Western Europe, beginning roughly two centuries ago. The accounts for a large part of that period are silent with regard to the appearance of such demands. It was only later that demands, such as those of women for emancipation, emerged in some formidable proportion. In terms of the history of Western Europe, the formation of such demands has been a slow and long process, instead of being condensed in the period of early industrialization. Further, historical accounts indicate decisively that their formation was the result of a large number of modernizing influences, such as communication, travel, education, the spread of democratic ideas, and the development of a variety of social movements. Their emergence is traceable more to a complex of social and ideological changes than to the industrializing process.

The linkage of these generalized demands to modernization rather than to industrialization is strongly affirmed by the fact of their contemporary rise in a number of so-called "underdeveloped" regions with insignificant industrialization. The appearance of new life demands in such nonindustrialized regions is a result of incorporation inside of the modern world. Such incorporation introduces new models and standards of life, new conceptions of rights and privileges, and new opportunities for education and sophistication. The demands for better schemes of living seem to be the stuff of modernization and not of industrialization.

Let us grant, however, that such generalized demands arise frequently in regions and countries undergoing industrialization. The point that should now be made is that such demands need not be disorganizing. The fact that women seek a better status and more privileges, or that youth seeks more freedom, or that people seek a higher standard of living, or that people strive for higher status, or that people elevate their aspirations to higher levels, does not signify a state of social disorganization. Such seekings and strivings may be accommodated inside of a changing system of life without that system falling apart or not being able to function. New channels of activity and new positions may be opened to women; husbands may accord greater privileges to wives; youth may be given wider ranges of freedom in socially regularized ways; people may achieve higher standards of living; channels for upward progression in status may be available; and people in general may see hope in the peaceful achievement of aspirations. The presence of means and facilities for the realization of generalized demands may permit their accommodation inside of functioning life, just as the absence of such means and facilities may lead to disorganization. The industrializing process has no responsibility for either the presence or the absence of the means and facilities.

Summary and conclusions

Scholarly thought is very confused regarding the relation of early industrialization to social disorganization. In noting the frequent incidence of disorganization in periods of early industrialization, scholars have been led to attribute the disorganization to the industrializing process. However, our remarks on the three major ways by which early industrialization is declared to produce disorganization indicate that the alleged connection is not tenable. There are five major considerations which compel us to reject the alleged connection. First, we have to note the instances of early industrialization, chiefly on the local community level, wherein disorganization is not present. Second, is the occurrence of disorganization in nonindustrial regions similar to that attributed to industrialization in regions undergoing early industrialization; this suggests that the causes of disorganization may lie outside of the industrializing process. Third, in the case of regions undergoing early industrialization the play of significant nonindustrial influences which may promote disorganization. Fourth, we see the crucial importance of the schemes of interpretation which are brought to the situations introduced under early industrialization; these schemes which set the lines of experience and response are not determined by the industrializing process. Finally, the social changes which are introduced, even though drastic, may be met and handled without the acting units becoming disorganized.

These considerations should make clear that the occurrence of social disorganization in periods of early industrialization is a complex matter. On the basis of a knowledge of the industrializing process, by itself, one cannot and should not assert that social disorganization will ensue as a consequence. One has to take account of other forces in play, such as the background of the people involved, the interpretation which they bring to their situations, and the capacity of the people to cope with the changes taking place in their lives. The industrializing process neither sets nor explains these decisive factors. It stands before them in a neutral and indeterminate position.

The occurrence of social disorganization in periods of early industrialization sets a problem and not a solution. It calls for the unraveling of the conditions which bring disorganization into being, instead of an attribution of the disorganization to the industrializing process. To treat industrialization as a cause or an independent variable responsible for or followed by disorganization is to tread perilous ground. The crucial factors lie outside of the industrializing process.

Sociological Theory in Industrial Relations*

This paper is confined to a consideration of the kinds of theorizing and research in the field of industrial relations being made today by sociologists and to an expression of judgment as to the reasons for the inadequacy of such theorizing and research.

Since much of this theorizing and research has blossomed forth under the current rubric of "Industrial Sociology" I think it is fitting first of all to say a few words about this recent sociological interest. It must be apparent to a sociologist that a great deal of the current interest in, and enthusiasm for, a field of industrial sociology has the aspects of faddish concern, paralleling similar outbursts of excitement by sociologists over new fields in the recent history of American sociology. The term, "Industrial Sociology," has an alluring ring. Supported by a generous amount of collectively generated enthusiasm it is not surprising that the field beckons to so many in our fold and attracts a lot on the basis of a spacious offer of great and easy rewards. The present faddish character of interest in Industrial Sociology is perhaps inevitable and since we are all human, merits nothing more than mere comment. What does occasion some misgiving, at least to me, is the delusion that the words, "Industrial Sociology" confer somehow an automatic assurance that sociologists who move into this field are equipped with an adequate fund of guiding principles and a pertinent set of instruments of research. As far as I can judge, the recent and current activities of students in the field of industrial sociology represent little more than the application of a conventional stock of ideas and methods of study to a new area of interest. In my opinion, this effort of application suffers from a double deficiency. First the students making the application are dread-

*Paper read before the annual meeting of the American Sociological Society, Chicago, Illinois, December 27-30, 1946.

fully naive with reference to the nature of industrial relations—I say they are naive because I think all of us are naive in this area. Second, the stock of conventional ideas and modes of research which we employ in our discipline are not suited to the study of industrial relations in our contemporary society. Such ideas and modes of research are essentially hackneyed, unrealistic and uninspiring. These are strong charges. Their validity may be judged by the content of the following discussion.

The evaluation of current theory and research in industrial relations requires as a background a brief sketch of the nature of industrial relations in our present-day American society. The primary parties to these relations are workers and management.[1] The extent and variety of the relations between workers and management cannot be dealt with in this paper. I wish merely to note the obvious point that these relations in American industry are not in the nature of a simple contact between a worker selling his labor and an employer purchasing that labor. That bare fundamental relation has been elaborated in our society into an extensive, diversified, complex and indirect network of relations in which the individual worker becomes an insignificant and inconspicuous figure. With unionization, especially with industrial unionization, workers have become incorporated in organizations, usually of vast dimensions. The relations of workers to management become increasingly led by, directed by, mediated by and expressed through such organizations. The organization as such functions through a hierarchy of officers and central committees who formulate policies, establish objectives, decide on strategy and tactics, and execute decisions. On the side of management one finds similar organization which takes out of the hand of the individual manager the determination of the major outlines of his relation to the worker. Relations between workers

[1] The relations which exist within the field of management, the relations between managers and owners, and the relations between managers of different industrial concerns and between owners of different industrial concerns—all are of admittedly great importance and deserve more than the negligible study that is being devoted to them today. Correspondingly, the myriad of relations between fellow workers ranging from contact at the work bench to the intricate indirect relations brought about by huge national unions are of definite importance. Such relations, likewise, have been studied only in a meager fashion. However, the relations between workers and management constitute what is centrally important in the field of modern industry.

and management become primarily a matter of relations between organized groups. The formation of huge national unions has especially given a new dimension and character to these relations.

To my mind the most noteworthy feature of the relations between workers and management in American industry is that the relations are dynamic, uncrystallized and changing. They may be regarded as in a state of continuous tension, even though the degree of this tension will vary significantly from time to time. The tension is, itself, an inevitable consequence of a variety of factors which lead workers and management to exercise pressure against each other at shifting points and in new ways. Each of these two parties is forced to meet such pressure to resist it if it can, to adjust to it in some way if it must. The result is that the relations are either moving, or if not moving, in tenuous accommodation poised to move.

That this is true should be apparent on an analysis of the basic and accessory conditions which impart impetus to the relations between workers and management. Fundamentally, workers and management in our economy are necessarily in conflict with each other. I don't say this in a Marxian sense. I refer merely to the fact that workers, especially in their organized groups, are seeking to secure benefits and to preserve benefits and that management is seeking managerial freedom and opportunities for business profit. As our economy is organized, these respective interests enter normally in opposition. As either of the two parties moves in the direction of what it is seeking, it encroaches on the interest of the other party. Thus, an advance is in the nature of pressure and as such encounters resistance. Whenever such advances are initiated the pattern of relations changes. This bare statement merely sketches the fundamental fact that industrial relations between workers and management under our economy are intrinsically unstable and inherently disposed toward rearrangement.

All that is needed to set such relations in movement is the initiation of seeking efforts by workers or by management. The conditions which initiate such seeking efforts are rife in our society and are likely to remain so. I call attention to only a few of the more conspicuous ones: competition in business with the inevitable effort to achieve efficient, low-cost production and managerial freedom; the effort of management to coup the gains of improved efficiency through technological improvements; the shifting and changing of management personnel with divergent philosophies; the development of new wishes and conceptions of rights on the part of workers; the exercise of pressure by the rank and file, particularly in large democratic unions; the formation of national unions, leading to uniform demands on diversified industrial concerns; the pressure on union leaders to produce increased benefits; the struggle for position on the part of union leaders or those seeking to be leaders; the development of a militant, aggressive psychology on the part of unions; the rivalry between unions for prestige, membership and the efforts to weaken rival unions; the change in price-wage relationships and the movement of the business cycle; shifts in political opinion which yield the same encouragement; and the appearance of new legislation or new judicial interpretation which open new vistas of what is permissible. Such conditions—and the list is by no means complete—lead and coerce workers and management into new relations as each part seeks to pursue and to protect its respective interests. In response to such forces, industrial relations in our society become tense, changeable and ever moving.

The mobile character of industrial relations has taken on a new dimension and nature with the organization of workers in vast national unions. The focal point of relationship has been shifted away from the contact between workers and local management to the contact between big union organization and management organization. Although there are exceptions, the usual consequence of the organization of workers on a national basis has been a centralized guidance of labor activities over an industry-wide area. Bargaining is done for the industry as a whole or for large segments of the industry represented by huge corporations. Thus labor relations become increasingly a matter of relationship between gigantic organizations of workers and management, each of which functions through central policy and executive groups. Relations between workers and management in the local plants in the industry tend to lose separate and autonomous character and instead are determined in their basic outlines by the policies, objectives, plans and strategy of the central organizations. Thus to suggest an analogy, workers and management become related and aligned like vast opposing armies, with

many outposts and points of contact but with the vast relationship operating along lines set up by the central organizations.

These two characteristics of industrial relations—their mobility and their guidance by organizations—may appear trite and
scarcely worthy of notice. If this is so, so much the better for the
presentation of my thesis. The very commonplace character of
the observations will help to establish the inadequacy of sociological theory and research in the field of industrial relations, especially so of the theory and research that parades under the ban-
ner of "industrial sociology." I can now address myself to this
matter.

In my judgment the theory and research by sociologists in
the field of industrial relations can be put conveniently into five
classes.

One body of theory and research rests on the proposition
that industrial relations are in the nature of organized practises
and customary routines. Thus, such relations are to be studied as
cultural data—as if they were expressions of a body of established regulations or definitions. In my judgment this type of
theory and research misses the central character of industrial relations in our society. As suggested in my previous remarks, industrial relations in our society are intrinsically tense, mobile and
unstable—not settled, regulated and set. They have a character
which arises less from the mere fact of what has been, and arises
more from what workers and management believe ought to be.
Anyone who is at all realistic about our industrial relations must
recognize that the wishes, hopes and intentions of workers and
management alike far transcend what the parties are actually getting out of their relations. These wishes, hopes and intentions
hover in the background as constant, impelling forces, exerting
pressure on the relations, eager to seize an opportunity to realize
themselves, and, consequently, breaking through or threatening
to break through. Personally, I find it unrealistic and fruitless to
try to study or interpret our industrial relations as if they were an
expression of a body of cultural norms, definitions or regulations. In my judgment, to press the point a little further, it is far-
fetched to try to study industrial relations in our society as one
might a medieval guild or a primitive tribe. For a long time, I
have believed that the conventional conception of culture which

302 Selected Works of Herbert Blumer

dominates so completely the thinking of sociologists, anthropologists, and fellow social scientists today is unrealistic and perverting as a scheme for the study of what is characteristic of modern social life. I am convinced that this is the case in current industrial relations. Such relations emerge from the energetic quest of active groups which are seeking new gains, advantages and protections and which are ever poised to seize and utilize the opportunities that arise. The wishes, intentions and calculations which underlie such efforts as well as the relations between workers and management that result therefrom are slippery matters that cannot be caught in the skeins of a cultural net.

These remarks apply in much the same manner to another body of sociological theory and research which rests on the premise that industrial relations are primarily a structure of stratified or status relationships. This premise does not seem to me to have much sense. Admittedly, the scheme of a hierarchy of status relationships may be applied with fruitfulness to various kinds of social organization. Also, it can be applied to the organization of personnel in an industrial concern although I doubt whether such an application would yield knowledge of any particular importance. It might also be applied, however with somewhat less ease and no greater fruitfulness, to the membership of a union. I do not see, however, that the scheme is meaningful when applied to the relations between workers and management. Undeniably in the shop, mill or other plant situations, workers and local management have status relations. I am unable to see how such local status relations either occasion, govern or explain the mobile industrial relations which have been referred to in the previous discussion. The resentments that may flow from a sense of inferior status on the part of individual workers and also the struggle for status on the part of unions are of significance in the moving relation with management—however, such individual resentments and such collective striving for status signify, if anything, a breaking down of a structure of status relations or an effort to create a new structure of such relations. The new activities are not ordered by the structure against which they are rebelling. Labor relations, as previously indicated, take the form of strivings and temporary accommodations in those strivings. This is an unsettled area which is not structured, or governed by a structure. The application of the conception of a structure of status relationship to the relations between workers and management in modern industry seems to me to be strained and barren.

There is a third body of sociological theory which regards modern industrial relations as products of long time trends or "super-organic" factors. There is considerable difference in what is taken as the significant trend or trends by different theorists or research students. The trend may be a class struggle, or a change in social stratification as a result of science or technology, or a change in the internal structure of industrial economy resulting from diverse inventions, or the operations of the business cycle, or it may be merely some kind of statistical trend. Whatever be the trend which is used, it becomes, logically, a kind of super-organic determinant of industrial relations. This type of approach seems to me to be markedly incapable of accounting for the mobile pattern of industrial relations, or interpreting what goes on in such industrial relations, or explaining the results or outcome of such relations. Admittedly, the activities between workers and management take place not in a vacuum, but in a historical context and in a field of pervasive social and economic factors. The context and the field undeniably provide stimulation and exercise constraints, opening lines of development and setting limits to developments. The fact that the context and the field constitute a framework does not mean, however, that the activities carried on in that framework are dictated or predetermined by that framework. The area of industrial relations, in particular, is marked by relatively constant striving of opposed parties requiring each to adjust to the other and imparting to their relation the condition of tension and uncertain outcome that has been referred to previously. What occurs in this area is forged from countless and varied discussions, from judgments of complicated situations, from calculations of the timeliness of action, from the threats and opportunities yielded by the play of events. Indeed these few remarks fail by far to depict the complicated and shifting arrangement of factors that must be calculated by the parties. It is not surprising that their relations are marked by compromise, expediency and by uncertain and tentative outcome. I do not find that the concept of trends or of superorganic factors is suited to the analysis of what goes on in industrial relations; indeed I believe such a concept to be intrinsically unfit for such an analysis.

A fourth body of sociological theory and research that is

particularly prominent in the field of industrial relations is associated with the gratuitous label of "human relations." No one can or should take serious issue with the view that industrial relations are human relations. However, one who proposes to study industrial relations as human relations should be faithful to the nature of human relations and should be sure that he is studying industrial relations. In my judgment the thinking and research in current studies of "human relations in industry" are deficient in either one or both of these two respects. In the studies, human relations are usually identified with and made synonymous with cultural relations or with structural relations. Here I merely repeat what I said above, namely, that it is inaccurate and misleading to regard dynamic human relations as predetermined or controlled by culture or structure. The other deficiency is more worthy of being noted. Current studies of "human relations in industry" rest, seemingly, on the premise that industrial relations are primarily direct relations between the people in the local plant or factory. Thus, studies may be made of the situation at a given work bench, assembly line, rolling mill or some other unit of operation. One may get information of cliques of workers, on alignments of supervisors or on how given workers and given supervisors get along with one another. The findings of such studies of this sort with which I am familiar have little relevance to industrial relations as they are developing in our society. It seems clear to me that industrial relations are becoming increasingly a matter of alignment of organizations—of unions on one side and industrial corporations and business federations on the other. What takes place on the front line of contact between worker and supervisor is admittedly of importance. However, unless the consideration of that front line of contact is made in the light of the relations between the organizations, the consideration will give rise to only a deceptive portrayal of industrial relations. In my judgment, this is a primary shortcoming of current studies of human relations in industry.

There is another body of sociological effort in the field of industrial relations that needs to be noted. It is in the form of quantitative studies of attitudes and opinions and sociometric studies of preferences, aversions and feelings. This body of study is attended by little coherent theory. The guiding idea seems to be that relations stem from attitudes and feelings and, consequently, are to be understood through the study of attitudes and feelings. This idea is fairly satisfactory. However, the studies being made of attitudes, opinions and feelings of workers and of managerial personnel fall short by far of coming to grip with the central character of industrial relations. Such studies consist usually of nothing more than the application of conventional techniques of "measuring attitudes" or constructing "sociograms" to any situation which is conveniently at hand. They seem to be conceived and made in complete innocence of the mobile and large dimensional character of contemporary industrial relations. A sociogram of clerks in an office, or the "scaled" attitudes of a given group of workers toward absenteeism, or a so-called study of morale of employees in a given work situation impresses me, frankly, as far away from the stream of present day industrial relations. Further, I doubt the efficacy of such devices if they were to be used in the study of current industrial relations in their mobile and large dimensional character. Assuming that what we commonly recognize as attitudes and feelings are faithfully caught by attitude scales or sociograms—and this assumption is actually not warranted—such attitudes and feelings in the field of industrial relations are subject to shifts, rearrangements, restraints, and replacements in the play of events in a dynamic moving situation. It is these latter conditions which are central. Consequently, I suspect that the application of our currently popular forms of scaled attitude studies and of sociometric studies would not yield analytical understanding. Such a pre-judgment, however, is not even called for since at present such studies do not seek to grapple with the mobile and complicated character of industrial relations.

I am acutely aware of the sketchy and cavalier summary of sociological theory and research in the field of industrial relations that I have made in the foregoing remarks. It is not possible to include in the scope of this paper a documented and detailed discussion of the individual works that fall under the types of theory and research which I have considered. I believe that the general points that I have made hold true. I do not wish to give the impression that all sociological studies made in the field of industry are valueless. Many of them, particularly those made by the "Harvard group" have been done carefully and conscientiously. Such studies have given telling accounts of the concrete situations studied and have helped to dispel inaccurate, fragmentary and biased ideas, particularly among members of higher management. Such studies have also given rise to generalizations which seem reasonable inside of certain limits. However, my judgment is that the value and validity of such studies become suspect at the precise point of entry into the area of mobile accommodative relations between organized workers and management. My point is that not only have these studies failed to deal with this new area of industrial relations, but that their generalizations, such as those on "morale," become suspect when applied to situations in this area. The question I have asked in reading such studies is whether they yield knowledge that is meaningful or relevant to an ordered understanding of industrial relations as we glimpse such relations in, let us say, news items appearing in our newspapers. My judgment is that the studies are not giving an ordered understanding of industrial relations in our society because of either a failure to see the outlines of contemporary industrial relations or because of intrinsic inability to fit such outlines.

A proper orientation to the study of industrial relations in our society must be based, in my judgment, on the recognition that such relations are a moving pattern of accommodative adjustments largely between organized parties. In a valid sense industrial relations may be likened to a vast, confused game evolving without the benefit of fixed rules and frequently without the benefit of any rules. The setting of this game is itself not stable, but instead is shifting and presenting itself in new forms. This occasions strains on the pattern of game. In addition, each of the parties is subject to the play of pressures and forces inside of its own ranks which impart further tension and shifts in the game situation. Still further, the participants are far from satisfying their respective wishes and objectives in the temporal accommodations which they make to each other, with a consequence of constant pressure on their relations and an opportunistic readiness to change them. I think that we deceive ourselves and perhaps engage in wishful thinking when we regard this shifting flow of relations in industry as temporary and transitory, to be followed by a shaking down of relationships into a permament orderly system. This, to my mind, is not at all likely as long as we live in a dynamic, democratic, competitive society. The degree of tension, the rapidity of accommodations and the extent of shifts in relations may vary from time to time, but the mobile character of the relations remains.

In my judgment the fruitful study of present day industrial relations requires a new perspective—one that is compatible with the mobile, indirect and large dimensional character of such relations. I sense the blurred outlines of such a perspective. It must visualize human beings as acting, striving, calculating, sentimental and experiencing persons and not as the automatons and neutral agents implied by the more dominant of our current scientific ideologies and methodologies. It must further visualize such human beings in their collective character—as arranged in diverse ways and incorporated in intricate and indirect network of relations. It must embrace the complicated behavior of these collectivities, particularly as they act and prepare to act toward one another.

The observation necessary to sharpen and fill in this vague perspective must meet the two requirements of intimate familiarity and broad imaginative grasp. That observation should be based on close familiarity with what is being observed is a truism and would require no mention here were it not for the woeful fact of the fashionable and respectful practise in our ranks to ignore and snub the truism. In addition to being based on intimate acquaintance with what is being observed, observation must be suited to the imaginative grasping of intricate complexes of data. It is unfortunate that observation in the field of industrial relations has to be made in the form of large intricate patterns—but it has to be, in order to be realistic. In a way, the necessities of observation in industrial relations are quite similar to those required in modern warfare. The individual soldier in his single observation post, regardless of how competent he may be as an observer, can understand little of what is taking place over the broad area of a campaign. A sociological investigator making observations in a single factory suffers, I believe, from a corresponding limitation. Effective observation requires the observer to sense the movement in the field to take many varied roles, to size up a variety of different situations and in doing so to perform the difficult task of fitting such things into somewhat of an integrated pattern. This type of observation, whether we like it or not, requires a high degree of imaginative judgment in order to be accurate. It may be noted, in passing, that this type of observation is not nurtured in our training programs for sociologists; indeed, our current conventions of research discourage this type of observation.

Assuming that observation based on intimate familiarity and using broad imaginative judgment is made of industrial relations, its findings, I suspect, will not lend themselves to treatment by our present kind or current stock of sociological theories. Our sociological thinking has been fashioned in the main from the consideration of matters which are quite apart from the central character of modern dynamic life. Our thinking has been derived from images of stable societies and of nicely ordered association; or from highly abstracted and emasculated data such as census and demotic items; or from a miscellany of imported theories which were formed when reference to matters different from those in our field; or from a variety of social philosophies which have appeared from time to time in our western civilization. Our sociological thinking has not been shaped from empirical consideration of the dynamic character of modern life. We need a scheme of treatment suited to the analysis of collective and mass interaction—the interaction between active and relatively free collectivities with different degrees and kinds of organizations. To formulate such a scheme is the theoretical task which confronts sociologists in the field of industrial relations. I do not believe that sociologists have begun this task.

Group Tension
and Interest Organizations

My assignment on this joint program is to discuss the problem of group tension arising in a society, such as ours, which is typified by the presence of economic power blocs. I am asked to treat particularly how such group tension may be lessened or controlled. The order of my discussion will be, first, to make some observations on the nature of economic power blocs in order to depict the character of the society in which they operate and, then, in the light of such a depiction to consider the problem of group tension.

ECONOMIC POWER BLOCS
NATURAL TO SOCIETY

I assume that in speaking of economic power blocs—the topic of this joint meeting—we refer to orgnaizations which by virtue of their size or strategic position exercise, directly or indirectly, significant control over various economic operations in our society. Some of these organizations like industrial corporations, cartels, combines, interests, and labor unions may exercise a direct control in certain areas over such items as prices, investments, wages, sources of raw material, and supply of goods. Other of these organizations like trade associations, industrial associations, agricultural associations, and labor associations may seek indirectly to achieve such control by exerting pressure on political institutions or governmental agencies.

The exercise of such direct and indirect control has made economic power blocs suspect in the eyes of many students. This is probably the reason why we are having the current program.

Many students regard economic power blocs as inimical to the operation of a free competitive system. Other students regard them as a threat to political democracy by virtue of the powerful pressure they allegedly exert on legislative and administrative agencies and by virtue of their efforts to influence public thought through propaganda and other means. Many students, further, believe that such organizations endanger the very existence of a unified society by their pursuit of special interests at the expense of communal interest. There lurks in these views an idea that economic power blocs are alien and threatening social forms that somehow have intruded themselves into a society whose intrinsic makeup is uncongenial to their presence. Thus, some economists think of them as unnatural and menacing because they do not fit the premises of a pure competitive economy; some political scientists think of them as alien and dangerous because they cut athwart the premise of a political democracy based on the principle of *vox populi;* and some sociologists think of them as strange and perilous social forms because they contravene the premise of shared community interest, without which, it is stated, no true society can exist.

In my judgment, however, any intelligent treatment of economic power blocs and kindred organizations in other areas of our life requires a recognition that they are natural products of our society, that they are congenial to the way in which our society operates and that they play an integral part in that operation. I wish to explain briefly why this seems to me to be true.

First, we may note that economic power blocs are fundamentally interest groups. They exist as tight or loose organizations seeking to advance or protect a given interest or combination of interests. As such, economic power blocs are like countless other organizations, big or small, in our society acting consciously to further or defend particular interests of the most diverse nature. In local communities, rural regions, cities, and states, in such broad areas as business, religion, politics, education, and popular arts, and in a variety of institutions, there are innumerable formal and informal organizations having their own particular interests which they seek to advance or to protect. Indeed, modern society is a vast network of such interest groups ranging from small combinations of few individuals to huge functioning organizations. What we refer to as economic power blocs are merely more conspicuous and formidable instances, in the economic and political realm, of such interest groups with which our society is rife.

In order that we not miss the full import of this generic similarity between economic power blocs and a host of other interest groups, small and large, in our society, we should note that in diverse ways and at different times other interest groups may acquire what amounts to a monopolistic or quasimonopolistic position similar to that which is alleged to exist in the case of economic power blocs. Thus, in the economic field a local employer may be in a position to depress wages, a union with a closed shop to elevate wages, a large purchaser to control the price of surplus products in a local market, a local combine to set the prices on some speciality item, or a local bank to control the extension of credit and to show favoritism in that extension. Such monopolistic or quasimonopolistic control on a small scale is not confined to the economic realm but may exist in other areas of interest—a local political machine may have a grip on local political life, a small administrative clique may "run" a college, a set of officials may dominate a church, or a gambling establishment may brook no opposition. Monopolistic control is in no sense confined to huge organizations nor is it limited to the economic field.

These trite observations are sufficient to emphasize (1) that in our type of society it is natural for a multitude of interest groups of the most diverse nature to arise and flourish, each seeking in its own way to advance or defend its own interest, and (2) that many of them, when opportunity affords and strategic position permits, may achieve a monopolistic position for a given time. We are compelled to recognize that economic power blocs are fundamentally like other interest groups in our society—they are organizations in pursuit of their particular interests in a setting which permits, invites, or compels their growth and facilitates their mode of operation.

What seems to be peculiar to economic power blocs in contrast to most other interest groups is their size and the more formidable power which they may exercise over wider areas of life. Yet even these elements of size and greater power are natural and congenial to our type of society. What I have in mind is that growth to huge size and increase in power occur naturally, under propitious circumstances, in the case of organizations pursuing their interests. There is nothing strange, unexpected, or unusual for a corporation which sees an opportunity for increased economic gain or economic security to absorb a series of competitors if its position enables it to do so; or for a number of concerns facing ruinous competition from each other to establish a combine which will enable their survival; or for a labor union, faced with widely differential wage rates and the presence of unorganized workers, to move toward complete coverage and control in its field; or for industrial associations, trade associations, agricultural groups, or labor organizations to combine, respectively, to exert political influence on behalf of their respective interests. All of such instances of growth are natural. And it should be noted that instances of natural growth to huge size are to be found not only in the economic field but in other fields—the professional field, the political field, the religious field, the educational field. Witness the American Medical Association, the American Legion, the Catholic Church in our country and may I say, the AAAS in whose embrace we find ourselves.

The emergence of huge interest organizations in our society should be easy to understand. After all our democratic type of society is committed to allowing people relatively wide latitude in the pursuit of their interests. The expansion of such a society in size, in diversification, and in resulting interdependency means a corresponding growth in the organization of interests. Our emerging society allows, encourages, or compels growth of large and powerful interest organizations. To some interest groups, a wider area of action is opened and they grow in response to the pursuit of their interest in that area. In the case of other interest groups, growth is almost compulsory if they are to protect their interests in the national arena; in the case of others, the mere peaking-up of function in an increasingly integrated society brings forth growth in size and strategic control. Frequently, the growth in size and power in some interest groups brings about almost inevitably such growth in the case of other interest groups. And, even though it may seem paradoxical to some, the growth in size and operation of government leads to growth in the case of some interest groups—if, for no other reason, than to exercise successful influence on such government.

It is such observations that lead me to believe that economic power blocs and other large interest organizations are natural and congenital products of our society and that they are integral parts of our society. Instead of viewing economic power blocs or other large interest organizations as alien or even dangerous to the nature of our society, I believe that we should view our emerging society as having increasingly a nature that is set by the presence and operation of large interest groups. It is doubtful if a massive and complex democratic society, set up to allow a relatively free play of interest, could operate without a developed structure of large interest organizations.

DYNAMIC ORGANIZATIONS IN A MOBILE WORLD

Having identified economic power blocs and other large interest organizations as natural parts of our society—as merely the larger and more formidable of the countless interest groups in our society—I would like to deal briefly with their nature and with the operating world in which they act. This knowledge will be helpful for the subsequent discussion of group tensions. The key to understanding large interest organizations, it seems to me, is to recognize that they are *dynamic organizations operating in a mobile world*. They should be seen as acting organizations and not as mere aggregations or classifications of inert individuals, allegedly having a common interest. Such classificatory groups as the proletariat, the bourgeoisie, farmers, laborers, or capitalists are not interest groups—and I venture to add do not play an important role in the shaping of our society. Interest groups are organizations set up to act. The large interest organization has a structure consisting of a top executive leadership, echelons of sub-leaders and officials with different authority, and a differentiated membership or following. In pursuit of its objectives the interest organization necessarily must act as an entity. This requires direction and gives rise to such functions as planning, the clarification of objectives, assessing the possibilities of action, setting policies, devising strategy and making decisions. In the case of large interest groups these functions are lodged increasingly and necessarily in the hands of a small executive or directing group who, as we are wont to say, guides the destiny of the organization.

The dynamic character of large interest organizations is clear from a scrutiny of the experience of any one of them. Such a scrutiny discloses a temporal succession of opportunities to be realized, of obstacles to be overcome, of threats to be forestalled, of encroachments to be beaten back, and of crises of varying severity to be met and surmounted. Such experiences bespeak an active and striving group which, in the pursuit of its interests, makes thrusts into its world, meets resistance to many of its thrusts, and is exposed to counter thrusts into its own area of interest. I doubt if there exists any large interest group in our modern American society which does not have to strive continuously to realize or defend its interests. Ask the directors if they have problems! The typical picture is one of constant effort and of new effort.

The dynamic character of large interest groups corresponds, of course, to the mobility of the world in which they operate and to which they have to adjust. Their operating worlds are arenas in which a new patterning is in process. Depending on the field of interest, there is emergence of new ideas, new inventions, new technologies, new encroachments, new oppositions, new alignments of power, new regulations, new laws, new possibilities, and new threats. And, added to this, is a play of events which frequently cannot be foreseen or controlled. The experience of a large interest organization, frozen in a single moment of its operation, may not disclose the mobility of its world; the experience over a reasonable period of time will surely do so. To invoke a serviceable simile, the experience of the large interest organization resembles less that of a standing army in peace-time and more that of such an army engaged in a military campaign.

The dynamic character of the large interest organization and the mobile nature of its operating world enable an appreciation of three items, significant for the subsequent discussion of group tension. One is that the large interest group is involved in a process of contest with its world and that an appreciable part of this struggle may be with groups having opposing interests. The second item is that the large interest organization operates in a precarious world. It is incorporated in a system that transcends it—a mobile system with an unfolding parade of events and developments bringing new opportunities, new obstacles, new threats, and new problems. In a sense its accustomed ground is slipping away from under it or threatening to do so. Despite its size, power, and strategic position, the large interest organization does not have the fixity of security, the freedom from concern, and the lasting triumph of control that popular imagery frequently assigns to it. Its power is something that waxes and wanes from situation to situation and from time to time. The third item is that by virtue of being in a shifting world and in an arena of opposition the large interest organization is perforce led to follow to a great extent a policy of workable adjustment or of expediential practice. It has to be flexible to meet the demands called for in exploiting opportunities, bulwarking against possible losses, and retrieving itself from setbacks.

NATURE OF GROUP TENSION

The foregoing discussion provides an appropriate background for a discussion of group tensions arising in a society with large interest organizations. The term "group tension" is a concomitant of conflict. It signifies a concern aroused in a group which believes that its security, well-being, interests, and values are being opposed, jeopardized, or undermined by the actions of another group. It means that the group with such a concern is poised to react in a hostile manner to what it construes to be an attack on it.

It should be clear from the previous discussion of interest groups that group tension is indigenous to the very process of operation of a society of interest organizations. The pursuit by groups of their interests usually brings them through one or another way of opposition or conflict with other organizations pursuing their interests. The clash of group interests in our society is so common that to cite even a few makes me feel that I am padding my paper. But I proceed to pad the paper. In my home community the apparently simple matter of formulating a building code has been held up for years as a result of an unbelievable strong clash of a variety of interests. In the economic domain of our society we may note the clash between competing business concerns; the clash between unions and companies; the conflict between unions; the conflict between so-called industry interests, such as coal and oil; the opposition between sectional producing groups; and the conflict between different farm organizations. Conflict of group interests may be seen easily in other areas such as religion, education, and politics. In all areas and at all levels of our society where there are interest organizations, there will be found opposition, conflict, and tension. The clashes of interest may differ in many ways. They may be momentary or long-lived, sporadic or continuous, frequent or infrequent, minor or grave. The chief point is that these clashes occur and that their occurrence is natural and inevitable by virtue of the very character of interest organizations and of the mobile world in which they operate.

CONTINUOUS WORKABLE ADJUSTMENTS

This picture of extensive, recurrent, and persistent conflict of interests in the world of interest organizations would suggest that the accompanying group tension would be formidable, serious, and very difficult to handle. Actually, such tension, by far, does not constitute a problem. I say this primarily because of the fact that just as the operations of interest organizations give rise continuously to conflict and tension, so similarly such operations provide continuously for the containment or liquidation of such conflict and tension. This may sound strange to some students; to others it will sound as the trite remark that it is. What I have in mind is that organizations who have occasion to come into opposition or conflict in the pursuit of their interests will almost always work out an adjustment between their respective actions. In the conflict situation an interest organization may refrain from pressing further its action; it may recede from the situation; it may make concessions or establish a compromise arrangement; or it may resign itself to a loss or a defeat. What is done will have the character of a workable adjustment. Sometimes the given workable adjustment covers the full scope of conflcit and thus leads to liquidation of tension. More frequently, the workable adjustment represents only a temporary accommodation, to be followed by further opposition and jostling which, in turn, gives rise to other workable accommodations. Such step by step adjustment may not reduce the tension, or sense of conflict, between the organizations. Indeed, in certain instances it may accentuate such tension. However, what is important to note is that the accommodations allow each organization to continue to function with regard to the other. Tension is contained in the sense that it is prevented from expressing itself in ways which would prevent such mutual functioning.

I submit that a survey of interest organizations in conflict, whether they be small organizations in a local community or huge economic blocks on the national scene, shows in amplitude a picture of continuous workable adjustment between them. Such workable adjustment is just as natural to the operation of interest organizations as is the opposition and conflict of which we have been speaking. It is a kind of corrective process which functions continuously to liquidate or contain the tension aroused by the conflict and opposition. Even in the area of labor management relations which is frequently regarded as showing the most acute and grievous conflict between interest organizations, the liquidation and containment of tension is by far the normal and dominant occurrence. It is very rare to find an instance of difference or of conflict in that area that is not resolved in a form of workable adjustment, however difficult it may be to reach that adjustment and however short-lived that adjustment may be. The pervasiveness of workable adjustment between interest organizations explains why the problem of tension in this field is, speaking generally, of no consequence.

PROBLEMS OF ADJUSTMENT

Yet there are problems—serious problems in the eyes of many people—which indicate an inability of a so-called process of workable adjustment to cope successfully with group tensions and which call for other means of eliminating or reducing such tensions. Let us mention a few of the more important of these problems. First, it is to be noted that in given instances the working out of adjustment by organizations in conflict may occasion appreciable social loss and inflict distress on innocent outsiders. The labor strike will serve as an example—it is a means, for both parties to it, of moving toward a workable adjustment. Many people would feel that when the process of adjustment involves social loss and public distress there is a clear need for the elimination or reduction of tension in place of relying on the normal working of such a process. Second, it is pointed out that frequently one of the interest organizations in conflict may have overwhelming strength and thus either force the weaker organization out of existence or else compel it to accept adjustment solely on the terms, so to speak, laid down by the stronger organization. Many people would feel that in such instances there is distinct need of resolving or abating tension in place of relying on a process of accommodation in which there is such unequal advantage between the conflicting groups. Third, one may note instances of a mounting up of tension despite the operation of workable adjustment, leading frequently to the transfer of the conflict to the political arena where it becomes a disturbing problem. Such a condition, as in the battle over labor legislation, signifies, seemingly, an inadequacy of the process of workable adjustment. To many it calls for positive efforts to eliminate or reduce tension.

However, we should be cautious in concluding that these conditions set a problem of group tension between interest organizations. I say this because such undesirable conditions seem to be natural concomitants of a system in which organizations are allowed relatively free play in the pursuit of their interests. By and large, this is recognized in our society; the conditions spoken of are generally tolerated. Thus, some degree of social harm or of distress attends many instances of group conflict and on some occasions may be quite pronounced as in the case of a strike, a filibuster, or a price war. Further, our society takes for granted the extinction of interest organizations in the conflict process, irrespective of unequal advantages between them; our history is a graveyard of organizations which have perished in the strife in the economic, political, or other fields. Also, our society has been, and is, rife with interest organizations, economic or otherwise, which because of relative weakness have been forced into extremely subordinate positions in relation to other interest organizations. Finally, the transfer of conflict between interest organizations into the political arena is, of course, a frequent occurrence and is acceptable in our political life. I make these observations not to justify or to deprecate the conditions but to point out that they occur repeatedly and that they are generally tolerated. The frequency of their occurrence suggests that they are indigenous to the conflict process in our society. They are taken as part of the game. They seem to be a price paid by a democratic society which is committed to the principle of relatively free pursuit of collective interests.

CONFLICTS AND THE PUBLIC INTEREST

As one runs his eyes over the American scene it becomes clear that such conditions as social loss, public distress, the extinction of interest organizations, and coerced adjustment of weaker organizations are regarded and treated as serious only when they are deemed to threaten what we vaguely call the public interest. When such conditions occur on a small scale they are tolerated; when they occur on a large scale there is likely to be a significant outcry and the intervention of the state is sought. A strike of a group of laborers in a local coal yard is viewed with comparative indifference; a national strike of coal miners becomes a matter of great concern. The smashing of a small union or the liquidation of a small business concern is accepted as part of the game; the undermining of a regional industry, in contrast, is viewed as serious. What I wish to note is that the same processes of conflict and accommodation with the same form of consequences are at work on a minor scale and on a major scale. What is accepted and taken as granted in the one instance is viewed with grave concern in the other. Tension between interest organizations becomes a problem of social significance only at the point where its expressions are felt to jeopardize the public interest. Consequently, the problem of coping with tension arises as important essentially only in the case of large interest organizations.

We can now address the question of what can be done to eliminate or reduce tension between large interest organizations, as in the case of economic power blocs. This question should be viewed in the light of the foregoing remarks, to wit, that conflict and tension are indigenous to a system of freely operating interest groups; that such tension is primarily resolved or contained through a process of point-to-point workable adjustment; that our social system accepts and tolerates in general deleterious consequences of such a process of adjustment as being part of the game; and that only in the event that such consequences are deemed to be adverse to public interest is action taken, and then in the form of the intervention of the state.

PROPOSALS TO REDUCE TENSION

There are, it appears, three general ways proposed to eliminate or lessen tension between interest organizations. These are: (1) to get them to follow a policy of understanding and good will, (2) to invoke effective control over them through public opinion, and (3) to apply to the problem the knowledge and techniques of social and psychological science.

In my judgment neither historic experience nor impartial analysis holds out much hope of eliminating or diminishing tension appreciably by having large interest organizations in conflict adopt a policy of good will and understanding toward one another. I will pass by the rather significant problem that is set in trying to get large organizations to adopt such a policy when they do not have it. The question of why such given organizations have not adopted such a policy, despite the general exhortation which we have in our society to do so, raises many interesting and important points which, however, we need not consider. Rather, I would assume that the large interest organizations have such a policy of good will and understanding which, incidentally, most of them would declare sincerely they did have. Such a policy would not, I think, appreciably affect conflict and tension if there were genuine conflict between vital interests. Where there is genuine conflict in interest, the problem does not lie in the area of ill will or misunderstanding—it exists, instead, in the fact that the respective interests and objectives of one of the organizations run athwart those of the other. If the organizations believe their respective interests and objectives to be valid and proper, it is somewhat presumptuous to expect them to desist from the pursuit of the interests and objectives, such as to surrender a vital advantage already secured or to refrain from pressing toward a vital accessible gain. If we as social scientists were organized as an interest group and were seeking, let us say, $5,000,000 of available federal funds for vital and cherished research, I do not think that out of a spirit of good will and understanding we would refrain from pressing our pursuit if one of our organized patriotic associations were seeking to secure that same $5,000,000 for the erection of statues and public plaques. Nor would the patriotic organization refrain from its pursuit out of consideration of good will to us, if it genuinely believed its objectives to be superior to ours. From everything I can find out, based in part on some direct observation of my own, the directors of large interest organizations have faith in the integrity and rectitude of their objectives. I am puzzled, accordingly, by the belief held by many thoughtful students that such organizations can be expected to curb or compromise their objectives solely out of sympathetic consideration for the opposed interest organizations. I would much rather expect interest organizations to compromise objectives because they found it judicious or expediential to do so.

The same observations may be made with regard to the tactics employed by interest organizations to realize objectives which they hold to be valid and proper. If the tactics, like that of the strike, are legal and sanctioned, it is fanciful to expect that their use will be forfeited out of sympathetic consideration for the interest organization which is blocking pursuit of the objectives. There is very little in historic experience to warrant such an expectation. These thoughts make me dubious about relying on good will and understanding to stay group tension in the case of large interest organizations.

However, one may ask, may not large interest organizations abandon or limit legitimate objectives and forfeit the use of sanctioned tactics out of consideration for the common welfare. This is a more reasonable expectation. Such a sacrifice—although with spottiness—does happen in times of dire danger such as war when the existence of the society, itself, is felt to be imperilled. The record for other times is very disappointing. It is not difficult to understand why. An understandable primacy attaches to the interests and objectives of the organization—a primacy, I wish to repeat, that is endorsed by the freedom accorded interest organizations in our democratic type of society. Further, as a sociologist would expect, the objectives become clothed in the eyes of the organization in a garment of rectitude and social good. Where the interests and objectives are viewed as legitimate and socially wholesome, an interest organization cannot be reasonably expected to sacrifice the objectives voluntarily out of consideration of a tenuous precept of common welfare.

This leads me to a second general type of proposal for handling tension between large interest organizations—namely, to invoke the pressure of public opinion. A critical public opinion, if formidable and unified, may unquestionably have an effect in given instances and at given times. The rub enters at this point. The opinion is not likely to be unified—large interest organizations have a habit these days of doing something themselves about the formation of public opinion. Further, even though a unified and formidable opinion may arise at certain critical points, there is little likelihood of forming a stable and durable climate of such opinion in our society with its given makeup. After all, our society, as one of interest organizations, works on the principle of allowing people to organize and act on behalf of collective interest as long as that interest is not illegal or does not contravene too grossly accepted norms of decency. There is, consequently, a strongly intrenched operating code which gives full support to interest organizations to defend tenaciously or follow vigorously what they believe to be vital and justifiable interests. Those who advocate control of interest organizations through public opinion should conjure with this deeply rooted operating code which impels in a direction opposite to that which they advocate. I think little reliance can be placed on public opinion as a stable means of controlling tension between large interest organizations.

This brings me to the third general type of proposal. The hope of eliminating or reducing tension between large interest organizations by applying the present-day knowledge and techniques of social sciences strikes me as futile and somewhat fanciful. I do not know where the relevant knowledge and techniques are to be found and I believe that I am familiar with the literature. There is a sizable literature on such varied topics as industrial peace, industrial unrest, the competitive process, social movements, political parties, interest politics, and group motivations—much of it concerned in one or another way with the world of interest organizations. The literature is full of proposals and blue prints; however, I do not find in it any formulae, tested propositions, or self-convincing knowledge which would assure the elimination or reduction of tension between large interest organizations in genuine conflict. Nor do I find among the variety of proposed techniques, such as two-way communication, the psychiatric interview, guided discussion, psycho-drama, social placement, status alignment, attitude studies, or opinion surveys any technique whose use offers any encouraging prospect of eliminating or reducing tension between large interest organizations in genuine conflict. To claim that they can, is little less than sheer pretension.[1] The discussions in the literature rarely address the central problem, to wit, how can consciously directed interest organizations in conflict be brought to renounce or to modify legitimate-appearing interests and to refrain from the use of sanctioned procedures when there is nothing in their appraisal of the situation to lead or compel them to do so. When such a problem is thought through with all of the breakdown that it requires in concrete situations, it becomes enormously complicated. What is there in our social science knowledge to prove to the directors of large interest organizations that their interests are wrong and need to be revalued? Even though there be such knowledge, suppose that the directors are unreasonable and stupid and refuse to heed such knowledge. Then, what social science propositions and techniques can be brought in to get them to heed such knowledge? Further, since frequently they are directing a collective entity with a following and inner groups to which they have to be

---

[1] I think that it must be admitted that present-day social and psychological science has done relatively little to study the world of interest organizations. There is, further, some legitimate doubt as to whether their prevailing imagery is suited to such study. I am fully satisfied that this doubt is justified in the case of my own discipline, sociology. Certainly, this world cannot be understood if it is viewed as a static equilibrium, or as a mere hierarchical structure, or as a differentiated aggregation of individuals; or if it is analyzed in terms of a simple community, or of an out-moded competitive market, or of an out-moded political forum. It is a complicated, dynamic, evolving world characterized by large organized collective striving. It must be studied in terms of an imagery that befits its character.

responsive in some manner, what reliable means does social science have for overcoming inner conflicts, changing traditional conceptions, and controlling the inner power process? Still further, what certainties does social science have to contribute to the appraisal that needs to be made of the concrete situation in which action is to take place? Such an appraisal requires an assessment of possibilities, a sensing of lurking tendencies, a calculation of risks, and a formation of synthetic judgment. What does present-day social and psychological science have to contribute to this highly complicated process of appraisal so as to assure that the appraisal will be made in a given specific way? There is no need to mention other parts of the central problem. Enough has been said to indicate that there is little in present-day social and psychological science that touches on the central problem.

CONCLUSION

If a policy of good will, the evoking of public opinion, and the use of present day knowledge and techniques of social and psychological science offer little secure promise of dealing with the problem of tension set by large interest organizations in genuine conflict, what is left? We should remember that by far interest organizations, themselves, handle this problem in a tolerable way through a process of workable adjustment, and that, as stated previously, the problem becomes serious when its expression is believed to jeopardize the public interest. At such a point the stage is set for the intervention of the state in one or another way. This is what our history has been and this is what I foresee will continue to happen. The intervention of the state as the only alternative means of controlling the problem of tension between large interest organization, which such organizations cannot themselves control, seems a dismal prospect, particularly since such control will be called for increasingly in the future. The intrusion of the state into the operation of huge interest groups and the accompanying intrusion of such interest groups into the political arena for the purpose of influencing the state raise many serious problems. My own opinion is that the problem of huge interest organizations, such as economic power blocs, is almost solely a problem of the relation between them and the state. Fortunately, my assignment does not require me to deal with this problem. It is left in the hands of a more competent scholar on this program.

Social Structure and Power Conflict

It is fitting in a symposium dealing with our industrial scene to view and discuss labor-management relations in terms of power conflict. Such a treatment is needed to portray our industrial life in one of its important dimensions and thus to complement the picture yielded by the bulk of studies being made by psychologists and social scientists. For reasons that need not be considered here these latter studies favor the premise that industrial relations are naturally cooperative and based on mutuality of interest. Opposition, strife, and conflict in industrial relations are regarded as unfortunate deficiencies that can and will give way before enlightened attitude, technical knowledge, and the application of scientific method. There is grave danger that studies and interpretations based on a premise which ignores or misconstrues power relations may yield a distorted and fictitious picture of contemporary industrial relations and thus may lead to unwise policy and to unfruitful methods of control.

INTRODUCTION

Several lines of consideration suggest not only the advisability but the necessity of viewing the industrial sector of our society in terms of power struggle. First, it should be noted that our society itself is clearly caught up in the play of power. The picture is one of innumerable groups and organizations relying on the exercise of power at innumerable points in seeking to maintain position, to achieve goals, and to ward off threats. To show this we need only refer to the operation of interest groups in our society.

Our American life invites, fosters, and sustains interest groups essentially everywhere: geographically from small villages at one extreme to our widespread national domain at the other and institutionally through the gamut of business, politics, education, science, religion, art, health, and recreation. Many people are erroneously inclined to think of interest groups as confined only to a few huge national organizations exerting pressure on governmental agencies or on public opinion. Actually, an interest group arises whenever individuals become organized or united in pursuit of some actual or imagined common interest and seek to forge in a recalcitrant world a line of action on behalf of that interest. Our democratic society gives extensive freedom to people everywhere to organize and act in response to a shared interest. Our national life, in one of its major dimensions, consists of the acts of such groups—local clubs, cliques in a church, chambers of commerce, businessmen groups, teachers' organizations, lodges, political clubs, trade associations, medical associations, veterans associations, church organizations, political parties, labor unions, educational societies, industrial corporations, and a variety of other organizations seeking to realize the special interests for which they exist.

This proliferation of interest groups imparts a vital power dimension to our national life. As these groups, ranging from small and loosely organized cliques to large tightly knit national federations, seek to further, sustain, or protect their respective interests, they are thrown at innumerable points into opposition and conflict with one another. It is at these points that power relations emerge and develop as a result of efforts to use strategic position, strength, influence, and skill to achieve or protect interests that are threatened, hindered, or blocked by opposing interests. It should be apparent that a large national society whose social and legal codes allow and indeed encourage people to act collectively on behalf of their group interests would inevitably be marked by extensive areas of power action. This must be recognized as true of our American society.

It would indeed be strange if our industrial arena did not show power situations comparable to those in other areas of our American life. The most careful observation of American industry reveals clearly the presence of power play and power conflict. Power actions are to be noted in the competitive struggles between business organizations, in the conflicts between different business interests, in the internal politics of large corporations, and in the half-hidden struggles between administrative units of production in factories and plants; in the factional strivings within labor unions and in the rivalries and disputes between labor unions; and in the relations between managements and labor unions. Power action in the industrial field varies greatly in intensity and persistency from place to place. It is likely to be casual, episodic, and minor on local levels and to be sustained and vigorous in the case of large national organizations. Whatever its variation in occurrence and degree from one point to another, its widespread existence suggests that it is an indigenous factor in our contemporary industrial organization.

Indeed the conditions in our industrial life are peculiarly conducive to the emergence of power relations. The sanctioning of success in business competition encourages vigorous action which may infringe on the acts of others; the extension and integration of the economic market bring in a larger number of economic-interests groups and increase the chances of opposition between their lines of interest; the dynamic changes in our economy open new areas for exploitation and thus for increased encroachment of groups on groups; the growth of huge organizations lays the stage for inner conflict and struggle for control; and the increasing unionization of industrial workers introduces a greater amount of union pressures. As a result of conditions and influences such as these, our industrial society becomes subject at innumerable points to power actions between trade associations, between business corporations, between units and echelons of management, between groups of stockholders, between occupational groups, between factions in unions, between labor unions, between unions and managements, and between aggregations of labor unions and aggregations of managements.

These casual observations are sufficient to invite a consideration of industrial relations from the standpoint of power effort. Further, they should be a signal of warning to the many of us who study the industrial arena with a disregard for the presence of power struggle and with a misconstruction of its play. They point particularly to the need for caution in recommending ways of handling industrial problems which are based on studies ignoring the factor of power action.

ANALYSIS OF POWER

It is advisable to make a brief analysis of power action. Power relations seem to be one of the basic forms of relationship between human beings and of human groups. The other important kinds of social relation are what may be termed "codified" relations and "sympathetic" relations. The distinctions between these three forms of social relation seem to be of crucial importance.

The drawing of the distinction can begin with codified relations. By such relations I have in mind those governed by rules, understandings, and expectations which are shared and followed by the parties to the relationship. How the parties stand with regard to rights, privileges, prestige, authority, and deference is laid out by a defining code; accordingly, the line of behavior of each in regard to the other is already established. Under such regulating social codes there is minimum occasion for conflict between the parties. Where such conflict arises or threatens to arise, the controls which are indigenous to the code are invoked as corrective devices for forcing the relations and the lines of behavior back into conformity with the code. Such codified relations are to be found wherever stable group relations exist. Concern for them has been particularly the stock in trade of sociologists and anthropologists in their preoccupation with custom, tradition, group norms, role relations, and culture.

It is important to see that these codified relations between groups and between individuals may involve significant differences in prestige, authority, and dominance between the participants. To take a few stray examples, we need merely think of master and slave, parent and child, feudal nobles and serfs, high and low castes, and military officers and private soldiers. It is a serious mistake, in my judgment, to regard such instances of codified relations as power relations because of the exercise of authority, prestige, and dominance by one party over the other. Where such dominance and directing control is prescribed and channelized and hence accepted and followed as the natural course, there is no power relation nor power action. In such a codified situation, there is no freedom of action, no pursuit of conflicting interest, no clash of lines of action, no jostling and maneuvering for advantageous position, and no test of strength.

A second major type of social relations I have termed sympathetic relations. In them the participants show sympathetic regard for each other's position and are guided by such appreciation. Such relations are marked by the presence of, and guidance by, personal sentiments and understanding—as in the case of sympathetic concern and care. While this kind of social relation and action is to be found particularly in friendly or intimate relations, it may occur between detached, remote, and even alien groups and individuals—as in the case of generosity of the victor, expressions of aid to the struggling, and sympathetic concern for those caught in a plightful conditions.

Again, it should be noted that in sympathetic relations there may be very obvious differences in positions of dominance. This does not establish the relation as a power relation. In sympathetic relations dominance, strength, and advantageous position, while present, do not set the goals of action; instead, action is formed and directed by appreciation and regard for the other party. Hence there is no struggle and hence no resolution of the relation in terms of respective strength.

In contrast to codified relations and sympathetic relations power relations are set and guided by respective positions of effective strength. This redundant statement points to a number of crucial features of power relations. First, a power relation is marked by an opposition of interests, intentions, and goals. In the pursuit of their respective objectives the parties are thrown into conflict with each other, and a contest of intention and will occurs. Second, in pursuing its objective each party uses and relies on its sources of strength instead of being confined to a codified channel of action or guided by sympathetic regard for the other. Third, because of freedom of action thus provided, there is elbow room for scheming, maneuvering, the devising of strategy and tactics, and the marshaling and manipulation of resources. Since action is neither held to an application of a code nor guided by a consideration for the other's welfare, a premium is placed on the successful pursuit of *one's own goal,* thus inevitably introducing egotism and possibilities of ruthlessness that have always made power action morally suspect. Where people in pursuit of goals are thrown into opposition to one another, with sanctioned or allowable leeway in the forging of actions to achieve success in the face of such opposition, and where the pursuit is not made subservient to consideration of each other's welfare, the stage is set for power action.

From this brief sketch of the generic nature of the power relationship it should be evident that power relations in our modern world are common and widespread. Conditions of our modern society are continuously at work to set and reset the stage for power action. The emergence of new groups or organizations, the development of new interests, the redirection of old interests under the dynamic play of events, the emergence of new uncodified areas, the crumbling away of old codifications, the increasing throwing together of groups who have little or no sense of common loyalty, and the absence of concern for the welfare of groups standing in opposition to one's own objective—all these factors, which are so pronounced in modern society, make power action widespread.

Most power relations in our society are localized and restricted, and the preponderant portion of them scarcely affects the welfare of the community life that embodies them. Power relations become a matter of concern in proportion to the size of power groups and to the extent of the ramified effect of their action. Thus it is "big power" that today awakens alarm and stimulates the interests of students—power relations as they appear in the strivings of nations on the international front and in the struggle of large interest groups in the domestic arena.

While power relations in the case of big power fit the generic pattern spoken of above, they show more pronouncedly certain features that should be noted. In the case of big-power groups power action comes to be more a matter of persistent policy and its pursuit more of a sophisticated art. Because a big-power group is subject recurrently to opposition and thwarting of its interests and aims over a lengthy span of time, it comes to be organized and girded in terms of a career of continuous power play. The big-power group is directed by an executive set of "full-time" individuals entrusted with the needs of understanding the developing world in which the power group operates, of coping with the immediate situation, of planning for the future, of developing policy, and of devising strategy and tactics to implement that policy. Power action thus tends to become a matter of studied group policy. Power policy and power action, one may say, become professionalized in the hands of experts. Power tends to be

332   Selected Works of Herbert Blumer

exercised calculatingly and rationally, *i.e.*, with constant and paramount regard to the advancement or protection of the interests of the power groups. There is likely to be more adroit and effective use of the power possibilities in the power situation and less restraint in the willingness to use such possibilities. Finally, it should be noted that the directorship of the big-power group, by virtue of its size and complexity of organization, is likely to be removed significantly from the direct and continuous participation of the membership or of the bulk of followers of the power group. All these mentioned considerations are equivalent to saying that power action comes to its "purest form" in the case of big-power groups.

This brief analysis of power action may be ended with a few words on controlling the power process. Oddly, the most effective restraint on the exercise of power is the calculation of the losses that might be sustained through its use in given situations. Power action, by definition, encounters resistance and is subject to assessment by opposing groups who seek in their own interest to locate its points of weakness and vulnerability. Thus its use and extension are subject to the limitations of possible failure, of exceeding its potential, of encountering the risks of unsustainable loss. This self-limitation inherent in the power process is far more effective than is realized. Without this self-correction, power struggle would attain the unrestrained viciousness which is usually and unwarrantedly ascribed to it. Yet this self-limitation clearly does not operate where there is a preponderance of power lodged in one of the parties to the power struggle or where there is a miscalculation of the costs and effects of a given line of power action.

Reliance on moral injunction or on exhortation to good will, while recognizably one of the conceivable methods of controlling power struggle, is essentially weak and nonenduring. Moral imperatives are not congenial to the power process; such imperatives tend to becloud that process, as each party proclaims and believes that its position and action are righteous.

Public opinion as a control of power struggle has greater influence; yet it is episodic, merely limiting at certain points, and susceptible at other points to direction by the parties to the struggle.

Control by law, if backed by effective punitive sanctions, has proved to be a more effective control of power action.

Finally, as reflecting such effectiveness of law, the state by virtue of its greater strength has the possibility of curbing power action, although at the expense, it must be seen, of becoming thereby the arena itself of the power process.

LABOR-MANAGEMENT RELATIONS AS POWER RELATIONS

Labor-management relations may now be considered in the light of the foregoing analysis of power.

The generic conditions of the power process clearly exist in labor-management relations. First, with the organizing of workers a genuine opposition arises between the interest of labor unions and of management. Such opposition in interest should not be regarded as an alien occurrence, as an imported deficiency, or as a breakdown of a natural harmony. Instead, it stems from the natural functions of management and of labor unions. The function of management is to operate the business enterprise efficiently; its paramount interests are to manage profitably and to have the right to exercise that management. The labor union has as its paramount interests (1) the protection and advancement of the industrial welfare of the workers and (2) the survival and growth of the union as an organization. That these respective sets of interests come naturally into opposition is evident. Actions on behalf of the welfare interests of workers and of the institutional interests of the union run athwart the actions stemming from the interests of management in the profitable operation of the business enterprise and in the right to manage. Any reader who is inclined to question the truth of this assertion needs only to reflect on the meaning of collective bargaining. Collective bargaining is a device for achieving the accommodation of opposed demands and positions, demands and positions that stem from, and reflect, the respective interests of organized workers and management. The very existence of collective bargaining (which in our industrial society is the law of the land and is recognized as the chief mediating agency of labor-management relations) bespeaks underlying opposition in interest between labor unions and managements.

We need to note further that, in the pursuit of their respective interests vis-à-vis each other, managements and unions are not under the dominance of codified relations. Each is granted a relative freedom of action in place of being compelled to abide by sanctioned regulations. Thus the parties may choose what to propose, what to reject, and what line of action to follow. This condition sets the stage for the use of available strength in pursuing interests—a practice which reaches its apogee in the test of power in the labor strike.

Finally, labor-management relations are marked by the remaining salient feature of power action: flexibility in maneuvering, in scheming, in marshaling resources, in grasping advantages in passing events, or in general exploiting whatever the situation seems to afford for the advancement or protection of interests, as immediately defined by each party.

Power action is usually not conspicuous nor striking in the relations of unions and managements on the local level, particularly when local unions enjoy a high degree of autonomy. It comes to be pronounced, however, in the case of large international unions which have to function *as single entities* vis-à-vis large corporations, trade associations, and employer organizations. My remaining remarks are devoted to a consideration of the power process in the case of big-power groups in labor-management relations in our society.

We should note, first, that the large union and the large management are steadily forced in their relations with each other to act as single entities. This creates in each the need for effective organization, effective inner control, and expert direction. The hierarchic structure of management readily allows, in its case, for meeting these needs. For its part the union in meeting these needs is increasingly forced to lodge the making of policies and of decisions in a top leadership and thus to strip away autonomy from the rank-and-file member and from the local union. The effort to achieve unitary direction on the part of a heterogeneous composition introduces an inner power process into the union—a condition which, in itself, is met in time by a concentration of control in a directing leadership. Just as a large army engaged in military campaign cannot allow autonomous policy and decision making to its units but must act concertedly, so similarly the large union and the large management are each under compulsion to act as single entities.

We should note in the case of large unions and large managements the fact that each organization has a career yielding memories of the past, giving a peculiar meaning to the needs of the immediate present, and requiring a girding for the proximate future. In an arena of opposing groups seeking to advance or protect their respective interests, this need on the part of professional leadership to preserve and further an *enduring* organization induces a working psychology of power orientation and power action.

What are the earmarks of such a power psychology? One of the essential features is a lively scrutiny of the operating situation to ascertain what threats it holds, what obstacles it sets, what advantages it contains, and what exploitable facilities it yields. The companion feature is an alertness in marshaling and in directing available sources of strength. The interaction of these two on behalf of sought objectives provides the working rationale of power action. Too much space would be required to trace out these features in practice amid the relations of big labor unions and big managements. However, a few general characteristics of their power action should be noted.

First, the fact that the arena in which big unions and big managements operate is subject to high dynamic play introduces a conspicuous fluidity into their relations. Such happenings as shifts in the economy, changes in the cost and the standard of living, political developments, new legislation and prospective legislation, judicial interpretation, stirring up of membership, and inner shifts of power are a few of the many factors at work in our modern society which impart a fluid and rather unpredictable character to big-power relations between labor and management.

Next, this dynamic setting leads conspicuously to rational expediency in the direction of power action. Policies in this shifting and uncertain setting become increasingly subject to compromise, tempering, and redirection under the impact of the passing array of newly developing situations.

Third, the relations between the parties become tenuous,

shifting, and tentative as each views the other and awaits developing action on the part of the other.

Finally, because of this tenuous and shifting nature of the relations between prodigious power groups operating in a dynamic arena, there is an increasing tendency for the power struggle to move over into the political arena. There is increased readiness to use the powers of the state through legislation, executive decision, and administrative action as the means of fortifying the security of one's own interests. The need of countering such efforts brings the other party into the political field. Further, a recurring inability to accommodate sucessfully their immediate opposed aims leads to intercession by the state on behalf of its own interests. This transferring of the power struggle between organized labor and management from the industrial arena to the political arena marks a major transformation in their relations, with consequences which, while only dimly foreseen, will be momentous.

The foregoing observations on the power process in labor-management relations are sketchy. However inadequate, they underline the need of recognizing that relations between managements and labor unions are set by each party acting faithfully on behalf of its respective interests and that these interests typically run counter to each other. This fundamental fact should not be veiled by a contention that, since management and workers are dependent on each other in the carrying on of the business enterprise, their interests are mutual. Such a contention is belied by the evident need of managements and labor unions to bargain and reach temporary agreements—to accommodate their respective wishes and demands in a workable adjustment. These conditions induce and sustain the use of power, a use which becomes pronounced in the alignment of large unions and large managements. Students of industrial relations will distort their subject matter and emerge with unrealistic results if they ignore the play of power or confuse codified and sympathetic relations with power relations.

The Concept of Mass Society

Pinpointing the special characteristics of modern society is a problem that is haunting and daunting sociologists. They feel—and proclaim at frequent intervals—that modern society exhibits a distinctive form which puts it in a class of its own, divorced alike from tribal, peasant and feudal societies, from ancient cultures and from the oriental cultures of more recent centuries. Nevertheless, they have not as yet been particularly successful in distilling and delineating the unique and specific character postulated of modern societies. Such is the conclusion forced on us by a critical exploration of the more prominent means by which sociologists have sought to identify and characterize the distinction. Putting aside for a moment the conception of modern society as a mass society, we find that sociologists have tried three main approaches: (1) Comparing specific institutions of modern societies with the corresponding institutions in other societies; (2) treating modern societies as antitheses of earlier societies; and (3) studying the particularity of modern society as manifested in its industrialized and urbanized structure. Each of these three conventional approaches requires a commentary.

Much has been done to compare certain of the institutions and social practices of present-day society with the corresponding institutions and practices of other, earlier societies. Such comparisons have focused upon an imposing number of variables: family, form of government, legal system, mores, educational system, class structure, systems of authority, types of religion, magic, folklore, beliefs, systems for economic production, forms of local government, and others. Many of the texts have attained a high scientific standard. To the surprise and disappointment of many, however, such comparative studies have not painted a clear, comprehensive picture of the general characteristics of modern society. To undertake the formidable task of piecing together the results of these studies in order to present a mosaic of modern society, or of putting them to work to provide a key to understanding the actual character of modern life, is to court disillusion and confusion. However successful the individual studies may be at unearthing specific differences, they fail to provide a general, congruent overview of the special features which distinguish modern society as such from other types of society.

To establish a general difference of this kind is precisely the aim of the second approach, which treats modern society as the antithesis of an earlier, simpler type of society. Good examples of this include such dichotomies as 'community' and 'society', mechanical and organic solidarity, primary and secondary association, and culture and civilization. Conventional pairs such as these single out an attribute or aspect of a difference, and go on to treat it as a continuum along which societies may be plotted. The opposite poles of the continuum are postulated as abstract ideal types, with one of them representing modern society. However, not one of these constructs has stood up to serious scientific scrutiny; it has been impossible to establish their empirical validity. More seriously still, such conventional constructs are able to offer little in the way of concepts for analyzing the forms of activity of modern society. The general features designed to characterize such antitheses may indeed assist us in drawing up rough formal differences between modern and earlier societies; as tools for analyzing what really goes on in a given sector of modern life, however, these differences are far from adequate. That this is in fact the case is indicated by the rarity with which such schemes are used in the study of modern communal life.

The third approach popular with scholars tackling this problem consists in affixing to modern society the traditional labels 'industrialized' and 'urbanized'. Wishing to characterize modern society, we speak of an industrialized and urbanized society, and are usually content to leave the matter there, as though use of these epithets were utterly sufficient to identify and clarify the specific nature of modern society. These adjectives, however, are at best quite general appellations—self-adhesive labels which remain unclear and confusing with regard to their denotation.

A reasonably comprehensive and painstaking inspection of the literature would probably expose the ambiguity of both words. We have no clear idea, let alone a consensus, of what 'industrialized' or 'industrialization' involves. Do these concepts refer only to manufacture, or to the whole of industry, or perhaps, too, to related forms of marketing, banking and commerce? Or, perhaps, in addition, to a host of social phenomena that in no ways appertain to industry, as, for example, education and schools, enfranchisements, the emancipation of women and young people, nascent hopes and expectations, democratic philosophy, and mounting professionalism? The fact that scholars have simply taken the concept 'industrialization' for granted cannot hide its manifest equivocality, its tangled nature and incoherence. The literature provides no clear delimitation of the concept, be it as a process, a form of organization, or a way of life. The same is true of the parallel concept 'urbanization'. Is urbanization a purely econological concept? Does it represent a kind of spatially limited economic system? Does it refer to a particular institutional system? Does it stand for a particular way of life? Is it true of a given framework of social relationships? Or is it a kind of collective term for all of these? Each of these possibilities has been selected for discussion by scholars—who have failed to clearly delimit a single one of them. Not one has proved able to elicit the collective agreement of competent critics. It is obvious that in the terms 'industrialization' and 'urbanization' we have a pair of empty formulae; they do not characterize a definite content in any explicit way. The most we can say of them is that they stand for two developments of obvious significance in modern life: they indicate the general makeup of the type of society they are said to engender.

The inadequacy of these traditional attempts to pinpoint a specific genre of modern society gives us further cause for considering carefully a new and seemingly more promising approach to the problem. I am referring here to the view that pictures modern society as a mass society. Even though the historic origins of this view are over a century old, it has become prominent only during the last thirty years. Although used in the literature only in a most nebulous and fragmentary manner, its main components may be arranged to form a reasonably coherent scheme. This is built around a chain of four basic properties that characterize modern society: (1) its massiveness; (2) the heterogeneous form of the society's structural elements; (3) unimpeded access to areas of public life, and (4) immersion in a constantly changing society. In what follows, I will discuss each of these constitutive characteristics and their implications.

The quantitative aspect of enormous dimensions is without doubt one of the main constituents of the academic conception of mass society. And a mass society is indeed characterized by colossal population statistics, and by particularly great population clusters, as, for example, in the big conurbations. This element of massiveness is mirrored in the size of its institutions, in the social potential, and in the scale of communal activities. Thus we speak, in connection with modern society, of mass sales, mass communications, mass transport, mass entertainment, mass education, mass legal systems and mass war. The related institutions and organizations, too, are as large as modern life: giant government departments, massive economic organizations, powerful industrial consortiums and extensive welfare systems. All these everyday examples show how considerations of extensive organization and mass activity yield an important yardstick for modern society, distinguishing it from earlier types.

Two provisos are necessary at this point. First, sheer size does not in itself confer or explain the specific character of a mass society. Societies of gigantic size (as conurbations) have existed earlier: some such societies continue to the present day but do not possess the other defining characteristics of a modern society. It remains true, nevertheless, that the element of mass is one of the prerequisites of the modern type of society. Second, this quantitative factor, that of size, is of particular importance because of the qualitative changes it induces in people's associations, in their modes of interaction, and in the way their institutions work.

Sociologists are agreed as to some of the qualitative features attending the formation of large-scale societies. They are clear about so-called secondary contacts—the gap between the majority of the employees and the management of big organizations, between delegates and their constituents, between those who produce and those who consume; about the resultant ignorance of the population concerning the mode of action of the institutions to which they belong; about their corresponding inability to take certain steps in connection with that mode of action; and, finally, about the opportunities for manipulation and exploitation open to a small number of strategically placed individuals, mostly within large complex social structures. Strangely enough, sociologists have made no attempt to investigate systematically the changes in social relations and human actions which depend on the factor of immense scale alone. We know enough, however, to realize that this factor gives human societies organized around large numbers of a qualitatively different character.

A second fundamental characteristic of mass society, following from the factor of sheer size just considered, is the heterogeneity of its constituent parts. A society on the scale of our modern society is composed of a great number of different parts, as we can see from a consideration of the plethora of professions. (If I am not mistaken, the latest official list published by the United States Census Bureau contains more than 13,000 trades and professions.) Even though such an index of differentiation might be important, it is hardly sufficient to document the extent of the distinctions in a mass society. Let us think rather of the many groups in localities spread over the country, the large number of formal associations growing out of institutional life, and the much larger number of informal associations; variety, or, better, variety on the largest of scales, is certainly a characteristic feature of a mass society.

The extent of the influence of this multiplicity of constituent parts has not yet been fully grasped by sociologists. The latter tend to regard this multiplicity merely as an extension of the division of labor, i.e., as a huge conglomerate of differentiated parts forming a widespread, more complex whole. The multiplicity of which we are speaking certainly possesses this integrating aspect, but it also exhibits another feature replete with consequences, a special quality arising from its solitary nature and from the relative autonomy of its single parts. In a mass society, the parts are not fused into an organic whole, as is, for example, the case in a primitive tribe or a peasant society. Instead, because of the overabundance of parts, many of these, as far as geographical distance or modes of action and perception are concerned, are far removed from one another. This means that groups and assemblies of such parts remain comparatively autonomous. They occupy relatively separate areas of operation, with the further consequence that their development proceeds independently. From this point of view, the diversity in a mass society extends so far beyond the diversity in a conglomerate that it takes in an inner diversity of

342   Selected Works of Herbert Blumer

development. The mutual adjustment of these differing developmental impulses is one of the basic, most important, and most idiosyncratic features of mass society.

The third fundamental characteristic of a mass society is found in those of its numerous areas of community life which have become generally accessible without reference to social or spatial position. The most obvious examples of such areas are: (1) the mass markets, in which people are assigned the anonymous and impersonal role of consumer; (2) mass communications, in which people form an indeterminate audience; and (3) the political arena, in which people exert influence through their membership in a party, through their right to vote, or through the voice of public opinion. The existence of these areas open to public participation means that mass society is something other than a structure compounded of geographically limited parts. Instead, such areas proclaim the mass of the people as a distinctive entity, and concede to it designation as a potent force in the life of the society. This decisive point needs further clarification. The people who take part in public life are drawn from all walks of life; they come from various professions, with varied status, from different localities, and belong to different organizations. In fact, to a great extent they mirror the multiplicity and heterogeneity found in a mass society. Despite this, however, in the public sectors they are engaged in common concerns that transcend the various areas of interest dependent on their fixed local positions. For them, the public sectors represent a wholly new world of involvement and action in which they exist as a huge, anonymous and relatively undifferentiated throng—without organization, status structure, fixed leadership or a codex or body of established regulations. To grasp this point, one has only to think of the mass of movie-goers or the mass of newspaper readers or the mass of consumers buying shoes.

In referring to a mass of this kind, it is justifiable to speak of a fully developed kind of group, for the mass, surprising though this may seem, does in fact really act. And this action consists in making choices: choosing products as a consumer at the market, choosing among mass media programs, choosing from among the array of suggestions, party policies, doctrines and candidates on the political battlefield. Although arguably an indeterminate, anonymous and unorganized group, the mass is treated and addressed as a structured being. The best examples are to be found in advertising, on radio and television programs, in newspaper editorials and in the hit parade.

This short presentation is designed to aid in the delineation of the mass as a particular kind of group, arising by virtue of its access to wide general areas of interest transcending the limitations of geographical position and local living areas. Our account, however, may also serve to correct specific misunderstandings and throw fresh light on others. First, and most important, the mass must not be interpreted as consisting merely of a large number of groups of low social status, as in Marx's conception of 'mass' as against 'class'. Rather, the mass consists of all those taking part in a certain area of mass action. In addition, as a distinctive type of group, the mass must not be confused with the 'crowd'. It is not a compact whole; there exists between its members practically no interaction or interstimulation, and it is not characterized by collective excitation. Third, the realization that the mass acts by choosing among available alternatives enables us to see the special character of its world, and to understand the potency of its actions. The world of its actions is characterized by a series of mutually competitive models—products, blueprints, suggestions, themes, etc.—all clamoring for attention and espousal. This world, in accordance with which the mass orients itself, is in a state of continuous movement and modification. It is perpetually subject to the introduction of new models, and to fluctuations in interests and tastes, which together shape the field of choice. It is surely unnecessary to add that changes in the consensus of selections may undermine institutions and at times ruin them; institutions dependent on a mass clientele for their survival cannot afford to take the risk of losing contact with the tastes and interests of the mass.

Various of the points mentioned up to now indicate a fourth fundamental characteristic of mass society, namely, the fact that it is caught up in a world in constant motion. The immense size and the heterogeneity of the mass society is enough in itself to induce continual reorganization. The freedom and relative independence with which its segments and sectors develop is the basis of a continuous transformation of mass society. Apart from anything else, an adaptation is made necessary merely by the fact that its various parts have been brought closer together by an expansion of the means of communication and transport. In addition, as we have already mentioned, access to further areas of mass participation leads to enduring competition to win and retain the recognition of the mass. Given the importance of these points, they will be elaborated further.

We must first realize the significance of the fact that the various parts and sectors of a mass society tend to develop relatively independently. Each has its own problems, presented for our appreciation and appraisal in a particular world of its own, and, further, its own innovators and innovations and its own internal competition. This is typical of the situation we meet when investigating social sectors like science, technology, industry, politics, education, entertainment and religion. Although these sectors are mutually related, each possesses a sphere of development of its own, reacting within this sphere to a process which remains relatively independent of the processes in other sectors. This being so, large areas of a mass society are typically prone to new, sporadic developments, which bring to the most varied phases of group life new and unexpected situations to be tackled: the development of the mass society is effected as the gradual advance of a number of disparate elements. We may add here that, to an astounding degree, the great institutions of a mass society are found to be in competition, rather than harmonious association. Moreover, mass society encourages the intrigues of interest groups, with consequent conflicts of values and designs. Finally, we must remember the following highly significant fact: mass society develops a characteristic sense of 'keeping in step with the times'. This sense—a feeling for modernity—encourages many to seek better methods, but, above all, it puts on the people the onus of not lagging too far behind what is considered up-to-date. All of these observations lead to the conclusion that the incentive, prerequisites and mechanics of continuous reshaping are the very essence of that natural melting pot which is mass society.

This brief review of the four factors—massiveness, heterogeneity, unlimited access to numerous areas of public life, and involvement in a changing world—that characterize mass society suffices to indicate that together they provide a framework for communal life unlike that obtaining in societies of a different type. It should be evident that the size of modern masses affects human relationships, the character of human institutions and organizations, and their relations to each other. Similarly, consider-able distinctions between the constitutive parts lead to novel out-ward forms; these parts are not combined to make a harmonious whole, like that evidenced by simple forms of society. Just as little, however, can they be said to exist in complete isolation from one another, as seems to have been the case among the large societies of antiquity. The opportunity offered by the largest and most heterogeneous human masses, namely, that of individuals separately or jointly, participating in decisive areas of social life, leads to an anomalous situation, one perhaps more problematic than any other. Ultimately the necessity of surviving in a world caught up in continual motion and continuous change gives a mass society its distinctive orientation.

The challenge facing sociologists is the task of identifying and analyzing the framework formed by these four factors, and showing how this framework influences the ordering of life going on within it. However, I believe we must admit that present-day sociology lacks the perspective and the conceptual models to suc-ceed in this task. The rest of this paper will be devoted to discuss-ing this extremely important matter.

Everyone conversant with the sociological literature on the nature of mass society is struck by the emphasis it places on such phenomena as disintegration and disorganization. The conven-tional argument goes roughly as follows: In a mass society people lack the props of proven tradition and established social station; they live in a world of confused values and uncertain status posi-tions; they have forfeited that sense of discipline and social respon-sibility which is the product of a mature culture and a regulated social structure—this being especially true of the vast majority who do not belong to the elite. Lacking a disciplined orientation and a cultivated taste, they resemble a big crowd, ruled by im-pulsive and sensual preoccupations, an easy prey for the dema-gogues, agitators, advertising specialists, and charismatic ad-venturers who profit from such interests; the existence of these undisciplined, unconditioned masses undermines established in-stitutions and regulated social control; the elite, as a cultivated di-recting force, is robbed of respect and authority; political life be-comes unsure and is converted into a crude struggle for power; institutions lose their ties to traditional obligations and cater in-stead to the transitory moods of their members; culture relinquishes its standards and sense of integrity, becoming a vulgar, decadent substitute, namely kitsch. Furthermore, the individuals who form the mass lack a social anchor of the sort that comes from either identification with an organization or the existence of stable social ties; they live, therefore, in an atmosphere of alienation and anonymity, a predicament that expresses itself in various forms of personal and social disorganization, e.g., in mental illness, personality disturbances, crime and other delinquencies, and in political unrest.

These are the characteristics most commonly used to describe mass society. They indicate only too clearly the tendency of many analysts to regard decadence and disorder as the earmarks of such a society. We are led to believe that mass society undermines a natural, traditional order of settled social relationships in the following ways; by enfeebling and unsettling social values; by driving people out of social roles and established status positions; by secularizing the content of life; by subverting traditional authorities and sacrosanctities; and by repudiating social ties. Such judgments, taking their points of departure from a conception of an established orderly and unified society, regard mass society—assumed to be attacking the former—as veritably seditious. To those who unconditionally endorse this view, the prospects for a future communal life are dark indeed. They can hardly suppose that (barring a world catastrophe, such as a nuclear holocaust) the advance of the four factors that have brought mass society about can be stemmed, let alone reversed. Whoever imagines the contrary has misunderstood the nature of the mass society.

[Nevertheless, such a contrary position can be argued.]* However, enormous they may be, however great the lack of intimate relationships between their members, the institutions of mass society do in fact fulfill their functions. And the parts of a mass society, however different and diverse they may be, do in fact achieve viable modi vivendi. It remains true, also, that the vital sectors open to mass participation—however variable their contents, arising out of their openness to the varying tastes and interests of the masses—are likely to attain long-term existence. Furthermore at all times, extreme crises excepted, there exists a

* Added by editors.

fairly reasonable accommodation to the novel situations that a changing world brings in its train. Thus, mass society cannot realistically be regarded to be in the throes of dissolution. We go wrong if, in our studies and analyses, we rate mass society not as a living order but as the decomposition of a living order. To analyze mass society by means of such concepts as 'aberration', 'dysfunction', 'Entfremdung' (alienation), 'anomaly' and 'disorganization' is to give a radically false picture of the situation. Mass society possesses a vital order, otherwise it would not be a society. Its members live a collective life, they interact in innumerable ways, they form groups of various kinds, within which they develop appropriate ways of life; they occupy various positions, they belong to active institutions, they have leaders and acknowledge other people possessed of authority, and they possess ritual and ceremony. Bearing in mind such facts as these, it is false to characterize mass society as disorganized or to equate it with a giant unordered crowd. Of course disorder and serious problems exist in mass society, but it would be ludicrous to regard such disorder as the essence of mass society.

A more reasonable view is that which sees disorder and serious problems for what they are, namely an inadequacy in achieving the mass society's own order. But such disorder and serious problems are not gotten rid of by returning to venerable and restrictive types of society, traditionally regulated and arranged as if mass society in embryo, but only by helping the specific order of the mass society to function more effectively.

In this connection the vital question is how the specific organization of a mass society is to be studied and analyzed. Which conceptual or theoretical frame of reference are we to use? The path most commonly chosen by sociologists attempting to analyze such an organization (assuming they do not prefer to treat it as a disorganization) must give us pause. There can be no doubt that they approach social organization in mass society with the same eyes, indeed with the identical tools that have been evolved for the analysis of other types of human social life. These are blinkers, and together with the conceptual apparatus designed to support them, at bottom presuppose the existence of the social order as a regulated, well-established, explicit and articulated social organization. Such a set of presuppositions is required by the analytical instruments that comprise no small part of the socio-

348   Selected Works of Herbert Blumer

logical toolbox: a human society is taken to be a social system organized of interwoven parts; it must have culture in the form of regulated practices controlled by values and norms held in common; it must have a social structure, consisting of a system of status positions; it must operate using a process of interaction in which members approach each other in well-determined social roles; it must depend on a process of socialization by means of which its members are integrated into an established social framework; it finally, must employ a system of social control, which enforces social conformity and prevents deviations. This collection of concepts, the sociologist's 'working heritage', is without doubt derived from the study of such ordered, determined and articulated living organizations, as those found in primitive societies, peasant societies, feudal societies, and ancient civilizations in their developed state.

This raises a general question: are these concepts, and the general point of view they stand for, adequate for analyzing mass society? Our discussion has tried to show that mass society exhibits a characteristic amalgam distinguishing it from other and earlier types of society. Therefore, important grounds for supposing that an effective analysis of this characteristic amalgam cannot be carried out by using ideas and the conceptual apparatus developed by the sociologist in his long preoccupation with simpler, more circumscribed and compact societies. It would take a full-fledged thesis to provide a reasonably complete justification for this claim. In the present essay we must confine ourselves to a few remarks demonstrating how ineffective our received sociological conceptual apparatus is for analyzing the mass society.

Let us begin with the concept of social change. In conventional sociological thinking, social change is regarded as typical of aberration from an established order. Consequently, it is to be explained in the form of factors or conditions pressing for the overthrow of a regularized item of social life. The established order (or a part thereof, a habit, belief, value or institution, for instance) is regarded as having attained a mature, established and determined form, so to speak, which betrays no inner impulse towards change. In this respect, order is equated with the old-fashioned psychological notion of habitualization. Change is regarded as something which occurs as a result of an external factor, destroying or calling into question the settled form. The organization of life in a mass society seems, however, to possess a different character, inasmuch as alteration and modification are immanent to it. Far from being established and determined, its natural state is that of continual adaptation to the fluctuating complex of factors with which it is constantly faced. A striking example is found in the stream of hit songs and popular dance tunes that are performed in modern society. The profusion of new songs and melodies, straining unceasingly for a breakthrough into the limelight of public recognition, renders this area one of natural and habitual change. Other examples are to be noticed in the fields of technical inventions and scientific discoveries, each characterized by continual innovation. Such areas of collective life, which because of their specific heterogeneity are in the grip of constant modification, cannot be analyzed in any realistic way by the conventional sociological conception of social change. We need a conception differing from that of a firmly established and determined order subverted by some disturbing factor only later to revert to another fixed order; we need a conception of continuous innovation or development. The idea that social change is natural, inherent in the order of life in a mass society, has as yet hardly penetrated the cognitive consciousness of present-day sociology, and has quite definitively not been written into its canon of traditional concepts.

A similar situation obtains with respect to the concept of culture when it is used in analyzing the mass society. As commonly understood by sociologists, culture appears in regulated and fixed forms of conduct, which are held in common by the members of a group and acquired by learning. These forms of conduct are regarded as directly or indirectly connected to each other; they constitute the organized social life of the group. Remarkable in regard to this view is the idea that these modes of conduct are the expression of common perceptions of the structure of rules, orders, standards and definitions. For the purposes of analysis these precepts are usually subsumed under the headings 'values' and 'norms', concepts that refer both to the goals of human desires and to the rules or standards followed in attaining these goals. Owing to the heterogeneity of mass society and to the changeable nature of the lives of its members, the application of this model to such a society is highly dubious. Differentiation within a mass society favors the formation of differing series of impermanent and often mutually opposed values and norms, which may very well coexist without correlation. Their introduction into the areas of the public life of a mass society gives rise to completely novel situations. The result is not so much a matter of confusion and chaos—as theory might lead one to expect— but rather a working arrangement between proponents of opposing precepts. This working arrangement is characterized by compromise, concessions and abstention from the complete exercise of rights, a blending of various precepts, and the search for novel, albeit perhaps merely temporary, bases for concerted action. Orderly life goes on, not as the result of values and norms held in common, but rather as the outcome of 'coming to terms'. The formation of public opinion, the play of fashion, political events, and mutual attempts by pressure groups to accommodate each other's interests are each examples of the widespread process of working compromise that occurs in mass society among people whose values, interests and recipes for confronting the world are divergent and shifting. The areas of living in which this process occurs cannot be analyzed with cultural concepts formulated once and for all, so to speak, valid for only fixed types of behavior.

Similar shortcomings and absurdities are apparent when other basic sociological concepts are applied to the analysis of mass society. The concept of the social system, so popular with today's sociologists, would seem unsuited to the character of mass society. Mass society is made up of a number of component parts, only loosely related to each other; each component reacts to surrounding happenings with a modicum of individual development, while still influenced by happenings in other sectors. The resultant picture is one of changing complexity, possessing neither stable nor even labile balance. Instead, we see an unequal flux throughout the mass society, a flux changing at different rates at different times and places, varying markedly in its effect on the various individual parts. The flux within mass society is so differentiated and multifariously oriented, is such a changing mixture of coordination and non-coordination that the logical prerequisites for a 'system' are absent.

The analysis of mass society that employs such structural terms as status positions or status systems leads to similar difficulties. The categories used to characterize social positions are extremely numerous. They interact in rather varied ways, each category fluctuating greatly in its meaning. Concomitantly, innumerable schemes are used to sort people into categories. These, too, vary from group to group and are subject to constant change. Mass society does not have a definitive structure of fixed social positions. Instead, they are realized in numerous, mutually unrelated dimensions; they vary greatly as to their definitions and enter into changing relationships. This characterization of status positions seems equally applicable to the concept of social roles in mass society. There exists no system of equably defined roles; rather, roles are noticeably different with respect to the behavior expected; they are subject to transformations as people adjust to each other in new relationships or new situations. In other words, in many areas of a mass society it is extremely difficult to use a role model to forecast how people will act.

The elements of variability and alterable states also lead to difficulties when the concept of socialization is applied to mass society. For socialization in mass society largely ceases to be the introduction of the individual into a determined social frame and becomes instead a question of participation and adaptation to worlds differing in appearance. A society that moves in various, non-parallel directions calls for a socialization of adaptable individuals who possess different outlooks, varying interests, and divergent conceptions of value; it remains unclear, how far the conventional concept of socialization is able to embrace such a process of adaptation.

In this connection, the terms social conformity and aberration make an extremely hazy impression, and they can all too easily be used in a distorted and arbitrary manner. For what from the standpoint of one group is seen as conformity may seem to be aberration from that of another. The variety of standards and values in mass society, the fact that one and the same person may often harbor opposing standards and values, and, finally, the change of value judgments and standards in the ongoing process of living make it difficult to apply terms like conformity and aberration to mass society. These terms have been inherited from the imagery of a society regulated by fixed and generally followed values and norms.

These few cursory observations may serve to draw attention to the fundamental problems facing contemporary sociologists in their analysis of society. There can be no doubt that present-day communal life manifests an order or a character essentially distinct from that found in earlier and simpler types of society. Notwithstanding, the standpoints and concepts which form the tools of sociology have evolved from the analysis of these other types of human society. Reliance on them for the study or analysis of mass society—the type that is coming more and more to occupy the foreground—is becoming more dubious. There can be no doubt of the need to undertake a drastic revision of the repertory of sociological concepts in order that there may be discovered those that are applicable to the distinctive social processes and ordering of life that we encounter in mass society.

Bibliography
and
Index

SELECTED BIBLIOGRAPHY OF HERBERT GEORGE BLUMER

Dissertation

1928   *Method in Social Psychology.* (Chicago: Department of Sociology and Anthropology, University of Chicago). March.

Books

1933   *Movies and Conduct.* (New York: The Macmillan Co.).

1933   *Movies, Delinquency, and Crime,* with Philip M. Hauser. (New York: The Macmillan Co.).

1935   Ed. with E. W. Burgess. *Human Side of Social Planning.* Selected Papers from the Proceedings of the American Sociological Society. (Chicago: American Sociological Society).

1939   *Critiques of Research in the Social Sciences: An Appraisal of Thomas and Znaniecki's "The Polish Peasant in Europe and America".* (New York: Social Science Research Council. Reprinted with a new introduction by the author, New Brunswick, N.J.: Transaction Books, 1979).

1969   *Symbolic Interaction: Perspective and Method.* (Englewood Cliffs, N.J.: Prentice-Hall. Reprint, Berkeley: University of California Press, 1986).

Monographs

1958   *The Rationale of Labor-Management Relations.* (Rio Piedras, Puerto Rico: Labor Relations Institute, University of Puerto Rico).

1967   *The World of Youthful Drug Use,* with assistance from Alan Sutter, Samir Ahmed, Roger Smith. ADD Center Final Report. (Berkeley: University of California School of Criminology).

Articles

1931   "Science Without Concepts", *American Journal of Sociology*. XXXVI (January), pp. 515–533.

1935   "Moulding of Mass Behavior Through the Motion Picture". *Publications of the American Sociological Society*. XXIX (August), pp. 115–127.

1936   "Social Attitudes and Non-Symbolic Interaction". *Journal of Educational Sociology*. IX (May), pp. 515–523.

1937   "Social Psychology", in *Man and Society*, ed. by Emerson P. Schmidt. (New York: Prentice-Hall), pp. 144–198.

1937   "Social Disorganization and Personal Disorganization". *American Journal of Sociology*. XLII (May), pp. 871–877.

1939   "Collective Behavior", in *An Outline of the Principles of Sociology*, ed. by Robert E. Park. (New York: Barnes and Noble, Inc.), pp. 219–280. Reprinted in revised edn., ed. by Alfred McClung Lee (New York: Barnes and Noble, 1946, 1951), pp. 167–224.

1939   "The Nature of Race Prejudice". *Social Process in Hawaii*. V (June), pp. 16–20.

1940   "The Problem of the Concept in Social Psychology". *American Journal of Sociology*. XLV (March), pp. 707–719.

1943   "Morale", in *American Society in Wartime*, ed. by William Fielding Ogburn. (Chicago: University of Chicago Press), pp. 207–231.

1947   "Sociological Theory in Industrial Relations". *American Sociological Review*. XII (June), pp. 271–278.

1948   "Public Opinion and Public Opinion Polling". *American Sociological Review*. XIII (October), pp. 542–554.

1949   "Group Tension and Interest Organizations". *Proceedings of the Second Annual Meeting, Industrial Relations Research Association*. No. 2 (December 29–30), pp. 151–164.

1949   "Leadership in Social Movements", in *Social Problems in America*, ed. by Alfred McClung Lee and E. B. Lee. (New York: Henry Holt and Co.), pp. 537–538.

1951   "Paternalism in Industry". *Social Process in Hawaii*. XV (n.m.1.), pp. 26–31.

1953   "Psychological Import of the Human Group", in *Group Relations at the Crossroads: The University of Oklahoma Lectures in Social Psychology*, ed. by Muzafer Sherif and M. O. Wilson. (New York: Harper and Brothers), pp. 185–202.

1954   "What is Wrong With Social Theory?" *American Sociological Review*. XIX (February), pp. 3–10.

1954   "The Sociologist Views the Problem of Old Age Retirement". *Paper Delivered During 48th Annual Conference, Public Employee Retirement Administration, San Francisco May 23–27.* (Chicago: Committee on Public Employee Retirement Administration of the Municipal Finance Officers Association of the United States and Canada), pp. 59–65.

1954   "Social Structure and Power Conflict", in *Industrial Conflict,* ed. by Arthur Kornhauser, Robert Dubin, Arthur M. Ross. (New York: McGraw-Hill), pp. 232–239.

1955   "Attitudes and the Social Act". *Social Problems.* III (October), pp. 59–65.

1955   "Reflections on Theory of Race Relations", in *Race Relations in World Perspective,* ed. by Andrew W. Lind. (Honolulu: University of Hawaii Press), pp. 3–21.

1956   "Foreword" to *Community Life and Social Policy: Selected Papers by Louis Wirth,* ed. by Elizabeth Wirth Marvick and Albert J. Reiss, Jr. (Chicago: University of Chicago Press), pp. v–x.

1956   "Social Science and the Desegregation Process". *Annals of the American Academy of Political and Social Science.* CCCIV (March), pp. 137–143.

1956   "Sociological Analysis and the 'Variable'". *American Sociological Review.* XXII (December), pp. 683–690.

1958   "Race Prejudice as a Sense of Group Position". *The Pacific Sociological Review.* I (Spring), pp. 3–7. Reprinted in *Race Relations: Problems and Theory,* ed. by Jitsuichi Masuoka and Preston Valien. (Chapel Hill: University of North Carolina Press), pp. 217–227.

1958   "Research on Race Relations: United States of America". *International Bulletin of Social Science.* X, pp. 403–447.

1959   "Collective Behavior", in *Review of Sociology: Analysis of a Decade,* ed. by Joseph B. Gittler (New York: John Wiley and Sons, Inc.), pp. 127–158.

1959   "Suggestions for the Study of Mass-Media Effects", in *American Voting Behavior,* ed. by Eugene Burdick and A. J. Brodbeck (Glencoe, Ill.: The Free Press), pp. 197–208.

1959   "The Study of Urbanization and Industrialization: Methodological Deficiencies", *Boletim de Centro Latino-Americano de Pesquisas em Ciencias Sociais.* II (May), pp. 17–34.

1960   "Early Industrialization and the Laboring Class". *The Sociological Quarterly.* I (January), pp. 5–14.

1962   "Society as Symbolic Interaction", in *Human Behavior and Social Processes,* ed. by Arnold M. Rose. (Boston: Houghton Mifflin Co.), pp. 179–192.

1964   "Industrialization and the Traditional Order". *Sociology and Social Research.* XLVIII (January), pp. 129–138.

1964   "Comments on Mr. Chasin's Article". *Berkeley Journal of Sociology.* Annual edn. IX, pp. 118–122.

1965   "The Future of the Color Line", in *The South in Continuity and Change,* ed. by John C. McKinney and Edgar T. Thompson. (Durham: Duke University Press), pp. 322–336.

1965   "Industrialisation and Race Relations", in *Industrialisation and Race Relations: A Symposium,* ed. by Guy Hunter. (New York: Oxford University Press), pp. 220–253.

1966   "Sociological Implications of the Thought of George Herbert Mead". *American Journal of Sociology.* LXXI (March), pp. 535–544. "Reply," pp. 547–548.

1966   "The Idea of Social Development", in *Studies in Comparative International Development.* II (St. Louis: Social Science Institute, Washington University), pp. 3–11.

1966   "Über das Konzept der Massengesellschaft", in *Militanter Humanismus: van den Aufgaben der modernen Soziologie,* ed. by Alphons Silbermann. (Frankfurt am Main: C. S. Fischer Verlag), pp. 19–35.

1967   "Reply to Woelfel, Stone, and Farberman". *American Journal of Sociology.* LXXII (January), pp. 411–412.

1967   "Threats from Agency-Determined Research", in *The Rise and Fall of Project Camelot,* ed. by Irving Louis Horowitz (Cambridge: Massachusetts Institute of Technology Press), pp. 153–174.

1968   "Fashion". *International Encyclopedia of the Social Sciences,* ed. by David L. Sills. (New York: The Macmillan Company and the Free Press). I, pp. 341–345.

1969   "Fashion: From Class Differentiation to Collective Selection". *The Sociological Quarterly.* X (Summer) pp. 275–291.

1971   "Industrialization and Problems of Social Disorder", in *Studies in Comparative International Development.* V: 1969–1970. No. 3. (New Brunswick, N.J.: Rutgers University. Distributed by Sage Publications), pp. 47–58.

1971   "Social Problems as Collective Behavior". *Social Problems.* XVIII (Winter), pp. 298–306.

1973   A Note on Symbolic Interaction". *American Sociological Review.* XXXVIII (December), pp. 797–798.

1974   "Exchange on Turner, 'Parsons as a Symbolic Interactionist': Comments by Herbert Blumer". *Sociological Inquiry.* XLIV (Fourth Quarter), pp. 59–62.

1974   "Exchange on Turner, 'Parsons as a Symbolic Interactionist': Reply to Parsons' Comments". *Sociological Inquiry.* XLIV (Fourth Quarter), p. 68.

1975   "Symbolic Interaction and the Idea of Social System". *Revue Internationale de Sociologie.* XI (Nos. 1–2), pp. 3–12.

1976   "A Tri-Fold Test of All Sociological Approaches". *The Wisconsin Sociologist.* XIII (Fall), p. 107.

1977   "Rejoinder to Bell". *The Wisconsin Sociologist.* XIV (Winter), p. 7.

1977   "Comment on Lewis' 'The Classic American Pragmatists As Forerunners to Symbolic Interaction'". *The Sociological Quarterly.* XVIII (Spring), pp. 285–289.

1978   "Social Unrest and Collective Protest", in *Studies in Symbolic Interaction,* I, ed. by Norman K. Denzin. (Greenwich, Ct.: J.A.I. Press Inc.), pp. 1–54.

1979   "Comments on George Herbert Mead and the Chicago Tradition of Sociology'". *Symbolic Interaction.* II (Fall), pp. 21–22.

1980.   "Theories of Race and Social Action", with Troy Duster, in *Sociological Theories: Race and Colonialism.* (Paris: United Nations Educational, Scientific, and Cultural Organization), pp. 211–238.

1980   "Comment: Mead and Blumer: The Convergent Methodological Perspectives of Social Behaviorism and Symbolic Interactionism". *American Sociological Review.* XLV (June), pp. 409–419.

1981   "George Herbert Mead", in *The Future of the Sociological Classics,* ed. by Buford Rhea. (London: George Allen and Unwin), pp. 136–169.

1981.   "Conversation with Herbert Blumer", interview in two parts by Thomas J. Morrione and Harvey A. Farberman. *Symbolic Interaction.* IV (Summer), pp. 113–128; (Fall), pp. 273–296.

1983   "Going Astray With a Logical Scheme". *Symbolic Interaction.* VI (Spring), pp. 123–137.

Review Essays

1965   "The Justice of the Crowd"—a review of *The Crowd in History* by George Rude. *Trans-Action*. II (September–October), p. 44.

1972.   "Action vs. Interaction"—a review of *Relations in Public: Microstudies of the Public Order* by Erving Goffman. *Society*. IX (April), pp. 50–53.

1981   "Review of *George Herbert Mead: Self, Language, and the World*" by David Miller. *American Journal of Sociology*. LXXXVI (January), pp. 902–904.

Obituaries

1952   "In Memoriam: Louis Wirth, 1897–1952". *American Journal of Sociology*. LVIII (July), p. 69.

1967   "Ernest Watson Burgess, 1886–1966". *American Sociologist*. II (May), pp. 103–104.

1968   "Joseph D. Lohman, 1910–1968". *American Sociologist*. III (August), pp. 255–256.

INDEX

Adorno, T. W.: socialization and race relations, 55

Affirmative action: xii; and Lipset, 8; debate over, 66–67; as a constitutional strategy, 66; Blumer's theory of, 69–70; and reverse discrimination, 73; consistent with Blumer's sociology, 73; opposition to, 73; and racial classification, 76, 83; and the badges and incidents of slavery, 80; programs, 83–84, 86; purpose of, 85–86; and the legatees of slavery, 89–90; and individual freedom, 118

Alienation: and the industrial worker, 273–74; and industrialization, 278; and the social order, 279; and mass society, 346, 347

Amendments, to the Constitution: intended to eliminate the vestiges of slavery, 69, 72; and segregation, 73; rights of picketers, 74; Civil War, 75; and racial classification, 77; and equal protection, 83; and affirmative action, 89–90; and freedoms, 104–05. *See also* Civil Rights Acts

American Cast Iron Pipe Company: and labor-management relations, 240

American Civil War: and public philosophy, 5; amendments, 72, 75, 79, 87; and racial prejudice, 186

American Civil Liberties Union: and Japanese internment, 32

American Enlightenment: and Protestantism, xii; and Lippmann's sociology, 11, 20–21, 21–22; and James Mill, 23; and reason, 25

American industry: and Croly's sociology, 17–18

American Jewish Committee: and civil rights, 77

American Jewish Conference: and civil rights, 77

American Legion: growth as a power bloc, 312

American Medical Association: growth as a power bloc, 312

American morale: during World War II, 178–80

American pragmatism: in World War II, 174, 176–77; and interest group conflict, 179–80

American Sociological Society: xvi

Anomie: and exclusion, 107; and industrialization, 271, 278

Anti-Defamation League of B'nai B'rith: and civil rights, 77

Anti-miscegenation: and blacks, 30

Anti-Semitism: Lippmann's view of, 29, 29–30; and group position, 205

Asian Americans: and Lippmann's public philosophy, 31–32

Authority: and social order, 20; public, 20; and motion pictures, 25; and the Catholic Church, 46–47; and civil liberty, 48–49; state, 76; and public philosophy, 100, 101;

Authority (*continued*)
  religious, 102; and mass society, 109

Bacon, Francis: 21
Badges and incidents of slavery: elimination of, 75–76; and Harlan's dissent, 75–76; and the state, 79; and affirmative action, 80, 85, 90; and racism, 86; beyond the black population, 89
Bellah, Robert: on secularization, 108
Biddle, Attorney General Francis: conflict with Lippmann, 32
Black, Hugo L.: liberal decisions of, 104–05
Blacks: post-Civil War relations with whites, 5; and affirmative action, 8; and Hughes's warranteeism, 19; and Mead's sociology, 19–20; and Lippmann's exclusion, 28–29; and Lippmann's sociology, 30–31; as a working class, 59; rejection of the term "Negro," 63; and economic subordination, 66; awareness of color line, 67; and employment, 68, 74–75; postwar migration of, 68; racial subordination of, 72; and slavery, 78–80; social disadvantage after slavery, 86; and Chinese, 88; whites' perception of, 91; and the Keynesian welfare state, 107; and conceptualized groups, 184–86; position in the social order, 208–09, 216; subordination of, 211, 216; in the South, 211; exclusion from the public arena, 214; acquisition of civil rights in the South, 215; and equal employment, 217–18; urbanization of, 218
Blumer, Herbert: secularization and public philosophy, xi–xii, xv–xvi, 6–7; and modernity, xv; biography, xv–xvii; public philosophy theory, 6–9, 35; and sociological instauration, 11; and the color bar, 30–31; on the hierarchy of reason and emotion, 35; perception of mass-media, 36; film studies, 36–42; film and mass behavior, 38–39; on the psychological effects of film, 40–41; and public opinion, 43–44; on wartime morale, 50–54; symbolic interaction, 56, 77; on interest groups, 57; on race relations, 57–61, 88; sympathetic relations, 60–61; on social problems and public discussion, 62; suggestions on race relations, 64; on desegregation, 65; and affirmative action, 66–67; on the color line, 66–69, 89, 91; and black employment, 68–69; emphasis on historical origins of prejudice, 69–70; seven theses on race relations, 71–72; on racial exclusion, 73; objects as social creations, 77–78; on segregation, 84–85; on racial and hierarchal order, 87–88, 91; on race and ethnic relations, 92; critique of industrialization theories, 92–93; study of industrialization and racial subordination, 94; studies of entrepreneurial organizations, 96; on industrial relations, 96–97; view of labor-management conflict, 98; power action, 98; recognition of legitimate labor strike, 99–100; civic virtue in the modern state, 101; character of the self in the modern world, 102; self-interest and civic virtue, 104–05; on mass society, 106–07, 110–12; and Keynesianism, 107; criticism of sociological studies of mass society, 109–11; model for a public philosophy, 114–15; on strikes, 114–17; misunderstanding of, 129 n.136; on public opinion and polling, 147–60; on morale, 161–81; on race prejudice, 183–95; on race prejudice and group position, 196–206; on the color line, 208–

22; on sociology and desegregation, 223–33; on labor-management relations, 234–69; on industrialization and social disorder, 270–96; on sociological theory in industrial relations, 297–308; on group tension and interest organization, 309–25; on social structure and power conflict, 326–36; on the concept of mass society, 337–52

Bourne, Randolph: Lippmann's opposition to, 29

Brotz, Howard: 7

Burger, Warren E.: on race consciousness in legislation, 85

California Supreme Court: and racially selective hiring, 74–75

Calvin, John: influence on Hughes, 14

Calvinism: in Parson's sociology, 46–47, 48, 49; separation of faith from work, 95

Capitalism: and labor-management relations, 240

Catholic Church: and growth as a power bloc, 312

Catholicism: and Parsons's sociology, 46–47

Censorship: and news media, 26–27; and film, 36, 36–37; Blumer's opposition to, 41; and democracy, 45

Chicago school of sociology: media studies and film, 37

Chinese; and labor exploitation, 88

Christianity: and morale, 165

Citizenship: and the disappearance of the color line, 215–16

Civil religion: and religiosity, xi

Civil rights: Constitutional, 63; and race, 76; attack on the color line, 210, 214; rural resistance to, 215; and removal of the color line, 215–16, 221; and racial consciousness, 216; and the intensification of blacks' sense of disadvantage, 217–18

Civil Rights Acts: and NAACP, 59; intended to eliminate the vestiges of slavery, 69–70; Post-Civil War, 75–76; and the color line, 78–79; and equal economic opportunity, 82; violation of, 84. *See also* Badges and incidents of slavery

Civil Rights Movement: and racial discrimination, 63–64; and the color line, 67–68

Clemenceau, George: 24

Codified relations: and power relations, 329; between union and management, 334

Collective bargaining: and the right to strike, 115, 252; and the government, 116–17; and industrial conflict, 244, 249; and strikes, 249–250, 252–54, 257; and major strikes, 262; and compulsory arbitration of strikes, 263; and state seizure of industry, 264–66; strike as integral to, 265; and power, 267; and the state, 268; and industrial relations, 300; and labor-management relations, 333–34

Collective behavior: and public opinion polling, 149; and war effort, 162; and group morale, 163–64, 169–70; and individualism, 168–69; and the goal attainment, 175–76; habituation in, 176

Collective experience: and the nature of a conceptualized object, 186; and racial prejudice, 191; and emotions, 191–92; and the breakdown of racial prejudice, 194–95

Collective image: and the subordinate racial group, 203–04; formed in the public arena, 204; and social position, 224; and interest groups, 205

Color bar: and social privilege, 30–31

Color line: and race relations, 66, 71–72; and affirmative action, 66–67, 73; in America, 67; and black employment, 69; future of,

Color line (*continued*)
69, 208–22; Post-Civil War institutionalization of, 79; transition
from rural to urban setting, 89;
and ethnography, 134 n.250; meaning of, 208; features of, 209; as a
definition of social position, 209;
and the organization of southern
life, 209; and the denigration of
blacks, 209–10; under attack, 210;
transformation of, 210–11; agents
of change of, 211; and the federal
government, 211; and national organizations, 211–12; and the media, 212; and the South, 212; the
national existence of, 214; not removed by civil rights, 215–16; and
economic barriers confronting
blacks, 217; and the status position
of blacks, 221
Committee on Educational Research:
film studies, 37
Compulsory arbitration: of strikes,
263
Comte, Auguste: and science of positive polity, xii–xiii; and Religion
of Humanity, xiii; *Cours de philosophie positive,* 11; and Mead,
19–20; on secularization, 108
Comteanism: xii; and Europe, xiii;
and America, xiv; and Herbert
Croly, xv, 10–11, 11, 18; and
David Croly, 11; and Constitution,
12; and interventionism, 12; and
Hughes, 13–14, 18; and Mead, 20;
and Lippmann, 21
Conceptualized objects: and racial
prejudice, 184–86; predetermining
the collective experience, 187; and
the breakdown of racial prejudice,
195
Conflict: and interest organizations,
316–18; and the public interest,
319–20. *See also* Group tension
Congress of Racial Equality: ascendency of, 59

Constitution of the United States of
America: and Croly's Comteanism, 12; and civil rights, 63, 72;
and the vestiges of slavery, 69–70;
and racial classification, 77. *See
also* Amendments
Counter-prejudice: 195
Cressey, Paul G.: Committee on
Educational Research, 37
Criminal behavior: and film, 38–39
Croly, David: and Comteanism, 11
Croly, Herbert: xiv–xv; and Comteanism, xv, 11–12; and Comte, 11;
and corporate society, 11; and
"new nationalism," 11, 15; proposals for reconstructing the
American economy, 12; and race
question, 14; and labor, 14–16;
federal-interventionist proposals,
15; collective effort and unlimited
competition, 16; work and social
value, 15–16; positivism and
leadership, 17; and secular theodicy of work, 18; and Mead, 20;
and Lippmann, 21
Crowd: and the mass, 343; and mass
society, 345, 348
Culture shock: and industrialization,
273

Daniel, Cletus: on Chinese exploitation, 89
Declaration of Independence: and
public philosophy, 5
Democracy: and plutocracy, 5–6; and
Blumer, 7, 114; and Myrdal, 7–8;
and affirmative action, 8; and
Sumner, 10; and Croly, 11, 13, 15,
18; and Mead, 19; and Lippmann,
20, 26, 29–30, 33; and the deliberative faculty, 23; and Kallen, 29;
and public discourse, 34; and Parsons, 47, 48; Lippmann's scheme
for reconstruction of, 82; and lobbying, 112–113; and public philosophy, 114; and freedom, 119; and

voting, 157; and industrial relations, 306; and interest organizations, 312, 327

Democratic Republicans: in Revolutionary era, 11–12

Demographics: and public opinion polling, 159; and the color line, 208; of black relocation, 218

Desegregation: as a deliberate action, 228; achievement of, 229; and the influence of functionaries, 229–230; and organizations, 231–233; conscious and natural, 233. *See also* Segregation

Dewey, John: and childhood socialization, 102

DeWitt, General John L.: and Lippmann, 31–32

Discrimination: and public and private rights, 226

Dixon, Thomas: *The Clansman,* 25

Durkheim, Emile: on secularization, 108

Duster, Troy: colleague of Blumer, 59; on race relations, 59, 60

Ecological differentiation: and the residential distribution, 224; and group exclusion, 225

Economic Bill of Rights: and the right to work, 82

Economic power blocs: natural to society, 310, 312–13; and interest groups, 310, 311–12; definition of, 309, 310–11; power of, 311–12; growth of, 311–12; reduction of tension between, 319–20; and the state, 325

Education: and positivism, 17; racially segregated, 72; and affirmative action, 73, 83–84; and civic consciousness, 102; and urban blacks, 219; and desegregation, 230

Employer-employee relations: and the direction of labor, 236; conflict of interests in, 237–40; structure of, 241; and the individual worker, 242; conflict as natural to, 242–43; and the changeability of conflict, 243; and collective bargaining, 244, 264–67; and the self-interest of unions, 244–45; and the self-interest of management, 245; and the state, 245–46; basic character of, 246; and strikes, 246–58; and the right to strike, 253, 258; and the abuse of strikes, 256; and compulsory arbitration, 263; and state seizure of industry, 264–66; and economic power blocs, 311. *See also* Labor-management relations

Ethics: and sociological positivism, 17; and the individual, 101, 103–04; and social order, 109

Ethnic diversity: xiv–xv

Ethnic groups: interaction and mutual conceptualization, 187; dominant and subordinate, 189–91; aversion between, 192

Ethnicity: and Lippmann, 28–29; and social classification, 78, 84; and the lobby, 113

Ethnocentrism: Protestant American, 87; and racial prejudice, 189, 190–91, 193–94

Ethnography: and the color line, 134 n.250

Europe: and Comteanism, xiii

Exclusion: and race relations, 57, 60, 67, 73; legislation, 88; and affirmative action, 90

Exploitation: and interest groups, 57; Blumer on, 61; labor, 89; in mass society, 340–41

Fact-finding committees: and strikes, 262–63

Family: nuclear, 45, 292; Parsons's view of, 46; urban black, 68; and the color line, 69; and mass society, 109; disorganization and in-

Family (*continued*)
dustrialization, 274; and early industrialization, 287; extended, 292

Faris, Ellsworth: and Jewish ethnicity, 29

Fascism: and Jews, 29–30n; and Parsons's sociology, 47, 48

Federalists: in Revolutionary era, 11–12

Feelings: and reason, 41; and racial prejudice, 196–200; and group position, 200

Film: social effects of, 25–26; censorship of, 36; Blumer's study of, 36, 37, 38–42; Munsterberg's study of, 36–37; and human values, 39; and modern warfare, 44–45; audiences paralleled to politically active citizenry, 110–11

Fitzhugh, George: 11

Folkways: Sumner on, 5; and the work ethic, 17; and stateways, 20–21; and film, 38; and crime, 38–39

Ford Motor Company: and workers, 234

Forman, Henry James: summary of Blumer's research, 129n.136

Freedom: and industrialization, 276–77

Freedom of speech: 35; and modern warfare, 44–45; and public philosophy, 61; and the state, 118

Functional groups: in American society, 150–51; organization in, 150–51; individuals in, 151; interaction of, 151–52; and public opinion, 155

Fuzzy-Wuzzies: and group morale, 164–65

Generalized other: in Mead's sociology, 102–03

Glazer, Nathan: opponent of affirmative action, 67, 76–77, 84, 85, 86

Goals: and morals, 163–71, 177, 179–81; and the individual, 168–69; rational, 170; romantic, 171–72, 181; sacred, 172–73, 181; and social disorganization, 279–80

Griffith, D. W.: *Birth of a Nation,* 25

Grocery Company: dispute with the New Negro Alliance, 73–74

Group exclusion: as indigenous to human societies, 224; and ecological differentiation, 225; and moral rights, 225; and segregation, 226; between racial groups, 227; and functionaries in the dominant racial group, 229–30. *See also* Racial exclusion

Group policy: and power action, 331–32

Group position: as the basis of racial prejudice, 197–98, 199–200; transcending the feelings of the individual, 200; and social status, 200–01; definition of, 201; variability of, 202

Group tension: and economic power blocs, 309; and the dynamics of interest groups, 315; definition of, 315; examples of, 316; not a problem, 316, 317, 318; reduction of, 319–20; and the public interest, 319; and good will, 320–21; and public opinion, 322

Harlan, John Marshall: dissent from Court decision, 75–76

Harvard group: study of industrial relations, 305

Harvard: and Lippmann, 20, 25, 29; and Munsterburg, 36; Faculty Defense Group, 45; human relations research, 96; letter from Lippmann, 126–27n

Hauser, Philip M.: Committee on Educational Research, 37; colleague of Blumer, 37, 38

Hawkins, Augustus: on unemployment, 82

Hawthorne studies: on worker motivation, 95

Hays, William: president of Motion Pictures Producers and Distributors Association, 37

Henderson, L. J.: edition of *Pareto's General Sociology*, 22–23

Heterogeneity: in mass society, 341, 349

Hilgard, Ernest: and Southern agriculture, 88–89

Hill, Herbert: and the Sinophobic invective, 88

History: and slavery, 86; industrial, 94

Hitler, Adolf: speeches of, 29–30n; and propaganda, 53; and dissension, 179

Hobbes, Thomas: 19

Hocking, William: and the morale of being, 165; on morale and psychology, 166

Holmes, George Frederick: 11

Holmes, Jr., Oliver Wendell: letter from Lippmann, 26

Hoyt, Palmer: correspondence with Lippmann, 32

Hughes, Henry: *Treatise on Sociology*, 11; and collective individualism, 13–14; and warranteeism, 14–15, 15, 19; and Comteanism, 18

Human relations in Industry: approach to industrial conflict, 97–98, 243–44; theoretical deficiency of, 304

Ideology: and public philosophy, 20

Immigrants: in Parsons's sociology, 47

Immigration: 5; restriction of Japanese, 89

Inclusion: and equality, 8; and the race relations cycle, 55; and minorities, 59; and social position, 67

Indians, American: protection of, 86; and race relations, 88; and institutionalized prejudice, 89

Individual opinion: and public opinion, 155

Individualism: in Croly's sociology, 13, 15–16, 18; and the family, 46; in mass society, 112; and morale, 168–69; subordinate to a collective purpose, 169

Industrial conflict: and differences between interest groups, 244

Industrial relations: Weber's view of, 95; and human relations, 96, 304; as a power relationship, 97–98; collective character of, 96; and sociological theory, 297–308; and industrial sociology, 297–98; instability of, 300; dynamic characteristics of, 300–01, 305, 306; and unions, 300; inadequacy of theory, 301; not organized, 301; superorganic factors in, 303; study of attitudes in, 304–05; nature of, 307; and human collective character, 307; observation of, 307; and mass interaction, 308; and power action, 327–28; and power relations, 336. *See also* Labor-management relations

Industrial revolution: and American republic, 11

Industrial sociology: academic, 96; and American sociology, 297; categorization of theory, 301–05; and imaginative judgement, 307; and census, 308; and power relations, 336. *See also* Industrial relations

Industrialization: Post-Civil War, 5; and social life, 64; and racism, 71, 80; Blumer's criticism of theories on, 92–93; and the significance of race, 93–94; as a sociological term, 110; and the preservation of the color line, 208; undermining the color line, 210; and employer-employee relations, 238; and social disorder, 270–96; social effects of, 270–72; and the working class, 271, 273; and the urban commu-

Industrialization (*continued*)
nity, 273–74; and women, 276–
77; and youth, 276–77; and rising
expectations, 276; and psychological disorder, 278; forms of behavior found in, 278; and traditional
authority, 278; and interest groups,
280; not an explanation of social
disturbance, 282–83; and the media, 283; and modernization, 283–
84, 294; and population growth,
284; and management, 285; people
and, 285–86; and the introduction
of alien situations, 288–89; and
situational interpretation, 289–90;
and the traditional order, 291–92;
and the shift in productive functions, 292–93; divergent responses
to, 291–92; and modern society,
338, 339
Integration: and Lippmann's race parallelism, 31; of blacks, 59; and the
change in the color line, 212; and
the South, 212
Interaction: and meaning, 35; collective and mass, 308
Interest groups: religions as, xiii; in
wartime, 53–54; and Blumer's sociology, 43, 57; and racial groups,
60; and the public, 103; in the
fifties and sixties, 107–08; and the
individual, 112; and social disorganization under industrialization,
280; economic power blocs as, 311;
growth of, 312; dynamic character
of, 313–14; in America, 314; and
group tension, 315–17; in conflict,
317; and workable adjustment,
317; extinction of, 318; transfer of
conflict between, 319; reduction of
tension between, 320; tactics employed by, 321; and the common
welfare, 321; and the state, 324–
25; and American life, 327; proliferation of, 327; and mass society, 344

Isolationism: and wartime morale,
174

James, William: and Lippmann's sociology, 33–34
Japanese: and Lippmann's exclusion,
28; post-Pearl Harbor incarceration of, 31–33; and the Keynesian
welfare state, 107
Jarvie, I. C.: on Payne Fund Studies,
37
Jehovah's Witnesses: and morale, 172
Jews: in Lippmann's sociology, 29–
30, 29–30n, 31; in the South, 86;
and conceptualized groups, 185
Jordan, Winthrop D.: and black freedom, 72

Kaiser Aluminum and Chemical
Corporation: and affirmative action, 86–87
Kellog, Paul U.: Pittsburgh survey,
26
Keynes, John Maynard: and Comteanism, 12
Keynesianism: 6, 15; and the New
Deal, 22; and the welfare state, 99;
and labor-management relations,
101; and Blumer, 107
Ku Klux Klan: and Hugo Black,
104–05

Labor: farm workers, 14–15; blacks,
14; and warranteeism, 14–15; and
Croly's conception of individuality, 15–16; motivation of workers, 95–96; authoritative direction
of, 235–36; and remuneration,
237; and job security, 237; and
working conditions, 237; and self-
respect, 237; and self-interest, 242;
and industrialization, 273. *See also*
Employer-employee relations; Labor-management relations
Labor-management relations: Blumer's examination of, 95; as collec-

tive, 96–97; and Taft-Hartley law, 99; compulsory mediation, 99; and legally codified procedure, 100; and public philosophy, 106; and strikes, 114–18; types of, 234–35; and common interest, 235; and self-interest, 239, 336; under capitalism, 239; and worker owned enterprises, 240–41; and industrial relations, 298; in American industry, 298–301; and status relations, 302–03; and historical factors, 303; and group tension, 317; and power conflict, 326; and power action, 328, 334, 335–36; as power relations, 333–34; and collective bargaining, 333–34; and big power groups, 336

Labor unions: Croly's vision of, 12, 14; and blacks, 68; racial discrimination in, 70, 73; and power psychology, 98; and the individual, 242; and employee interests, 242; intrusion into labor-management relations, 244; self-interest of, 244–45; protected by strikes, 249, 250, 253–54; as not essential to the industrial enterprise, 250; as a foreign element in labor-management relations, 250–51; sources of threat to, 251; abuse of strikes, 256; deprivation and, 267–68; seizure of, 268; and status relations, 302–03; and economic power blocs, 309; and power action, 328; and the power process, 333. *See also* Industrialization; Labor; Labor-management relations; Management; Unionization

Laissez-faire: and public philosophy, 6; and leadership, 19

Le Bon, Gustave: on the crowd and group interest, 111

Le Conte, Joseph: 11; Southern Comtean, 15; and Southern agriculture, 88–89

Lippmann, Walter: xiv, xv; and Protestantism, xv; and Enlightenment, 11; public philosophy, 11, 20–34; influence of *Pareto's General Sociology,* 22–23; perception of Utilitarianism, 23–24; and Munsterberg, 25; and Sumner, 27; and popular government, 28; exclusion of deviants, 28; on rationality in a multi-ethnic society, 28–29; attitude toward Jews, 29–30n; and race parallelism, 31; and Japanese internment after Pearl Harbor, 31–33; rejection of religion, 33; and natural law, 33; and public opinion, 35; and *Birth of a Nation,* 36; public philosophy and modern warfare, 45, 52; distrust of wartime governments, 50; and natural rights, 81–82; on job entitlement, 81, 82; on social scientist, 124n; on social control, 124n.61; on law and power, 124n.63; and Weber, 126n.87; letter to Harvard, 126–27n.100

Lipset, Seymour Martin: view of American public philosophy, 7; and affirmative action, 8

Lobbying: and the mass democratic society, 112–13; incompatibility with a public philosophy, 113; regulation of, 113; and public opinion, 152–53

Lutheranism: and Parsons' sociology, 46–47

Management: and power psychology, 98; and paternalism, 100, 245; and the authority over workers, 235–36; and profit, 235, 236–37, 266–67; and the interests of workers, 239–40; and worker owned enterprises, 240–41; necessity of self-interest of, 239–42, 248; abuse of strikes, 256; in industrial societies, 285. *See also* Industrial

Management (*continued*)
  relations; Labor; Labor-management relations
Marx, Karl: rationalization and racial prejudice, 93
Marxism: and industrialization theory, 92–93; and low status groups, 111; and indutrial conflict, 299; conception of mass, 343
Mass: definition of, 343; and individuals, 345–46
Mass behavior: and film, 38; and human values, 39
Mass media: Croly's anticipation of, 18; and stereotypes, 23–24; Lippmann's view of, 25; and public affairs, 26; and news, 26–27; and morality, 36; Lippmann's skepticism of, 42–43; Blumer's position towards, 43–44; and mass consensus, 103. *See also* Film
Mass opinion: 8; and stereotypes, 27–28
Mass society: and secularization, 108; socio-cultural losses of, 109; central characteristics of, 110–11; and film audiences, 110; as an unorganized group, 110–11; and information assimilation, 111; non-geographical, 111; group independence within, 111; and the individual, 112; and lobbying, 112–13; states's role in, 118; as modern society, 339; population and, 340; heterogeneity of, 341, 349; and mass markets, 342–43; and mass communications, 342–43; public participation in, 342; and change, 343, 344, 350–51; development of, 343–44; and modernity, 344; competition in, 344; and sociology, 345; and decadence, 346; institutions of, 346; and collective life, 347; order within, 347–48; and earlier societies, 348; analysis of, 347–48; differentiation within, 349–50; and social positions, 351;

and social roles, 351; socialization in, 351; conformity and aberration in, 351; sociological analysis of, 351–52
McReynolds, James C.: dissent from Court's majority, 74
Mead, George Herbert: xvi; and black freedom, 19; and civic consciousness, 102
Mead, Lawrence M.: and neo-Crolyism, 18–19; and warranteeism, 18–19
Media: and racial prejudice, 197; as a challenge to the color line, 212; and heterogeneity in mass society, 342
Merriam, Charles: and Social Science Research Council, 22
Miles, Robert: class consciousness in Britain, 93–94
Mill, James: faith in reason, 23
Mill, John Stuart: rationalization and racial prejudice, 93
Millerites: and group morale, 164
Minority groups: not a danger to morale, 178
Minority rights: lack of in Lippmann's sociology, 32–33
Miscegenation: *See* Anti-miscegenation
Modernity: in Lippmann's sociology, 24–25
Modernization: and industrialization, 283–84; and social change, 294; and society, 337
Mohammedanism: and religious ethnocentrism, 191
Monopolies: and interest groups, 311
Montesquieu, Charles De: on freedom, 33
Moore, Wilbert E.: on the institutionalized degradation of blacks, 79; on the effects of slavery, 85–86
Morale: and public philosophy, 8; and modern warfare, 44–45; and immigrants, 48; in wartime, Lippmann on, 50; Blumer on, 50–54;

industrial, 95; modern war and, 161; formation of, 161; misuse of the term, 162; and groups, 163–64; and goals, 163–64, 168–69; as a collective undertaking, 164–66; in adverse conditions, 167, 176; and a collective enterprise, 165–67; and technology, 168; and entertainment, 168; and social adjustment, 169; psychiatric view of, 169; types of, 170–73; in unfavorable settings, 173; in America during wartime, 174–75; clear goals and the maintenance of, 175; and goals of practical necessity, 177, 179–80; public participation as a measure of, 177; dangers to, 178–79; and industrial relations, 306

Morality: and mass media, 18; and censorship, 26; and social interaction, 78; and public opinion, 103; and action, 103; and Blumer's writings, 104

Mores: Sumner on, 5; and the work ethic, 17; and the filmgoer, 39; and democracy, 41–42

Motion Picture Production Code: and Payne Fund Studies, 37

Motion Picture Research Council: 37; and Blumer, 129n.136

Motion Pictures Producers and Distributors Association: and self-censorship, 37

Movies: See Film

Munsterberg, Hugo: studies in perception, 25; film study, 36–37; studies on industrial morale, 95; and personnel testing, 125n.81

Myrdal, Gunnar: and the race question, 7–8

Myths: and sacred goals, 173; and race prejudice, 196

National Association for the Advancement of Colored People: and film banning, 36; decline of, 59; attacking the color line, 212

National Resources Planning Board: proposal for full employment, 82

Natural rights philosophy: and the framers of the Thirteenth Amendment, 80–81; and employment, 81–82; decline of, 82–83

New Deal: Lippmann's dissatisfaction with, 22; legislation, 52; and racial conflict, 101

New nationalism: and Croly's sociology, 18

New Negro Alliance: picketing The Grocery Company, 74

New Republic, The: and Lippmann and Croly, 20

News media: in Sumner's sociology, 27

Norms: and mass society, 349–51

Ogburn, William Fielding: and Social Science Research Council, 22

Operationalism: and public opinion polling, 148–49

Organic solidarity: and society, 338

Pacifism: and wartime morale, 174

Paris Peace Conference: and Lippmann, 24

Park, Robert: student of Munsterberg, 37; and Committee on Educational Research, 37; race relations cycle, 55

Parsons, Talcott: xv; and the race question, 7–8; public philosophy and modern warfare, 45–46; on occupational mobility and frustration, 45–46; and religion, 46–47; and the struggle against fascism, 47–48; and Calvinism, 49; and social scientific propaganda, 49; and wartime morale, 51–52; formulation of race relations, 55; theory of roles, 55–56; and secularization, 108

Paternalism: and union organization, 100; and employer-employee rela-

Paternalism (*continued*)
tions, 235, 245; and industrialization, 275, 291
Patriotism: and American morale, 175
Payne Fund: support of Motion Pictures Research Council, 37
Pearl Harbor: and goal formation, 174
Phizacklea, Annie: class consciousness in Britain, 93–94
Pisani, Donald J.: study of Japanese farm workers, 89
Pluralistic mass societies: equity in, 93
Plutocracy: and democracy, 5–6; and Comteanism, 11
Polling: *See* Public opinion polling
Population: and mass society, 340
Positivism: and functionalism, xii–xiii; and Comteanism, 13; and America, 17; and Lippmann, 21, 33
Power action: and interest groups, 328; analysis of, 330–32; morality of, 330; and group policy, 331; control of, 332–33; and good will, 332; opposition to, 332; and public opinion, 332; and the state, 333; and union-management relations, 333; psychology of, 335; and labor-management relations, 335–36
Power psychology: and industrial relations, 98, 335
Power relations: and American industry, 327–28; characteristics of, 330–31; in modern society, 331; and big power groups, 331; as unpredictable, 335; and the state, 336
Pragmatism: and the morality of society, 102
Preindustrial societies: breakdown of, 270, 280–81; and industrialization, 272–73, 280–81
Prejudice: *See* Racial prejudice

Profit: and management, 235, 236–37, 239
Progressive Citizens of America: dispute with Lucky Stores, 74–76
Propaganda: and news media, 26–27; and censorship, 36; and patriotism, 44; and Calvinism, 46; in Parsons's sociology, 49; Lippmann on, 50; and morale, 161; not a danger to morale, 179; and economic power blocs, 310
Protestant Ethic: and democracy, 6; and worker motivation, 95
Protestantism: and sociology, xii; and Lippmann, xv, 34; and public philosophy, 6; and film, 39; and work, 95; and the state, 101–02; and secularization, 108
Proudhon, Pierre-Joseph: and atheism, 109
Psychological disorder: and industrialization, 278; and rising expectations, 284
Psychological warfare: and the problem of morale, 161
Psychology: and the American Enlightenment's, 25; geisteswissenschaftliche, 36; and popular film, 39–42; and mental life, 56; and race relations, 58; and morale, 213, 229–30; and the study of racial prejudice, 196–97; and desegregation, 229; of industrialization and social disorder, 272; and protest, 281–82; of unions, 300; and interest group conflict, 320, 323–24, 323n; order and habitualization, 348
Public interest: and Lippmann's sociology, 28; and emotion, 35–36; and film, 36–37; and national consensus, 101; and Tussman, 101; and corrective action, 104; and competition, 106; and strikes, 115, 117–18; and the labor strike, 259–261, 268–69; state seizure of in-

dustry and the protection of, 263–65

Public opinion: concerns of, xi; and Lippmann's positivism, 21, 42; Lippmann's theory of, 42–43; Blumer's theory of, 43–44, 52; and propaganda, 50; and affirmative action, 76; and moral consensus, 103; and polling studies, 147–48; as a generic object, 148–49; and operationalism, 148–49; functional nature of, 149; as a function of society, 151; and group interaction, 151; individuals and the formation of, 153; expression of, 154; not a quantitative distribution of individual opinions, 154–55; the individual's participation in the forming of, 154–55; as a function of a structured society, 156; in a complex society, 160; suggestions for a model of, 160; and fact-finding committees, 262–63; and interest group conflict, 320, 322; and interest groups, 327; and power action, 332; and modern society, 342; and compromise in mass society, 350

Public opinion polling: and the character of the object under study, 147–48; analysis of techniques of, 148–49; and operationalism, 148–49; deficiency of, 154; sampling procedure of, 154; assessing the findings of, 156; distortions in, 158–59; and sampling, 159–60. See also Public opinion

Public philosophy: xi, xii; and the Civil War, 5; necessity of formulating a, 10; and Croly, 10–19; and Croly's sociology, 18–19; and Mead's Comtean-Crolyeanism, 20; and Lippmann, 20–34; and newspapers, 26–27; and public interest, 28; and affirmative action, 66–67; and the Civil War Amendments, 72; and industrialization, 94; and the individual, 112; and lobbying, 113; and the right to strike, 115; and industrial conflict, 117–18; and the state, 118–119. See also Affirmative action; Blumer; Natural Rights Philosophy

Public policy: and Lippmann's sociology, 22, 23

Public rights: and discrimination, 226; and group exclusion, 226

Puritanism: in Croly's sociology, 17; loss of power, 102

Race: and Lippmann's sociology, 28–33; and social classification, 78, 79–80; and morale, 165–66

Race parallelism: in Lippmann's sociology, 31

Race relations: in Lippmann's sociology, 30; in Blumer's sociology, 58–61; as a power relation, 60; as a social problem, 62–64; and racial hierarchy, 64; and color line, 66, 66–67; Blumer's study of, 71–72; and racial subordination, 72; and employment practices, 73–75; types of, 88; and industrialization, 92–93; like industrial relations, 97; and legally codified procedure, 100; variable nature of, 183; not consistent with racial prejudice, 184, 197; and group position, 201–02; and interest groups, 205; in the South, 209–10, 213–14; and urbanization, 219; and the equalization of status positions, 221; and racial exclusion, 228

Racial classification: and symbolic interaction, 77; as a social construct, 78; and reverse discrimination, 80; benign, 85; and affirmative action, 86–87, 90

Racial conflict: xiv–xv; in Chicago, 30; and wartime morale, 52–53; assimilation and separation, 60;

Racial conflict (*continued*)
and strikes, 101; and the New
Deal, 101; and wartime morale,
174; as a national problem, 213
Racial exclusion: and social position,
214; and the breakdown of the racial order, 228; and desegregation,
228–29; complexity of, 229
Racial prejudice: Blumer's theory of,
70–71; and the color line, 71; as a
consequence of slavery, 79–80;
following the Civil War, 86; variations of, 88; institutionalized, 89;
origin of, 90; as a variable phenomenon, 183–84; as a collective
attitude, 185; and the interaction
of concept and experience, 187–
88; attitudes of, 187–88; the perception of threat and, 190, 191–92,
193, 194, 199; and tribal preservation, 190, 192–93; a product of
collective experience, 191; on the
history of, 191; and the scape goat
mechanism, 193; modern efforts
to break down, 193–95; and its relation to group position, 196; and
racial identification, 197; and the
feeling of superiority, 198; and racial difference, 198; and the proprietary claim to privilege, 198–
99; and the fear of the subordinate
racial group, 199; as a protective
device, 201; and group position,
203–06; and the authoritarian personality, 203; conditions that cause
the decline of, 205
Rationality: Lippmann's emphasis on,
21, 28, 33; and public opinion,
42–43; and the formation of collective goals, 170
Rationalization: and industrialization,
64
Reason: in Lippmann's sociology,
21–22; and the American Enlightenment, 23; and public philosophy, 35, 41
Reconstruction: and blacks, 88

Redemptionist Era: and black-white
relations, 78
Rehnquist, William H.: on racially
discriminatory practices, 91
Religion: and American social compact, xi; and Lippmann's sociology, 28–29, 34; and Parsons's
sociology, 46–47; and American
society, 108–09; and morale, 166;
and the formation of collective
goals, 172–73. *See also* Comteanism; Protestantism; Puritanism; Secularization
Reverse discrimination: and affirmative action, 73, 80, 90; Glazer
on, 77; and benign racial classification, 85
Rogers, Edith Nourse: letter from
Parsons, 48
Romanticism: and the formation of
collective goals, 172
Roosevelt, Franklin Delano: and federal intervention, 6; and Japanese
internment, 32; and labor organization, 101
Ross, Edward Alsworth: on the immoral effects of film, 37

Sampling: *See* Public opinion polling
Saxton, Alexander: on the Chinese
and emancipated blacks, 88
Schutz, Alfred: crisis in the lebenswelt, 40
Secular theodicy: of work, 18
Secularization: xv; and Lippmann's
sociology, 34; and work, 95; and
religious values, 108; and industrialization, 275; and mass society,
346
Securities Exchange Commission: 113
Segregation: Supreme Court decision
on, 61; as a result of prejudice and
discrimination, 64–65; desegregation, 65; and the color line, 67–
68; and the urban black enclave,
68; and white supremacy, 83; and
societal organization, 84; and the

subordinate ethnic group, 194; and
the color line, 210; and the position of blacks in the public arena,
214; voluntary black, 222; as a
natural process, 223, 225; and the
organization of society, 223; ecological allocation as a cause of,
224; and exclusion, 224–25; as a
racial problem, 225–26; and racial
and social difference, 227; conventional view of, 229; causes of,
229–30; functionaries in the operating pattern of, 230; enactment of
laws against, 231
Short, Rev. William H.: director of
Motion Picture Research Council,
37
Simmel, Georg: rationalization and
racial prejudice, 93; and social
conflict, 114
Slavery: and Croly, 14; and work
ethic, 18; and race prejudice, 70,
79; and the color line, 75; legacy
of and affirmative action, 85–86,
118; and racial prejudice, 186
Social action: and racial segregation,
230
Social change: and industrialization,
281, 295; adaptation to, 288; and
modernization, 294; not an aberration, 348
Social control: over workers in Croly's
sociology, 13–14
Social disorganization: definition of,
279; chronic, 279; and interest
groups, 280; in early industrialization, 281–82, 294; and protest,
281–82; not caused by industrialization, 282, 288, 295; in non-in-
dustrial regions, 284–85, 295; and
society, 286–87; and the inability
to cope with change, 286–87; and
concerted action, 287; and alien
situations, 288–89; and situational
interpretation, 289–90, 295; and
the traditional order, 290–93; in
Great Britain, 293; in Western Eu-

rope, 293; and rising expectations,
294
Social Gospel: and American sociology, xiii–xiv, 10; fulfillment of, 11
Social objects: Blumer's theory of,
77–78
Social position: and the color line,
208–09, 211; and black-white relations, 213; black resistance to, 219;
and industrialization, 275. See also
Group position
Social Science Research Council: 22
Social status: opportunities for advancement of under industrialization, 277
Social structure: and the formation of
public opinion, 154–55
Socialization: and national stereotypes, 24; and prejudice, 55; of
children, 69, 102; theory, 104; in
mass society, 351
Society, modern: and the conflict of
interests, 114; and public opinion,
149–50; and organization, 150,
153; and social disorganization,
286–87; studies of, 337; and earlier, 338; mass and, 339, 340; characteristics of, 339–44; and population, 340; and heterogeneity, 341;
and the mass market, 342–43; and
mass communications, 342–43;
and change, 343. See also Mass
society
Sociograms: and industrial sociology,
305
Sociology: and Comteanism, xii–
xiii; and positivism, xii–xiii; and
functionalism, xii–xiii; and Social
Gospel, xiii–xiv; functionalist and
positivist, 8; and the Social Question, 10; and news gathering, 26–
27; and race relations, 55; Blumer
on race relations research, 58–59,
61; focus on strikes, 96; and socialization theory, 104; and secularization, 108; studies of mass
society, 109; and public opinion

Sociology (*continued*)
polling, 147–60; and the study of segregation, 223–24; and desegregation, 228–29; and labor-management relations, 239–40; and the study of employer-employee relations as pathological, 243–44; and the study of strikes, 247; and the study of industrialization, 270–75; and the study of industrialization and social disorganization, 283–84, 288, 295; study of economic power blocs, 309–10; and interest group conflict, 320, 322–23, 323n; and the study of modern society, 337–39; on the formation of large-scale societies, 340–41; and the heterogeneity of modern society, 341; and the study of mass society, 345–48, 350–51, 351–52; working heritage of, 348; on social change, 348. *See also* Industrial sociology

South Africa: industrialization and racial order, 92, 93

Southern Comteanism: and collective individualism, 13–14; and the race question, 14

Sowell, Thomas: opponent of affirmative action, 67; on racial classification, 90

Spanish American War: 5

State: and labor unions, 12; and warranteeism, 14–15; Croly's vision of, 16–17; seizure of business, 116–17; intrusion into labor management relations, 244, 245; justified control of strikes, 261; seizure of industry, 263–65; and group tension, 324–25; and economic power blocs, 324–25; and power action, 333; and power groups, 336

State ownership: and labor-management relations, 234–35

Status relations: and worker-management relations, 302–03; and the analysis of mass society, 350–51

Stereotypes: in Lippmann's sociology, 24; Lippmann on, 26, 28; and propaganda, 50

Stewart, Potter: on the prohibition of racial discrimination, 81

Strikes: and worker dissatisfaction, 95–96; and ethics, 99; legitimate and unwarranted, 99–100, 100; as natural to labor relations, 114–15, 254–55, 257; and the public interest, 115–16; and government intervention, 116–18; and wartime morale, 179; public attitude toward, 246–47; as indispensable to labor management relations, 247, 249–50; and the maintenance of labor unions, 250, 251; and the recognition of labor unions, 251; and collective bargaining, 252; right to, 252–53; avoiding, 253–54; and the resolution of conflict, 255; the legitimate role of, 255; abuse of 256, 259; control of, 257; value of, 257–58; infrequency of abuse of, 259; and the public welfare, 259–61; and the Taft-Hartley Act, 261; and fact-finding committees, 262–63; and compulsory arbitration, 263; and state seizure of industry, 263–65, 268–69; and the deprivation of the involved parties, 266–67, 268; as a contest of power, 267; and group tension, 318; and the freedom of action, 334

Structural-functionalist sociology: and Parsons, 45; and race relations, 59

Sullivan, William M.: the social self and public philosophy, 102

Sumner, William Graham: xiv, 17; and Puritanism, xv, 5; theory of self interest, 6; and federal power, 10–11; and plutocracy, 11; and

Lippmann, 20–21; on judgement in mass society, 27–28

Supreme Court: decision on school segregation, 61, 63; and equal protection, 73, 83; decision on NNA picketers, 74; and black equality, 75; and the color line, 78–79; and natural rights, 81; and affirmative action, 90; liberal decisions, 104

Symbolic interaction: and Blumer, xi–xii; and Croly's sociology, 18; in Blumer's sociology, 56; and racial classification, 77; and special legislation, 83

Symbols: and group moral, 164

Sympathetic relations: definition of, 60–61; and social relations, 329, 330

Taft-Hartley Act: and labor-management relations, 99; and strikes, 116; and the prohibition of strikes, 261

Taylor, Paul S.: Hispanic American studies, 89

Technology: and morale, 168; and mass society, 344, 349

Teggart, Frederick: on social convention, 40

ten Broek, Jacobus: research of the Thirteenth Amendment, 80–81; and benign racial classification, 85–86

Thomas, W. I.: crises and conduct, 40

Thrasher, Frederick M.: and Committee on Educational Research, 37

Tinder, Glenn: civility, 8

Tocqueville, Alexis De: on egalitarianism and commercialism in America, 104

Traditional values: and industrialization, 273, 274–75, 279–80, 291–93

Treaty of Guadalupe Hidalgo: and farm labor, 15

Truth: and news media, 26–27; and propaganda, 49

Tussman, Joseph: and benign racial classification, 85; on public interest, 101

U.S.S.R.: and management and worker interest, 240; and employer-employee relations, 245; and the suppression of strikes, 253

Unionization: industrial, 298, 300. See also Labor unions

Unions: and strikes, 117

United States Census Bureau: 341

United States Steel Corporation: xvi

United Steelworkers of America: and affirmative action, 86–87; use of the strike, 255

Urbanization: post-Civil War, 5; Blumer on, 71, 80; as a sociological term, 110; of blacks, 218, 220; and black-white relations, 219; and group exclusion, 225; and modern society, 338, 339

Utilitarianism: and the triumph of reason, 23; and freedom of expression, 41; and exclusion, 107

Values: and mass society, 349, 350, 351

Voluntarism: Parsons's assertion of, 55

Voting: and the accuracy of public opinion polling, 156–57; and the expression of public opinion, 157–58

War: and morale, 161, 167; and American morale, 174–77; and interest groups, 321

Ward, Lester Frank: xiv; proposal for American technocratic sociocracy, 22; and social telesis, 22–23

Warranteeism: in California, 14–15; Hughes's public philosophy, 19

Watts: riot in, 61

Weber, Max: on labor management
conflict, 95; on the lack of ethics
in the modern state, 101–02; on
the press, 126 n.87
Welfare state: and sociological theory,
8; and Mead's sociology, 18–19;
and Keynesianism, 99, 107
Wellington, Arthur Wellesley: on
morale, 167
Whites: and the color line, 209; perception of the color line, 214
Wilson, William J.: on the decline of
racial significance in America, 93
Women: emancipation of and industrialization, 276–77, 293, 294, 339

Work: as social obligation, 19; in
modern society, 95
Workable adjustment: and interest
group conflict, 317–18, 324; and
strikes, 318; and economic power
blocs, 320
Working class: in the new industrial
establishments, 273
Wright, Quincy A.: and Lippmann,
20

Young, Kimball: criticism of Forman, 129 n.136
Youth: emancipation of and industrialization, 276–77, 293, 294, 339